CB128372

NATURAL SCIENCE
PRIMARY 4

TEACHER'S BOOK

BY ME

TABLE OF CONTENTS

Introduction to ByME Natural Science

Who the course is for

ByME Natural Science is a six-level course for pupils studying the subject of Natural Science in a bilingual context. Level 4 is for pupils in year 4 of Primary.

Aims of the course

The course follows the Natural Science syllabus as laid out by the LOMCE. It is an introduction to the natural sciences, leading learners through their first experiences of Biology, Chemistry and Physics. *ByME Natural Science* aims to develop pupils' scientific knowledge and language skills. Given the challenge of teaching Natural Science in a bilingual classroom, it is important that language does not overwhelm the content, nor vice versa. For that reason, this programme was designed to ensure a unique balance between language and content.

The guiding principles are **simplicity** and **motivation** – *ByME Natural Science* is interesting and engaging for the pupil and user-friendly for the teacher. It features:

- A simple, fixed unit structure to ensure easy navigation.
- A fresh and clear design with a dynamic mix of age-appropriate illustrations and attractive photography, providing visual aids that facilitate comprehension.
- A focus on **scientific method** in order to develop pupils' **investigative and presentation skills**.
- A real sense of **progression** through the levels with a fun, accessible feel to the early levels – with songs, characters and stories – and a more **mature and scientific approach at higher levels-** a clear **bridge to Secondary**.
- **Flexibility**, with many extra, non-content pages, allowing for easy adaptation to specific teaching situations.
- **Scientific literacy** instruction to support content learning in English through reading, writing, speaking and listening activities.
- A wide range of **additional resources**.

This course also aims to address the children's education beyond the scope of Natural Science through:

- Activities designed to prepare children for the question types found in the most common **external exams**.
- **Study skills sections** where children are introduced to techniques for improving their own learning.
- **Cooperative Learning projects** designed to instil collaboration and teamwork as important life skills.
- A strong focus on **ethics** and **values**, encouraging children to engage with the world around them, appreciate its complexities and problems, and develop a sense of **social responsibility**.
- Attention to **higher order thinking skills** to give children opportunities to apply what they know.
- Problem-based activities to encourage **critical thinking**.

Course components

Pupil's materials

Pupil's Book

A 152-page Pupil's Book including:

- a two-page introductory unit introducing pupils to the characters that will accompany them on their learning experience: Alex and Carla in the case of Natural Science 4
- nine main units of 12–16 pages
- three end-of-term review sections
- a picture dictionary.

Activity Book

An optional 64-page Activity Book comprised of six full-colour pages per unit that offers:

- a range of engaging exercises to consolidate and extend the topics covered in the Pupil's Book
- additional reading and writing practice of the science content
- a mini-project designed to encourage pupils to explore scientific concepts and methods at home or in the classroom
- a bilingual glossary to support language learning.

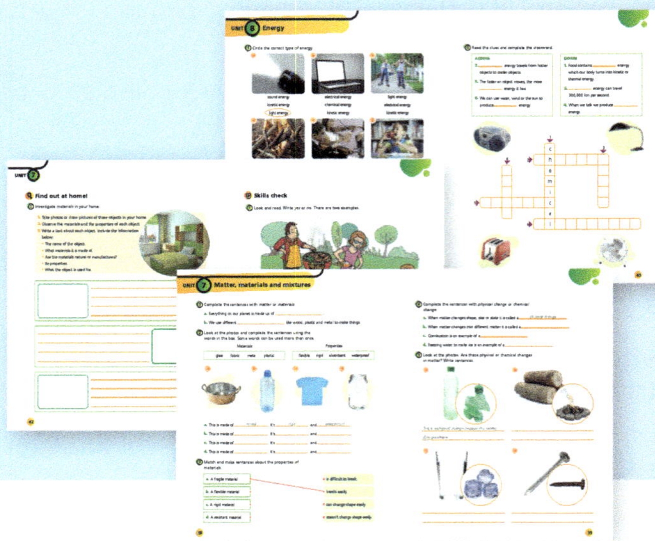

Modules

The modules offer an ideal solution to teaching contexts where only a limited amount of hours in English are available. Each module combines a unit of the Pupil's Book with the corresponding Activity Book unit.

Teacher's materials

Teacher's Book

The full-colour Teacher's Book includes easy-to-follow, flexible lesson plans and practical support specially designed for English teachers teaching Science. A clear, simple design helps ease-of-reference even in the most challenging teaching situations. The Teacher's Book fully addresses the LOMCE curriculum through:

- careful attention to content, evaluation criteria and learning standards
- treatment of the updated key competences in correlation with learning standards
- clearly identified key content and extras sections, enabling teachers to focus on minimum content or to extend their lessons according to their timetable
- a full answer key to all the questions and activities in the Pupil's Book and the Activity Book.

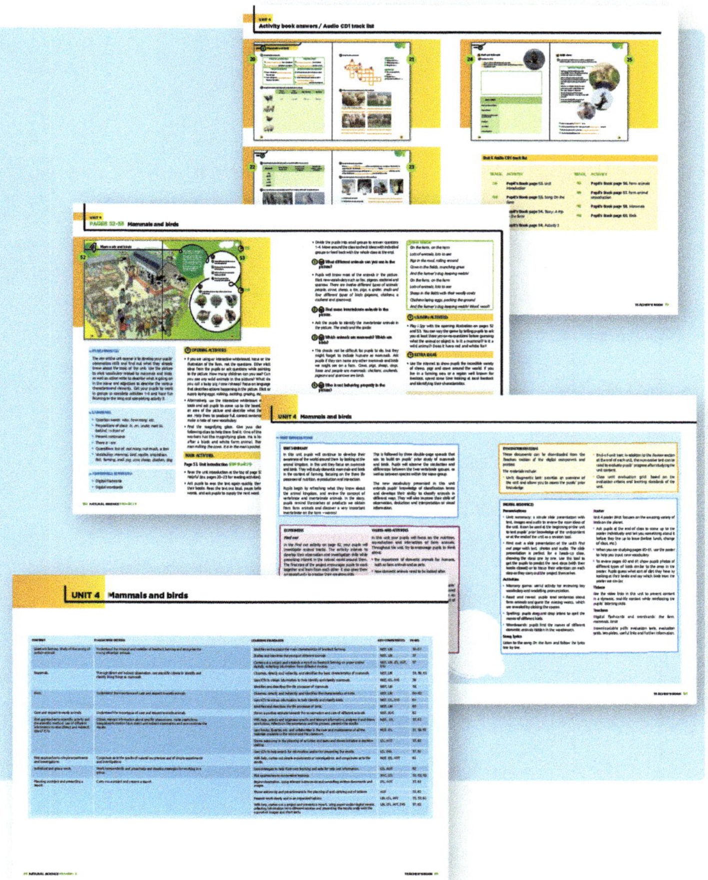

Class audio CD

Included with the Level 4 Teacher's Book, the Class audio CD offers the key recordings for the Pupil's Book in a traditional, easily accessible format. It can be played on dedicated audio players or on the computer. It includes:

- recordings of the main texts of the content pages
- external exam-style recordings for listening skills practice
- quiz answer audio for self-assessment of end-of-term reviews.

Free access to the complete, unabridged audio is available through the Digital resources, where recordings of all the reading texts in the Pupil's Book can be found.

Classroom materials

Posters, digital flashcards and wordcards

Large-scale printed posters are available for added visual support in the classroom, providing additional opportunities for vocabulary practice and revision.

In Levels 1 and 2, flashcards are available in printed format, or in digital format from Level 3 upwards.

Wordcards are provided through the digital resources and can be downloaded and printed.

Ideas for using these classroom materials are provided in the Teacher's Book.

- Full-colour posters to illustrate the most important topics and vocabulary
- Full-colour flashcards (available through the digital resources)
- A large number of wordcards featuring key content vocabulary for each unit (available for print through the digital resources).

Printable resources

Extra printable resources are provided online through the digital resources. These include:

- unit tests
- end-of-term tests
- evaluation grids
- letters to family to help involve parents and carers in their children's learning.
- worksheets

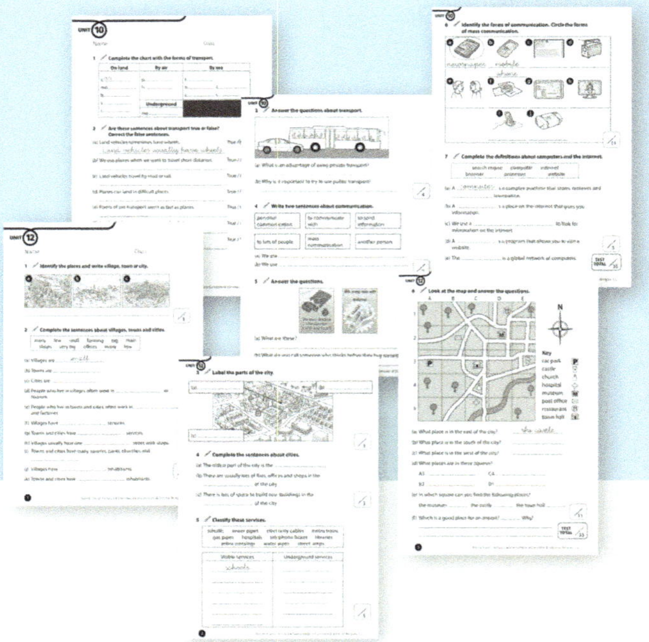

Digital resources

Extensive digital resources are provided. Their focus is a projectable, fully navigable version of the Pupil's Book. This includes a spot-zoom facility to increase ease-of-use and facilitate navigation in dynamic classroom moments. It also provides direct access to the entire course audio as well as the Activity Book, Teacher's Book, interactive digital resources and the printable classroom materials already mentioned.

Interactive digital resources include:

- **Slide shows:** Two types are provided:
  - Step-by-step experiments and projects from the Pupil's Book
  - Unit review presentations to be used as an introduction to or revision of key content
- **Activities:** A variety of activities to revise vocabulary and concepts: Definitions, Wordsearches, Memory games, Classification, Labelling, Spelling, Read-and-reveal activities
- **Posters:** Interactive versions of the printed posters
- **Flashcards:** The aforementioned flashcards available in digital format provide a practical image bank
- **Audio:** Complete, unabridged audio expanding on the Class audio CD. All the Pupil's Book reading texts can be found here. An excellent pronunciation aid and useful for dictations
- **Songs:** Especially oriented towards younger learners; however, also available for higher levels for those teachers whose method is especially dynamic or musical
- **Videos:** Links to useful videos chosen to highlight and expand on key topics in a fun and dynamic way.

bilingualbyme.com

The ByME website is home to a wealth of articles, videos, activities and useful links. It also provides support for parents, providing tips and ideas on how to assist with their children's learning.

How to use the Pupil's Book

Unit introduction

Opening spread

Each unit opens with a vibrant double-page spread. These introductory pages maximise motivation by showing that pupils' prior knowledge of key topics is often already considerable. Key content and vocabulary is introduced though attractive large-scale illustrations, songs and engaging activities.

The opening double page introduces children to the key vocabulary and concepts of the unit in an entertaining and accessible way. The illustrations always feature the Level 4 *Natural Science* course characters **Alex** and **Carla** on a school field trip.In some units you will also be able to find **Ana** and **Tom**, their *Social Science* friends, creating a charming visual link between the two subjects.

Activities can be formulated as group activities or discussions to encourage cooperative learning. They are designed to encourage pupils to think for themselves and to draw on their prior knowledge.

A **song** with a related activity reviews key vocabulary from the illustration.

Story, external exam practice and project worke

Page three and four of every unit follows the course characters on a school field trip.

On the opposite page, pupils are introduced to the concept of organising and presenting their knowledge in different ways. The content is presented in the form of Alex and Carla's school trip project.

Page three features a fun but informative story that shows the children enjoying an adventure on their field trip. A dramatisation of the story can be listened to on the class CD or on the digital component. The story activities are designed to reflect the most common activities found in external exams.

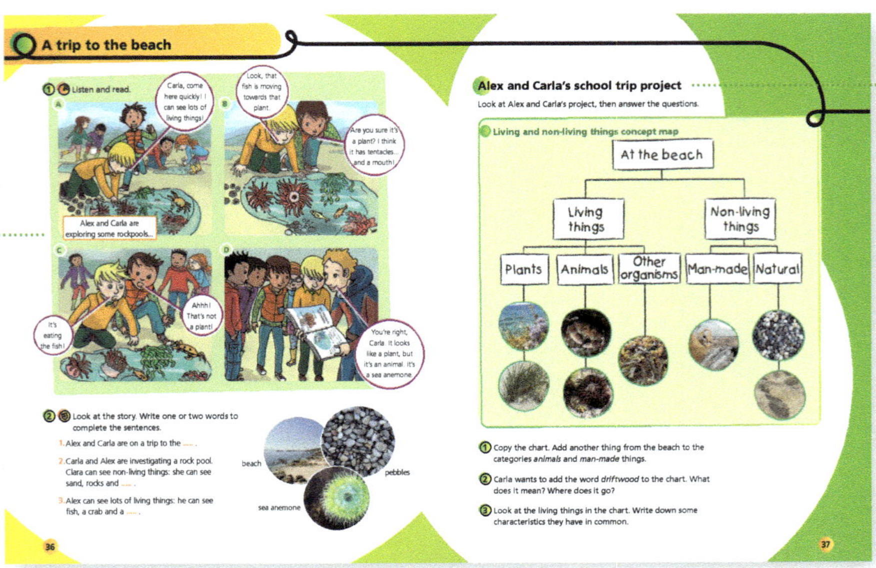

Unit development

The content pages allow pupils to build on their prior knowledge through highly visual content and a wide variety of activities, presenting different levels of cognitive challenge.

Content pages are richly illustrated with a careful balance of photography and age-appropriate illustration, in order to facilitate comprehension in all learner types and maximise engagement with the content.

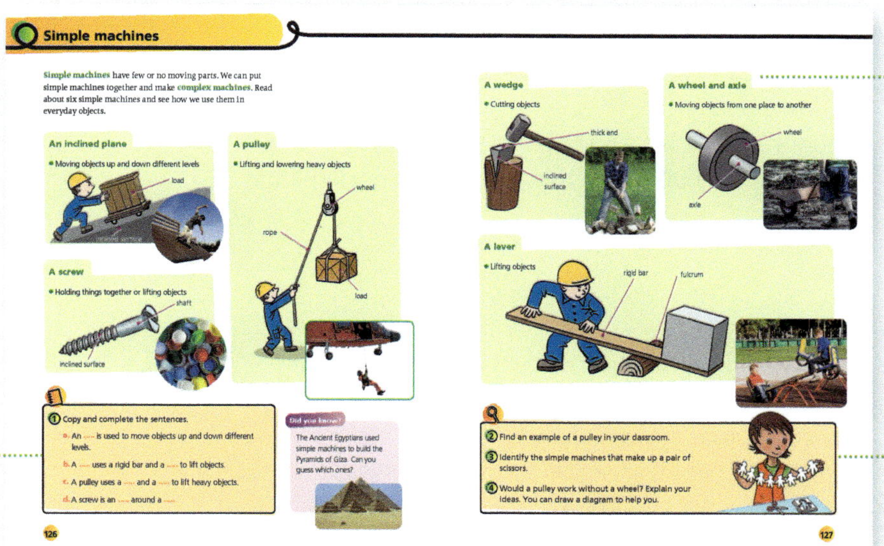

Higher order thinking skills are introduced through the use of graded activities. Activities on the left are revision questions directly related to the content on the double page, while activities on the right provide greater **challenge**, encouraging children to think, investigate and make connections.

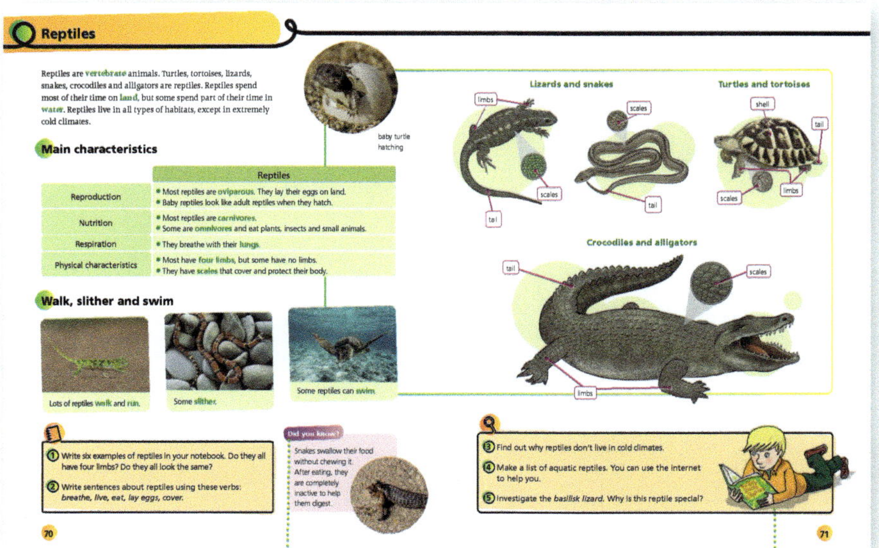

Did you know and **In other words** boxes provide pupils with fun snippets of information or explain complex terms with a twist.

Course characters are repeated throughout the unit presenting the key concepts visually in order to facilitate comprehension.

Unit conclusion

Each unit closes with four pages in which content is extended and revised. These pages can be extended depending on each teacher's timetable and requirements.

Find out

This page extends the content through an accessible, fun experiment, investigation or project.

Think about it

On the opposite page pupils are offered a values-oriented link to the same content. Pupils are also given the opportunity to develop their presentation skills.

Find Out: Fun projects and simple experiments provide children with an age-appropriate introduction to **scientific methods** (idea, test, conclusions) from the very beginning. Projects are carefully designed to be accessible and appropriate for young children and only require the use of everyday materials. Studio photography, including real children of the same age as the pupils, helps them relate to the content.

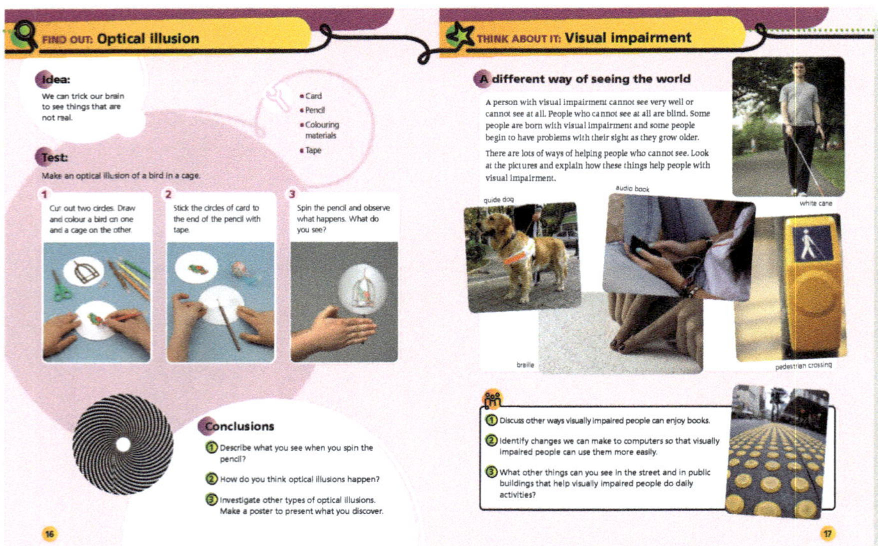

FIND OUT: Optical illusion

Idea:

We can trick our brain to see things that are not real.

- Card
- Pencil
- Colouring materials
- Tape

Test:

Make an optical illusion of a bird in a cage.

1 Cut out two circles. Draw and colour a bird on one and a cage on the other.

2 Stick the circles of card to the end of the pencil with tape.

3 Spin the pencil and observe what happens. What do you see?

Conclusions

1. Describe what you see when you spin the pencil?
2. How do you think optical illusions happen?
3. Investigate other types of optical illusions. Make a poster to present what you discover.

16

THINK ABOUT IT: Visual impairment

A different way of seeing the world

A person with visual impairment cannot see very well or cannot see at all. People who cannot see at all are blind. Some people are born with visual impairment and some people begin to have problems with their sight as they grow older.

There are lots of ways of helping people who cannot see. Look at the pictures and explain how these things help people with visual impairment.

1. Discuss other ways visually impaired people can enjoy books.
2. Identify changes we can make to computers so that visually impaired people can use them more easily.
3. What other things can you see in the street and in public buildings that help visually impaired people do daily activities?

17

Think about it: Pupils are introduced to values and ethics in relation to the scientific project. They are presented with situations designed to encourage **reasoning** and an engagement with their immediate surroundings, in order to develop their independence and the beginnings of a sense of **social and personal responsibility.** There are also further ideas for projects and class presentations.

Look back

Unit revision pages ensure that pupils' progression is regularly checked and reviewed. Each review section is divided into Study Skills and more traditional review activities, designed to check the learning of both content and language.

More traditional review questions check progress while also providing ample opportunity for language practice with reading and writing activities.

Study skills: pupils are introduced to a variety of visual organisers. The aim is to help pupils further their own learning process.

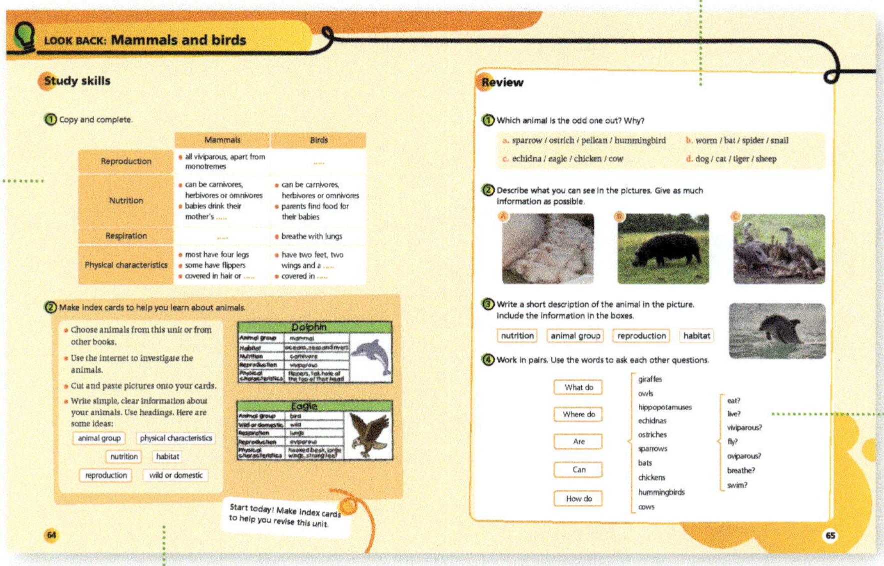

LOOK BACK: **Mammals and birds**

Study skills

1. Copy and complete.

	Mammals	Birds
Reproduction	• all viviparous, apart from monotremes	.....
Nutrition	• can be carnivores, herbivores or omnivores • babies drink their mother's	• can be carnivores, herbivores or omnivores • parents find food for their babies
Respiration	.....	• breathe with lungs
Physical characteristics	• most have four legs • some have flippers • covered in hair or	• have two feet, two wings and a ..... • covered in .....

2. Make index cards to help you learn about animals.

- Choose animals from this unit or from other books.
- Use the internet to investigate the animals.
- Cut and paste pictures onto your cards.
- Write simple, clear information about your animals. Use headings. Here are some ideas:

animal group | physical characteristics | nutrition | habitat | reproduction | wild or domestic

Dolphin	
Animal group	mammal
Habitat	oceans, seas and rivers
Nutrition	carnivore
Reproduction	viviparous
Physical characteristics	flippers, tail, hole at the top of their head

Eagle	
Animal group	bird
Wild or domestic	wild
Respiration	lungs
Reproduction	oviparous
Physical characteristics	hooked beak, large wings, strong feet

Start today! Make index cards to help you revise this unit.

64

Review

1. Which animal is the odd one out? Why?

a. sparrow / ostrich / pelican / hummingbird
b. worm / bat / spider / snail
c. echidna / eagle / chicken / cow
d. dog / cat / tiger / sheep

2. Describe what you can see in the pictures. Give as much information as possible.

A B C

3. Write a short description of the animal in the picture. Include the information in the boxes.

nutrition | animal group | reproduction | habitat

4. Work in pairs. Use the words to ask each other questions.

What do / Where do / Are / Can / How do — giraffes / owls / hippopotamuses / echidnas / ostriches / sparrows / bats / chickens / hummingbirds / cows — eat? / live? / viviparous? / fly? / oviparous? / breathe? / swim?

65

Each unit contains a different dynamic revision activity, which allows pupils to build up their own set of revision materials and have fun with their classmates at the same time.

A final pairwork activity encourages self-evaluation while also providing opportunities for speaking and listening, and practice for language structures.

Term pages

Four end-of-term pages provide additional progress-checking activities as well as the opportunity to practise different communicative skills.

Think together

Cooperative learning project: A final group project takes these communication and collaboration skills further and gives students the opportunity to engage with a key theme from a different point of view while having fun at the same time. These cooperative activities are carefully adapted to the age group. The group dynamics used are fully described in the Cooperative Learning pages.

The different activities are conducted following different Cooperative Learning structures that provide an optimal learning experience for students and guarantee the involvement of all team members. Different structures include Round robin, Think-pair-share, Jigsaw, etc.

Before doing the activities, teams are formed by the teacher. Pupils are assigned roles and an explanation is given on the procedures to follow according to the relevant Cooperative Learning structure.

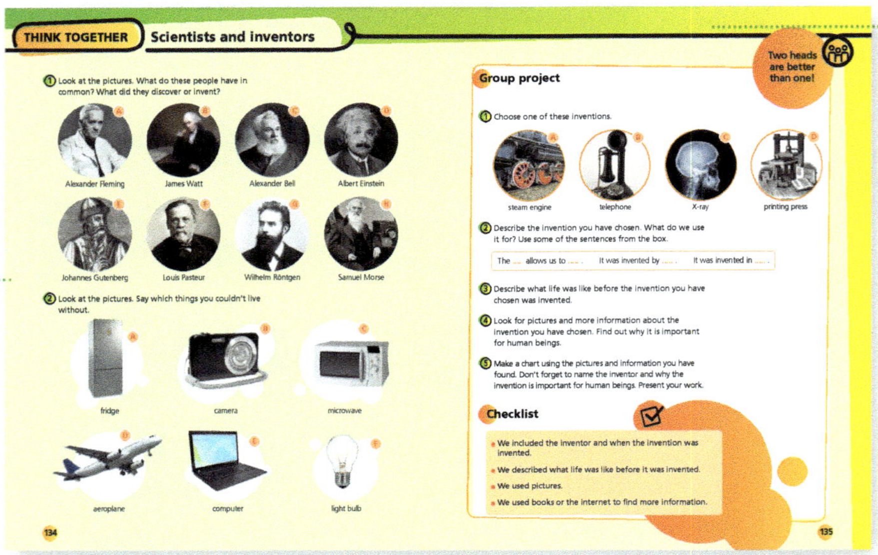
THINK TOGETHER Scientists and inventors

1 Look at the pictures. What do these people have in common? What did they discover or invent?

Alexander Fleming, James Watt, Alexander Bell, Albert Einstein, Johannes Gutenberg, Louis Pasteur, Wilhelm Röntgen, Samuel Morse

2 Look at the pictures. Say which things you couldn't live without.

fridge, camera, microwave, aeroplane, computer, light bulb

134

Group project

Two heads are better than one!

1 Choose one of these inventions.

steam engine, telephone, X-ray, printing press

2 Describe the invention you have chosen. What do we use it for? Use some of the sentences from the box.

The ... allows us to ... . It was invented by ... . It was invented in ... .

3 Describe what life was like before the invention you have chosen was invented.

4 Look for pictures and more information about the invention you have chosen. Find out why it is important for human beings.

5 Make a chart using the pictures and information you have found. Don't forget to name the inventor and why the invention is important for human beings. Present your work.

Checklist

- We included the inventor and when the invention was invented.
- We described what life was like before it was invented.
- We used pictures.
- We used books or the internet to find more information.

135

Term review

Science Quiz follows a traditional question and answer format as well as offering the opportunity for practising listening skills.

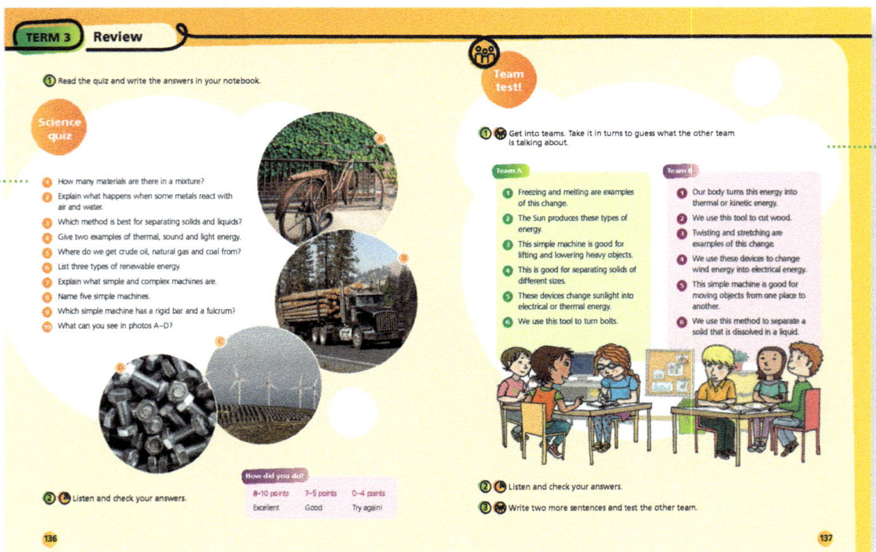
TERM 3 Review

1 Read the quiz and write the answers in your notebook.

Science quiz

1 How many materials are there in a mixture?
2 Explain what happens when some metals react with air and water.
3 Which method is best for separating solids and liquids?
4 Give two examples of thermal, sound and light energy.
5 Where do we get crude oil, natural gas and coal from?
6 List three types of renewable energy.
7 Explain what simple and complex machines are.
8 Name five simple machines.
9 Which simple machine has a rigid bar and a fulcrum?
10 What can you see in photos A–D?

2 Listen and check your answers.

How did you do?

8–10 points	7–5 points	0–4 points
Excellent	Good	Try again!

136

Team test!

1 Get into teams. Take it in turns to guess what the other team is talking about.

Team A
1 Freezing and melting are examples of this change.
2 The Sun produces these types of energy.
3 This simple machine is good for lifting and lowering heavy objects.
4 This is good for separating solids of different sizes.
5 These devices change sunlight into electrical or thermal energy.
6 We use this tool to turn bolts.

Team B
1 Our body turns this energy into thermal or kinetic energy.
2 We use this tool to cut wood.
3 Twisting and stretching are examples of this change.
4 We use these devices to change wind energy into electrical energy.
5 This simple machine is good for moving objects from one place to another.
6 We use this method to separate a solid that is dissolved in a liquid.

2 Listen and check your answers.

3 Write two more sentences and test the other team.

137

Team test! allows pupils to compete against their classmates while revising content and practising speaking and listening skills.

End pages

Picture dictionary

The book ends with an extensive easy-reference picture dictionary with the focus on photography to help memory and recognition.

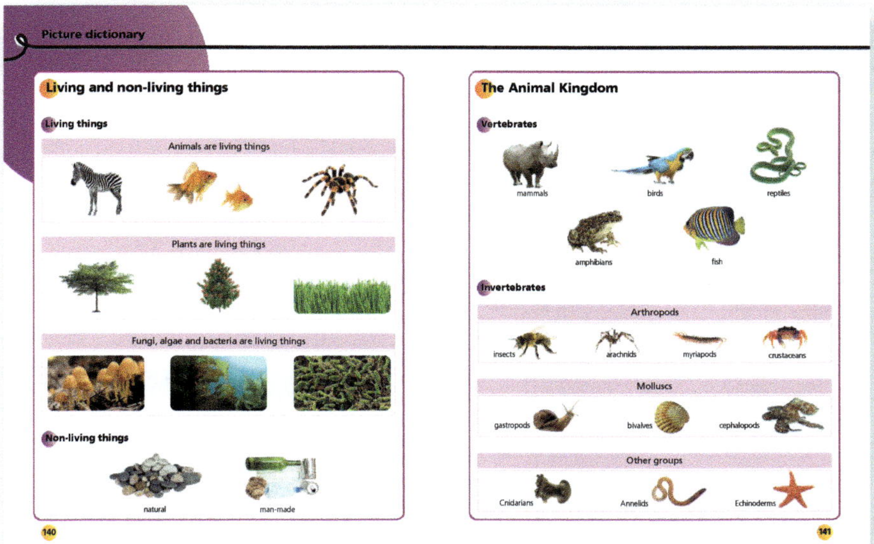

Optional Activity Book

The Activity Book is ideal for homework or for increasing the amount of pupils' reading and writing practice. There are also innovative new sections to encourage family participation and practice with the question types that are found in the most common external exams.

Find out at home! projects are designed to encourage parents or carers to engage with pupils' learning through simple investigative projects to be carried out in the home.

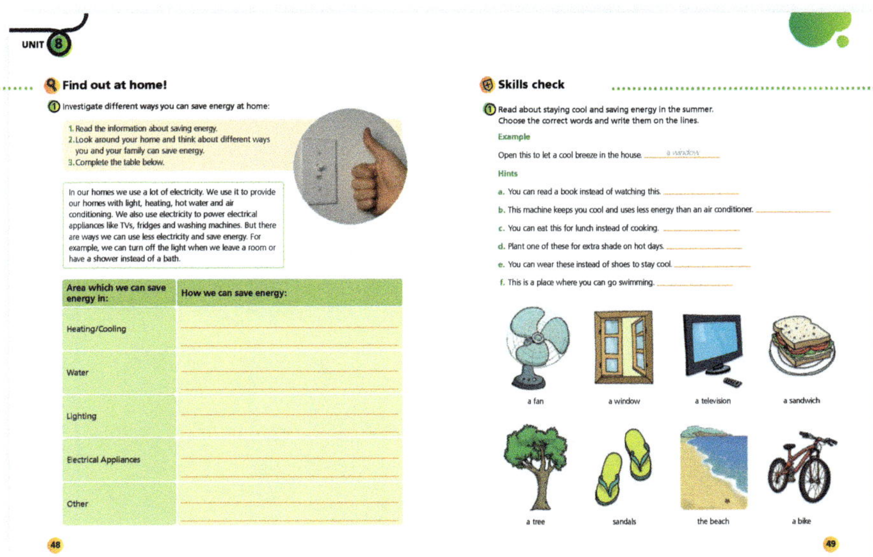

Skills check helps pupils to review content while also offering them extensive practice with the most common activity and question types found in external language exams.

How to use the Teacher's Book

Preliminary pages

The Teacher's Book includes a variety of articles with practical ideas on how to get the most out of the lesson.

Helpful tips & Classroom management

The section *Helpful tips* is set out as a reference resource. There are countless ideas on setting up reading tasks, maximising the benefits of classroom materials, and keeping your pupils motivated through a variety of activity types.

The *Classroom management* section provides some general ideas on managing your class in order to create a productive environment in which all pupils are able to flourish.

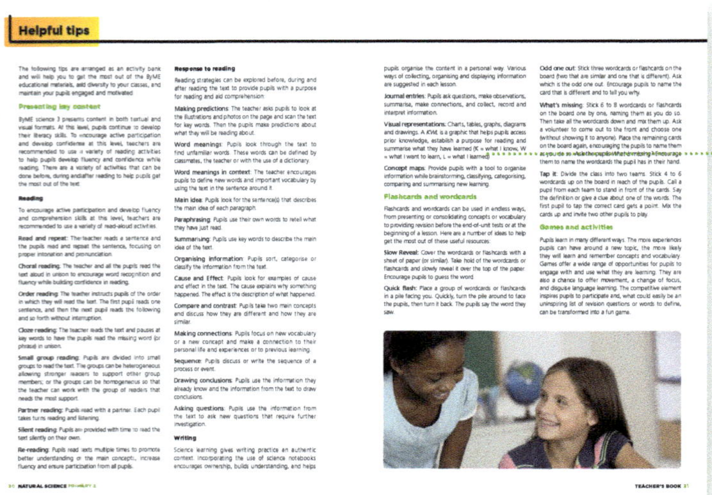

Flashcards and wordcards: flashcards and wordcards are incredibly effective tools if used appropriately. This section offers a wide range of suggestions on how to make these useful resources work for you.

Games and activities: additional activities that can be adapted to specific teaching contexts, for revision, reinforcement or extension in mixed-ability situations, or to keep fast finishers busy while the rest of the class completes the task.

Presenting key content: this section addresses the perennial problem of how to make reading in class dynamic, productive and stimulating.

Time management: suggestions for working to a limited timetable. ByME Teacher's Books give teachers the option of focusing on key content, incorporating clearly marked extras only if time allows.

Classroom organisation: provides clear rules for behaviour which the pupils themselves are asked to help define.

Procedures: ways of sequencing a class session, with suggestions for routines that can be repeated from class to class.

Cooperative Learning

An article on Cooperative Learning (CL) offers an introduction to this innovative method of teaching. This section complements the end-of-term Teamwork sections, explaining in simple language how to set up each CL structure referenced there.

Further reading: a brief bibliography for those who would like to deepen their knowledge of CL.

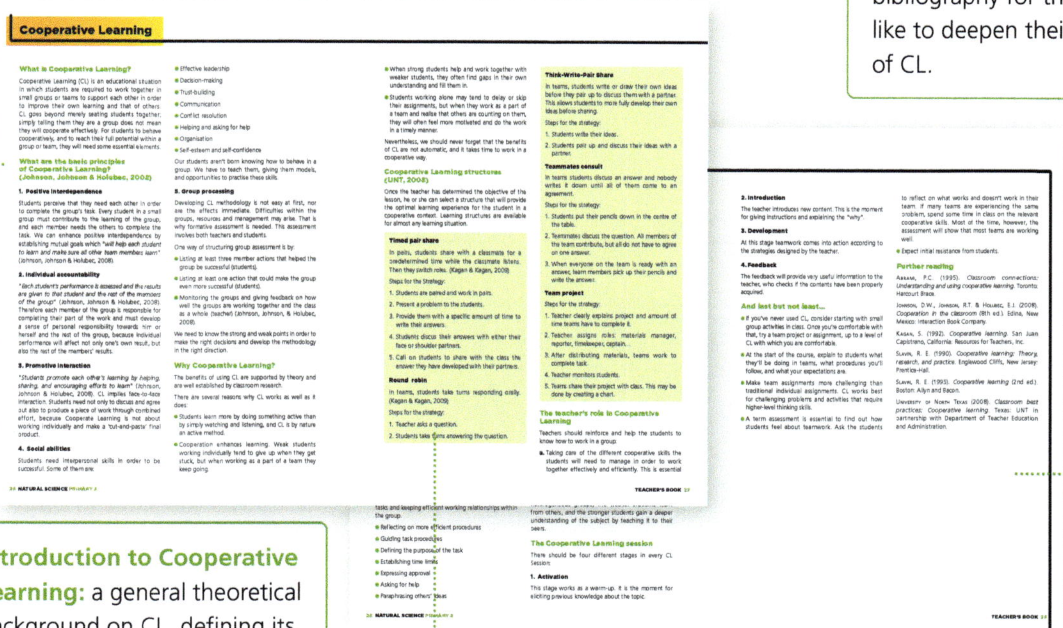

Introduction to Cooperative Learning: a general theoretical background on CL, defining its main principles and benefits.

Cooperative Learning structures: specific information on the different group dynamics referenced in the lesson plans. Here you'll find easy-to-follow instructions on how each CL structure is set up.

How to use the Teacher's Book

Content maps

Each unit and Cooperative Learning section begins with a content map, fully compatible with the LOMCE curriculum, to help the teacher see at a glance the content, evaluation criteria, learning standards and key competences ahead.

Learning standards, evaluation criteria and content: all key elements of the LOMCE curriculum are clearly mapped out for each unit.

Key competences: related to each learning standard.

LIN: Competence in linguistic communication
MST: Competence in mathematics, science and technology
DIG: Digital competence
LTL: Competence in learning to learn
SOC: Competence in social awareness and citizenship
AUT: Competence in autonomous learning and personal initiative
CUL: Competence in artistic and cultural awareness

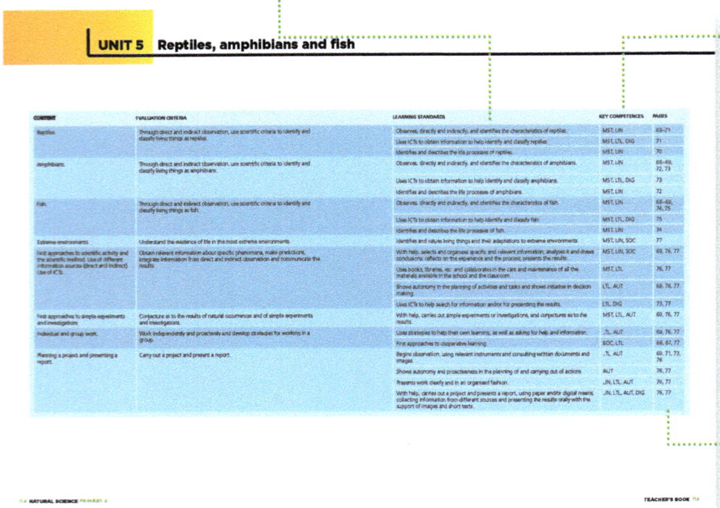

Page references: these indicate where each learning standard is covered.

Unit information

Unit summary: an overview of the lesson, highlighting the main topics and outcomes, as well as identifying areas that are popular with or difficult for pupils.

Materials: materials required for each lesson and reminders for pupils of the materials they should bring from home for upcoming activities.

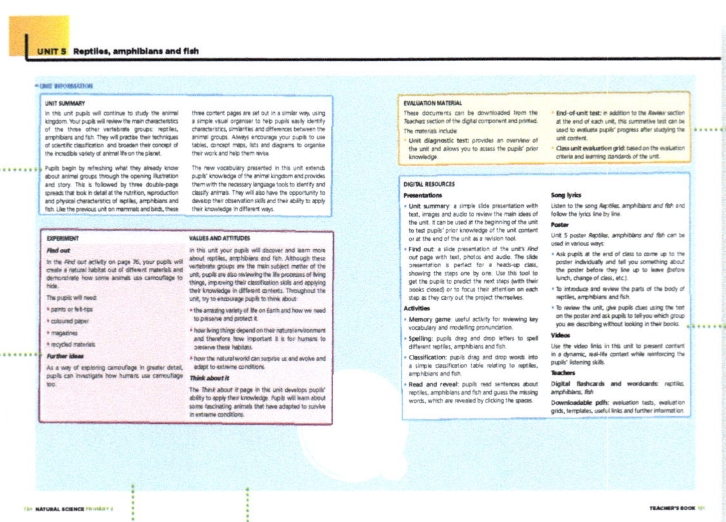

Evaluation material: a short description of the evaluation aids available.

digital resources: an index of the materials and activities available through the Digital resources.

Experiment: helps prepare for the science project ahead of time. Especially important when experiments require pupils to bring in materials.

Values and attitudes: aims to make the content relevant to pupils, helping them understand how it affects them directly and why it should matter to them.

Lesson plans

There are step-by-step lesson plans for all units and term sections.

Step-by-step lesson plans: teacher tips on presenting textual and graphic content, and instructions for guiding pupils through the activities.

Visual page reference: a full-colour image of the Pupil's Book for the teacher's reference.

Lesson information at a glance: lesson summary, language focus and materials to help prepare lessons ahead of time.

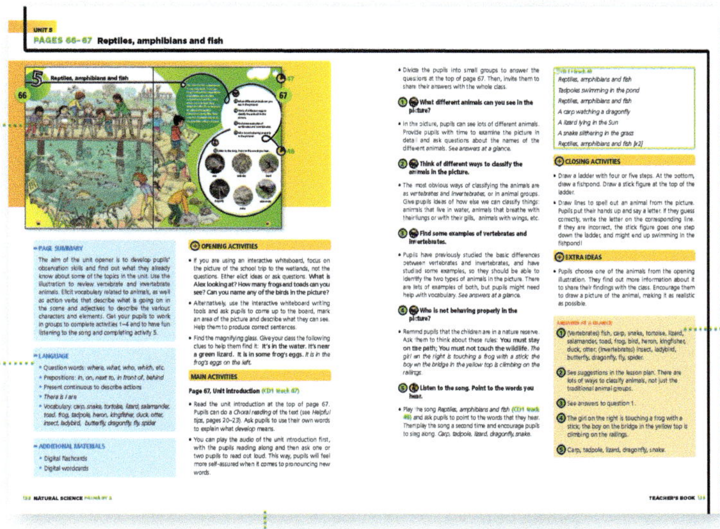

Extra ideas: activities for pupils who finish the lesson early.

Opening and closing activities: each lesson begins and ends with flexible activities that can be reduced or extended according to the time available.

Activity Book solutions & Audio track lists

Activity Book solutions: provided at the end of the unit, making the Teacher's Book a one-stop reference point for all the materials of each course.

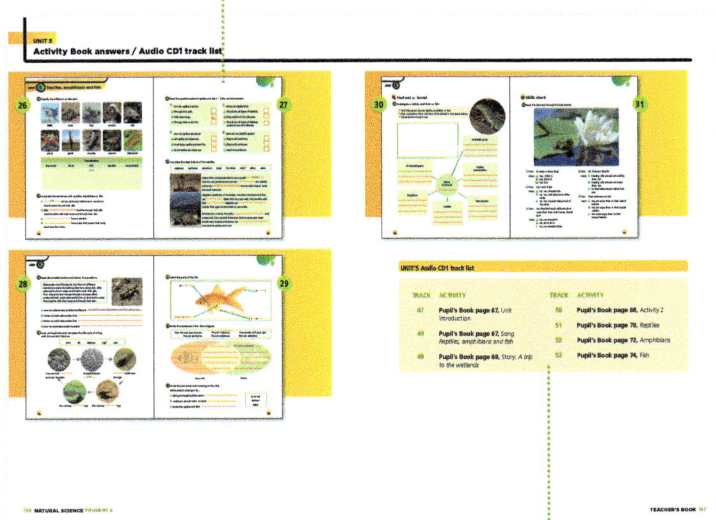

Audio tracks: the last page of each unit of the Teacher's Book has a simple to use audio track reference. The audio tracks are also marked clearly on each page image in the lesson plans.

How to use the Digital resources

All teachers using *ByME Natural Science:* have free access to the ByME Digital resources. Users of the Pupil's Book or Activity Book have access to the complete books. Module users have individual access to the specific units they are using of both the Pupil's Book and Activity Book.

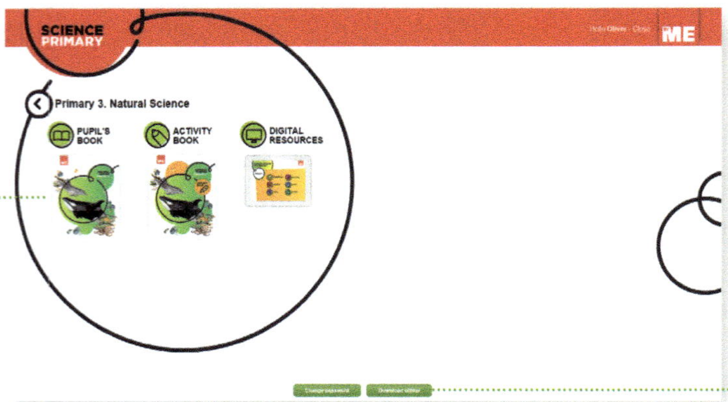

The Digital resources are available both on-line and off-line. Both versions are accessed with a specific code that all users will receive.

The digital component also provides easy navigation between the Pupil's Book and the Activity Book, and direct access to extensive digital resources.

The user has access to projectable, fully-navigable versions of the Pupil's Book and the Activity Book.

Through an innovative, easy-to-use spot-zoom tool, there is easy access to the complete audio.

The Digital resources include:

- extensive interactive activities (see images below)
- accessible unit review and experiment presentations with integrated audio
- all the songs with the lyrics and a karaoke effect
- access to videos which bring key topics to life
- interactive versions of the course posters
- access to printable resources and a PDF version of the Teacher's Book.

Digital activities to practise key vocabulary vary for each level but include:

- Labelling activities
- Memory games
- Read and reveal activities
- Wordsearches
- Classification and definition activities

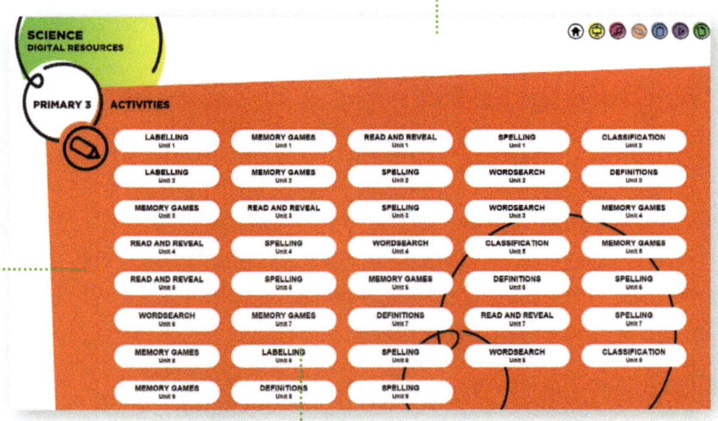

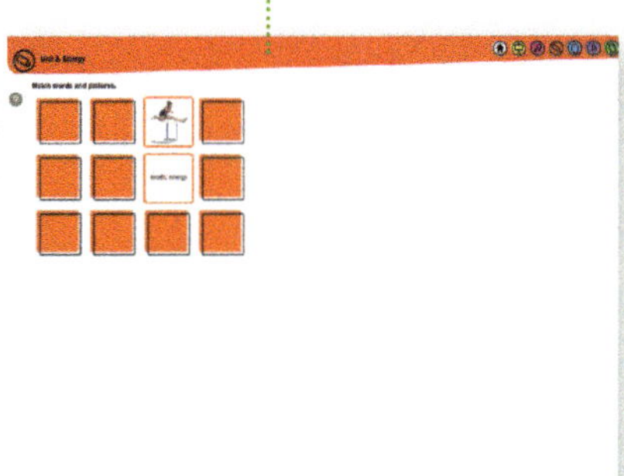

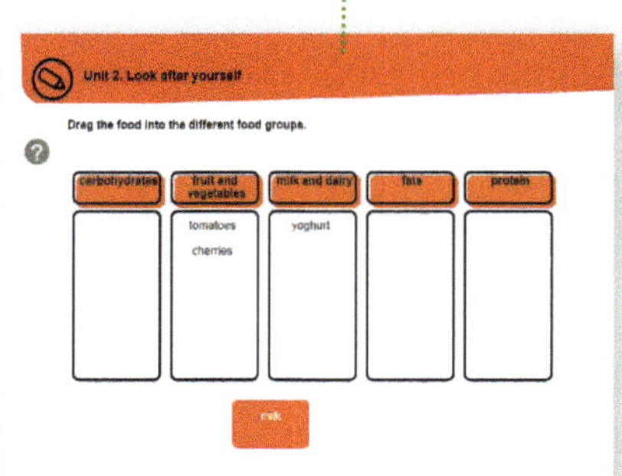

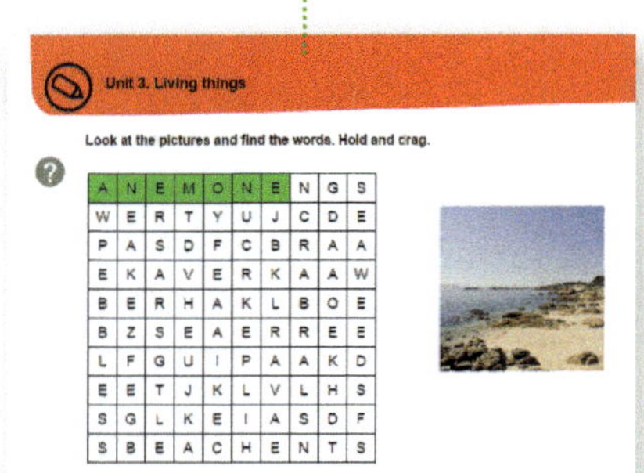

Helpful tips

The following tips are arranged as an activity bank and will help you to get the most out of the ByME educational materials, add diversity to your classes, and keep your pupils engaged and motivated.

Presenting key content

ByME science 4 presents content in both textual and visual formats. At this level, pupils continue to develop their literacy skills. To encourage active participation and develop confidence at this level, teachers are recommended to use a variety of reading activities to help pupils develop fluency and confidence while reading. There are several activities that can be used before, during and after reading to help pupils get the most out of the text.

Reading

To encourage active participation and develop fluency and comprehension skills at this level, teachers are recommended to use a variety of read-aloud activities.

Read and repeat: The teacher reads a sentence and the pupils read and repeat the sentence, focusing on proper intonation and pronunciation.

Choral reading: The teacher and all the pupils read the text aloud in unison to encourage word recognition and fluency while building confidence in reading.

Order reading: The teacher instructs pupils of the order in which they will read the text. The first pupil reads one sentence, and then the next pupil reads the following and so forth without interruption.

Cloze reading: The teacher reads the text and pauses at key words to have the pupils read the missing word (or phrase) in unison.

Small group reading: Pupils are divided into small groups to read the text. The groups can be heterogeneous allowing stronger readers to support other group members; or the groups can be homogeneous so that the teacher can work with the group of readers that needs the most support.

Partner reading: Pupils read with a partner. Each pupil takes turns reading and listening.

Silent reading: Pupils are provided with time to read the text silently on their own.

Re-reading: Pupils read texts multiple times to promote better understanding of the main concepts, increase fluency and ensure the participation of all pupils.

Response to reading

Reading strategies can be explored before, during and after reading the text to provide pupils with a purpose for reading and to aid comprehension:

Making predictions: The teacher asks pupils to look at the illustrations and photos on the page and to scan the text for key words. Then the pupils make predictions about what they will be reading about.

Word meanings: Pupils look through the text to find unfamiliar words. These words can be defined by classmates, the teacher or with the use of a dictionary.

Word meanings in context: The teacher encourages pupils to define new words and important vocabulary by using the text in the sentence around it.

Main idea: Pupils look for the sentence(s) that describes the main idea of each paragraph.

Paraphrasing: Pupils use their own words to retell what they have just read.

Summarising: Pupils use key words to describe the main idea of the text.

Organising information: Pupils sort, categorise or classify the information from the text.

Cause and Effect: Pupils look for examples of cause and effect in the text. The cause explains why something happened. The effect is the description of what happened.

Compare and contrast: Pupils take two main concepts and discuss how they are different and how they are similar.

Making connections: Pupils focus on new vocabulary or a new concept and make a connection to their personal life and experiences or to previous learning.

Sequence: Pupils discuss or write the sequence of a process or event.

Drawing conclusions: Pupils use the information they already know and the information from the text to draw conclusions.

Asking questions: Pupils use the information from the text to ask new questions that require further investigation.

Writing

Science learning gives writing practice an authentic context. Incorporating the use of science notebooks encourages ownership, builds understanding, and helps pupils organise the content in a personal way. Various ways of collecting, organising and displaying information are suggested in each lesson.

Journal entries: Pupils ask questions, make observations, summarise, make connections, and collect, record and interpret information.

Visual representations: Charts, tables, graphs, diagrams and drawings. A *KWL* is a graphic that helps pupils access prior knowledge, establish a purpose for reading and summarise what they have learned (K = what I know, W = what I want to learn, L = what I learned)

Concept maps: Provide pupils with a tool to organise information while brainstorming, classifying, categorising, comparing and summarising new learning.

Flashcards and wordcards

Flashcards and wordcards can be used in endless ways, from presenting or consolidating concepts or vocabulary to providing revision before the end-of-unit tests or at the beginning of a lesson. Here are a number of ideas to help get the most out of these useful resources:

Slow Reveal: Cover the wordcards or flashcards with a sheet of paper (or similar). Take hold of the wordcards or flashcards and slowly reveal it over the top of the paper. Encourage pupils to guess the word.

Quick flash: Place a group of wordcards or flashcards in a pile facing you. Quickly, turn the pile around to face the pupils, then turn it back again. Pupils say the word they saw.

Odd one out: Stick three wordcards or flashcards on the board (two that are similar and one that is different). Ask which is the odd one out. Encourage pupils to name the card that is different and to tell you why.

What's missing: Stick 6 to 8 wordcards or flashcards on the board one by one, naming them as you do so. Then take all the wordcards down and mix them up. Ask a volunteer to come out to the front to choose one (without showing it to anyone). Place the remaining cards on the board again, encouraging pupils to name them as you do so. Ask pupils *What is missing?* Encourage them to name the wordcards the pupil has in their hand.

Tap it: Divide the class into two teams. Stick 4 to 6 wordcards up on the board in reach of the pupils. Call a pupil from each team to stand in front of the cards. Say the definition or give a clue about one of the words. The first pupil to tap the correct card gets a point. Mix the cards up and invite two other pupils to play.

Games and activities

Pupils learn in many different ways. The more experiences pupils can have around a new topic, the more likely they will learn and remember concepts and vocabulary. Games offer a wide range of opportunities for pupils to engage with and use what they are learning. They are also a chance to offer movement and a change of focus, as well as providing an opportunity for language learning. The competitive element inspires pupils to participate and, what could easily be an uninspiring list of revision questions or words to define, can be transformed into a fun game.

Helpful tips

I-Spy: Use the classroom, the playground, a poster or the opening illustration for a unit to say *I spy with my little eye something beginning with (/k/).* Pupils suggest words beginning with that letter to guess your word.

Pictionary: Divide the class into two teams. Start to draw an item on the board very slowly. In turns, teams have 30 seconds to guess what you are drawing. You'll need a timer! Once pupils are familiar with the game, they can play in threes. One pupil begins to draw an item from the unit or the Picture dictionary. The other two pupils in the group must guess what it is. The first to guess can draw the next picture.

Picture snap: Pupils draw one item from the unit e.g. something they have for breakfast, their favourite animal, a machine in their kitchen. Pupils must keep their picture a secret and must not show others. Provide pupils with the sentence starter you would like them to use e.g. *For breakfast I have ...; my favourite animal is ...; In my kitchen there's a ...* Pupils must walk around the classroom repeating their sentence to as many classmates as possible. If they hear somebody say the same item as them, they must shout Snap! and show each other their picture. Check at the end how many pupils had the same item as somebody else.

Stand up if...: Pupils listen to the statements you make. If they think your statement is true, they stand up. If they think it is false, they remain seated. Between statements, pupils sit down. The game can also be played with flashcards. Hold up a flashcard and make a true or false statement about what is on the flashcard. Pupils stand up if it is true.

Repeat if true: Pupils listen to your statements. If they think your statement is true, they repeat it. If they think it is false, they shake their heads and remain silent.

Chinese whispers: Have pupils stand one behind the other, in 3 lines of equal numbers. Whisper a sentence to the pupil at the end of each line at the same time. Pupils must whisper the sentence to the next person in their line, who whispers it to the next until it is passed down all the way to the first person in the line. The pupil at the front of the line puts up their hand when they think they know the sentence or runs and circles a flashcard or wordcard on the board).

Backs to the board: Divide the class into two teams. Place two chairs at the front of the class, each chair facing a team. Ask one pupil from each team to come and sit in the chair, facing their team but with their backs to the board. Write a word or put up a flashcard on the board behind the pupil's backs and insist that they do not turn round. (Ensure the class understand the word you have written). Encourage the teams to mime the word on the board to their team member who must guess what it is. The team member who guesses first gains a point for their team. Two new team members then come to the chairs.

Noughts and crosses: Draw a noughts and crosses grid on the board and write numbers in each square. Divide the class into two teams and choose one team to be *noughts* and one team to be *crosses*. For each number prepare a question or true false statement. Each team takes turns to choose a number. If they answer your question correctly, a team member can come up to the board and replace the number with a nought or a cross. The winning team is the first to get three noughts (or crosses) in a line.

Bingo: Pupils fold an A5 piece of paper in half, in half again, and in half one more time. When they open the paper up, they should have a grid with eight squares. Pupils draw (or write) 8 items from your lesson (food, animals, machines, etc.). Draw a grid with eight squares on the board. Draw items one at a time in your grid. If pupils have that same item in their grid, they can cross it out. When a pupil has crossed out all the items in their grid that are the same as yours, they can shout Bingo! Use the other side of the paper to start a new game.

Listen and do: Pupils listen carefully to two instructions at the same time e.g. *Wiggle your hips. Make an angry face; Touch something made of wood with your elbow. Scratch your head.* When pupils get good at remembering and following two instructions at a time, increase it to three.

Run to the corners: This is best played in the playground or gym. Label the corners of the space you are in with different categories. Organise pupils into groups. Give names to the different groups (animals, professions, food names). Call out the group name and a vocabulary item. The group must run to the correct corner.

Hangman (man on a raft): Instead of a hanging man, draw a man standing on a raft (ten circles under him on a rough river or sea). Draw a crocodile or shark in a corner of the board. Draw spaces for the letters of a word you want pupils to guess. If pupils guess a letter in the word correctly, write it in the correct space. If the letter does not appear in the word, write it under the crocodile or shark, and rub out a circle of the raft. Pupils must guess the word before the raft is totally rubbed away (and the man is eaten by the shark or crocodile!).

Quiz makers: At the end of a unit ask the pupils to work with a partner or divide the class into groups and invite them to make questions for a quiz about the topic. Tell them that they can use the Pupil's Book to help them. Remind them that they must also supply the answers to their questions. Take in their papers and use the questions to give the class a quiz. Read the questions to the class and ask them to write their answers on a paper. Paraphrase the questions so that the pupils can answer in a few words. They then exchange papers and the quiz is corrected collectively.

Vocabulary storms: As an introductory activity to a new topic, divide the class into groups and ask them to write down as many words as they can that are related to the topic that is going to be studied. At the end of the group activity, invite pupils to share their work with the rest of the class. Encourage pupils to come to the board to draw mind maps in order to organise the words from their lists.

Scrabble: Have sets of plastic alphabet letters, scrabble letters, and/or letter sets cut up on card. Divide the class into small groups. Give each group a set of letters. The groups spell the word you have read out loud.

Ready, steady, spell: Mini-white boards are a great learning aid! Say a word and have pupils spell it on their mini-white board and hold it up to show you. The boards also provide an easy opportunity for pupils to practise spelling a word before writing it in their books.

Classroom management

Assessment

Formative and summative assessments are essential in any Science class. In order to develop scientific competences, pupils need to reflect on their work, as well as the work of others. In addition to the printable tests available in the Digital resources, there are also evaluation sheets for each unit to help keep track of your pupils' progress. These are fully compliant with the evaluation criteria and learning standards as set out by the Spanish curriculum.

Classroom management

As with all ages, the establishment of clear rules for behaviour is key to successful classroom management. As the pupils are now older and more mature, encourage them to participate in the process of establishing these rules. You may want to explain to pupils that, as in society, they have rights and responsibilities in their Science class.

Elicit ideas from the pupils about the rights they feel they should have and the responsibilities they need to accept so that everyone can share those same rights. Possible rights and responsibilities include:

1. I have the right to share my ideas. I have a responsibility to listen to the ideas of others.

2. I have the right to feel safe sharing my work. I have a responsibility to contribute constructive criticism.

3. I have the right to use a variety of resources in my work. I have a responsibility to take care of those resources and to use them safely.

Classroom organisation

The physical arrangement of the classroom varies greatly from school to school and from teacher to teacher. Often, many different specialist teachers share one classroom and need to be sensitive to the needs of their fellow teachers. Depending on the extent of Cooperative Learning, it can be important that pupils are seated in groups of four to six in order to share ideas and complete projects in pairs or small groups. If the classroom is set up in rows, pupils can be taught to move their desks quickly and quietly into groups at the beginning of class. It is a routine that needs to be practised but one that can easily be mastered. Some activities can be completed whilst seated in rows.

Time management

Many pupils have limited time for their Science class each week. This means that the teacher needs to have all the materials prepared before class and establish procedures and routines in order to use the time effectively. Opening and closing activities can be shortened and lengthened depending on the time allotted for Science class. Holidays, excursions and absent pupils can interfere with the rhythm of the class. If needed, some activities from *Analyse and organise*, *Fragile world* or *Revise* can be sent home as homework.

Procedures

Procedures and routines are essential in class. These should be introduced gradually throughout the first term and practised on a regular basis. Positive reinforcement can help the acquisition of these procedures and routines.

Helpful procedures and routines for Science class include:

Listening routine

Use a quick and simple chant to get pupils' attention.

Teacher: *1, 2, 3. Look at me.*

Pupils: *1, 2. I'm looking at you.*

Attention routine

Sometimes during class, the teacher may need to stop the pupils in order to give them further instructions. Many pupils find it difficult to stop working and choose to keep reading, writing, discussing, etc. Using a bell, xylophone or other musical instruments can be useful to get pupils' attention, or the teacher can use a quick chant:

I've got something important to say.

Put your hands on your (head) and look my way.

Pupils have to stop working and put their hands on their heads. The teacher can change the word head for other parts of the body (e.g. *knees, shoulders,* etc.).

Moving desks procedure

Design a seating arrangement that will require the least amount of moving. Have pupils practise moving their desks quickly, quietly and carefully from rows to groups and back to rows again. Placing coloured tape on the floor can be helpful.

Distributing materials procedure

Design a procedure for handing out materials. A helper (or helpers) can be selected every week to help hand them out. This role can be used as a reward for good behaviour.

Cleaning up procedure

Design a procedure for cleaning up different types of science projects. Helpers can be useful in this procedure. There are many cleaning up songs on YouTube. You can choose one and play it while pupils clean up.

Cooperative Learning

What is Cooperative Learning?

Cooperative Learning (CL) is an educational situation in which students are required to work together in small groups or teams to support each other in order to improve their own learning and that of others. CL goes beyond merely seating students together; simply telling them they are a group does not mean they will cooperate effectively. For students to behave cooperatively, and to reach their full potential within a group or team, some essential elements need to be put in place.

What are the basic principles of Cooperative Learning? (Johnson, Johnson & Holubec, 2008)

1. Positive interdependence

Students perceive that they need each other in order to complete the group's task. Every student in a small group must contribute to the learning of the group, and each member needs the others to complete the task. We can enhance positive interdependence by establishing mutual goals which *"will help each student to learn and make sure all other team members learn"* (Johnson, Johnson & Holubec, 2008).

2. Individual accountability

"Each student's performance is assessed and the results are given to that student and the rest of the members of the group" (Johnson, Johnson & Holubec, 2008). Therefore, each member of the group is responsible for completing their part of the work and must develop a sense of personal responsibility towards him or herself and the rest of the group, because individual performance will affect not only one's own result, but also the results of the wider team.

3. Promotive interaction

"Students promote each other's learning by helping, sharing, and encouraging efforts to learn" (Johnson, Johnson & Holubec, 2008). CL implies face-to-face interaction. Students need not only to discuss and agree but also to produce a piece of work through combined effort, because Cooperate Learning is not about working individually and making a 'cut-and-paste' final product.

4. Social abilities

Students need interpersonal skills in order to be successful. Some of these include:

- Effective leadership
- Decision-making
- Trust-building
- Communication
- Conflict resolution
- Helping and asking for help
- Organisation
- Self-esteem and self-confidence

Students aren't born knowing how to behave in a group. We have to teach them, giving them models, and opportunities to practise these skills.

5. Group processing

Developing CL methodology is not easy at first, nor are the effects immediate. Difficulties within the groups, resources and management may arise. That is why formative assessment is needed. This assessment involves both teachers and students.

One way of structuring group assessment is by:

- Listing at least three member actions that helped the group be successful (students).
- Listing at least one action that could make the group even more successful (students).
- Monitoring the groups and giving feedback on how well the groups are working together and the class as a whole (teacher) (Johnson, Johnson, & Holubec, 2008).

We need to be aware of the strong and weak points in order to make the right decisions and develop the methodology in the right direction.

Why Cooperative Learning?

The benefits of using CL are supported by theory and are well established by classroom research.

There are several reasons why CL works as well as it does:

- Students learn more by doing something active than by simply watching and listening, and CL is by nature an active method.
- Cooperation enhances learning. Weak students working individually tend to give up when they get stuck, but when working as a part of a team they keep going.

- When stronger students help and work together with weaker students, they often find gaps in their own understanding and do something about filling in those gaps.
- Students working alone may tend to delay or skip their assignments, but when they work as a part of a team and realise that others are counting on them, they will often feel more motivated and do the work in a timely manner.

Nevertheless, we should never forget that the benefits of CL are not automatic, and it takes time to learn to work and function in a cooperative way.

Cooperative Learning structures (UNT, 2008)

Once the teacher has determined the objective of the lesson, he or she can select a structure that will provide the optimal learning experience for the student in a cooperative context. Learning structures are available for almost any learning situation.

Timed pair share

In pairs, students share ideas with a classmate for a predetermined time while the classmate listens. Then they switch roles. (Kagan & Kagan, 2009)

Steps for the Strategy:

1. Students are paired and work in pairs.
2. Present a problem to the students.
3. Provide them with a specific amount of time to write their answers.
4. Students discuss their answers with other students either in front of or beside them.
5. Call on students to share with the class the answer they have developed with their partners.

Round robin

In teams, students take turns responding orally. (Kagan & Kagan, 2009)

Steps for the strategy:

1. Teacher asks a question.
2. Students take turns answering the question.

Think-Write-Pair Share

In teams, students write or draw their own ideas before they pair up to discuss them with a partner. This allows students to more fully develop their own ideas before sharing.

Steps for the strategy:

1. Students write their ideas.
2. Students pair up and discuss their ideas with a partner.

Teammates consult

In teams students discuss an answer and nobody writes it down until all of them come to an agreement.

Steps for the strategy:

1. Students put their pencils down in the centre of the table.
2. Teammates discuss the question. All members of the team contribute, but they don't all have to agree on one answer.
3. When everyone on the team is ready with an answer, team members pick up their pencils and write the answer.

Team project

Steps for the strategy:

1. The teacher clearly explains the project and the amount of time teams have to complete it.
2. The teacher assigns roles: materials manager, reporter, timekeeper, captain…
3. After distributing the materials, teams work to complete the task.
4. The teacher monitors students.
5. Teams share their project with the class. This may be done by creating a chart.

The teacher's role in Cooperative Learning

Teachers should reinforce and help the students to learn how to work in a group:

a. Taking care of the different cooperative skills the students will need to manage in order to work together effectively and efficiently. This is essential because all the elements derived from social interaction in the classroom depend on these cooperative skills.

b. Turning social interaction into promotive interaction. Teachers should ask students reflect on the way they address their teammates: what they mean and how they sound.

c. Creating opportunities for inter-individual information intake (or processing), making students aware of their individual accountability.

d. Contemplating group assessment as an instrument for cooperative reflection to ensure the improvement of the cooperative structure. Teachers should help students identify their weak and strong points as a group and to take the necessary steps to improve.

Cooperative skills

Cooperative skills can be classified as (Johnson, Johnson, & Holubec, 2008):

Organisation skills: those related to group formation and organisation as well as establishing behavioural rules.

- Encouraging every member to participate
- Turn-taking
- Forming groups quickly with minimum noise
- Staying in the group
- Managing noise level
- Respecting other members' personal space
- Taking care of materials
- Paying attention to the person talking
- Respecting everybody's opinions

Working out skills: those devoted to completing the tasks and keeping efficient working relationships within the group.

- Reflecting on more efficient procedures
- Guiding task procedures
- Defining the purpose of the task
- Establishing time limits
- Expressing approval
- Asking for help
- Paraphrasing others' ideas
- Resolving conflicts
- Making shared decisions by negotiating and reaching a consensus

Formulation skills: those needed for a deep understanding of the concepts the students have acquired.

- Summarising
- Correcting others and adding information
- Scaffolding with previously seen concepts
- Creating memorisation strategies
- Checking understanding
- Explaining how the task should be done

Processing skills: those targeted as raising socio-cognitive awareness to cultivate a more in-depth understanding. For example:

- Discussing ideas
- Integrating different ideas in one conclusion
- Improving the answers of other group members
- Verifying and contrasting the work produced with the instructions given

Team formation

Teachers should form the teams rather than letting the students to choose their own teammates.

One of the fundamental aspects in structuring CL activities is the size of the groups. Ideally, form teams of 3–4 students. Pair work doesn't usually produce the diversity of ideas and approaches common to CL. In teams of five or more, some students are likely to be inactive.

Make the teams heterogeneous in ability level. In heterogeneous groups, the weaker students learn from others, and the stronger students gain a deeper understanding of the subject by teaching it to their peers.

The Cooperative Learning session

There should be four different stages in every CL Session:

1. Activation

This stage works as a warm-up. It is an opportunity for eliciting previous knowledge about the topic.

2. Introduction

The teacher introduces new content. This is the moment for giving instructions and explaining the 'why'.

3. Development

At this stage, teamwork comes into play according to the strategies designed by the teacher.

4. Feedback

The feedback session will provide very useful information for the teacher, who checks if the concepts have been properly understood.

And last but not least...

- If you've never used CL, consider starting with small group activities in class. Once you're comfortable with that, try a team project or assignment, up to a level of CL with which you are comfortable.
- At the start of the course, explain to students what they'll be doing in teams, what procedures you'll follow, and what your expectations are.
- Make team assignments more challenging than traditional individual assignments. CL works best for challenging problems and activities that require higher-level thinking skills.
- A term assessment is essential to find out how students feel about teamwork. Ask students to reflect on what works and doesn't work in their team. If many teams are experiencing the same problem, spend some time in class on the relevant cooperative skills. Most of the time, however, the assessment will show that most teams are working well.
- Expect initial resistance from students.

Further reading

ABRAMI, P.C. (1995). *Classroom connections: Understanding and using cooperative learning*. Toronto: Harcourt Brace.

JOHNSON, D.W., JOHNSON, R.T. & HOLUBEC, E.J. (2008). *Cooperation in the classroom* (8th ed.). Edina, New Mexico: Interaction Book Company.

KAGAN, S. (1992). *Cooperative learning*. San Juan Capistrano, California: Resources for Teachers, Inc.

SLAVIN, R. E. (1990). *Cooperative learning: Theory, research, and practice*. Englewood Cliffs, New Jersey: Prentice-Hall.

SLAVIN, R. E. (1995). *Cooperative learning* (2nd ed.). Boston: Allyn and Bacon.

UNIVERSITY OF NORTH TEXAS (2008). *Classroom best practices: Cooperative learning*. Texas: UNT in partnership with Department of Teacher Education and Administration.

PAGES 4–5 Meet Alex and Carla

PAGE SUMMARY

The aim of these introductory pages is to introduce the course characters, Carla and Alex. There are a few different pairwork activities to encourage pupils to work with their classmates. This is a good opportunity to mix the class up and get pupils working with different people. If you have new pupils in your class this year, use the activities to help the class get to know their new classmates.

LANGUAGE

- Vocabulary: free time activities, professions, living things
- *Like / don't like* + verb + ing

ADDITIONAL MATERIALS

- Digital flashcards
- Digital wordcards

MEET THE COURSE CHARACTERS

Carla and Alex are the ByME Natural Science 4 course characters. They guide the pupils through the units and go on school trips to places your pupils might not have had the opportunity to visit. If you are also studying ByME Social Science 4, you will see that Tom and Ana are present too, as members of the class.

OPENING ACTIVITY

- Before the class begins, open the digital Pupil's Book on page 4 and click on the illustration of Carla and Alex. Black out the text in the speech bubbles.
- Ask the pupils some questions about the characters: **Where are they? What are they doing? How old do you think they are? What do you think they like doing?**

MAIN ACTIVITIES

(1) Answer Carla and Alex's questions.

- Ask the pupils to open their books on page 4. Ask two pupils to read what Carla and Alex say, and choose a few different pupils to answer the questions.
- If you have time, you could carry out a quick survey: **What do you want to be when you grow up?** Collect answers on the board and draw any conclusions, e.g. five boys want to be footballers, four girls want to be doctors. Do boys and girls prefer different professions?

(2) Match these living things to Alex and Carla's clues.

- Ask the pupils to look at the pictures and read the clues in activity 2 for 20 seconds, then close their books. Ask them to work in pairs and write down the key words from the questions. Write them on the board.
- Ask pupils to open their books and match the photos to their definitions. *1-C, 2-A, 3-D, 4-B*
- Ask pupils to think of more living things, write descriptions and test their partner.

(3) In pairs, say what you can see in the photos. Use each object or living thing in a sentence.

- In pairs, pupils look at the photos for ten seconds, before closing their book.
- Ask each pair to try and remember what the photos were.
- Ask them to open their books and look at the photos. Check understanding of the objects or living things in the photos. Some of them will be new to the pupils, e.g. the ultrasound machine. **What do we use this machine for? Who uses it?** *See Answers at a glance.*
- Ask pairs to think of sentences using each of the objects or living things. If the pupils are struggling, give them some assistance.

(4) Read about some of the things you will learn in your Natural Science book.

- Write the following words on the board in circles: **body systems, medical advances, forces, machines, plants** and **animal nutrition, respiration and reproduction**. Check their understanding of these words.
- Ask for ideas for each category and add the words to the circles.
- Carry out a class race. Ask pupils to find out which unit covers the topics they have brainstormed. The pupils flick through their books and put their hands up when they have the unit number or the page number *(body systems – unit 1/pages 10-14; medical advances – unit 2/pages 22-23; forces – unit 7/pages 106-107; machines – unit 9; plants – unit 5; animal nutrition, respiration and reproduction – unit 4)*

(+) CLOSING ACTIVITIES

- Ask pupils to look at the photos from activity 3. Ask them, in pairs, to put the objects or living things into the categories from activity 4. For example, the ultrasound machine would belong to the *medical advances* category.

(+) EXTRA IDEAS

- Make a class vocabulary poster, using the categories from activity 4. Pupils can add words (they could be accompanied by illustrations) to the poster in this lesson, and then add more words over the course of the year. You could make one big poster, or a poster for each category, depending on how much space there is in the classroom.

ANSWERS AT A GLANCE

(1) Open answer.

(2) 1-C, 2-A, 3-D, 4-B.

(3) Clockwise from the top left: a butterfly and a flower, a lemon tree, an ultrasound machine, a lion and a cub, a model heart, a seesaw.

(4) Body systems – unit 1/pages 10-14; medical advances – unit 2/pages 22-23; forces – unit 7/pages 106-107; machines – unit 9; plants – unit 5; animal nutrition, respiration and reproduction – unit 4.

UNIT 1 Body systems

CONTENT	EVALUATION CRITERIA
Parts of the body.	Know the parts of the human body: internal and external.
Nutrition.	Know the different organs and systems involved in nutrition.
Interaction.	Know the different organs and systems involved in interaction.
Reproduction.	Know the different organs involved in reproduction, and the difference between the male and female reproductive systems.
First approaches to scientific activity and the scientific method. Use of different information sources (direct and indirect). Use ICTs.	Obtain relevant information about specific phenomena, make predictions, integrate information from direct and indirect observation and communicate the results.
First approaches to simple experiments and investigations.	Conjecture as to the results of natural occurrences and of simple experiments and investigations.
Individual and group work.	Work independently and proactively and develop strategies for working in a group.
Planning a project and presenting a report.	Carry out a project and present a report.

LEARNING STANDARDS	KEY COMPETENCES	PAGES
Knows the parts of the body: internal and external.	MST	7–15
Explains the process of nutrition, and knows the organs and systems involved.	MST, LIN	10, 11
Explains the process of interaction and knows the organs and systems involved.	MST, LIN	12, 13
Knows the different organs involved in reproduction and the difference between the male and female reproductive systems.	MST	14
Understands how human beings are born.	MST	15
With help, selects and organises specific and relevant information; analyses it and draws conclusions; reflects on the experience and the process; presents the results.	MST, LTL	9, 16, 17
Use books, libraries, etc. and collaborate in the care and maintenance of all the materials available in the school and the classroom.	MST, LTL	6–19
Shows autonomy in the planning of activities and tasks and shows initiative in decision taking.	LTL, AUT	9, 16, 17
With help, carries out simple experiments or investigations, and conjectures as to the results.	MST, LTL, AUT	16, 17
Uses strategies to help their own learning, as well as asking for help and information.	LTL, AUT	9, 16–18
First approaches to Cooperative Learning.	SOC, LTL	7, 17
Begins observation, using relevant instruments and consulting written documents and images.	LTL, AUT	16
Shows autonomy and proactiveness in the planning of and carrying out of actions.	AUT	16, 17
Presents work clearly and in an organised fashion.	LIN, LTL, AUT	16, 17
With help, carries out a project and presents a report, using paper and/or digital means, collecting information from different sources, presenting the results orally and with the support of images and short texts.	LIN, LTL, AUT, DIG	16, 17

UNIT INFORMATION

UNIT SUMMARY

In this unit, pupils will review and extend their knowledge of the human body, looking at different body systems and the organs that work together to make up these systems. They will study the digestive, circulatory, respiratory and the male and female reproductive systems. This year they will also gain insight into the development of a human baby in the uterus, and childbirth.

At the beginning of the unit, pupils will revise the body systems they studied the previous year and also extend that knowledge. This subject area is covered in the opening illustration with the help of the course characters, Carla and Alex, who are on a school trip to a biology fair. The school trip continues in the story and, on their return to school, Alex and Carla carry out a *School trip project* to review all the parts of the digestive and respiratory systems. These opening pages are designed to test pupils' prior knowledge and ease them into the subject matter of the unit, stimulating interest and participation.

They will move on to study body systems and look at how these systems work together. The aim of this unit is to focus on the idea that our body is made up of systems that work together like a complex machine and to look in more detail at how these systems work.

EXPERIMENT

Find out

In the *Find out* activity on page 16, pupils will prepare a model to observe how the diaphragm helps us breathe by changing the amount of space inside our chest when we breathe in and out.

Pupils will need:

- a plastic bottle (with the bottom cut off)
- a plastic bag
- two balloons
- two straws
- some tape
- scissors
- some plasticine

VALUES AND ATTITUDES

In this unit, pupils will learn to appreciate how important our body systems are and how they are connected. Throughout the unit, try to encourage pupils to think about the purpose of each system and the importance of keeping them healthy and in good condition.

Think about it

The *Think about* it page in this unit focuses on the way that the pupils now have to face more responsibilities at home and at school. They are encouraged to think and talk about the things that worry them and to realise that these worries are normal but can affect their behaviour. They will be shown how to control their emotions by using a calm breathing method.

EVALUATION MATERIAL

These documents can be downloaded from the *Teachers* section of the digital component and printed.

The materials include:

- Unit diagnostic test: provides an overview of the unit and allows you to assess the pupils' prior knowledge.
- And end-of-unit test: in addition to the *Review* section at the end of each unit, this summative test can be used to evaluate pupils' progress after studying the unit content.
- A class unit evaluation grid: this is based on the evaluation criteria and learning standards of the unit.

DIGITAL RESOURCES

Presentations

- Unit summary: a simple slide presentation with text, images and audio to review the main ideas of the unit. It can be used at the beginning of the unit to test pupils' prior knowledge of the unit content, or at the end of the unit as a revision tool.
- Find out: a slide presentation of the unit's *Find out* page with text, photos and audio. The slide presentation is perfect for a heads-up class, showing the steps one by one. Use this tool to get pupils to predict the next steps (with their books closed) or to focus their attention on each step as they carry out the project themselves.

Activities

Activities vary by unit and include:

- A memory game: a useful activity for reviewing key vocabulary and modelling pronunciation.
- Labelling: pupils label a diagram by dragging and dropping key terms.
- Spelling: pupils drag and drop letters to spell key terms.
- Read and reveal: pupils read sentences and guess the missing words, which are revealed by clicking the spaces.
- Classification: pupils drag and drop concepts and key terms in a simple classification table.
- A wordsearch: pupils find key terms hidden in the wordsearch.
- Definitions: pupils drag and drop words to complete definitions.

Song lyrics

Listen to the song *Body systems* and follow the lyrics line by line.

Posters

Attractive and informative posters to display in class. You can use them to review key concepts and vocabulary.

Videos

Use the video links in this unit to present content in a dynamic, real-life context while reinforcing pupils' listening skills.

Teachers

Digital flashcards and wordcards: topics include *Nutrition*, *Interaction* and *Reproduction*.

Downloadable PDFs: evaluation tests, evaluation grids, templates, useful links and further information.

PAGES 6–7 Body systems

6

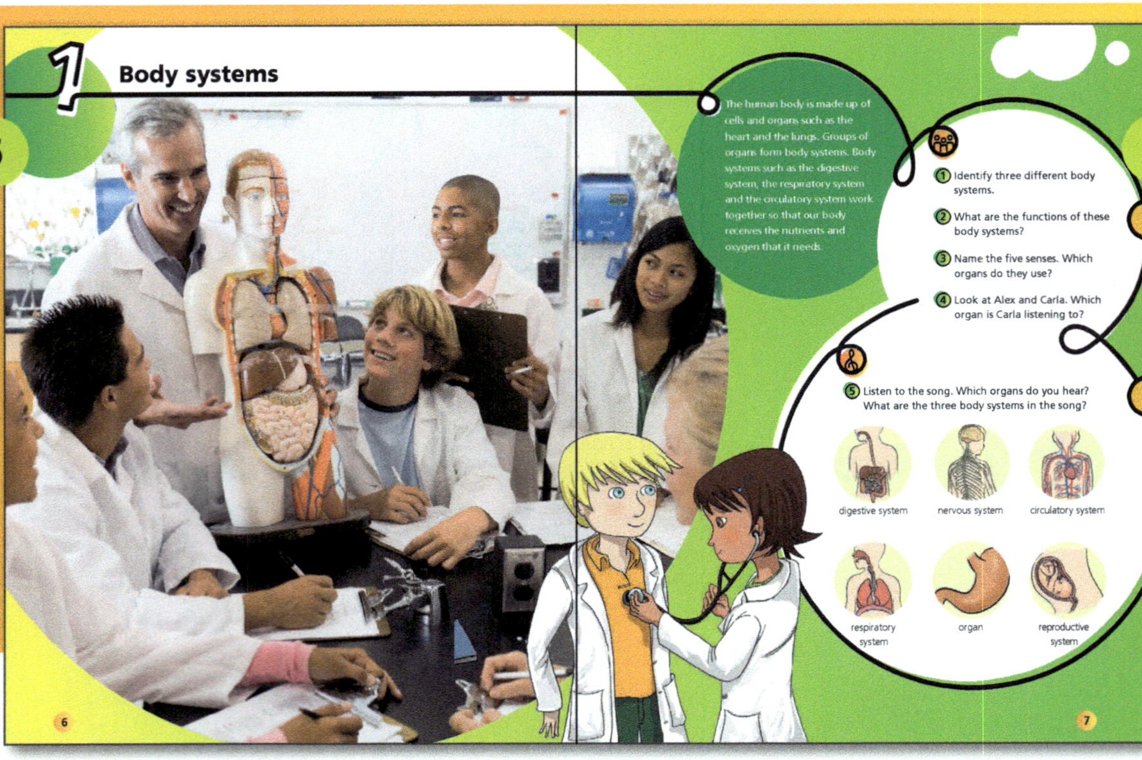

7

02

03

PAGE SUMMARY

The aim here is to develop your pupils' observation skills and discover what they already know about the unit topic. Use the picture to elicit vocabulary related to the human body and body systems. Get pupils to work in groups to complete activities 1–4 and to have fun listening to the song and completing activity 5.

LANGUAGE

- Question words: *what, which*
- Present tense
- Prepositions: *on, in, in front of, behind, next to, between*
- Present continuous: *What is he doing?*
- Vocabulary: *respiratory system, circulatory system, digestive system, nervous system, brain, heart, lungs, stomach, intestines, eye, ear, nose, tongue, skin, organs, sight, hearing, smell, touch, taste, stethoscope*

ADDITIONAL MATERIALS

- Digital flashcards
- Digital wordcards

OPENING ACTIVITIES

- If you are using an interactive whiteboard, focus only on the illustration of the biology fair, not the questions. Either elicit ideas (*The man is holding a model. He is talking about the human body,* etc.) or ask questions indicating the relevant picture part: **What's Carla doing? What are the pupils doing?**
- Make false statements about the picture and encourage pupils to correct you. **I can see four people in the room. Carla is testing Alex's eyes,** etc.

MAIN ACTIVITIES

Page 7, Unit introduction (CD1 track 02)

- Ask pupils to brainstorm as many body parts as possible. Write their suggestions on the board. Make two groups of words: external body parts and internal body parts. Highlight any tricky spellings such as *knee, tongue*, etc. Elicit why there are two groups. Ask pupils if they can think of other subgroups, e.g. bones, joints, parts of the face, etc.
- Now focus their attention on the opening text. Play the audio while pupils read, then ask one or two pupils to read out loud . This way, pupils will feel more assured when pronouncing new words. (See *Helpful tips*, pages 20-23.)

* Divide pupils into small groups to answer the questions (top of page 7). Then invite different groups to compare their answers.

1 Identify three different body systems.

* Point to the model of the human torso on the table and see if they can name the internal organs shown. (*Lungs, heart, stomach, intestines.*) Place the wordcards on the board and elicit which body systems they belong to. Ask **Which organ controls all our body systems?** Elicit that the brain is part of the nervous system. Tell pupils to work in pairs to identify the body systems they can see. *The circulatory, digestive and respiratory systems*

2 What are the functions of these body systems?

* If pupils find this question difficult, help by asking questions. **Which system helps us digest our food?** *(Digestive system.)* **Which system helps us breathe?** *(Respiratory system.)* **Which system takes blood around the body?** *(Circulatory system.) See Answers at a glance*

3 Name the five senses. Which organs do they use?

* Ask **Which system gives us information about the things around us?** Elicit the organs of the five senses and place the wordcards on the board. Invite volunteers to place the corresponding sense next to the sense organ. Tell pupils to find examples of people using their senses in the picture. *See Answers at a glance.*

4 Look at Alex and Carla. Which organ is Carla listening to?

* Ask pupils which organ Carla is listening to. *She's listening to Alex's heart.*

5 Listen to the song. Which organs do you hear? What are the three body systems in the song?

* Focus pupils' attention on the five photos. Ask them to read and repeat the words. Check for understanding. Play the song *Body systems* **(CD1 track 03)** and ask pupils to point to the body parts they hear. Then play the song again and encourage pupils to sing along (use the *Song lyrics* section on the digital component to display the words as you listen). *Heart, intestines and lungs. The circulatory, digestive and respiratory systems*

CD1 • Track 02

Body systems, body systems
So many systems
What do they do?
What do they do?
The heart pumps your blood
All around your body
Never stopping
The circulatory system
A transport line to all your cells
Taking nutrients from the small intestine
Oxygen from the lungs
To all your body parts
The circulatory, digestive and respiratory systems working together
Keeping the cells alive
Helping us survive

+ CLOSING ACTIVITIES

* Label the corners of the classroom with the names of the different body systems: digestive, circulatory, respiratory and nervous systems. Organise pupils into groups (Group A, Group B, etc.). Call out the names of different organs. Groups must move to the correct corner. For example, **Group A: Heart**. A walks to the circulatory system corner.

ANSWERS AT A GLANCE

1. The circulatory, digestive and respiratory systems.
2. The digestive system breaks down food into nutrients. The respiratory system gets oxygen from the air and expels carbon dioxide. The circulatory system takes nutrients and oxygen to all parts of the body.
3. Sight – eye; Smell – nose; Hearing – ear; Taste – tongue; Touch – skin.
4. Carla's listening to Alex's heart.
5. Heart, intestines and lungs. The circulatory, digestive and respiratory systems.

PAGES 8–9 A trip to the biology fair

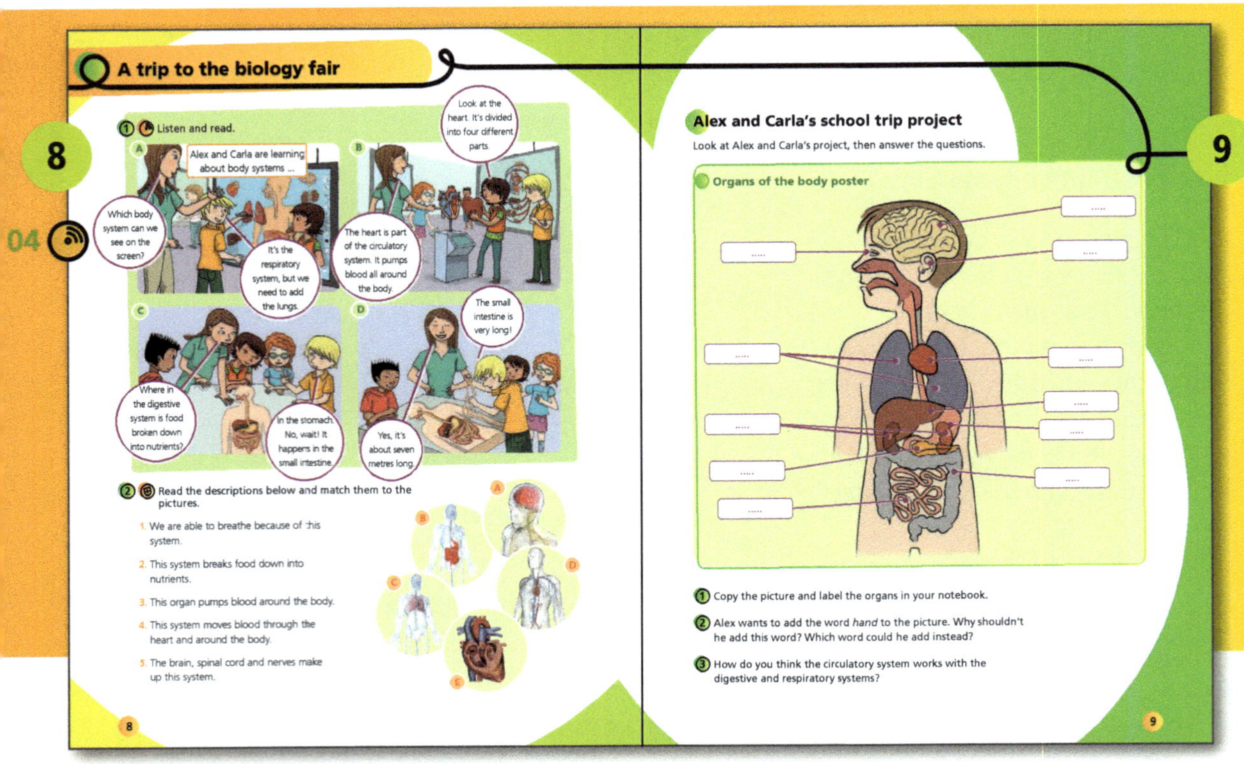

PAGE SUMMARY

This spread opens by following Carla and Alex's biology fair story. They are talking to the guide, showing their knowledge of body systems. The story is reinforced with an exam-style matching activity, related to the story and the opening double-page spread. On page 9, pupils can study Carla and Alex's school trip project about the organs that make up different body systems.

LANGUAGE

- Question words: *which, where, how long, how*
- *Should / shouldn't*
- Vocabulary: *respiratory system, circulatory system, digestive system, lungs, heart, blood, stomach, small intestine, large intestine, brain, eye, ear, liver, stomach, pancreas, kidneys, pump*

MATERIALS

- Digital flashcards
- Digital wordcards
- Extra materials: Tissue paper, shiny paper, cellophane, newspaper, etc.

OPENING ACTIVITIES

- Play the *Body systems* song **(CD1 track 03)** and encourage pupils to sing along.
- Place wordcards on the board. Invite pupils to group the cards into systems. (There will be some unknown wordcards left over. Ignore for now but leave them on the board for the *School trip project*.) Now ask volunteers to add other words to the systems. **Can you add more words to the nervous system?** Tongue, skin, nose, etc.

MAIN ACTIVITIES

1 Listen and read. (CD1 track 04)

- Draw pupils' attention to the story (top of page 8) and explain that they are going to listen to a story about Alex and Carla's biology fair trip. Say **Let's listen and read**. Play the audio.
- Ask pupils to look at each of the illustrations and describe what is happening using their own words. For example, *Alex is adding the lungs to the respiratory system. Carla is looking at a model of a heart.*
- Divide pupils into groups of three and ask them to choose a character from the story – Alex, Carla or the guide. Pupils then read their part of the story aloud in their small group. Invite a group to the front of the class to act the story out.

② Read the descriptions below and match them to the pictures.

- This activity reinforces what pupils have learned and refreshes concepts studied at previous levels. Focus pupils' attention on the illustrations first. Ask them to work in pairs to identify the systems. Ask **Why is picture E the odd one out?** *It is an organ, not a system.*
- Now ask them to take turns to read the definition for their partner to identify the illustration.

1-C (respiratory system), 2-B (digestive system), 3-E (heart), 4-D (circulatory system), 5-A (nervous system)

SCHOOL TRIP PROJECT

- Before pupils open their books, copy the outline of the picture (page 9) onto the board. Invite pupils to come up and to draw the organs they are familiar with inside the outline. (*Brain, eye, ear, lungs, heart, stomach, small intestine, large intestine*)
- Look at the illustration on page 9 and ask for volunteers to label the picture on the board with the wordcards (*liver, pancreas* and *kidneys* are new vocabulary). Give clues to help identification. **The largest organ is called the liver. The pancreas is a small organ under the stomach. The kidneys are two small bean-shaped organs.**

① Copy the picture and label the organs in your notebook.

- Prepare a photocopied outline for pupils, or get them to copy the picture. Suggest they use different colours for each organ (but the same colour for the two kidneys). Alternately, tell them the colours for each organ and use this as a colour dictation.
- Ask pupils which system the liver and pancreas belong to. Explain that they help break down food. Explain that the kidneys are part of the excretory system, which eliminates liquid waste from the body. *Labels: brain, eye, ear, lungs, heart, liver, stomach, kidneys, pancreas, large intestine, small intestine*

② Alex wants to add the word *hand* to the picture. Why shouldn't he add this word? Which word could he add instead?

- Elicit that a hand isn't an organ. *Alex should add the word skin because it's the sense organ for touch.*

③ How do you think the circulatory system works with the disgestive and respiratory systems?

- Organise the class into small groups to work together and answer the question. Write on the board. **What does the digestive system do? What does the respiratory system do? What does the circulatory system do?** *The blood in the circulatory system carries nutrients from the digestive system and oxygen from the respiratory system to all parts of the body.*

⊕ CLOSING ACTIVITIES

- Play *Quick flash* with the wordcards/flashcards. Place a group of wordcards / flashcards in a pile, facing you. Quickly, turn the pile around to face the pupils, then turn it back. Pupils say the word they see. (See *Helpful tips*, pages 20 -23.)

ANSWERS AT A GLANCE

Page 8

② 1–C (respiratory system), 2–B (digestive system), 3–E (heart), 4–D (circulatory system), 5–A (nervous system).

Page 9

① Brain, eye, ear, lungs, heart, liver, stomach, kidneys, pancreas, large intestine, small intestine.

② No, he shouldn't. The hand isn't an organ. He could label skin, the sense organ for touch.

③ Model answer: The blood in the circulatory system carries nutrients from the digestive system and oxygen from the respiratory system to all parts of the body.

PAGES 10–11 Nutrition

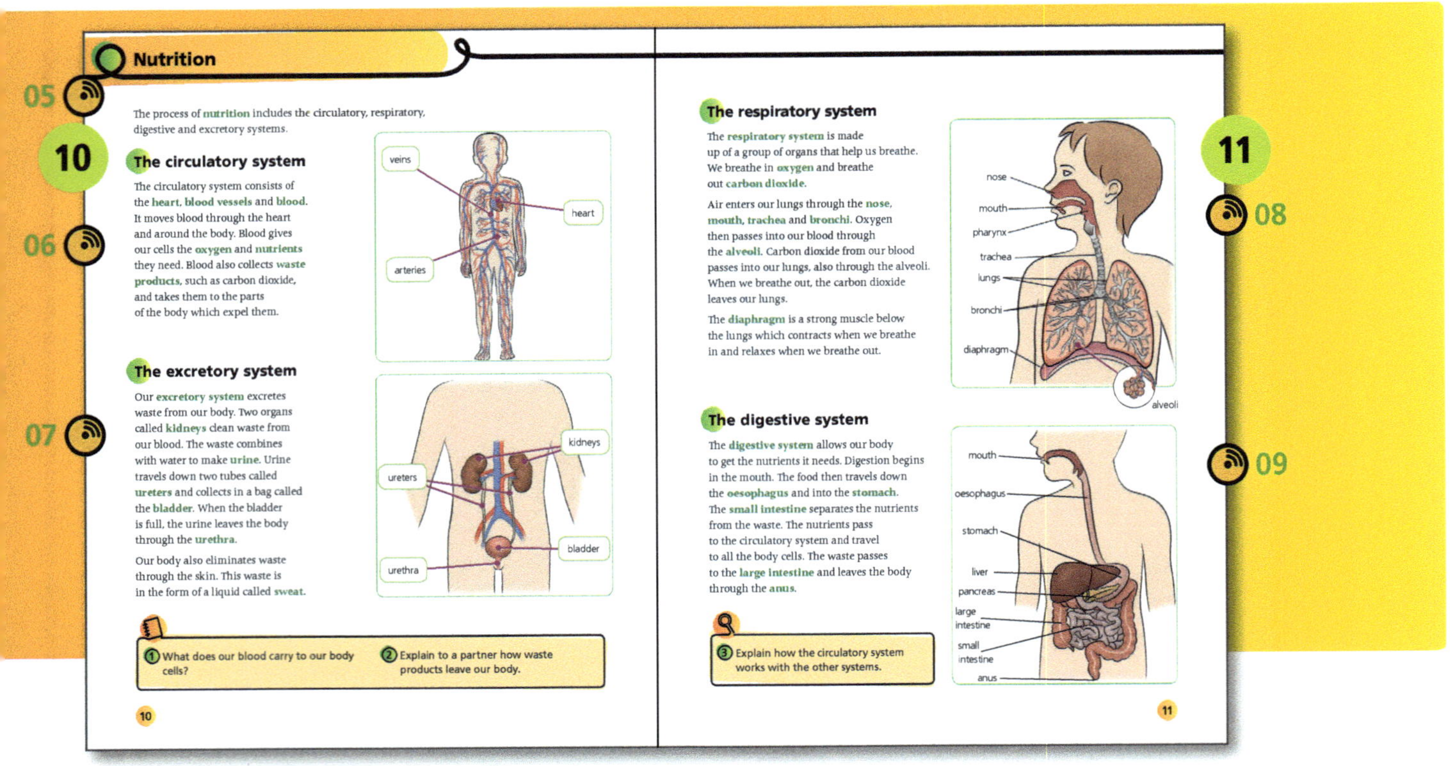

05 06 07 08 09

10

Nutrition

The process of **nutrition** includes the circulatory, respiratory, digestive and excretory systems.

The circulatory system

The circulatory system consists of the **heart**, **blood vessels** and **blood**. It moves blood through the heart and around the body. Blood gives our cells the **oxygen** and **nutrients** they need. Blood also collects **waste products**, such as carbon dioxide, and takes them to the parts of the body which expel them.

The excretory system

Our **excretory system** excretes waste from our body. Two organs called **kidneys** clean waste from our blood. The waste combines with water to make **urine**. Urine travels down two tubes called **ureters** and collects in a bag called the **bladder**. When the bladder is full, the urine leaves the body through the **urethra**.

Our body also eliminates waste through the skin. This waste is in the form of a liquid called **sweat**.

1. What does our blood carry to our body cells?
2. Explain to a partner how waste products leave our body.

10

11

The respiratory system

The **respiratory system** is made up of a group of organs that help us breathe. We breathe in **oxygen** and breathe out **carbon dioxide**.

Air enters our lungs through the **nose**, **mouth**, **trachea** and **bronchi**. Oxygen then passes into our blood through the **alveoli**. Carbon dioxide from our blood passes into our lungs, also through the alveoli. When we breathe out, the carbon dioxide leaves our lungs.

The **diaphragm** is a strong muscle below the lungs which contracts when we breathe in and relaxes when we breathe out.

The digestive system

The **digestive system** allows our body to get the nutrients it needs. Digestion begins in the mouth. The food then travels down the **oesophagus** and into the **stomach**. The **small intestine** separates the nutrients from the waste. The nutrients pass to the circulatory system and travel to all the body cells. The waste passes to the **large intestine** and leaves the body through the **anus**.

3. Explain how the circulatory system works with the other systems.

11

PAGE SUMMARY

This spread introduces pupils to the life process of nutrition. A lot of new vocabulary and concepts are covered here. Do not expect pupils to absorb everything at once; the main learning aim is to understand the purpose of the four body systems (circulatory, excretory, respiratory and digestive) and understand how they work together.

LANGUAGE

- Present simple
- Sequencing words: *first, next, then, after that, finally*
- Vocabulary: *heart, blood, oxygen, nutrients, waste, kidneys, urine, urethra, ureters, sweat, oxygen, carbon dioxide, nose, mouth, trachea, bronchi, diaphragm, oesophagus, stomach, small intestine, large intestine, anus, circulatory system, excretory system, respiratory system, digestive system*

MATERIALS

- Digital flashcards
- Digital wordcards

OPENING ACTIVITIES

- Put your hand on your heart and ask pupils to copy you. Ask which organ is underneath (*the heart*). Now ask **If you fall over and cut yourself, what liquid comes out of your body?** (*Blood.*) Place the wordcards *heart* and *blood* on the board. Elicit that the heart and blood are part of the circulatory system and that in this lesson they are going to find out more about the circulatory system and other body systems involved in the vital life process of nutrition.

MAIN ACTIVITIES

Page 10, Nutrition (CD1 track 05)

- Before you read the text, ask pupils to look at the illustrations. If you are using an interactive whiteboard, black out the text. Ask the pupils which body systems they can see. Elicit that these body systems all play a vital part in the vital life process of nutrition.
- Play the audio track **(CD1 track 05)** for the introductory text on page 10 and say **Let's listen and read**.
- Ask the pupils to write the four body systems in their notebooks as headings in a table. Then ask them to close their Pupil's Book. Pupils, in pairs, write down any organs or body parts under the relevant heading/body system. They will check to see if these body parts are under the right body system during the course of the lesson.

Page 10, The circulatory system (CD1 track 06)

- Play the audio track **(CD1 track 06)** for the circulatory system and say **Let's listen and read.**
- Ask pupils questions to check their understanding. **What does the circulatory system consist of? What does our blood give to our cells? Which waste product does our blood help get rid of?**
- Pupils can check the section for the circulatory system in the table they made and add to it.

Page 10, The excretory system (CD1 track 07)

- Play the audio track **(CD1 track 07)** for the excretory system and say **Let's listen and read.**
- Ask pupils questions to check their understanding. **What does the excretory system consist of? Which organs clean waste from our blood? Where does urine collect before it leaves the body?**
- Pupils can check the section for the excretory system in the table they made and add to it.

1 What does our blood carry to our body cells?

- Encourage pupils, in pairs, to think what our blood gives our body cells. (*Oxygen and nutrients.*) You could also ask them what our blood removes from our body cells. (*Waste products such as carbon dioxide.*)

2 Explain to a partner how waste products leave our body

- You can help pupils answer this question by writing the main stages of the excretory process on the board in a random order, e.g. *The waste combines with water to make urine; Urine leaves the body through the urethra, etc.* Ask pupils, in pairs or small groups, to order the sentences. *See Answers at a glance*

Page 11, The respiratory system (CD1 track 08)

- Play the audio track **(CD1 track 08)** for the respiratory system and say **Let's listen and read.**
- Ask pupils questions to check their understanding. **What does the respiratory system do? Which muscle, found below the lungs, helps us to breathe?**
- Pupils can check the section for the respiratory system in the table they made and add to it.

Page 11, The digestive system (CD1 track 09)

- Play the audio track **(CD1 track 09)** for the digestive system and say **Let's listen and read.**
- Ask pupils questions to check their understanding. **What does the digestive system do? How does food travel to our stomach?**
- Pupils can check the section for the respiratory system in the table they made and add to it.

3 Explain how the circulatory system works with other systems.

- Refer pupils to their answer for question 1. Ask them questions to connect the circulatory system with the other body systems. **Where do the nutrients that our blood carries to our cells come from? How do they become nutrients? Our circulatory system collects carbon dioxide – how does it leave our body? How do other waste products leave our body?** *See Answers at a glance*

ANSWERS AT A GLANCE

1. The circulatory system gives our cells the oxygen and nutrients it needs.
2. Our kidneys clean waste from our blood. The waste combines with water to make urine. Urine travels down the ureters and collects in the bladder. Finally, the urine leaves the body through the urethra.
3. The circulatory system carries the nutrients provided by the digestive system. It carries the oxygen provided by the respiratory system and returns waste carbon dioxide. The excretory system cleans the waste carried by our blood in the circulatory system.

PAGES 12–13 Interaction

12

10

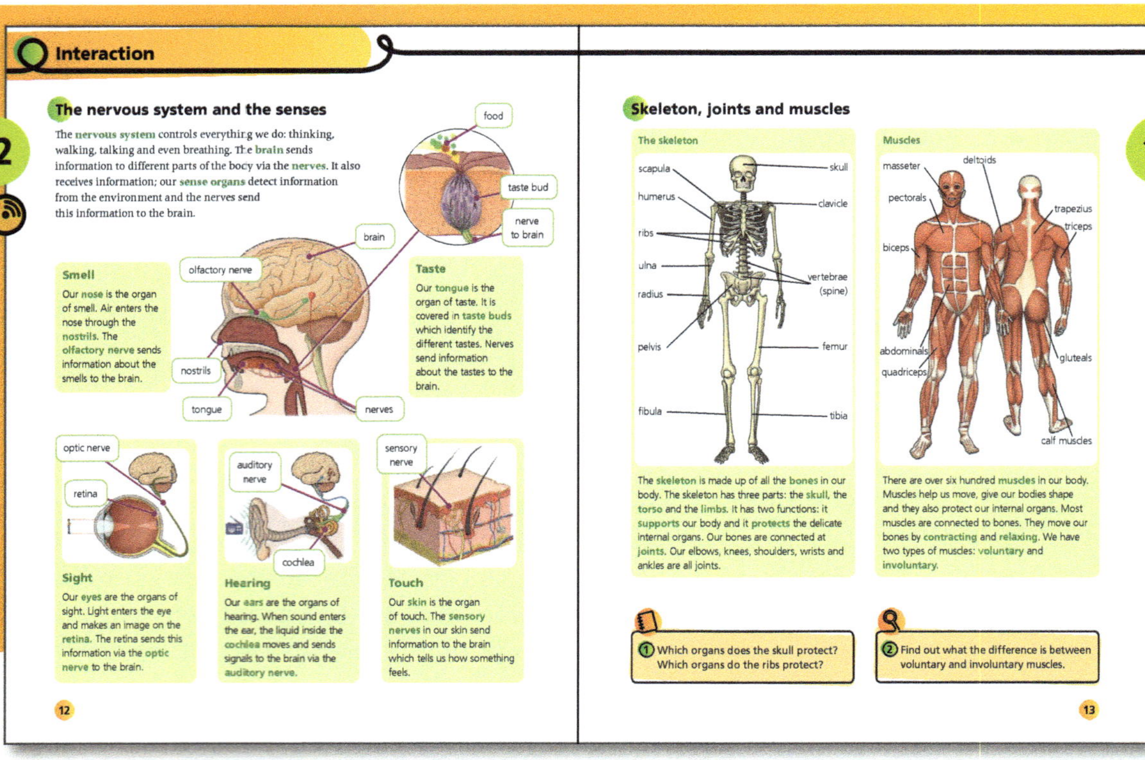
Interaction

The nervous system and the senses

The nervous system controls everything we do: thinking, walking, talking and even breathing. The brain sends information to different parts of the body via the nerves. It also receives information; our sense organs detect information from the environment and the nerves send this information to the brain.

Smell

Our nose is the organ of smell. Air enters the nose through the nostrils. The olfactory nerve sends information about the smells to the brain.

Taste

Our tongue is the organ of taste. It is covered in taste buds which identify the different tastes. Nerves send information about the tastes to the brain.

Sight

Our eyes are the organs of sight. Light enters the eye and makes an image on the retina. The retina sends this information via the optic nerve to the brain.

Hearing

Our ears are the organs of hearing. When sound enters the ear, the liquid inside the cochlea moves and sends signals to the brain via the auditory nerve.

Touch

Our skin is the organ of touch. The sensory nerves in our skin send information to the brain which tells us how something feels.

12

Skeleton, joints and muscles

The skeleton

The skeleton is made up of all the bones in our body. The skeleton has three parts: the skull, the torso and the limbs. It has two functions: it supports our body and it protects the delicate internal organs. Our bones are connected at joints. Our elbows, knees, shoulders, wrists and ankles are all joints.

Muscles

There are over six hundred muscles in our body. Muscles help us move, give our bodies shape and they also protect our internal organs. Most muscles are connected to bones. They move our bones by contracting and relaxing. We have two types of muscles: voluntary and involuntary.

1 Which organs does the skull protect? Which organs do the ribs protect?

2 Find out what the difference is between voluntary and involuntary muscles.

13

13

PAGE SUMMARY

The aim of this double page spread is to review and extend pupils' knowledge of the life process of interaction and the five senses. The main learning aim is to understand the function of the nervous system and the senses, and how they work together.

LANGUAGE

- Present simple
- Vocabulary: *nervous system, brain, sense organs, smell, taste, sight, hearing, touch, olfactory nerve, taste buds, retina, optic nerve, cochlea, auditory nerve, sensory nerve, skeleton, muscles, joints, limbs, torso, bones, skull*

MATERIALS

- Digital flashcards
- Digital wordcards

OPENING ACTIVITIES

- Get pupils to engage with their senses. You can have pupils do a taste, smell, hearing or touch test. These tests involve pupils closing their eyes and using their other senses. For example, put objects of different materials and different textures in a bag and ask them what they think the objects are and how they feel. Or bring in differently flavoured foods and ask pupils to describe the smell, or taste, and then to say what they are.

MAIN ACTIVITIES

Page 12, The nervous system and the senses (CD1 track 10)

- Read the introductory text (page 12). Read the text again but ask pupils to finish your sentences. **The nervous system __________ everything we do: thinking, walking, talking and even breathing. The _________ sends information to different parts of the body via the __________.**
- Pupils read the information boxes on page 12. Ask questions to check understanding. **What is the tongue covered in? Which nerves send information from our skin to our brain?**

- If you are using an interactive whiteboard, black out the labels in each illustration. Divide the class into groups and ask them to try and label the different parts of each picture. If groups are struggling, you can write the name of the nerves (olfactory, optic, auditory and sensory) on the board to help them.

Page 13, Skeleton, joints and muscles

- Write the following words on the board: *skull, torso, limbs, six hundred, contact and relax* and *voluntary and involuntary.* Before reading, ask pupils to look at the pictures and then categorise the words as *skeleton* or *muscles*.
- Pupils then read the texts underneath the pictures and see if their categorisation was correct.
- Ask questions to check understanding. **Where are our bones connected to each other?** *(At the joints.)* **How do our muscles move our bones?** *(By contracting and relaxing.)*

1 Which organs does the skull protect? Which organs do the ribs protect?

- Ask pupils to point to their skull and then their ribs, before discussing the answer in pairs. *The skull protects the brain, eyes and nose. The ribs protect the lungs.*

2 Find out what the difference is between voluntary and involuntary muscles.

- Pupils can answer this question at home, with the help of their parents, using the internet or reference books. They could also do this as a group project at school. Pupils can make a note of different examples of voluntary and involuntary muscles. *See Answers at a glance*

CLOSING ACTIVITIES

- Pupils, in groups or pairs, can make their own poster which includes the different senses.
- Alternatively, you could draw or print out the different sense organs and stick them around the room. Say sentences about each sense, e.g. *This is the organ of touch* and ask pupils to point at the correct picture.

EXTRA IDEAS

- If you have a model skeleton, you can ask groups to write down the names of bones of small, sticky notes and then attach them to the model. Alternatively, you can draw a skeleton or find a picture from the internet.
- Play *Simon says*. Say the names of some of the more known bones and muscles, e.g. pelvis, skull, ribs, biceps, abdominals. Pupils touch the correct part of their body when you say *Simon says (touch your skull.)* If you don't say *Simon says* however, pupils shouldn't do anything.

ANSWERS AT A GLANCE

1. The skull protects the brain, eyes and nose. The ribs protect the lungs.
2. Voluntary muscles are the ones we can control. Involuntary muscles don't need the brain to send them messages. They keep doing their job without us thinking about it. Examples include, the muscles in your heart and stomach.

PAGES 14–15 Reproduction

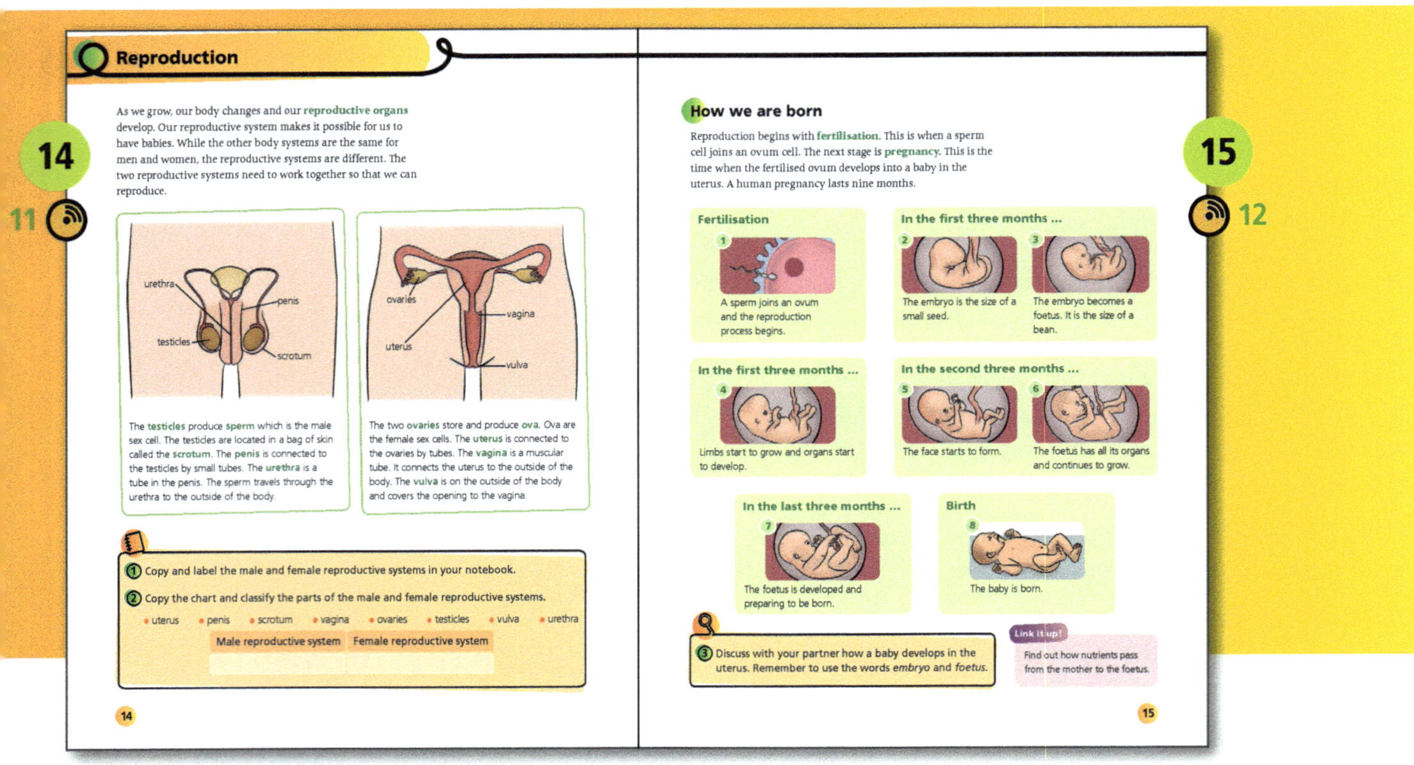

PAGE SUMMARY

In this double page spread pupils gain an understanding of the male and female reproductive systems. They identify and differentiate the reproductive organs and study how these systems work. They also gain insight into the development of a human baby in the uterus and childbirth.

LANGUAGE

- Present simple
- Vocabulary: *reproductive system, male, female, testicles, sperm, scrotum, penis, urethra, ovaries, ova, uterus, vagina, vulva, fertilisation, pregnancy, birth, embryo, foetus, develop, connect*

MATERIALS

- Digital flashcards
- Digital wordcards

OPENING ACTIVITIES

- Tell pupils that, so far, the different systems they have seen are the same for both men and women. Ask them if they can tell you which system in the human body is different in men and women. (*The reproductive system.*) Explain that in this lesson they are going to find out more about the reproductive system. Write on the board **Men have a male reproductive system. Women have a female reproductive system.**

MAIN ACTIVITIES

Page 14, Reproduction (CD1 track 11)

- Ask pupils to turn to page 14 in their Pupils' Books. Draw their attention to the introductory text. Play the audio. Ask them to listen and read. Check for understanding. **Do men and women have the same reproductive systems?** *(No.)* **What do our reproductive organs make it possible for us to do?** *(To reproduce or have babies.)* Reiterate how important it is for male and female organs to work together so that we can reproduce.
- Draw pupils' attention to the diagram of the male reproductive system (if you are using the digital whiteboard you can play the audio). Go over the key vocabulary by saying a word and asking pupils to repeat the word and to point to the correct part on the diagram.

- Now draw pupils' attention to the diagram of the female reproductive system (if you are using the digital whiteboard you can play the audio). Repeat the procedure used for the male reproductive system to go over key vocabulary.

1 Copy and label the male and female reproductive systems in your notebook.

- Encourage pupils to take their time to copy these diagrams. Walk around and help if necessary. As you monitor the activity, ask questions to check understanding. **What do the testicles produce?** (*Sperm.*) **What are ova?** (*The female sex cells.*) **Where is the vulva?** (*On the outside of the female's body.*), etc.

2 Copy the chart and classify the parts of the male and female reproductive systems.

- Place the wordcards on the board and invite volunteers to group them into parts of the male reproductive and female reproductive systems. Encourage pupils to say something about each one. **It's a tube in the penis.** *(The urethra.)* **The testicles are in this bag of skin.** *(Scrotum.) Male reproductive system: penis, scrotum, testicles, urethra. Female reproductive system: vagina, ovaries, vulva.*

Page 15, How we are born (CD1 track 12)

- Before beginning the main activity of the lesson, ask pupils what they think the answers to these questions are: **Are humans oviparous or viviparous?** *(Viviparous.)* **Where does a baby grow before it's born?** *(The uterus.)* **What do we call the time when a baby is developing inside the mother?** *(Pregnancy.)* **What do we call a baby when it's developing?** *(Embryo and foetus.)* **What parts of the baby grow first?** *(The limbs.)*
- Tell pupils to open their books on page 15. Play the audio. Pupils listen and read. Go back to the original questions and check their answers. Invite volunteers to read the texts again. Suggest they highlight or underline the key vocabulary. **Which word should we highlight in this text?** If you are using an interactive board, use the highlighting tool. *Fertilisation, pregnancy, sperm, ovum, embryo, foetus, limbs, organs, face, grow, born.*

3 Discuss with your partner how a baby develops in the uterus. Remember to use the words *embryo* and *foetus*.

- Encourage pupils to write down the key vocabulary in order before they begin to speak. Suggest they take turns to give information. *Open answer*

+ CLOSING ACTIVITIES

- Play the *Definitions game*. Divide the class into two teams. Give definitions of the key vocabulary and ask the teams to identify the body part. The teams win a point for each correct answer. **This part protects the vagina.** *(Vulva.)* **They produce sperm.** *(Testicles.)* **This part is connected to the ovaries.** *(Uterus.)*

+ EXTRA IDEAS

- Ask pupils to do some research on what pregnant women should or shouldn't do to make sure they have healthy babies. (The pupils could ask their parents at home so internet research isn't necessary.) As the baby develops inside the mother, it's very important that she is healthy. Suggest they look into diet and exercise.

ANSWERS AT A GLANCE

1 Open answer.

2 Male reproductive system: Penis, scrotum, testicles, urethra. Female reproductive system: vagina, ovaries, vulva.

3 Open answer.

PAGES 16–17 Find out / Think about it

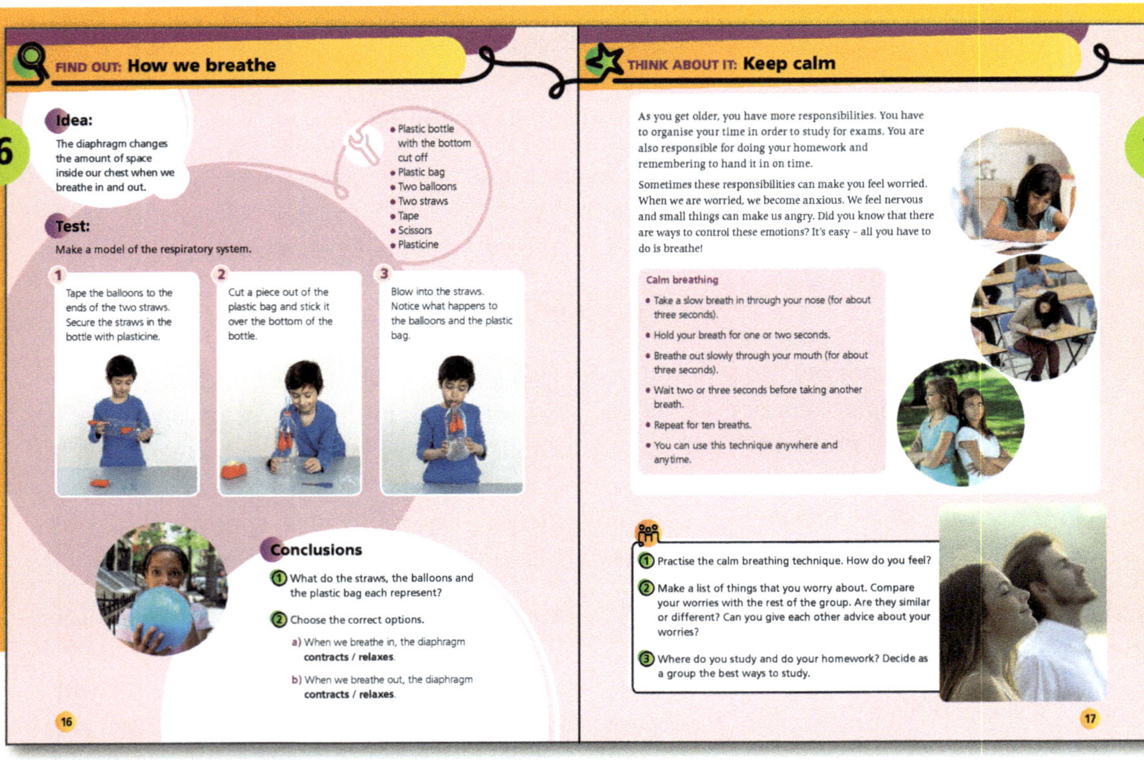
16

FIND OUT: How we breathe

Idea:

The diaphragm changes the amount of space inside our chest when we breathe in and out.

- Plastic bottle with the bottom cut off
- Plastic bag
- Two balloons
- Two straws
- Tape
- Scissors
- Plasticine

Test:

Make a model of the respiratory system.

1 Tape the balloons to the ends of the two straws. Secure the straws in the bottle with plasticine.

2 Cut a piece out of the plastic bag and stick it over the bottom of the bottle.

3 Blow into the straws. Notice what happens to the balloons and the plastic bag.

Conclusions

1 What do the straws, the balloons and the plastic bag each represent?

2 Choose the correct options.

a) When we breathe in, the diaphragm **contracts / relaxes**.

b) When we breathe out, the diaphragm **contracts / relaxes**.

16

17

THINK ABOUT IT: Keep calm

As you get older, you have more responsibilities. You have to organise your time in order to study for exams. You are also responsible for doing your homework and remembering to hand it in on time.

Sometimes these responsibilities can make you feel worried. When we are worried, we become anxious. We feel nervous and small things can make us angry. Did you know that there are ways to control these emotions? It's easy – all you have to do is breathe!

Calm breathing

- Take a slow breath in through your nose (for about three seconds).
- Hold your breath for one or two seconds.
- Breathe out slowly through your mouth (for about three seconds).
- Wait two or three seconds before taking another breath.
- Repeat for ten breaths.
- You can use this technique anywhere and anytime.

1 Practise the calm breathing technique. How do you feel?

2 Make a list of things that you worry about. Compare your worries with the rest of the group. Are they similar or different? Can you give each other advice about your worries?

3 Where do you study and do your homework? Decide as a group the best ways to study.

17

PAGE SUMMARY

On the first page *(Find out)*, pupils make a model of the lungs to demonstrate how the diaphragm works with the lungs to help us breathe. The second page *(Think about it)* provides pupils with the opportunity to learn a simple breathing technique to help them control their anxiety levels when worried. They will think about their own and other people's feelings and become aware of the importance of staying calm to resolve conflicts.

LANGUAGE

- Imperatives: *cut, stick, tape, secure, blow, notice*
- Vocabulary: *straws, plasticine, bottle, tape, contracts, relaxes, breathe in, breathe out, emotions, calm, responsibilities, hand in*

FIND OUT

OPENING ACTIVITIES

- Ask pupils to stand up and place their hand on their chest. Tell them to inhale deeply and observe/feel what happens to their ribcage. Repeat the observation when they exhale. Now ask them to place their hands on their diaphragm and breathe in and out slowly. Ask them if they can feel the diaphragm change.
- Now ask the class to jump on the spot 20 times. When finished, ask them to put their hand on their chest. **What is happening?** *(Breathing faster.)* **Why are you breathing more quickly? What does your body need?** *(The body's cells need oxygen as a result of exercising.)* Ask **Which other organ is working harder?** Elicit that the heart has to work harder to send oxygen to the body's cells.

MAIN ACTIVITIES

- Explain that pupils will make a simple model with basic materials to observe how the diaphragm changes the amount of space inside our chest when we breathe in and out.
- Ask pupils to read the steps (page 16), and then write the materials and the three steps in their notebooks. If you are using the book on the interactive whiteboard, play the audio related to the steps.

- You may do this investigation as a class or let small groups go through the steps independently. Monitor the model construction carefully. Ensure plenty of tape is used to secure the balloons so air can't escape. Check enough straw is left poking through the plasticine to blow through.

(+) CLOSING ACTIVITIES

1 What do the straws, the balloons and the plastic bag each represent?

- Give pupils time to enjoy observing their working model. Let the class compare models. Encourage pupils to answer with full sentences. *The straws represent the trachea and bronchi. The balloons represent the lungs. The plastic bag represents the diaphragm.*

2 Choose the correct options

- Suggest pupils check what happens to the diaphragm when they inhale and exhale by repeating the opening activity. *a) When we breathe in, the diaphragm contracts. b) When we breathe out, the diaphragm relaxes.*

THINK ABOUT IT

(+) OPENING ACTIVITIES

- Draw a large happy face and a large sad face on the board. Ask: **How is this person feeling? What about this one?** Point out that sometimes a person's face shows how they are feeling but sometimes it's difficult to know. Brainstorm vocabulary about feelings and emotions. **What other emotions can we feel?** Write positive words under the happy face and negative ones under the sad face. Write words that can be both negative and positive between the two faces. *Proud, excited, scared, worried, nervous, guilty, lonely, annoyed, confident, cross,* etc.

MAIN ACTIVITIES

- Ask pupils to open their books (page 17) and say **Let's read about emotions and how to control them.** If using the interactive whiteboard, play the audio and encourage pupils to read along in their books. Draw pupils' attention to the box about *Calm breathing*. Invite volunteers to read the steps again to the rest of the class.
- Then, ask pupils to look at the pictures in pairs and to describe what they can see. Ask them to think about how the people in the photos are feeling. *She is doing her homework. They are doing an exam. I think they are angry.*

(+) CLOSING ACTIVITIES

1 Practise the calm breathing technique. How do you feel?

- Ask pupils to work in pairs. One reads the instructions for *Calm breathing* and the other follows them. You may like to play some calm atmospheric music during this activity. Pupils then change roles. Ask them: **How do you feel? Do you feel calm?** Ask them if they think this will work in a real situation. Ask them when a good time would be to use this technique. *(Before an exam, when you are getting angry, etc.)*

2 Make a list of things that you worry about. Compare your worries with the rest of the group. Are they similar or different? Can you give each other advice about your worries?

- Tell pupils to make a list of things that worry them. Then form small groups and ask them to discuss their worries. Encourage groups to think about whether they can do anything about their worries or not. Ask: **Do any of you have the same worries?** Give groups time to talk and then ask them to share their information with the class. Ask the class if they have any advice to help with the worries.

3 Where do you study and do your homework? Decide as a group the best ways to study.

- Pupils work in small groups and discuss the best ways to study. To help the discussion ask: **Where do you study and do your homework? Do you study with music or in silence? What do you have on your desk?** At the end, ask each group to choose a spokesperson and tell the class their thoughts. Allow time for class comments and discussion.

PAGES 18–19 Look back: Body systems

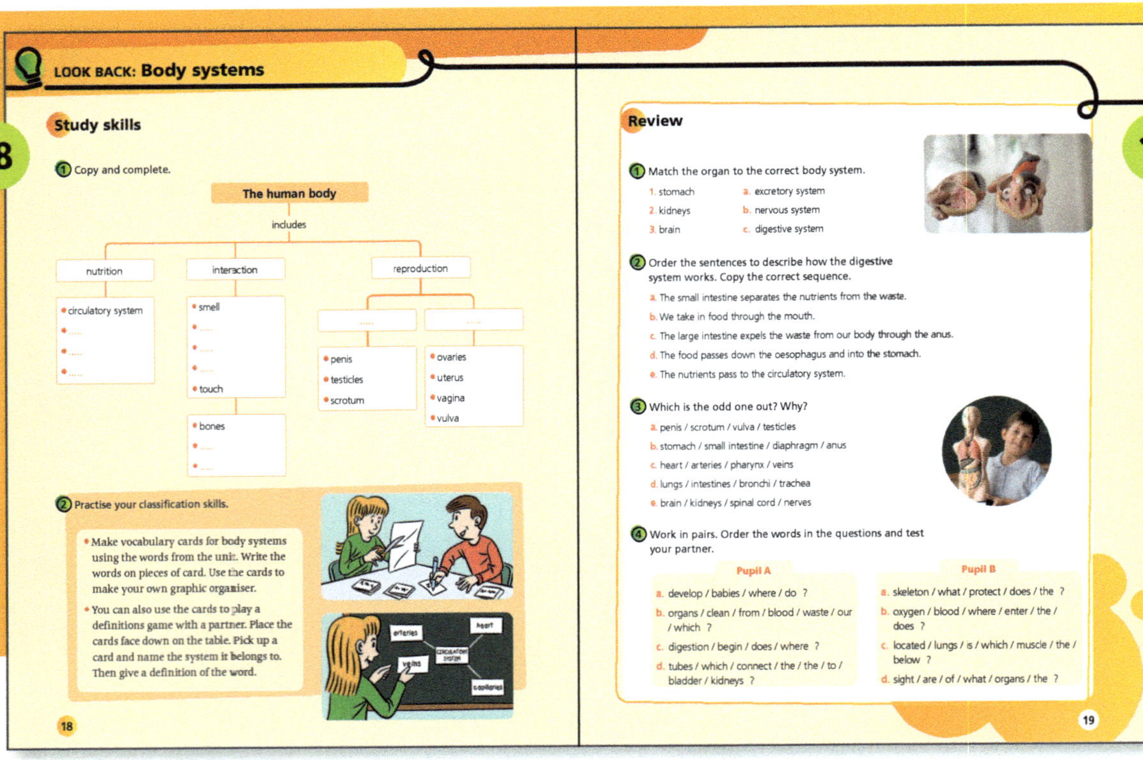

18

LOOK BACK: Body systems

Study skills

1. Copy and complete.

The human body
includes
nutrition
interaction
reproduction
• circulatory system
• ......
• ......
• ......
• smell
• ......
• ......
• ......
• touch
• bones
• ......
• ......
......
......
• penis
• testicles
• scrotum
• ovaries
• uterus
• vagina
• vulva

2. Practise your classification skills.

• Make vocabulary cards for body systems using the words from the unit. Write the words on pieces of card. Use the cards to make your own graphic organiser.
• You can also use the cards to play a definitions game with a partner. Place the cards face down on the table. Pick up a card and name the system it belongs to. Then give a definition of the word.

18

19

Review

1. Match the organ to the correct body system.

1. stomach a. excretory system
2. kidneys b. nervous system
3. brain c. digestive system

2. Order the sentences to describe how the digestive system works. Copy the correct sequence.

a. The small intestine separates the nutrients from the waste.
b. We take in food through the mouth.
c. The large intestine expels the waste from our body through the anus.
d. The food passes down the oesophagus and into the stomach.
e. The nutrients pass to the circulatory system.

3. Which is the odd one out? Why?

a. penis / scrotum / vulva / testicles
b. stomach / small intestine / diaphragm / anus
c. heart / arteries / pharynx / veins
d. lungs / intestines / bronchi / trachea
e. brain / kidneys / spinal cord / nerves

4. Work in pairs. Order the words in the questions and test your partner.

Pupil A

a. develop / babies / where / do ?
b. organs / clean / from / blood / waste / our / which ?
c. digestion / begin / does / where ?
d. tubes / which / connect / the / the / to / bladder / kidneys ?

Pupil B

a. skeleton / what / protect / does / the ?
b. oxygen / blood / where / enter / the / does ?
c. located / lungs / is / which / muscle / the / below ?
d. sight / are / of / what / organs / the ?

19

PAGE SUMMARY

This double page spread lets pupils organise what they've learned in the unit using a concept map. They can also learn a new study skill – classification. Pupils make their own vocabulary cards for the three body systems to use in classification activities. On the *Review* page, pupils complete activities individually to check their understanding of this unit's material. Activity 4 is a pairwork speaking activity to encourage them to create complete, accurate sentences and to identify and use a simple structure (*should / shouldn't*). It is also an opportunity for peer evaluation.

LANGUAGE

- Imperatives: *complete, match, order, write, copy, correct, talk, test, and work*
- Encourage pupils to speak and write in complete sentences.

ADDITIONAL MATERIALS

- Digital flashcards
- Digital wordcards
- Coloured A4 cards for classification cards

OPENING ACTIVITIES

- *Spelling game.* Tell pupils to work in pairs. Ask them to look through the unit and choose five key vocabulary words. Pupil 1 reads the words to their partner, who must write down what they hear. Pupils then change roles. To correct the spelling test, pupil 1 spells out their five words for pupil 2. Pupil 2 then spells out their words. At the end of the activity the pupils check answers together.
- *Classification game.* Place the wordcards *circulatory system, respiratory system* and *reproductive system* on the board. Place the other wordcards, ones related to these body systems, randomly. Invite pupils to come to the board to classify the cards into the three body systems.
- Carry out a group quiz. Organise the class into three groups. Assign each group a body system: circulatory system, respiratory system and reproductive system. Tell each group to work together to write five questions about their system for the rest of the class. Monitor the groups to ensure they are forming questions correctly.

MAIN ACTIVITIES

Page 18, Study skills

1 Copy and complete.

- Remind pupils that when we organise new information, it is easier to understand and remember it. Focus pupils' attention on the concept map and ask them to tell you what the missing words are. Encourage them to make full sentences, such as *There are four body systems which help carry out the process of nutrition. They are…*
- Tell them to copy and complete the concept map in their notebooks.

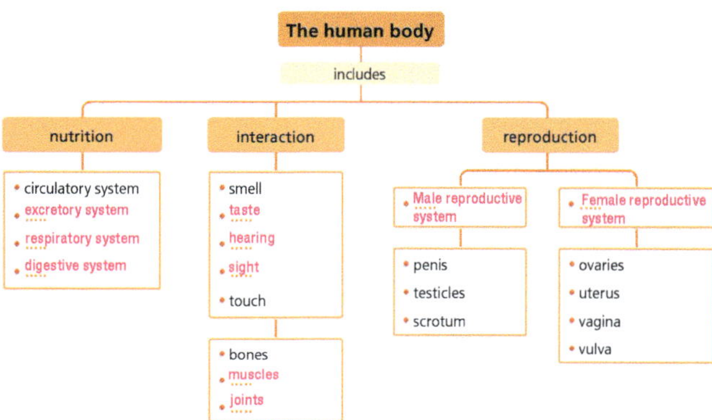

2 Practise your classification skills.

- Hand out three different coloured A4 pieces of card to each pupil. Explain that they are going to use the different coloured cards to make their own wordcards to practise classifying the different organs into the correct body system. Each A4 card can be divided into eight rectangles simply by folding in three. Tell pupils to look back at the Pupil's Book and to copy the names of the organs that comprise each body system. Check spelling and presentation. These cards can also be used to practise spelling and definitions. Consider giving pupils plastic envelopes to keep the cards clean and organised.

Page 19, Review

Note: This part of the review can be done with minimal teacher guidance. You may wish to work through the activities as a class or in small groups or pairs.

Alternatively, you can ask pupils to do them individually as self-evaluation. This review could also be done as homework.

1 Match and write sentences about the circulatory system

1. c **2.** a **3.** b

2 Order the sentences to describe how the respiratory system works. Copy the correct sequence.

b. We take in food through the mouth.

d. The food passes down the oesophagus and into the stomach.

a. The small intestine separates the nutrients from the waste.

e. The nutrients pass to the circulatory system.

c. The large intestine expels the waste from our body through the anus.

3 Which is the odd one out? Why?

a. The **Vulva** is part of the female reproductive system. The others are part of the male reproductive system.

b. The **Diaphragm** is part of the respiratory system. The others are part of the digestive system.

c. The **pharynx** is part of the respiratory system. The others are part of the circulatory system.

d. **Intestines** are part of the digestive system. The others are part of the circulatory system.

e. The **kidneys** are part of the excretory system. The others are part of the nervous system.

4 Work in pairs. Order the words in the questions and test your partner.

Pupil A

a. Where do babies develop? *(In the uterus)*

b. Which organs clean waste from our blood? *(The kidneys)*

c. Where does digestion begin? *(In the mouth)*

d. Which tubes connect the kidneys to the bladder? *(The ureters)*

Pupil B

a. What does the skeleton protect? *(The internal organs)*

b. Where does oxygen enter the blood? *(In the alveoli)*

c. Which muscle is located below the lungs? *(The diaphragm)*

d. What are the organs of sight? *(The eyes)*

Activity Book answers / Audio CD1 track list

2

UNIT 1 Body systems

1 Label the organs of the body.

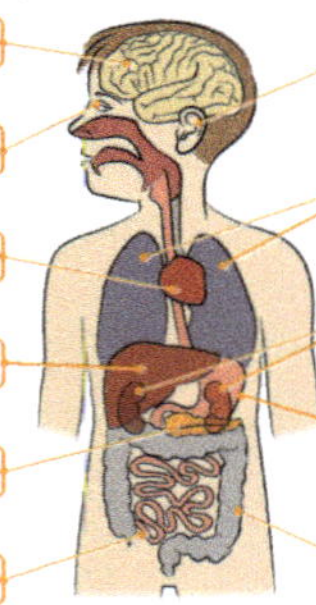

a. brain
b. eyes
c. heart
d. liver
e. pancreas
f. small intestine
g. ears
h. lungs
i. kidneys
j. stomach
k. large intestine

2 Complete each sentence with the correct body system. Match the picture to the correct sentence.

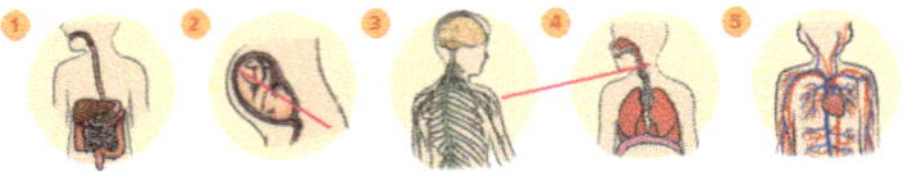

a. 4 We are able to breathe because of the respiratory system.
b. 1 The digestive system breaks food down into nutrients.
c. 5 The circulatory system moves blood through the heart and around the body.
d. 2 The reproductive system makes it possible to have babies.
e. 3 The nervous system includes the brain, spinal cord and nerves.

2

3

3 Complete the sentences about the circulatory system.

~~waste~~ ~~vessels~~ ~~cells~~ ~~carbon dioxide~~ ~~nutrients~~ ~~heart~~ ~~circulatory~~

a. The circulatory system consists of the heart, blood vessels and blood. It moves blood through the heart and around the body.
b. Blood gives our cells the oxygen and nutrients they need.
c. Blood also collects waste products, like carbon dioxide, and takes them to the parts of the body which expel them.

4 Label the parts of the excretory system.

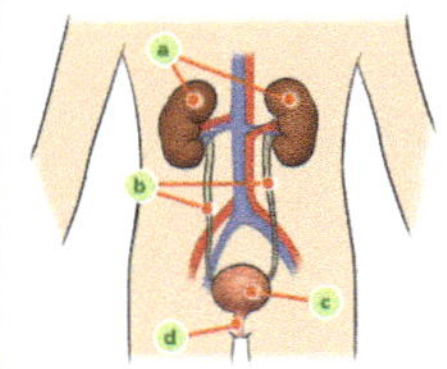

a. kidneys
b. ureters
c. bladder
d. urethra

5 Use your answers from Activity 4 to complete the sentences. Order the sentences to describe the excretory system.

a. The urine then collects in a bag called the bladder. 3
b. Urine travels down two tubes, called ureters. 2
c. Two organs, called kidneys, clean waste from our blood. The waste combines with water to make urine. 1
d. When the bladder is full, the urine leaves the body through the urethra. 4

3

4

UNIT 1

6 Look at the diagram. Complete the sentences to describe how the respiratory system works.

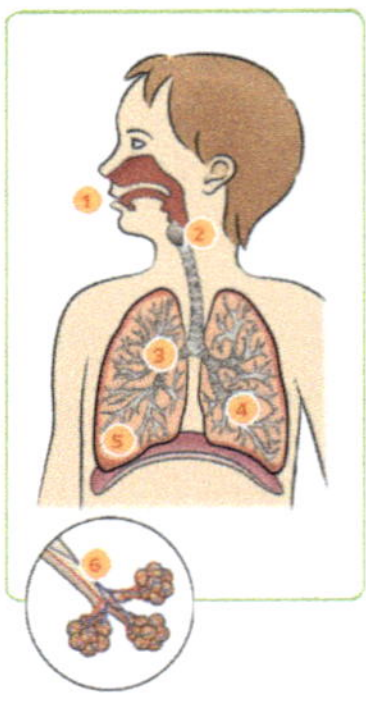

~~nose~~ ~~trachea~~ ~~carbon dioxide~~ ~~alveoli~~ ~~lungs~~ ~~pharynx~~ ~~mouth~~ ~~oxygen~~ ~~bronchi~~

1. We breathe in through our nose and mouth.
2. The pharynx opens and the air goes down a tube called the trachea.
3. The trachea divides into two tubes called bronchi.
4. The air passes through the bronchi and enters the lungs.
5. Inside the lungs, the bronchi divide into smaller tubes. At the end of these tubes, there are tiny sacs called alveoli which are covered in capillaries.
6. It is here that oxygen passes from our lungs into our blood and carbon dioxide passes from our blood into our lungs.

7 Match the words in the box to the correct definition.

~~oesophagus~~ ~~small intestine~~ ~~large intestine~~ ~~anus~~ ~~circulatory system~~

a. This tube carries food from your mouth to your stomach. oesophagus
b. In the digestive system, this organ separates the nutrients from the waste. small intestine
c. This is where the nutrients go, after being separated from the waste. circulatory system
d. This is where the waste goes, after being separated from the nutrients. large intestine
e. This is where the waste leaves the body. anus

4

5

8 Label the male and female reproductive organs.

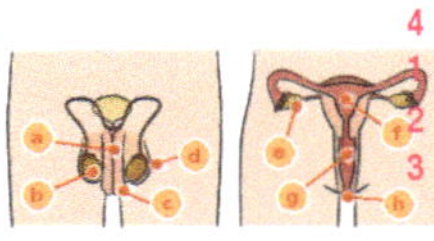

a. uretha
b. testicles
c. penis
d. scrotum
e. ovaries
f. uterus
g. vagina
h. vulva

9 Identify and order the stages of reproduction.

~~foetus~~ ~~birth~~ ~~fertilisation~~ ~~embryo~~

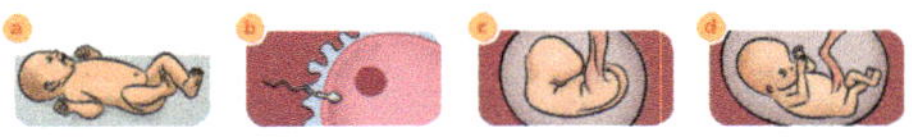

earliest → latest

b fertilisation, c embryo, d foetus, a birth

10 Read about how a baby is born. Match to identify each stage.

Fertilisation	The embryo becomes a foetus. Limbs and organs start to grow.
First three months	The baby is born.
Second three months	A sperm joins an ovum.
Last three months	The foetus is developed and prepares for birth.
Birth	The face starts to form.

5

UNIT 1

Find out at home!

1. Investigate how fast your heart beats:

1. Do you know your heart rate? Put your first two fingers on your right hand on your left wrist below your left thumb. Can you feel your heart beating?
2. Using a clock, count how many times your heart beats in 60 seconds.
3. Do you think your heart always beats at the same rate? Check your heart rate at different times during the day and after different activities. Write the results in the table. Compare your results with someone else in your family.

2. Complete the chart.

	My heart rate	My family member's heart rate
In the morning, before getting out of bed		
When watching TV or reading		
After walking	Open answers.	
After running or playing sport		

6

7

Skills check

1. Look and read. Write some words to complete the sentences below. You can use 1, 2 or 3 words.

Look after your heart and lungs

The circulatory system and the respiratory system work together. Your heart, blood and lungs help transport oxygen and nutrients to all your body's cells. There are lots of things you can do to look after them.

Keep your heart strong by exercising for at least 30 minutes every day. Breathing hard also makes the muscles around your lungs stronger.

You also need to eat healthy food, drink lots of clean water and get plenty of sleep every night.

Finally, it's important not to smoke and to stay away from any sort of strong chemical smell. These can damage your lungs.

Take good care of your heart and lungs and they will take care of you for a long time!

a. Together the circulatory system and the respiratory systems transport *oxygen and nutrients* to all the cells in the body.
b. Exercising for around **30 minutes** every day helps keep your heart strong.
c. It is important to eat **healthy food** and drink lots of water every day.
d. Remember not to **smoke** because this can damage your lungs.

7

Unit 1 Audio CD1 track list

TRACK	ACTIVITY
02	**Pupil's Book page 7,** Unit introduction
03	**Pupil's Book page 7,** Song *Body systems*
04	**Pupil's Book page 8,** Story: *A trip to the biology fair*
05	**Pupil's Book page 10,** Nutrition
06	**Pupil's Book page 10,** The circulatory system
07	**Pupil's Book page 10,** The excretory system
08	**Pupil's Book page 11,** The respiratory system
09	**Pupil's Book page 11,** The digestive system
10	**Pupil's Book page 12,** The nervous system and the senses
11	**Pupil's Book page 14,** Reproduction
12	**Pupil's Book page 15,** How we are born

UNIT 2 Looking after yourself

CONTENT	EVALUATION CRITERIA
Healthy habits.	Understand different healthy habits and their benefits for our health.
Unhealthy habits.	Understand different unhealthy habits and the damage they can do to our health.
Emotions and feelings.	Understand their own emotions and feelings and those of others.
Scientific developments.	Identify some scientific advances that have improved our lives.
First aid.	Know the basics of first aid.
First approaches to scientific activity and the scientific method. Use of different information sources (direct and indirect). Use ICTs.	Obtain relevant information about specific phenomena, make predictions, integrate information from direct and indirect observation and communicate the results.
First approaches to simple experiments and investigations.	Conjecture as to the results of natural occurrences and of simple experiments and investigations.
Individual and group work.	Work independently and proactively and develop strategies for working in a group.
Planning a project and presenting a report.	Carry out a project and present a report.

LEARNING STANDARDS	KEY COMPETENCES	PAGES
Identifies, understands and adopts different healthy habits and their importance for our health: diet, exercise, sleep, hygiene, medical check-ups.	MST, SOC	23, 24, 25
Understands different unhealthy habits and the damage they can do to our health.	MST, LIN	26, 27
Adopts a critical attitude towards habits that can damage our health.	MST, SOC	26, 27
Accepts the toxic effects of alcohol and tobacco on the health, above all when consumed at a young age.	MST,SOC	27
Understands and identifies their own emotions and feelings, and those of others.	MST, SOC	28, 29
Displays empathy towards other children and adults.	SOC	29
Observes, identifies and describes some scientific and investigative advances that have improved our lives.	MST, SOC	21-23
Knows the basics of first aid.	MST, SOC	31
With help, selects and organises specific and relevant information; analyses it and draws conclusions; reflects on the experience and the process;	MST, LTL	23, 30, 31
Use books, libraries, etc. and collaborate in the care and maintenance of all the materials available in the school and the classroom.	MST, LTL	20-33
Shows autonomy in the planning of activities and tasks and shows initiative in decision taking.	LTL, AUT	23, 30, 31
With help, carries out simple experiments or investigations, and conjectures as to the results.	MST, LTL, AUT	30, 31
Uses strategies to help their own learning, as well as asking for help and information.	LTL, AUT	23, 30-32
First approaches to Cooperative Learning.	SOC, LTL	21, 31
Begins observation, using relevant instruments and consulting written documents and images.	LTL, AUT	30
Shows autonomy and proactiveness in the planning of and carrying out of actions.	AUT	30, 31
Presents work clearly and in an organised fashion.	LIN, LTL, AUT	30, 31
With help, carries out a project and presents a report, using paper and/or digital means, collecting information from different sources, presenting the results orally and with the support of images and short texts.	LIN, LTL, AUT, DIG	30, 31

UNIT INFORMATION

UNIT SUMMARY

In this unit, pupils will review and extend their knowledge of how to take care of their body and how to look after their health. They will review healthy habits and also become aware of the dangers of unhealthy habits. As they are becoming older, they should understand that they are responsible for looking after their health. In this unit, they will begin to learn about medical advances and to recognise the importance of medical technology.

At the beginning of the unit, pupils will be introduced to the positive changes that have happened in society which allow us to lead much healthier lives than in the past. This subject area is covered in the opening illustration with the help of the course characters, Carla and Alex, who are on a school trip to a hospital to learn about medical technology. The school trip continues in the story and, on their return to school, Alex and Carla carry out a *School trip project* to review the information they have seen. They will also classify the medical advances into three groups: prevention, diagnosis and treatment. These opening pages are designed find out the pupils' prior knowledge and to stir interest about the unit subject matter.

They will move on to review healthy habits and to look at unhealthy habits. The final section of this unit focuses on behaviour and emotions. It encourages the pupils to be aware of other people's feeling and to adopt a responsible and empathic attitude towards people who are different from them.

EXPERIMENT

Find out

In the *Find out activity* on page 30, pupils will prepare an investigation about how germs can spread from one person to another. The results of this investigation should lead to a discussion about the importance of washing your hands.

The pupils will need:

- dark sheets of card
- flour
- plastic plates

Further ideas

This investigation can be extended by having the pupils work in groups of four. The first pupil places their hand in the flour and shakes hands with pupil 2 as before. Then pupil 2 shakes hands with pupil 3, and pupil 3 with pupil 4. Each one makes a hand print on dark card.

VALUES AND ATTITUDES

In this unit, pupils will learn the importance of adopting healthy habits and avoiding unhealthy habits in order to keep themselves in good health: physically, emotionally and socially. Throughout this unit, encourage them to take responsibility for their actions regarding their health. Encourage them to think about how they could improve their diet, the importance of basic hygiene and sleep. It is also important that they recognise how technology has changed and improved our lives.

Think about it

The *Think about it* page in this unit focuses on first aid and what the pupils should do if they, or someone they know, has an accident. The intention of this section is to make pupils aware of how, by taking appropriate actions, as well as behaving responsibly, they can stay safe and healthy.

EVALUATION MATERIAL

These documents can be downloaded from the *Teachers* section of the digital component and printed.

The materials include:

- **Unit diagnostic test:** provides an overview of the unit and allows you to assess the pupils' prior knowledge.
- **End-of-unit test:** in addition to the *Review* section at the end of each unit, this summative test can be used to evaluate pupils' progress after studying the unit content.
- **Class unit evaluation grid:** based on the evaluation criteria and learning standards of the unit.

DIGITAL RESOURCES

Presentations

- **Unit summary:** a simple slide presentation with text, images and audio to review the main ideas of the unit. It can be used at the beginning of the unit to test pupils' prior knowledge of the unit content or at the end of the unit as a revision tool.
- **Find out:** a slide presentation of the unit's *Find out* page with text, photos and audio. The slide presentation is perfect for a heads-up class, showing the steps one by one. Use this tool to get the pupils to predict the next steps (with their books closed) or to focus their attention on each step as they carry out the project themselves.

Activities

Digital activities vary per unit and include the following:

- **Memory game:** useful activity for reviewing key vocabulary and modelling pronunciation.
- **Labelling:** pupils label a diagram by dragging and dropping key terms.
- **Spelling:** pupils drag and drop letters to spell key terms.
- **Read and reveal:** pupils read sentences and guess the missing words, which are revealed by clicking the spaces.
- **Classification:** pupils drag and drop concepts and key terms in a simple classification table.
- **Wordsearch:** pupils find key terms hidden in the wordsearch.
- **Definitions:** pupils drag and drop words to complete definitions.

Song lyrics

Listen to the song *Germs* and follow the lyrics line by line.

Posters

Attractive and informative posters to display in class. You can use them to review key concepts and vocabulary.

Videos

Use the video links in this unit to present content in a dynamic, real-life context while reinforcing the pupils' listening skills.

Teachers

Digital flashcards and wordcards: topics include *Healthy habits*, *Unhealthy habits* and *We are all equal*.

Downloadable pdfs: evaluation tests, evaluation grids, templates, useful links and further information.

PAGES 20–21 Looking after yourself

PAGE SUMMARY

The aim of the unit opener is to develop pupils' observation skills and find out what they already know about the unit topic. Use the picture to elicit vocabulary related to the human body and healthy habits. Encourage pupils to talk about their own experiences in hospitals and at the doctor's. Get pupils to work in groups to complete activities 1–4 and to have fun listening to the song and completing activity 5.

LANGUAGE

- Present tense
- Past tense
- Vocabulary: *advances, white blood cells, red blood cells, bacteria, virus, flu, measles, smallpox, disease, vaccination, treat, X-ray*

ADDITIONAL MATERIALS

- Digital flashcards
- Digital wordcards
- Photocopies of the Autonomous Community's vaccination calendar (it can be in Spanish)
- Examples of X-rays (brought in by the pupils)

⊕ OPENING ACTIVITIES

- Introduce the class to the topic by asking them to remember the last time they were ill and couldn't come to school. Write their answers on the board and ask them to comment on the findings. Elicit that often a virus can affect many people in the same class.
- Prepare cards with descriptions of various health problems: *You have a headache. There is a problem with your arm. You have hurt your ankle.* Choose members of the class to mime the symptoms on the card for the class. The rest of the class assumes the role of the doctor and diagnoses the problem and suggests a form of treatment.

MAIN ACTIVITIES

Page 21, Unit introduction (CD1 track 13)

- Read the unit introduction at the top of page 21. Pupils can do a *read and repeat* of the text (see *Helpful tips*, pages 20–23). Read a sentence and ask the pupils to read and repeat the sentence, focusing on proper intonation and pronunciation. Invite volunteers to read the text.
- Divide the pupils into small groups to answer the questions at the top of page 21. Then, invite different groups to compare their answers with each other.

1 Explain why we live longer nowadays compared to one hundred years ago.

- Before dividing the class into groups, ask them how they think life was like one hundred years ago. Give clues by asking: **What do we have today to help keep us healthy? What do you think houses were like? Try to imagine the hospitals. Were they like our hospitals?** *Open answer.*

2 What can you do to keep healthy?

- Ask pupils to work with a partner to talk about rules they should follow in order to lead a healthy lifestyle (*exercise, healthy diet, sleep, etc.*). Invite the pupils to share their ideas with the rest of the class and write their ideas on the board. Afterwards, invite pupils to talk more about these ideas. **What is a healthy diet? How many hours should you sleep?** *See Answers at a glance.*

3 What are the girl and the doctor looking at in the photo?

- Ask: **What are the girl and the doctor looking at in the photo?** *(An X-ray).* Encourage the pupils to talk about their own experiences with X-rays. **Have you ever had an X-ray? Why did they do an X- ray? What happened?**

4 Have you ever had a vaccination?

- Hand out the copies of the vaccination calendar for pupils to read in pairs. Give the names of the illnesses in English (tetanus, meningitis, chickenpox, etc.). Ask the pupils to think about why it is necessary to have vaccinations. *Open answer*

5 Listen to the song. Point to the words you hear.

- Focus the pupils' attention on the six photos. Ask them to read and repeat the words. Check for understanding.
- Play the song *Germs* **(CD1 track 14)** and ask pupils to point to the words that they hear. *White blood cell, vaccination, virus, bacteria.*

CD 1 • track 14

Much too small to see
They're invisible to you and me, yeah!
But germs are everywhere
On your hands, in the air!
Germs! Germs! Germs!
(Rapped) Trying to make us sick
Germs! Germs! Germs!
Attacking our defenses!
Germs! Germs! Germs!
(Rapped) That invade our blood
Germs! Germs! Germs!
Attacking all our systems!
When germs attack
The white blood cells fight back!
Vaccinations keep us safe
From the viruses and bacteria!
[chorus] Germs! Germs! Germs!...

CLOSING ACTIVITIES

- Prepare a list of sentences which describe conditions today and conditions in the past. Get pupils to decide if they refer to the present or the past.
- Ask the class to make up two sentences about their lifestyle. Explain that they can be true or invented. When they say their sentences, the rest of the class has to indicate if it is a healthy habit or an unhealthy habit by giving a thumbs up or a thumbs down.

EXTRA IDEAS

- Pupils have learned that white blood cells are part of the body's defense system. Ask them to find out the work of the other parts of blood. Discuss their findings in the next class.

ANSWERS AT A GLANCE

1 Open answer.

2 Exercise, hygiene, sleep, a healthy diet, medical checkups and enjoying your free time.

3 An X-ray.

4 White blood cell, vaccination, virus, bacteria.

PAGES 22–23 A trip to the hospital

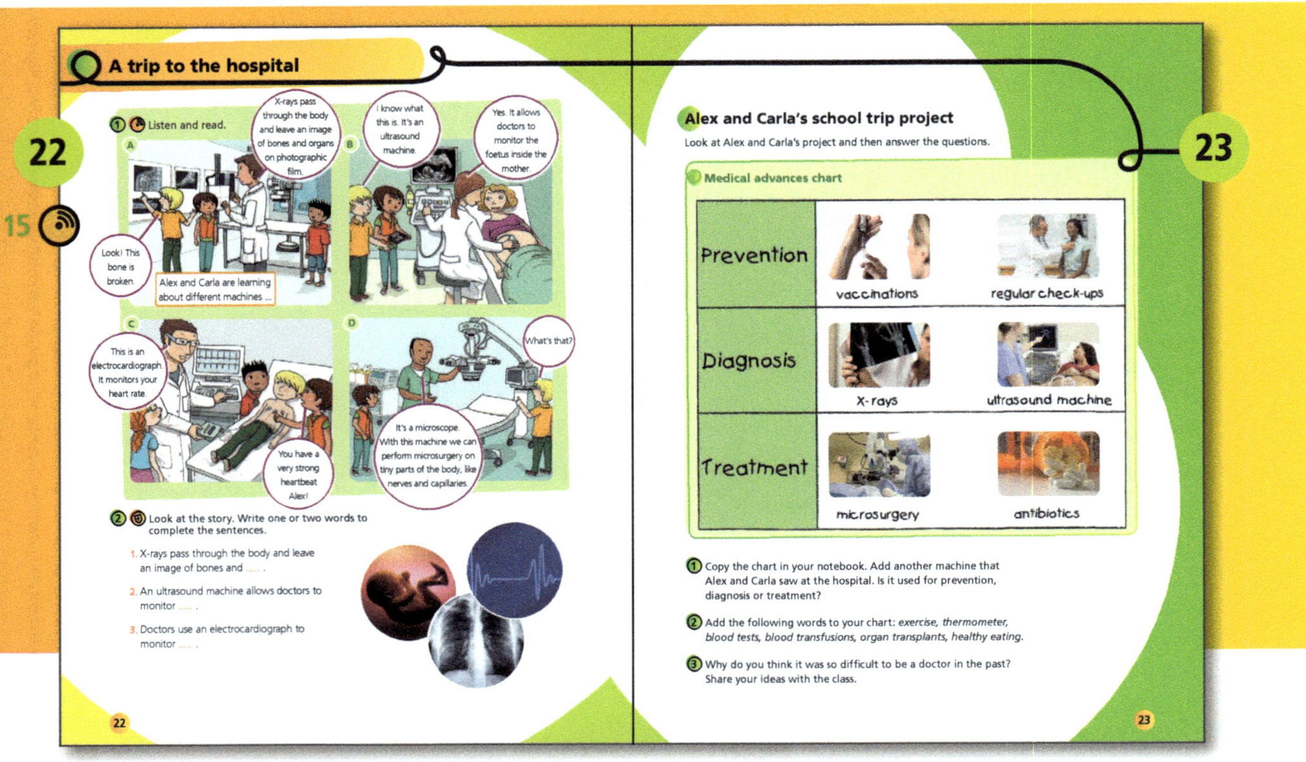

22

15

A trip to the hospital

1 Listen and read.

A
Look! This bone is broken.
Alex and Carla are learning about different machines ...
X-rays pass through the body and leave an image of bones and organs on photographic film.

B
I know what this is. It's an ultrasound machine.
Yes. It allows doctors to monitor the foetus inside the mother.

C
This is an electrocardiograph. It monitors your heart rate.
You have a very strong heartbeat Alex!

D
What's that?
It's a microscope. With this machine we can perform microsurgery on tiny parts of the body, like nerves and capillaries.

2 Look at the story. Write one or two words to complete the sentences.

1. X-rays pass through the body and leave an image of bones and ..... .
2. An ultrasound machine allows doctors to monitor ..... .
3. Doctors use an electrocardiograph to monitor ..... .

22

23

Alex and Carla's school trip project

Look at Alex and Carla's project and then answer the questions.

Medical advances chart

Prevention	vaccinations	regular check-ups
Diagnosis	X-rays	ultrasound machine
Treatment	microsurgery	antibiotics

1 Copy the chart in your notebook. Add another machine that Alex and Carla saw at the hospital. Is it used for prevention, diagnosis or treatment?

2 Add the following words to your chart: *exercise, thermometer, blood tests, blood transfusions, organ transplants, healthy eating.*

3 Why do you think it was so difficult to be a doctor in the past? Share your ideas with the class.

23

PAGE SUMMARY

This double-page spread opens with a story about Carla and Alex on a school trip to the hospital. Carla and Alex are talking to the doctor and showing their knowledge of medical technology. The story is reinforced with an exam style matching activity that is related to the story and opening double page spread. On page 23, pupils can study Carla and Alex's school trip project about prevention, diagnosis and treatment.

LANGUAGE

- *This / that*
- Present tense
- Vocabulary: *prevention, diagnosis, treatment, X-ray, ultrasound, electrocardiograph, microsurgery, vaccinations, antibiotics, check-up, blood tests, blood transfusions, organ transplants, healthy eating, exercise, thermometer, foetus, bones, organs, heart rate, nerves, capillaries, monitor, perform*

ADDITIONAL MATERIALS

- Digital flashcards
- Digital wordcards

OPENING ACTIVITIES

- Point out that today we have many machines at home, school and at work to help us in our daily lives. Brainstorm a list of different machines that we use. **Who can name a machine we use at home? What machines can you see in class?**
- Ask the class to choose a machine and give a definition of it so that the rest of the class can identify it. **I use this machine to wash clothes. I can make toast with this machine.** The pupil that identifies the machine can then give the next definition.
- Play the *Germs* song **(CD1 track 14)** and encourage pupils to sing along. Explain that nowadays we have many machines which help doctors look after our health. Say **Let's find out more about medical technology**.

MAIN ACTIVITIES

1 Listen and read (CD1 track 15)

- Draw pupils' attention to the story at the top of page 22 and explain to pupils that they are going to hear a story about Alex and Carla's trip to a doctor's surgery. Say **Let's listen and read**. Play the audio.
- Say sentences and ask pupils to identify the correct box. For example, *The doctor is using an ultrasound machine. (B) This machine performs microsurgery. (D)*

- Divide pupils into groups of three and ask them to choose a character from the story – Alex, Carla or the doctor. Pupils then read their part of the story aloud in their group. You can invite a group to the front of the class to act the story out.

② Look at the story. Write one or two words to complete the sentences.

- Ask the pupils to prepare this activity in pairs. Invite volunteers to give their answers. Now tell pupils to copy the activity into their notebook.

1. X-rays pass through the body and leave an image of bones and ***organs***.
2. An ultrasound machine allows doctors to monitor ***a foetus***.
3. Doctors use an electrocardiograph to monitor ***heart rate***.

SCHOOL TRIP PROJECT

- Explain to pupils that following their trip to the hospital, Alex and Carla have done a project about medical advances.
- Tell pupils to look at the photo on page 23 and ask for volunteers to read the words. Place the wordcards *prevention*, *diagnosis* and *treatment* on the board. Ask if anyone can describe what these words mean. *Prevention stops you getting ill. Diagnosis is when the illness is identified and treatment helps you recover.*

① Copy the chart in your notebook. Add another machine that Alex and Carla saw at the hospital. Is it used for prevention, diagnosis or treatment?

- Ask pupils which machine is missing from the chart. (*An electrocardiograph*). Elicit that the machine monitors heart rate. Ask **Is this machine for prevention, diagnosis or treatment?** (*Diagnosis*). Tell pupils to copy the pictures and words from the book. *Electrocardiograph - diagnosis*

② Add the following words to your chart: *exercise, thermometer, blood tests, blood transfusions, organ transplants, healthy eating.*

- Place the wordcards *prevention, diagnosis* and *treatment* on the board. Read out the names of the words from the question, one by one: *X- ray, ultrasound, electrocardiograph*, etc. Invite pupils to come and write the words in the correct group *(prevention, diagnosis or treatment).* Now ask the pupils to add the words to their chart. *Prevention: exercise and healthy eating. Diagnosis: thermometer and blood tests. Treatment: blood transfusions and organ transplants.*

③ Why do you think it was so difficult to be a doctor in the past? Share your ideas with the class.

- Organise the class into small groups to discuss this question. Write some questions on the board to give them some guidelines and ideas. *What happens when you have an operation? How do we get a doctor in an emergency? What can we take when we are in pain?* Allow time for pupils to discuss these ideas. Ask each group to choose a spokesperson to share their ideas with the rest of the class. *Open answer.*

⊕ CLOSING ACTIVITIES

- Choose words from the key vocabulary and spell them out letter by letter. Tell pupils to write down the letters they hear. At the end of the activity invite pupils to come to the board to write the words for the rest of the class. Ask another pupil to explain what it is. *Microsurgery. This allows doctors to perform surgery on tiny parts of the body.*

⊕ EXTRA IDEAS

- Tell pupils that they are going to carry out a survey about the different illness people in the class have had. Encourage them to design the questions and help with vocabulary when necessary. Use the structure: *Have you ever had _____?* Possible ideas: *Have you ever had flu / chickenpox / a cold?* When they have collected the information, get them to represent the results using a bar chart.

ANSWERS AT A GLANCE

① Electrocardiograph – diagnosis.

② Prevention: exercise and healthy eating. Diagnosis: thermometer and blood tests. Treatment: blood transfusions and organ transplants.

③ Open answer.

PAGES 24-25 Healthy habits

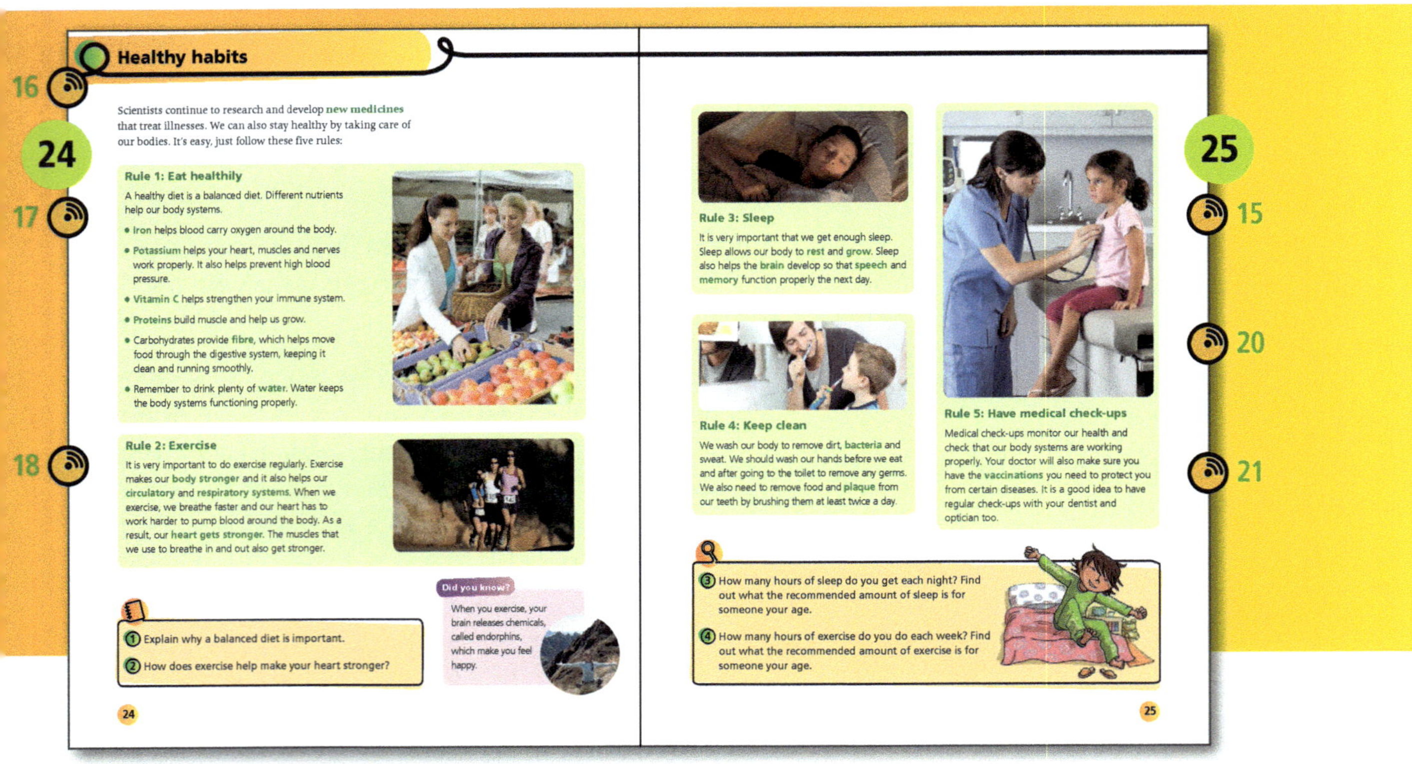

16
24
17
18

Healthy habits

Scientists continue to research and develop **new medicines** that treat illnesses. We can also stay healthy by taking care of our bodies. It's easy, just follow these five rules:

Rule 1: Eat healthily

A healthy diet is a balanced diet. Different nutrients help our body systems.

- **Iron** helps blood carry oxygen around the body.
- **Potassium** helps your heart, muscles and nerves work properly. It also helps prevent high blood pressure.
- **Vitamin C** helps strengthen your immune system.
- **Proteins** build muscle and help us grow.
- Carbohydrates provide **fibre**, which helps move food through the digestive system, keeping it clean and running smoothly.
- Remember to drink plenty of **water**. Water keeps the body systems functioning properly.

Rule 2: Exercise

It is very important to do exercise regularly. Exercise makes our **body stronger** and it also helps our **circulatory** and **respiratory systems**. When we exercise, we breathe faster and our heart has to work harder to pump blood around the body. As a result, our **heart gets stronger**. The muscles that we use to breathe in and out also get stronger.

1. Explain why a balanced diet is important.
2. How does exercise help make your heart stronger?

Did you know?

When you exercise, your brain releases chemicals, called endorphins, which make you feel happy.

24

25
15
20
21

Rule 3: Sleep

It is very important that we get enough sleep. Sleep allows our body to **rest** and **grow**. Sleep also helps the **brain** develop so that **speech** and **memory** function properly the next day.

Rule 4: Keep clean

We wash our body to remove dirt, **bacteria** and sweat. We should wash our hands before we eat and after going to the toilet to remove any germs. We also need to remove food and **plaque** from our teeth by brushing them at least twice a day.

Rule 5: Have medical check-ups

Medical check-ups monitor our health and check that our body systems are working properly. Your doctor will also make sure you have the **vaccinations** you need to protect you from certain diseases. It is a good idea to have regular check-ups with your dentist and optician too.

3. How many hours of sleep do you get each night? Find out what the recommended amount of sleep is for someone your age.
4. How many hours of exercise do you do each week? Find out what the recommended amount of exercise is for someone your age.

25

PAGE SUMMARY

The main learning aim of this double page spread is to understand that by having a healthy lifestyle pupils can keep their body systems in good condition and avoid becoming ill.

LANGUAGE

- Question words: *how, why, how much*
- Comparatives: *stronger, faster, harder*
- *Should / shouldn't*
- Vocabulary: *balanced diet, nutrients, iron, potassium, vitamin C, proteins, carbohydrates, fibre, water, speech, memory, bacteria, germs, sweat, dirt, plaque, muscles, heart, lungs, brain, blood, teeth*

ADDITIONAL MATERIALS

- Digital flashcards
- Digital wordcards
- Extra materials: picture of a healthy boy and girl for opening activities, picture of a food wheel, card and art materials for each group

OPENING ACTIVITIES

- Show a picture of a healthy-looking boy and girl. Explain that these two children both lead a very healthy lifestyle. Ask them to suggest things that they do and don't do in order to look so well.
- Revise food groups and nutrients. Show a picture of a food wheel on the board. Ask the pupils if they can name the food groups in the wheel *(meat and fish, fruit and vegetables, milk and dairy, fats and sugars)*. Now ask them if they can name the nutrients in the food wheel *(proteins, vitamins and minerals, carbohydrates and fats)*. Ask them to work with a partner to decide how each of these nutrients help our body *(They help us grow, give us energy and keep us healthy.)*

MAIN ACTIVITIES

Page 24-25, Healthy habits (CD1 track 16)

- Ask pupils to open their books on page 24 and read the introductory text. Play the audio and ask the pupils to listen and read. Focus their attention on Rule 1: Eat healthily **(CD1 track 17)**. Ask them to work with a partner to decide how eating healthily is good for our body. Ask them to make notes. Repeat with the other four rules. **(CD1 tracks 18-21)**
- Now ask the pupils to close their books and to only use the notes they have made. Invite pupils to explain how a balanced diet can help our body systems.

- Draw the pupils' attention to the *Did you know?* box. Invite someone to read the box for the rest of the class. Ask **What other activities make you feel happy?**

1 Explain why a balanced diet is important.

- Organise the class into small groups and ask them to work together to answer this question. To guide the discussion write *growth*, *health* and *energy* on the board. Remind them that different foods and nutrients are good for different body systems. Write *digestive system, circulatory system, nervous system, immune system and respiratory system* on the board. Allow time for the groups to organise their ideas and say which foods and nutrients benefit these body systems. *Open answer*

2 How does exercise help make your heart stronger?

- Write this sentence on the board. When we exercise, we breathe _________ and our heart has to work _________ to pump blood around the body. As a result, our heart gets _______. Ask the pupils to work with a partner to complete the sentence. *When we exercise, we breathe faster and our heart has to work harder to pump blood around the body. As a result, our heart gets stronger.*

3 How many hours of sleep do you get each night? Find out what the recommended amount of sleep is for someone your age.

- This activity can be done at home with the help of parents or in small study groups. *10 hours*

4 How many hours of exercise do you do each week? Find out what the recommended amount of exercise is for someone your age.

- This activity can be done at home with the help of parents or in small study groups on a computer or in the library. *At least an hour a day.*

CLOSING ACTIVITIES

- Write the following example of a balanced meal on the board- *Mixed salad, fish and rice and yohurt.* Ask pupils if they think this is a balanced meal. Invite pupils to come out to write the names of the nutrients next to each food. *(vitamins and minerals; proteins, carbodyhdrates and fibre; calcium)* Now, ask them to work with a partner to design their own balanced meal.
- Invite pupils to describe their balanced meal to the rest of the class. The class decides if the meal is balanced or not.
- Explain that they are going to make a word chain. The first pupil names a food, for example *ham*. The next one names the nutrients in ham *(proteins and iron)* and names another food, e.g. *oranges*. The next pupil says *vitamins* and so on.

EXTRA IDEAS

- Organise the class into small groups and ask them to design a poster about healthy habits. Tell them they can focus on one rule or on the five rules for healthy habits.

ANSWERS AT A GLANCE

1 Open answer.

2 When we exercise, we breathe faster and our heart has to work harder to pump blood around the body. As a result, our heart gets stronger.

3 10 hours.

4 At least one hour a day.

PAGES 26-27 Unhealthy habits

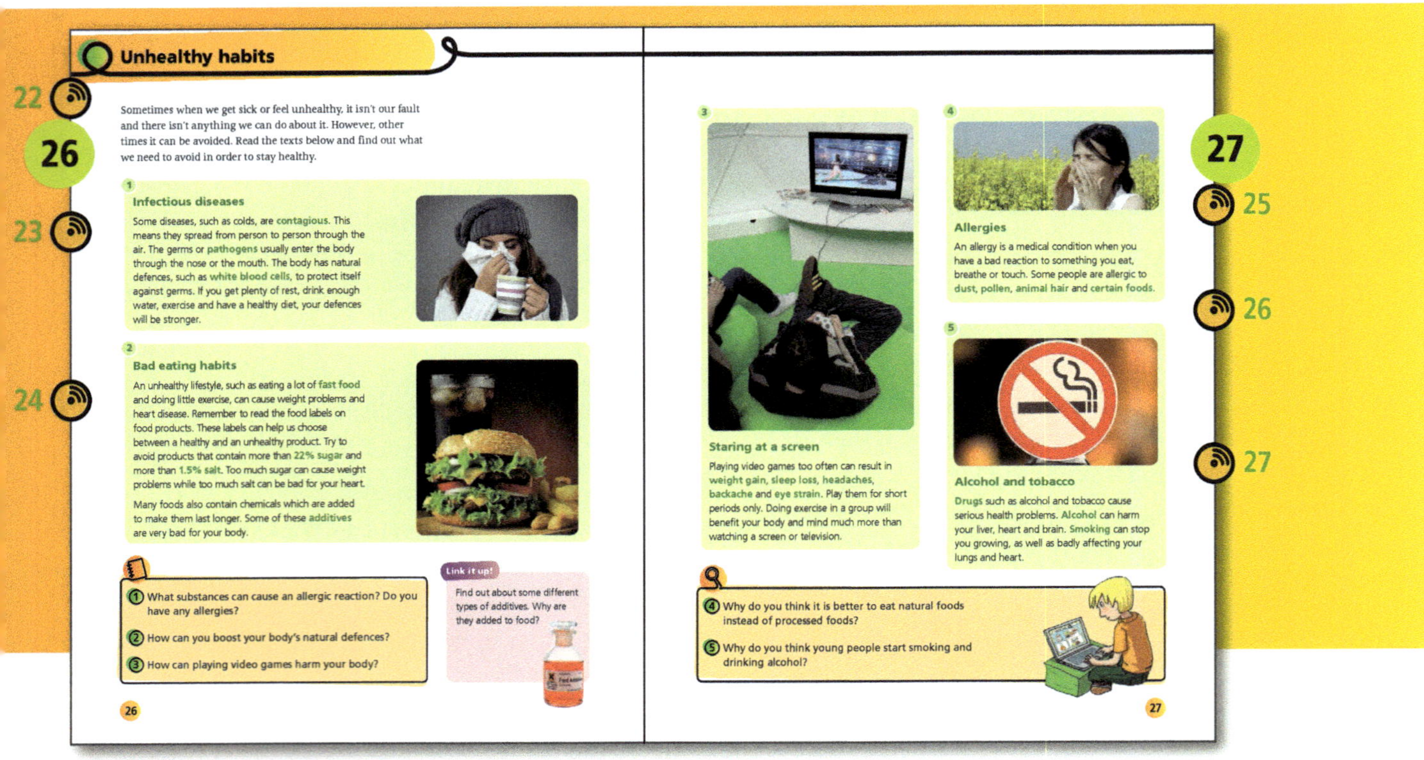

22 23 24 25 26 27

Unhealthy habits

26

Sometimes when we get sick or feel unhealthy, it isn't our fault and there isn't anything we can do about it. However, other times it can be avoided. Read the texts below and find out what we need to avoid in order to stay healthy.

1 **Infectious diseases**

Some diseases, such as colds, are contagious. This means they spread from person to person through the air. The germs or pathogens usually enter the body through the nose or the mouth. The body has natural defences, such as white blood cells, to protect itself against germs. If you get plenty of rest, drink enough water, exercise and have a healthy diet, your defences will be stronger.

2 **Bad eating habits**

An unhealthy lifestyle, such as eating a lot of fast food and doing little exercise, can cause weight problems and heart disease. Remember to read the food labels on food products. These labels can help us choose between a healthy and an unhealthy product. Try to avoid products that contain more than 22% sugar and more than 1.5% salt. Too much sugar can cause weight problems while too much salt can be bad for your heart.

Many foods also contain chemicals which are added to make them last longer. Some of these additives are very bad for your body.

1. What substances can cause an allergic reaction? Do you have any allergies?
2. How can you boost your body's natural defences?
3. How can playing video games harm your body?

Link it up! Find out about some different types of additives. Why are they added to food?

26

27

3 **Staring at a screen**

Playing video games too often can result in weight gain, sleep loss, headaches, backache and eye strain. Play them for short periods only. Doing exercise in a group will benefit your body and mind much more than watching a screen or television.

4 **Allergies**

An allergy is a medical condition when you have a bad reaction to something you eat, breathe or touch. Some people are allergic to dust, pollen, animal hair and certain foods.

5 **Alcohol and tobacco**

Drugs such as alcohol and tobacco cause serious health problems. Alcohol can harm your liver, heart and brain. Smoking can stop you growing, as well as badly affecting your lungs and heart.

4. Why do you think it is better to eat natural foods instead of processed foods?
5. Why do you think young people start smoking and drinking alcohol?

27

PAGE SUMMARY

This double-page spread introduces pupils to the concept of infectious diseases and pathogens or germs. The main aim of this lesson is to show pupils the effect that unhealthy habits have on our body.

LANGUAGE

- Questions words: *what, why, how, etc.*
- Vocabulary: *disease, infectious, contagious, pathogens, fast food, weight, label, avoid, additives, benefit, gain, strain, allergy, reaction, dust, drugs, alcohol, tobacco, harm, smoking*

ADDITIONAL MATERIALS

- Digital flashcards
- Digital wordcards
- Extra materials: A4 card, food labels from home

OPENING ACTIVITIES

- Place the wordcards from the lesson *Healthy habits* on the board. Ask pupils to identify the five rules for a healthy lifestyle (eat healthily, exercise, sleep, etc.). Invite pupils to classify the wordcards under the correct heading and ask them to justify why they placed the card where they did. *Potassium is in the eat healthily group because it's a mineral and helps the circulatory system.*

MAIN ACTIVITIES

Page 26-27, Unhealthy habits (CD1 track 22)

- Before reading ask pupils to look at the photos on pages 26 and 27. Ask them to predict what the texts will be about. **Look at the first photo. What do you think is the matter with her? The hamburger looks delicious, doesn't it? What will the text be about?**
- Play the audio to pupils. Play one information box and stop to check for understanding. Now ask the pupils to read the box again in *Order reading* (see *Helpful tips* pages 20 -23).

① Ⓓ What substances can cause an allergic reaction? Do you have any allergies?

- Ask pupils if they have any allergies and ask them what they are allergic to? Write the allergies on the board. Ask them how they react when they have contact with these substances. **What happens to you? Do you sneeze? Do you have a rash?** (Mime these reactions if necessary.) *Dust, pollen, animal hair and certain foods.*

② Ⓓ How can you boost your body's natural defences?

- Play the *Germs* song **(CD1 track 14)** and encourage pupils to sing along. Say **Our white blood cells protect us against germs. How can we make sure our natural defence system is in good condition?** Tell the pupils to look for the answer in the first box. *If you get plenty of rest, drink enough water, exercise and have a healthy diet, your defences will be stronger.*

③ Ⓓ How can playing video games harm your body?

- Ask pupils to work with a partner to talk about this question. Write on the board questions about video games: *Do you play video games? How often do you play them?* Tell pupils to interview their partner and to make a note of their answers. Then suggest they look for the answer to the question in box 3. *Playing video games too often can result in weight gain, sleep loss, headaches, backache and eye strain.*
- Get feedback from the class and note how long pupils spend playing video games. Ask: **Do you think you spend too much time in front of a screen? What could you do instead?**

④ Why do you think it is better to eat natural foods instead of processed foods?

- Organise the class into small groups and ask them to work together to answer question 4. Ask them to think about why people buy processed foods. Draw their attention to the *Link it up* box. Suggest they conduct a mini investigation at home with the help of parents. Point out that additives are called by a letter and a number. *See Answers at a glance*

⑤ Why do you think young people start smoking and drinking alcohol?

- Ask pupils what the dangers of smoking and drinking alcohol are. Point out that both habits are really bad for you and can cause serious health problems. Ask **So why do young people start doing this if they all know how dangerous these habits are?** Encourage everyone to take part in the class discussion. *See Answers at a glance*

⊕ CLOSING ACTIVITIES

- Place the wordcards *infectious diseases, bad eating habits, allergies, video games and drugs* on the board. Read out sentences from pages 26 and 27 and ask pupils to identify the information box. *Many foods contain chemicals. (Bad eating habits); Pathogens usually enter the body through the nose or mouth. (Infectious diseases)*

⊕ EXTRA IDEAS

- Ask pupils to bring in food labels from home. Ask them to stick the label onto a piece of card and to write the ingredients in English and the percentages of its contents. Ask them to pay special attention to the amount of sugar, salt and additives.

ANSWERS AT A GLANCE

① Dust, pollen, animal hair and certain foods.

② If you get plenty of rest, drink enough water, exercise and have a healthy diet, your defences will be stronger.

③ Weight gain, sleep loss, headaches, backache and eye strain.

④ Processed foods contain chemical additives which can harm the body.

⑤ Open answer. (They want to seem older. They think it's cool. They don't want their friends to laugh at them. They want to disobey their parents.)

PAGES 28–29 We are all equal

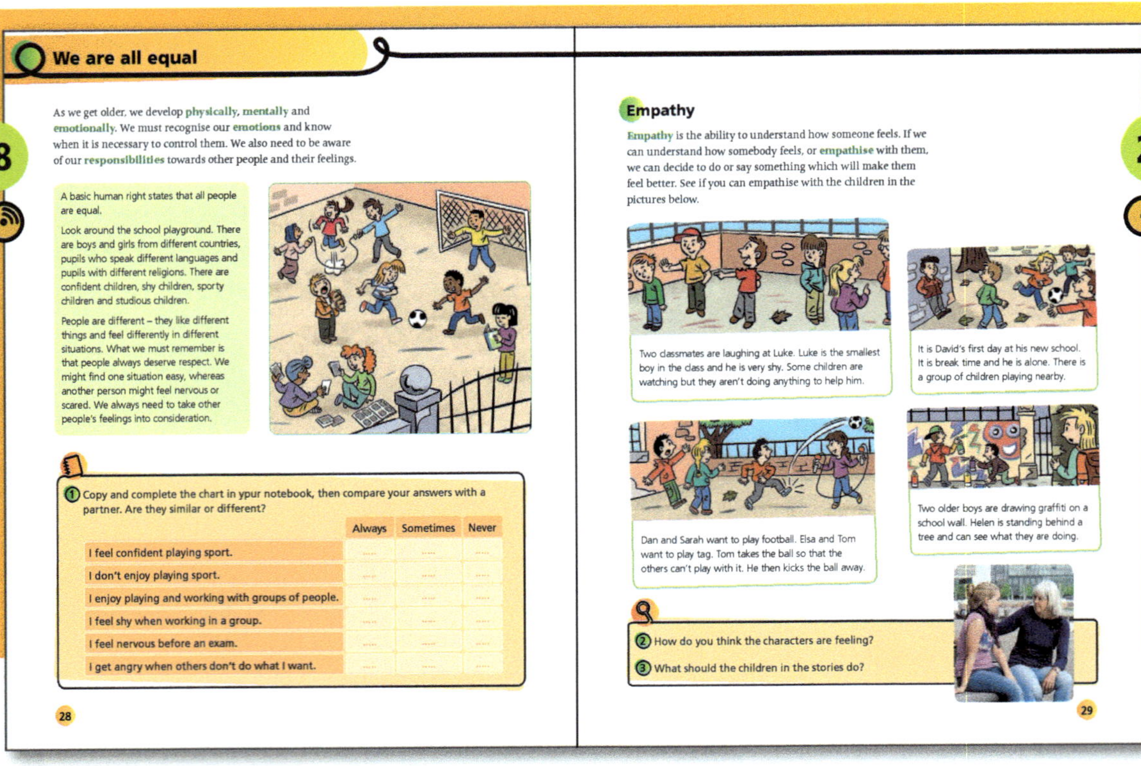

We are all equal

28

As we get older, we develop **physically**, **mentally** and **emotionally**. We must recognise our **emotions** and know when it is necessary to control them. We also need to be aware of our **responsibilities** towards other people and their feelings.

A basic human right states that all people are equal.

Look around the school playground. There are boys and girls from different countries, pupils who speak different languages and pupils with different religions. There are confident children, shy children, sporty children and studious children.

People are different – they like different things and feel differently in different situations. What we must remember is that people always deserve respect. We might find one situation easy, whereas another person might feel nervous or scared. We always need to take other people's feelings into consideration.

1 Copy and complete the chart in ypur notebook, then compare your answers with a partner. Are they similar or different?

	Always	Sometimes	Never
I feel confident playing sport.	.....	.....	.....
I don't enjoy playing sport.	.....	.....	.....
I enjoy playing and working with groups of people.	.....	.....	.....
I feel shy when working in a group.	.....	.....	.....
I feel nervous before an exam.	.....	.....	.....
I get angry when others don't do what I want.	.....	.....	.....

28

Empathy

29

Empathy is the ability to understand how someone feels. If we can understand how somebody feels, or **empathise** with them, we can decide to do or say something which will make them feel better. See if you can empathise with the children in the pictures below.

Two classmates are laughing at Luke. Luke is the smallest boy in the class and he is very shy. Some children are watching but they aren't doing anything to help him.

It is David's first day at his new school. It is break time and he is alone. There is a group of children playing nearby.

Dan and Sarah want to play football. Elsa and Tom want to play tag. Tom takes the ball so that the others can't play with it. He then kicks the ball away.

Two older boys are drawing graffiti on a school wall. Helen is standing behind a tree and can see what they are doing.

2 How do you think the characters are feeling?

3 What should the children in the stories do?

29

PAGE SUMMARY

This double-page spread asks pupils to reflect on the ways people are different and also to be aware of their responsibilities towards other people and their feelings.

LANGUAGE

- Questions words: *what, how, etc.*
- Adverbs of frequency: *always, often, never*
- *Should / shouldn't*
- Present continuous
- Adjectives: *confident, shy, sporty, studious*
- Vocabulary: *responsibilities, emotions, confident, shy, sporty, studious, respect, empathy, empathise, tag, graffiti*

ADDITIONAL MATERIALS

- Digital flashcards
- Digital wordcards
- Extra materials: A4 paper cut into quarters

OPENING ACTIVITIES

- Announce suddenly that you are going to give the class a surprise exam today. Wait a few moments before telling them that you aren't going to do it. Ask: **How many of you felt worried? How many felt happy? How many felt angry?** Point out that they felt different emotions about the same situation.
- Brainstorm different emotions. Invite pupils to talk about these emotions. **When do you feel worried? What can make you feel annoyed? What makes you sad? When do you get really angry?**
- Remind the pupils about the *Calm breathing* technique that they learned in the previous unit. Ask them to sit comfortably on their chair and close their eyes. Tell them to follow your instructions. Read the steps of *Calm breathing* to the pupils.

MAIN ACTIVITIES

- If you are using an interactive whiteboard, focus only on the illustration of the playground on page 28. If not, ask pupils to look at the picture on page 28. Elicit ideas about what is happening. *Some children are playing football. A boy and a girl are swopping cards, etc.* Ask: **Do the children look happy? Do they all look the same? How are they different?**

Page 28, We are all equal (CD1 track 28)

- Read the text on page 28.(See *Helpful tips* pages 20 – 23). Pause at key words to have the pupils read the missing word or phrase together. Ask the pupils what the text is telling us. *We are all equal. People are different. We must respect other people, etc.*

1 Copy and complete the chart in your notebook, then compare your answers with a partner. Are they similar or different?

- Ask pupils to copy and complete the chart in their notebooks. When they have finished, tell them to compare their answers with their partner. *Do you feel confident playing sport? Do you enjoy playing sport?* Ask them if their answers are similar or different. *Open answer*

Page 29, Empathy (CD1 track 29)

- Before you read the text, ask pupils to look at the illustrations. Elicit what is happening in each story. Read the introductory text and ask pupils to listen and read. Ask the pupils how you can know what a person is feeling. *(It often shows on their faces.)* Invite a volunteer to explain the word empathy. *(It is understanding how somebody feels.)*
- Organise the class into small groups and assign a story to each group. Tell the group to read the story and work together to answer questions 3 and 4. Ask them to read the story first and then to give their ideas about how the characters are feeling. Then ask them what they think the children in the story should do.

2 How do you think the children are feeling?

- Ask pupils to discuss this question in pairs or small groups, before reporting back to the class. *Open answer*

3 What could you do to help them feel better?

- Ask pupils to discuss this question in pairs or small groups, before reporting back to the class. *Open answer*

+ CLOSING ACTIVITIES

- Chinese whispers. Have the class stand one behind another in two lines. Give a piece of paper to the two pupils at the front of their line. They must read the sentence and whisper it to the next person in their line, who whispers it to the next until it is passed all the way to the end. The pupil at the end of the line comes and writes the sentence they've heard on the board. *I feel worried when I go to the dentist. I'm sad when I have an argument with my friends. I get angry when people don't listen to me*, etc.

+ EXTRA IDEAS

- Take sheets of A4 paper and cut the sheets into four pieces. Hand out a piece to each pupil. Tell them to fold the paper again and again and then to smooth it out. Now tell them to make the paper into a ball. Tell them to throw the ball against the table. Tell them to drop the paper onto the floor and jump on it. Now ask them to smooth the paper out again on the table. Ask **Is the paper the same as it was?** Tell the pupils to say sorry to the paper. Ask: **Is the paper better now?** Explain that this is what happens when we upset another person. The hurt stays inside for a long time.

ANSWERS AT A GLANCE

1 Open answer.

2 Open answer.

3 Open answer.

PAGES 30-31 Find out / Think about it

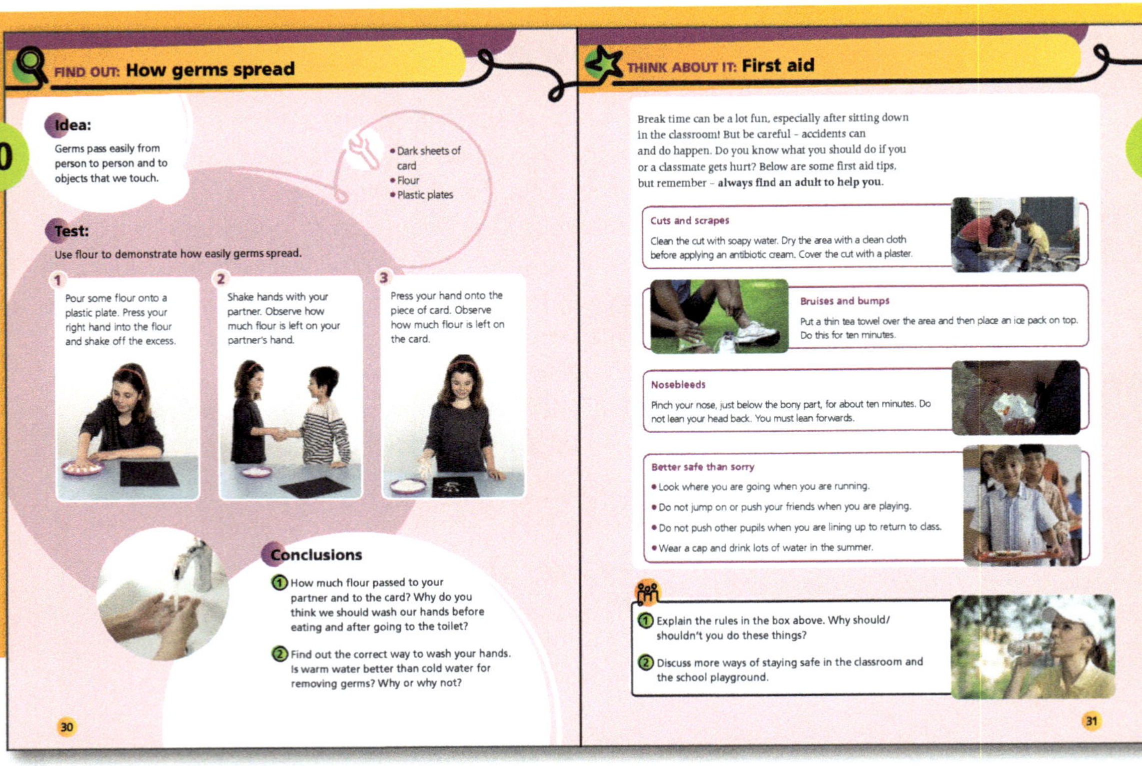

PAGE SUMMARY

In the first of these two pages *(Find out)*, pupils investigate how germs pass easily from person to person. The second page *(Think about it)* provides pupils with the opportunity to learn about first aid procedures and what pupils should do if they, or someone they know, is hurt.

LANGUAGE

- Imperatives: *pour, press, shake, observe*
- Past tense
- Vocabulary: *cut, scrape, bruise, bump, nosebleed, pinch, plaster*

MATERIALS

- Digital flashcards
- Digital wordcards

FIND OUT

OPENING ACTIVITIES

- Play the game *Correct me please* to test pupils on the concepts from pages 24-27. *(Healthy and unhealthy habits)*. Say sentences with mistakes that pupils have to correct. *An allergy is an infectious disease. Pathogens enter the body through the feet. The dentist makes sure you have the correct vaccinations.*
- Remind pupils that there are healthy habits and unhealthy habits. Ask them to work with a partner to prepare a mime to illustrate one of the examples from the unit. For example, they could mime washing their hands or doing an eye test at the optician's.

MAIN ACTIVITIES

- Explain to pupils that they will be doing a simple investigation to observe how easily germs can spread from person to person.
- Ask pupils to read the steps on page 30. If you are using the book on the interactive whiteboard, you can play the audio of the steps.

CLOSING ACTIVITIES

- Give pupils time to compare the hand print on their piece of card with their classmates' hand prints. Point out that germs are so small that we can't see them and therefore we sometimes forget that they exist. Ask: **You know that you should cover your nose and mouth when you sneeze or cough but why is it wrong to cover your nose and mouth with your hand?** (*The germs pass on to your hand and then to other people or things.*) **If you have to use your hand, what should you do immediately?** *(Wash your hands.)*

CONCLUSIONS

1 How much flour passed to your partner and to the card? Why do you think we should wash our hands before eating and after going to the toilet?

- Ask the pupils if they know how many times they wash their hands during the day. Ask them to work with a partner to write a list of the times when they should wash their hands. *You should wash your hands after touching an animal. You should wash them after going to the toilet.* etc. Ask them to explain the reason for washing our hands. *(Washing removes the germs that are on our hands.)*

2 Find out the correct way to wash your hands. Is warm water better than cold water for removing germs? Why or why not?

- This activity can be done at home for homework using a computer. *Warm water is more effective at removing germs.*

THINK ABOUT IT

OPENING ACTIVITIES

- Ask pupils if they have ever hurt themselves at school. Ask them: **How did the accident happen? What were you doing? Which part of your body did you hurt?** Encourage them to talk about their experiences. Ask the class: **Could they have stopped this accident from happening?**

- Borrow the school's first aid kit. Before you open it, explain that it is called a first aid kit and ask them to guess what is inside it. Take out the different items and name them. Ask the pupils what they are used for. **This is a band aid or plaster. When do we use them? This is antibiotic cream. Why do put this on a cut or a scrape?** Try to show the pupils the following items: a thermometer, a plaster, gauze, a bandage, scissors, tweezers, antibiotic cream and an ice pack.

MAIN ACTIVITIES

- Ask pupils to open their books on page 31 and ask them look at the pictures and describe what they can see in pairs. Encourage them to use complete sentences when speaking about the photos. Encourage them to speculate about what has happened. Remind them about: *prevention*, *diagnosis* and *treatment*. Ask: **Which photos show treatment and which show prevention?** Say **Let's read about first aid**. If you are using the interactive whiteboard, you can play the audio and encourage pupils to read along in their books.

CLOSING ACTIVITIES

1 Explain the rules in the box above. Why should/shouldn't you do these things?

- Ask the pupils to work with a partner to answer this question. You may like to model an answer, e.g. *You should look where you are going when you are running because if you don't you can run into a person or an obstacle, like a wall or a tree.* Ask them to talk about each point and to think about the consequences of not following this advice. Invite volunteers to read the advisory sentences and encourage the other pupils to give their opinions.

2 Discuss more ways of staying safe in the classroom and the school playground.

- Pupils can talk about this question in small groups or as a class activity. Take the opportunity to talk about specific situations that affect the group e.g. swinging on chairs, over-enthusiastic tackling when playing football, jumping down the stairs, etc. The pupils could draw up their list of rules for keeping safe and design posters to be used around the school.

PAGES 32–33 Look back: Looking after yourself

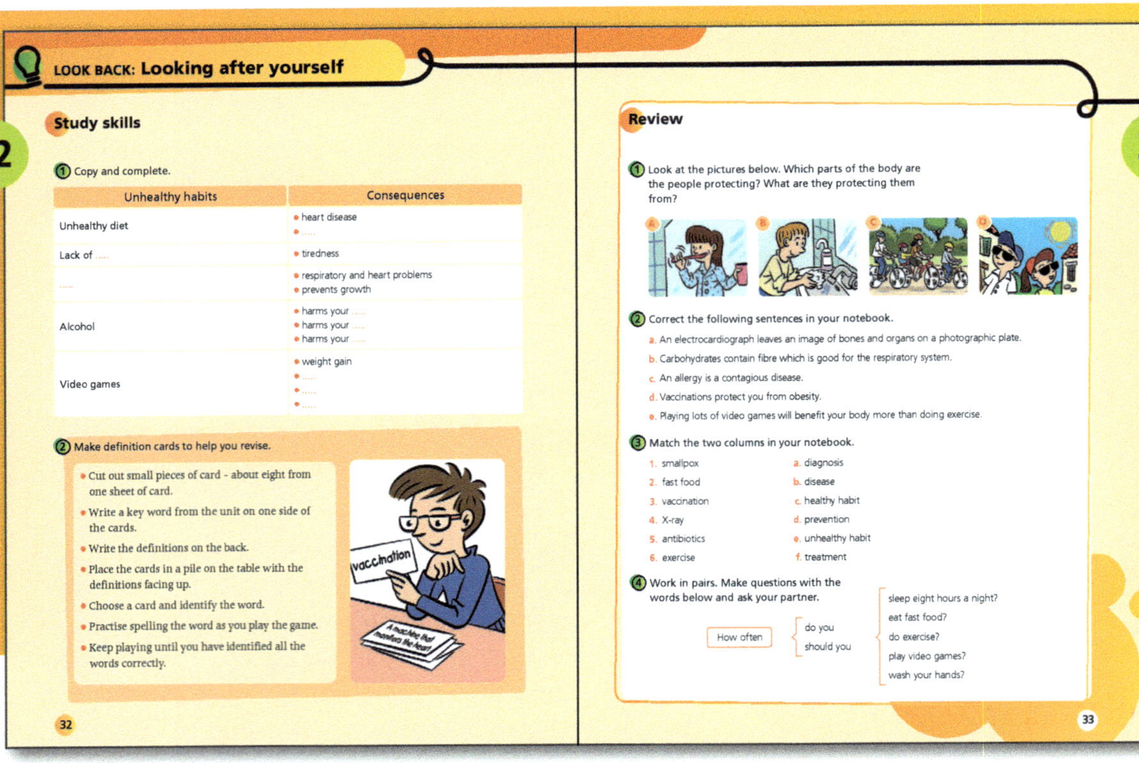

32

LOOK BACK: Looking after yourself

Study skills

1 Copy and complete.

Unhealthy habits	Consequences
Unhealthy diet	• heart disease • ......
Lack of	• tiredness
......	• respiratory and heart problems • prevents growth
Alcohol	• harms your ...... • harms your ...... • harms your ......
Video games	• weight gain • ...... • ...... • ......

2 Make definition cards to help you revise.

- Cut out small pieces of card - about eight from one sheet of card.
- Write a key word from the unit on one side of the cards.
- Write the definitions on the back.
- Place the cards in a pile on the table with the definitions facing up.
- Choose a card and identify the word.
- Practise spelling the word as you play the game.
- Keep playing until you have identified all the words correctly.

32

33

Review

1 Look at the pictures below. Which parts of the body are the people protecting? What are they protecting them from?

a b c d

2 Correct the following sentences in your notebook.

a. An electrocardiograph leaves an image of bones and organs on a photographic plate.
b. Carbohydrates contain fibre which is good for the respiratory system.
c. An allergy is a contagious disease.
d. Vaccinations protect you from obesity.
e. Playing lots of video games will benefit your body more than doing exercise.

3 Match the two columns in your notebook.

1. smallpox	a. diagnosis
2. fast food	b. disease
3. vaccination	c. healthy habit
4. X-ray	d. prevention
5. antibiotics	e. unhealthy habit
6. exercise	f. treatment

4 Work in pairs. Make questions with the words below and ask your partner.

How often — do you / should you — sleep eight hours a night? / eat fast food? / do exercise? / play video games? / wash your hands?

33

PAGE SUMMARY

This double-page spread allows pupils the opportunity to organise what they've learned in the unit by means of a classification table. On the *Review* page, pupils complete activities individually to check their understanding of the material covered in this unit. Activity 4 is a pairwork speaking activity to encourage them to create complete, accurate sentences, and use a simple structure (*How often do you …*?). They will also use the structure (*How often should you …*?).

LANGUAGE

- Imperatives: *look, match, write, copy, correct, work, make, cut, place, choose, write, work*
- *Should / shouldn't* + infinitive
- *How often do you …? (Every day, twice a day, three times a day)*
- Frequency adverbs: *always, sometimes, never*
- *How often should you …?*

ADDITIONAL MATERIALS

- Digital flashcards
- Digital wordcards

OPENING ACTIVITIES

- Review vocabulary by placing wordcards from the unit on the board. Say a definition of a word and choose a pupil to find the word on the board. Put the word back on the board in a different place. Define another word and choose a different volunteer. Pupils can also take turns to provide definitions.
- Ask pupils to work with a partner. Tell pupils to look at the Pupil's Book to help them make two sentences about the contents of this unit. One sentence must be true and the other one false. One of them says the true sentence and the other one says the false sentence. *Allergies are infectious diseases. An ultrasound machine monitors the foetus inside the mother.* The class repeats the true sentence and corrects the false one.
- Ask the class to think of a healthy habit to tell the rest of the class. Make a challenge that each one must give an example that hasn't been said before.

MAIN ACTIVITIES

Page 32, Study skills

1 Copy and complete

- Remind pupils that when we organise new information, it is easier to understand and remember it.

- Focus the pupils' attention on the classification table and ask them to tell you what the missing words are.
- Tell them to copy and complete the classification table in their notebooks.

Unhealthy habits	Consequences
Unhealthy diet	• heart disease • Weight problems
Lack of sleep	• tiredness
Smoking	• Respiratory and heart problems • Prevents growth
Alcohol	• harms your liver • harms your heart • harms your brain
Video games	• Weight gain • Sleep loss • Headaches • Backaches • Eye strain

2 Make definition cards to help you revise

- Hand out A4 pieces of card to the pupils. Show them how to cut the card into eight smaller pieces. Tell them that you want them to write a key word – *electrocardiograph* - on one side of the card. Explain that on the other side of the card, they must write the definition of the word, e.g. *A machine that monitors the heart.*
- Pupils can work individually, in pairs or in groups to make their cards. Monitor the activity careful to ensure correct spelling and accurate definitions.
- When the cards are ready, pairs can test each other or groups can test other groups.

Page 33, Review

Note: This part of the review can be done with minimal teacher guidance. You may wish to work through the activities as a class or in small groups. Alternatively, you can ask pupils to do them individually as a self-evaluation. This review can also be done as homework.

1 Look at the pictures below. Which parts of the body are the people protecting? What are they protecting them from?

a. Teeth: protecting them from tooth decay.

b. Skin: protecting it from germs and bacteria.

c. Heart and lungs: protecting them from heart and respiratory problems.

d. Eyes: protecting them from harmful rays from the Sun.

2 Correct the following sentences in your notebook.

a. An X-ray leaves an image of bones and organs on a photographic plate.

b. Carbohydrates contain fibre which is good for the digestive system.

c. An allergy is a medical condition when you have a bad reaction to something. It isn't contagious.

d. Vaccinations protect you from certain diseases.

e. Doing exercise will benefit your body more than playing lots of video games.

3 Match the two columns in your notebook.

1. smallpox – b. disease
2. fast food – e. unhealthy habit
3. vaccination – d. prevention
4. X-ray – a. diagnosis
5. antibiotics – f. treatment
6. exercise – c. healthy habit

4 Work in pairs. Make questions with the words below and ask your partner.

- How often do / should you sleep eight hours a night?
- How often do / should you eat fast food?
- How often do / should you do exercise?
- How often do / should you play video games?
- How often do / should you wash your hands?
- Encourage pupils to answer the questions with full sentences. *I never eat fast food. You should do exercise every day. I play video games at the weekend. You shouldn't play video games for too long.*

Activity Book answers / Audio CD1 track list

8

UNIT 2 Looking after yourself

1 Complete the sentences about machines we can find at a hospital.

~~electrocardiograph~~ ~~microscope~~ ~~ultrasound~~ ~~X-ray~~

a. An *ultrasound* machine allows doctors to monitor a foetus inside the mother.
b. An **electrocardiograph** monitors heart rate.
c. An **X-ray** machine makes an image of bones and organs inside the body.
d. A **microscope** can be used to perform microsurgery on tiny parts of the body.

2 Complete the table of medical advances.

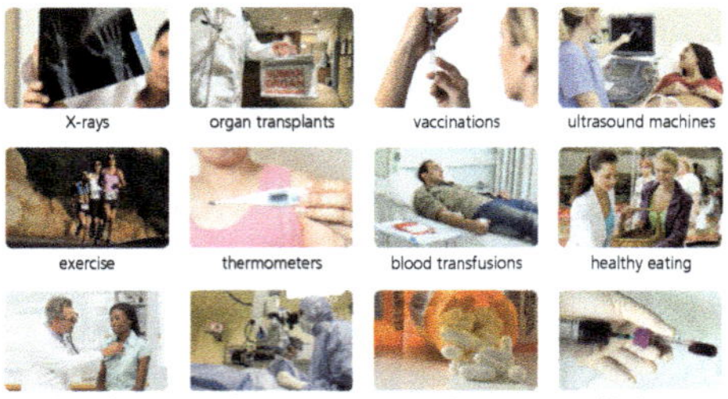

X-rays, organ transplants, vaccinations, ultrasound machines, exercise, thermometers, blood transfusions, healthy eating, regular check-ups, microsurgery, antibiotics, blood tests

Medical advances		
Prevention	Diagnosis	Treatment
vaccinations	*X-rays*	organ transplants
regular check-ups	ultrasound machines	microsurgery
healthy eating	thermometers	antibiotics
exercise	blood tests	blood transfusions

8

9

3 Complete the sentences about healthy habits.

~~wash~~ ~~memory~~ ~~respiratory~~ ~~brain~~ ~~balanced~~ ~~grows~~ ~~stronger~~ ~~nutrients~~ ~~teeth~~ ~~heart~~

Rules of healthy living

Rule 1: Eat healthily *b*
We need to eat a *balanced* diet. Different **nutrients** from a variety of foods help our body systems.

Rule 2: Exercise **d**
Regular exercise helps our circulatory and **respiratory** systems. Our **heart** and the muscles we use to breathe get **stronger**.

Rule 3: Sleep **c**
When we sleep our body rests and **grows**. Our **brain** develops so that speech and **memory** function properly the next day.

Rule 4: Keep clean **a**
We must always **wash** our hands before eating and after using the toilet. We also have to brush our **teeth** twice a day.

4 Complete the crossword about healthy living.

Clues down:
1. This helps move food through the digestive system.
2. This helps your heart, muscles and nerves work properly.
3. This is the body system that breaks down food.

Clues across:
4. This vitamin helps strengthen your immune system.
5. You need to drink plenty of this every day.
6. This nutrient helps carry oxygen around the body.

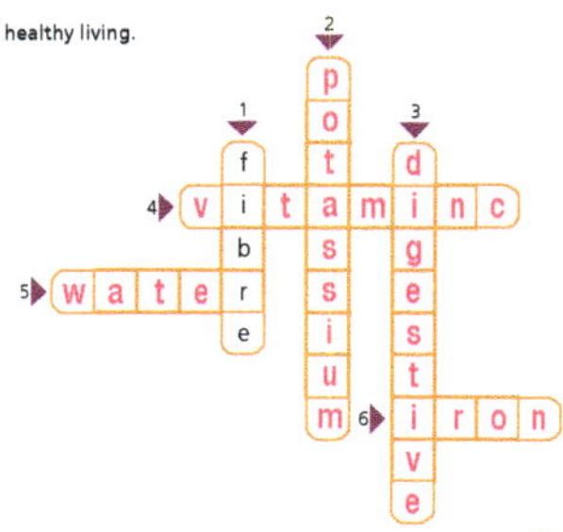

9

10

UNIT 2

5 Tick (✓) the consequences of unhealthy habits.

	unhealthy eating	video games	smoking	drugs and alcohol
It causes heart disease and obesity.	✓			
It harms your lungs.			✓	
It harms your liver and heart.				✓
It can cause weight gain, backache and eye strain.		✓		

6 Cross out the mistake in each sentence. Write the correct word or words.

a. Some ~~allergies~~ are contagious, which means that they spread from person to person. **infectious diseases**
b. Some people are allergic to dust, pollen, animal hair and certain ~~people~~. **foods**
c. The body has natural defences, such as ~~red~~ blood cells, to protect itself against germs. **white**

7 Read the labels. Why aren't these foods healthy?

Fizzy drink	
Nutritional information	Typical values
Per	330ml (% of recommended daily amount)
Energy	122kcal (6%)
Fat	0g (0%)
Carbohydrate	26g (11%)
Sugars	28g (31%)
Protein	0g (0%)
Sodium/Salt	0g (0%)

This drink isn't healthy because **it contains too much sugar**.

Pizza	
Nutritional information	Typical values
Per	140g - 2 small slices (% of recommended daily amount)
Energy	407kcal (20%)
Fat	18g (24%)
Carbohydrate	29g (12%)
Sugars	5g (6%)
Protein	10g (20%)
Sodium/Salt	1.5g (25%)

This pizza isn't healthy because **it contains too much fat and salt**.

10

11

8 Match and write true sentences about equality and empathy.

A basic human right	that all people	feel differently in different situations.
Empathy is	different things and	deserve respect.
People like	states that	understand how someone feels.
We must remember	the ability to	all people are equal.

a. *A basic human right states that all people are equal.*
b. **Empathy is the ability to understand how someone feels.**
c. **People like different things and feel differently in different situations.**
d. **We must remember that all people deserve respect.**

9 Look at the photos and consider how each person feels.

a. I think he feels ______ because ______
b. ______ **Open answers**
c. ______

10 What would you do to help the people in the photos?

a. ______
b. **Open answers**
c. ______

11

UNIT 2

Find out at home!

1 Do you take care of yourself? Keep track of your habits for five days.

What do you eat each day?				
Day 1	Day 2	Day 3	Day 4	Day 5
		Open answers.		

How much time do you spend exercising each day?				
Day 1	Day 2	Day 3	Day 4	Day 5
		Open answers.		

How many hours do you sleep each night?				
Day 1	Day 2	Day 3	Day 4	Day 5
		Open answers.		

How much time do you spend playing video games, using a device or watching TV?				
Day 1	Day 2	Day 3	Day 4	Day 5
		Open answers.		

2 Write down two things you do well and two things you would like to do better. Compare with your classmates.

My healthy habits	Things I should change
1. Open answers.	1. Open answers.
2.	2.

12

Skills check

1 Look and read. Write *yes* or *no*. There are two examples.

1. The children are playing outside in the playground. yes
2. It is cold and rainy. no
3. Two children are exercising. no
4. A girl wearing a blue shirt is skipping over a rope. no
5. The girl standing near the gate is reading a book. yes
6. There are two children eating a healthy snack. no
7. The pupil standing in the goal is drinking water. no
8. The boy sitting on the ground has cards in his hands. yes
9. The boy in front of the goalkeeper has short hair. yes
10. There are two children wearing religious headwear. yes

13

13

Unit 2 Audio CD1 track list

TRACK	ACTIVITY
13	**Pupil's Book page 21,** Unit introduction
14	**Pupil's Book page 21,** Song *Germs*
15	**Pupil's Book page 22,** Story: *A trip to the hospital*
16	**Pupil's Book page 24,** Healthy habits
17	**Pupil's Book page 24,** Rule 1: Eat healthily
18	**Pupil's Book page 24,** Rule 2: Exercise
19	**Pupil's Book page 25,** Rule 3: Sleep
20	**Pupil's Book page 25,** Rule 4: Keep clean
21	**Pupil's Book page 25,** Rule 5: Have medical check-ups

TRACK	ACTIVITY
22	**Pupil's Book page 26,** Unhealthy habits
23	**Pupil's Book page 26,** Infectious diseases
24	**Pupil's Book page 26,** Bad eating habits
25	**Pupil's Book page 27,** Staring at a screen
26	**Pupil's Book page 27,** Allergies
27	**Pupil's Book page 27,** Alcohol and tobacco
28	**Pupil's Book page 28,** We are all equal
29	**Pupil's Book page 29,** Empathy

UNIT 3 Living things

CONTENT	EVALUATION CRITERIA
Characteristics of living things.	Know the basic characteristics of living things.
Classifying living things.	Classify living things according to their kingdom.
Respect for living things.	Display attitudes and conduct of respect towards living things.
First approaches to scientific activity and the scientific method. Use of different information sources (direct and indirect). Use ICTs.	Obtain relevant information about specific phenomena, make predictions, integrate information from direct and indirect observation and communicate the results.
Individual and group work.	Work independently and proactively and develop strategies for working in a group.
Planning a project and presenting a report.	Carry out a project and present a report.

LEARNING STANDARDS	KEY COMPETENCES	PAGES
Knows the structure of living things: cells, tissues, organs, systems, functions and processes.	MST	38
Understands that living things can be unicellular and multicellular.	MST	35-37
Understands that all living things carry out the same life processes and explains the basic characteristics of each one.	MST	39
Uses a magnifying glass and other tools in the study and observance of living things.	MST, LTL	42
Classifies living things according to their kingdom and identifies the characteristics of each: monera, protest, fungus, animal and plant kingdoms.	MST, LTL	40, 41
Adopts a critical attitude towards habits that can damage our health.	MST, SOC	26, 27
Accepts the toxic effects of alcohol and tobacco on the health, above all when consumed at a young age.	MST, SOC	27
Displays attitudes and conduct of respect towards living things.	MST, SOC	43
Helps actively in the conservation of animals and plants.	MST, SOC	43
With help, selects and organises specific and relevant information; analyses it and draws conclusions; reflects on the experience and the process; presents the results.	MST, LTL	37, 42, 43
Use books, libraries, etc. and collaborate in the care and maintenance of all the materials available in the school and the classroom.	MST, LTL	34-45
Shows autonomy in the planning of activities and tasks and shows initiative in decision taking.	LTL, AUT	37, 42, 43
Uses strategies to help their own learning, as well as asking for help and information.	LTL, AUT	37, 42-44
First approaches to Cooperative Learning.	SOC, LTL	35,43
Begins observation, using relevant instruments and consulting written documents and images.	LTL, AUT	42
Shows autonomy and proactiveness in the planning of and carrying out of actions.	AUT	42, 43
Presents work clearly and in an organised fashion.	LIN, LTL, AUT	42, 43
With help, carries out a project and presents a report, using paper and/or digital means, collecting information from different sources, presenting the results orally and with the support of images and short texts.	LIN, LTL, AUT, DIG	42, 43

UNIT INFORMATION

UNIT SUMMARY

In this unit, pupils will review and extend their knowledge of living and non-living things. At the beginning of the unit, pupils will be introduced to the concept of cells. This subject area is covered with the help of the course characters, Carla and Alex, who are on a school trip to a science laboratory. The school trip begins in the story and, on their return to school, Alex and Carla carry out a *School trip project* to review what they have learned about unicellular and multicellular living things. These opening pages are designed to test pupils' prior knowledge. They will move on to look in detail at cell organisation and what an organism is made up of. They will also review and extend their understanding of the life processes of living things.

EXPERIMENT

Find out

In the *Find out* activity on page 42, your pupils will carry out a hands-on activity about the living things found in the local environment. This activity requires them to use their observation, research and classification skills.

The pupils will need:

- a notebook
- a pencil
- colouring materials
- a magnifying glass
- a camera (optional)

Further ideas

Pupils can research the living things in a different area of Spain, using the internet or reference books. You could allocate different areas to different groups and ask each group to make a poster.

VALUES AND ATTITUDES

In this unit, your pupils will learn that all living things carry out basic life processes. Throughout the unit, try to encourage pupils to think about how they interact with the world around them and how we should respect all living things. Encourage them to see how varied and fascinating life on Earth is and motivate them to find out more.

Think about it

The *Think about it* page in this unit focuses on the precarious situation of bees today. The pupils learn about the importance of bees and also about ways of helping and protecting these insects.

EVALUATION MATERIAL

These documents can be downloaded from the *Teachers* section of the digital component and printed.

The materials include:

- **A unit diagnostic test**: this provides an overview of the unit and allows you to assess pupils' prior knowledge.
- **An end-of-unit test**: in addition to the *Review* section at the end of each unit, this summative test can be used to evaluate pupils' progress after studying the unit content.
- **A class unit evaluation grid**: this is based on the evaluation criteria and learning standards of the unit.

DIGITAL RESOURCES

Presentations

- **Unit summary**: a simple slide presentation with text, images and audio to review the main ideas of the unit. It can be used at the beginning of the unit to test pupils' prior knowledge of the unit content, or at the end of the unit as a revision tool.
- **Find out**: a slide presentation of the unit's *Find out* page with text, photos and audio. The slide presentation is perfect for a heads-up class, showing the steps one by one. Use this tool to get pupils to predict the next steps (with their books closed) or to focus their attention on each step as they carry out the project themselves.

Activities

Activities vary by unit and include:

- **A memory game**: a useful activity for reviewing key vocabulary and modelling pronunciation.
- **Labelling**: pupils label a diagram by dragging and dropping key terms.
- **Spelling**: pupils drag and drop letters to spell key terms.
- **Read and reveal**: pupils read sentences and guess the missing words, which are revealed by clicking the spaces.
- **Classification**: pupils drag and drop concepts and key terms in a simple classification table.
- **A wordsearch**: pupils find key terms hidden in the wordsearch.
- **Definitions**: pupils drag and drop words to complete definitions.

Song lyrics

Listen to the song *Living things* and follow the lyrics line by line.

Posters

Attractive and informative posters to display in class. You can use them to review key concepts and vocabulary.

Videos

Use the video links in this unit to present content in a dynamic, real-life context, while reinforcing pupils' listening skills.

Teachers

Digital flashcards and wordcards: topics include *What do living things have in common?* and *How are living things classified?*

Downloadable pdfs: evaluation tests, evaluation grids, templates, useful links and further information.

PAGES 34–35 Living things

PAGE SUMMARY

The aim of the unit opener is to develop your pupils' observation skills and find out what they already know about the topic of the unit. Use the picture to elicit vocabulary related to living and non-living things, as well as action verbs that describe what is going on in the scene. Get your pupils to work in groups to complete activities 1–4 to encourage participation and peer support. Play the song and have fun listening to it and completing activity 5.

LANGUAGE

- Question words: *who, what, where, how many, etc.*
- Prepositions of place: *in, on, under, next to*
- *There is / are*
- Passive: *are made up / is made up of*
- Vocabulary: *cell, unicellular, multicellular, nutrition, interaction, repodruction, bacteria, wet suit, mask, oxygen tank, flippers, turtle, fish, coral, survive, share*

ADDITIONAL MATERIALS

- Digital flashcards
- Digital wordcards

⊕ OPENING ACTIVITIES

- If you are using an interactive whiteboard, focus only on the illustration, not the questions. Either elicit ideas (*Alex is looking at a turtle; Carla is wearing flippers, etc.*) or ask questions indicating each part of the picture.
- Alternatively, use the interactive whiteboard writing tools and ask pupils to come up to the board, mark an area of the picture and describe what they can see. Help them to produce full, correct sentences.

MAIN ACTIVITIES

Page 35, Unit introduction (CD1 track 30)

- Read the unit introduction at the top of page 35. Pupils can do a choral reading of the text (see *Helpful tips*, pages 20–23).
- You can play the audio of the unit introduction first, with the pupils reading along with it, and then ask one or two pupils to read out loud. This way, pupils will feel more self-assured when it comes to pronouncing new words. Check for comprehension: **What is the smallest living unit?** (*A cell*); **Which living thing is made up of only one cell?** (*Bacteria*); **Are we unicellular or multicellular?** (*Multicellular*); **What is another name for living things?** (*Organisms*)

- Divide pupils into small groups to answer the questions at the top of page 35. Then invite different groups to compare their answers with each other.

1 What characteristics do living things have in common?

- This is a good opportunity to review vocabulary from year 3. Pupils can answer using the information in the introductory text. *Nutrition, interaction* and *reproduction. Living things are born and they die. They eat, grow, move, breathe, excrete, reproduce and interact.*

2 What is the difference between a unicellular and multicellular organism?

- Suggest to pupils that they look at the photos on page 36. Ask them to identify the unicellular organisms in the photos (bacteria and yeast). *Unicellular organisms are made up of one cell and multicellular organisms are made up of more than one cell.*

3 Which living things can you see in the picture?

- Ask pupils to identify the living things in the picture and then ask them to make a list of other living things found under the sea. You may also ask them to make a list of natural non-living things under the sea. Remind them that non-living things can be natural or man-made. *A turtle, fish, people, coral reef*

4 What do living things need to survive?

- Ask the groups to call out one basic need and write them on the board. Invite volunteers to talk about how the needs vary from organism to organism. *There are five basic needs that all living things have: water, air, sunlight, food (energy) and shelter.*

5 Listen to the song. Which characteristics of living things are represented by the photos below?

- Focus the pupils' attention on the six photos. Ask them to describe what they can see in each photo. Play the song *Living things* **(CD1 track 31)** and ask pupils to point to the characteristics in the photos that they hear. Then play the song a second time and encourage pupils to sing along (you can use the *Song lyrics* section on the digital component to display the song line by line and listen to the song). *Movement, nutrition, interaction, reproduction, respiration/excretion and growth*

CD1 • track 31

Does it need food?
Does it interact?
Does it reproduce?
Does it breathe?
If it does, if it does
It's a living thing
Does it move?
Does it grow?
Does it excrete the waste
It doesn't need?
If it does, if it does,
It's a living thing
Does it need food?
Does it interact?
Does it reproduce?
Does it breathe?
If it doesn't, if it doesn't
It's a non-living thing
Does it move?
Does it grow?
Does it excrete the waste
It doesn't need?
If it doesn't, if it doesn't
It's a non-living thing

ANSWERS AT A GLANCE

1. Living things are born and they die. They eat, grow, move, breathe, excrete, reproduce and interact.
2. Unicellular organisms are made up of one cell and multicellular organisms are made up of more than one cell.
3. A turtle, fish, people, coral reef.
4. Water, air, sunlight, food (energy) and shelter.
5. Movement, nutrition, interaction, reproduction, respiration/excretion and growth.

PAGES 36–37 A trip to science lab

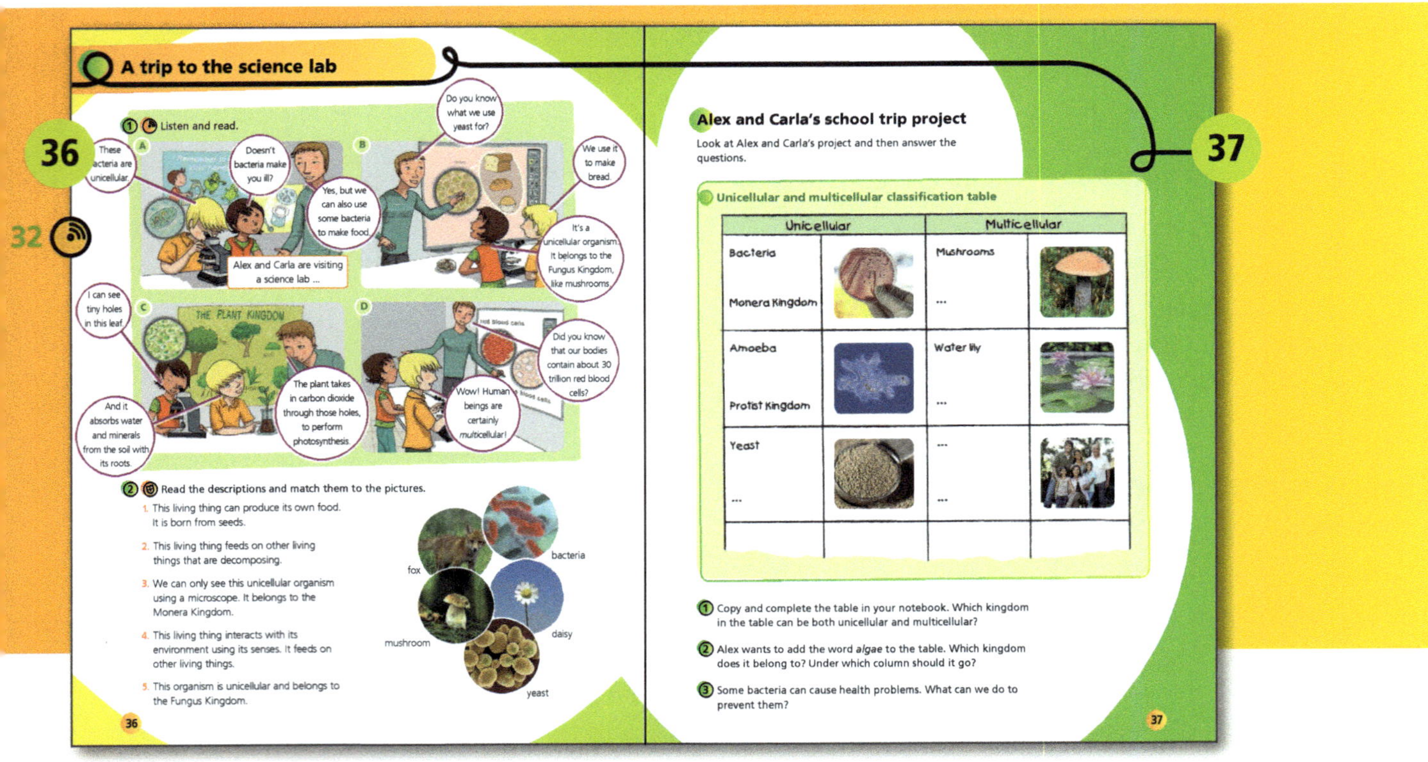

36

32

A trip to the science lab

① Listen and read.

② Read the descriptions and match them to the pictures.

1. This living thing can produce its own food. It is born from seeds.
2. This living thing feeds on other living things that are decomposing.
3. We can only see this unicellular organism using a microscope. It belongs to the Monera Kingdom.
4. This living thing interacts with its environment using its senses. It feeds on other living things.
5. This organism is unicellular and belongs to the Fungus Kingdom.

36

37

Alex and Carla's school trip project

Look at Alex and Carla's project and then answer the questions.

Unicellular and multicellular classification table

Unicellular		Multicellular	
Bacteria Monera Kingdom		Mushrooms ...	
Amoeba Protist Kingdom		Water lily ...	
Yeast ...		... ...	

① Copy and complete the table in your notebook. Which kingdom in the table can be both unicellular and multicellular?

② Alex wants to add the word *algae* to the table. Which kingdom does it belong to? Under which column should it go?

③ Some bacteria can cause health problems. What can we do to prevent them?

37

PAGE SUMMARY

This double-page spread opens with a story in which your pupils have the opportunity to see Carla and Alex at a particular moment of their school trip to the science lab. Carla and Alex are talking to the scientist and showing their knowledge of living things. The story is reinforced with an exam style matching activity that is related to the story. On page 37, the pupils can study Carla and Alex's school trip project about unicellular and multicellular organisms.

LANGUAGE

- Present simple
- Infinitive of purpose
- Vocabulary: *unicellular, multicellular, bacteria, yeast, mushroom, daisy, amoeba, water lily, Monera Kingdom, Protist Kingdom, Fungus Kingdom, Plant Kingdom, Animal Kingdom*

ADDITIONAL MATERIALS

- Digital flashcards
- Digital wordcards
- Extra classroom materials: A plant, a rock, leaves, magnifying glasses

OPENING ACTIVITIES

- Bring a plant and a rock to class. Ask pupils to explain the differences between the two items. *A plant is a living thing. It breathes and grows, etc.*

MAIN ACTIVITIES

① Listen and read. (CD1 track 32)

- Before you listen and read, ask the pupils to look at each frame and describe what is happening using their own words. If you are using an interactive board, prepare the story before class, blocking out the dialogue with the black paint tool. Elicit that the children are looking at bacteria, yeast, a plant and red blood cells.
- Tell the pupils they are now going to listen to the story of Alex and Carla's trip to the science lab. Ask **Which organisms in the story are unicellular?** (*Bacteria and yeast*); **Which group of living things has blood?** (*Animal vertebrates*); **Which group carries out photosynthesis?** (*Plants*); **Do you think bacteria and yeast belong to the same group?** (*No*) Explain that living things can be classified into groups which are called kingdoms. Mushrooms and yeast belong to the Fungus Kingdom. Place the wordcard *Fungus Kingdom* on the board.

(2) Read the descriptions and match them to the pictures.

- This activity aims to introduce some new vocabulary, reinforce what pupils have learned in the story and refresh concepts studied in previous levels. Ask the pupils to work with a partner to match the statements to the photos. Ask a volunteer to read the first statement and invite another to give the answer. *See Answers at a glance*

SCHOOL TRIP PROJECT

- Before the pupils open their books, ask them to give examples of members of the different kingdoms. Say **Who can come and write the name of an organism that belongs to the Monera Kingdom?** (*Bacteria*); **Can you name organisms that belong to the Fungus Kingdom?** (*Mushrooms and yeast*) Encourage volunteers to write examples of plants and animals. Remind them that invertebrates belong to the Animal Kingdom.
- Explain to the pupils that following their trip to the science lab, Alex and Carla have done a project to summarise what they have learned about unicellular and multicellular organisms.
- Tell pupils to look at the photo on page 37 and ask for volunteers to read the words. Place the wordcard *Protist Kingdom* on the board. Explain that these can be unicellular or multicellular.

(1) Copy and complete the table in your notebook. Which kingdom in the table can be both unicellular and multicellular?

- Tell the pupils to copy and complete the table from the book, then share their ideas with a partner. Encourage peer correction of spelling if appropriate. *See Answers at a glance*

(2) Alex wants to add the word *algae* to the table. Which kingdom does it belong to? Under which column should it go?

- This activity can be done at home with the help of parents or in small study groups on a computer or in the library. You may prefer to tell them that it belongs to one of the groups and ask them to guess. Point out that it is a multicellular protist. *Algae are multicellular and belong to the Protist Kingdom.*

(3) Some bacteria can cause health problems. What can we do to prevent them?

- This activity can be done at home with the help of parents or in small study groups on a computer or in the library. You may prefer to guide them to the answer by prompting. *See Answers at a glance for model answer*

(+) CLOSING ACTIVITIES

- Make a word chain. Name an organism and explain that the next person must say which kingdom it belongs to. If they are correct, they then name another organism and the next person classifies it, and so on. *Daisy – Plant Kingdom – amoeba – Protist Kingdom – fox – Animal Kingdom,* etc.
- Organise the class into small groups and give each group a selection of leaves and a magnifying glass. Encourage them to look at the underside of the leaves through the magnifying glass to see the small holes (stomata) there.

(+) EXTRA IDEAS

- Pupils find pictures of organisms from the five kingdoms at home and make a display. They label the organisms as unicellular or multicellular.
- Ask the pupils to investigate yeast in bread making or the importance of bacteria in the making of yoghurt.

ANSWERS AT A GLANCE

Page 36

(2) 1–daisy, 2–mushrooms, 3–bacteria, 4–fox, 5–yeast

Page 37

(1) Yeast – Fungus Kingdom; Mushrooms – Fungus Kingdom; Water lily – Plant Kingdom; Humans – Animal Kingdom. The Fungus Kingdom and Protist Kingdom can be both unicellular and multicellular.

(2) Algae are multicellular and belong to the Protist Kingdom.

(3) (Model answer) We should wash our hands before eating and after going to the toilet. Brush your teeth after eating. Keep fresh food in a fridge. Check sell-by dates on food. Clean cuts and scrapes when you fall.

PAGES 38–39 What do living things have in common?

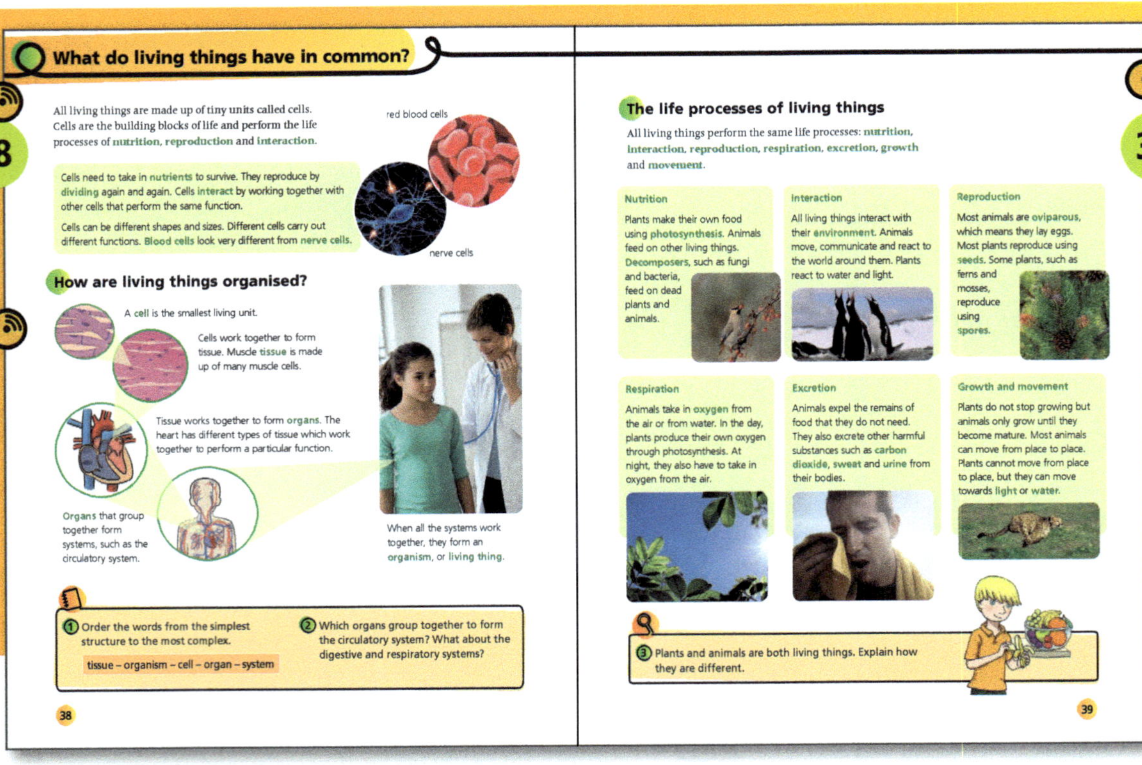

33 34 35 38 39

What do living things have in common?

All living things are made up of tiny units called cells. Cells are the building blocks of life and perform the life processes of **nutrition**, **reproduction** and **interaction**.

Cells need to take in **nutrients** to survive. They reproduce by **dividing** again and again. Cells **interact** by working together with other cells that perform the same function.

Cells can be different shapes and sizes. Different cells carry out different functions. **Blood cells** look very different from **nerve cells**.

red blood cells

nerve cells

How are living things organised?

A cell is the smallest living unit.

Cells work together to form tissue. Muscle **tissue** is made up of many muscle cells.

Tissue works together to form **organs**. The heart has different types of tissue which work together to perform a particular function.

Organs that group together form systems, such as the circulatory system.

When all the systems work together, they form an **organism**, or **living thing**.

1 Order the words from the simplest structure to the most complex.

tissue – organism – cell – organ – system

2 Which organs group together to form the circulatory system? What about the digestive and respiratory systems?

38

The life processes of living things

All living things perform the same life processes: **nutrition**, **interaction**, **reproduction**, **respiration**, **excretion**, **growth** and **movement**.

Nutrition

Plants make their own food using **photosynthesis**. Animals feed on other living things. **Decomposers**, such as fungi and bacteria, feed on dead plants and animals.

Interaction

All living things interact with their **environment**. Animals move, communicate and react to the world around them. Plants react to water and light.

Reproduction

Most animals are **oviparous**, which means they lay eggs. Most plants reproduce using **seeds**. Some plants, such as ferns and mosses, reproduce using **spores**.

Respiration

Animals take in **oxygen** from the air or from water. In the day, plants produce their own oxygen through photosynthesis. At night, they also have to take in oxygen from the air.

Excretion

Animals expel the remains of food that they do not need. They also excrete other harmful substances such as **carbon dioxide**, **sweat** and **urine** from their bodies.

Growth and movement

Plants do not stop growing but animals only grow until they become mature. Most animals can move from place to place. Plants cannot move from place to place, but they can move towards **light** or **water**.

3 Plants and animals are both living things. Explain how they are different.

39

PAGE SUMMARY

This double-page spread introduces pupils to the concept of cells and cell organisation and reviews and extends their knowledge about life processes. There is a lot of new vocabulary and concepts on this double page. Do not expect pupils at this stage to absorb all of the information; the main learning aim is to understand how cells work together to form an organism and how the organisms carry out the life processes.

LANGUAGE

- Questions words: *where, what, why, how, etc.*
- Present simple
- Superlative adjectives: *simplest, smallest*
- Vocabulary: *cells, tissue, organs, systems, nutrition, interaction, reproduction, respiration, excretion, growth, movement*

ADDITIONAL MATERIALS

- Digital flashcards
- Digital wordcards
- Extra classroom materials: photos of bacteria, yeast, an amoeba, an animal and cells

OPENING ACTIVITIES

- Place photos of bacteria, yeast, an amoeba and an animal on the board or show a slide show of these organisms. Ask pupils to identify the organisms in the photos and ask: **Are they all living things?** (*Yes, they are.*) **How are they different?** (*Bacteria, yeast and amoebas are unicellular and animals are multicellular.*) **What do they have in common?** (*They perform the life processes.*)
- Place the wordcards *nutrition, interaction, reproduction* and *respiration* on the board. Ask: **Which body system helps us carry out the process of nutrition?** (*Digestive*); **Which body system helps us interact?** (*Nervous*); **Which body system helps us carry out the process of reproduction?** (*Reproductive*) Ask pupils to work with a partner to name the organs that are part of these body systems. Correct as a class activity, inviting pupils to give their answers.

MAIN ACTIVITIES

Page 38, (CD1 track 33)

- Ask pupils to open their books on page 38 and read the introductory text together. Play the audio **(CD1 track 33)** and ask pupils to listen and read. Alternatively, keep the books closed and present this lesson on the interactive whiteboard. Read the introductory text again as a *Cloze reading*. Pause at key words and have pupils read the missing word in unison. Check for understanding. Ask: **How do cells reproduce?** (*By dividing*); **How do they interact?** (*They work together*); **Do they perform the process of nutrition?** (*Yes, they take in nutrients*)

Page 38, How are living things organised? (CD1 track 34)

- Before you read the text, ask pupils to look at the illustrations. Explain that these pictures show us how cells are organised. Read the text on page 39 and check understanding. **What is the smallest unit?** (*A cell*); **What makes up a body system?** (*Organs*); **What makes up tissue?** (*Cells*); **What does a group of tissues make up?** (*An organ*)

1 Order the words from the simplest structure to the most complex.

- Place the wordcards *cell, tissue, organ, body system* and *organism* randomly on the board. In groups, pupils organise the cards and write the correct order in their notebook. *Cells – tissue – organ – system - organism*

2 Which organs group together to form the circulatory system? What about the digestive and respiratory systems?

- Write the words *circulatory, digestive* and *respiratory* on the board. Ask pupils to work with a partner to write the names of the organs that make up the three systems. Correct as a class activity. *Circulatory – heart; Digestive – stomach, liver, pancreas, intestines; Respiratory – lungs, mouth, nose*

Page 39, The life processes of living things (CD1 track 35)

- Tell pupils to close their books. Read the introductory text and ask pupils to listen. Ask them to name the seven life processes and place the wordcards on the board as they are named.
- If you are using an interactive whiteboard, block out the texts that accompany the photos with the black paint tool. Zoom in on each photo and ask the pupils to say which life process they can see in each photo.
- Organise the class into six groups. Assign one information box to each group. Ask the groups to read only their assigned box and to make notes about the important information. Rearrange the groups so that each new group has a member from each reading group. Ask the pupils to share what they have learned with their new group.

3 Plants and animals are both living things. Explain how they are different.

- Organise the class into groups and tell them to use the information on page 39 to answer this question. *See Answers at a glance*

CLOSING ACTIVITIES

- Test pupils on a few basic concepts from pages 38 and 39 using the *True or False game*. Divide the class into two teams to make it more exciting. **Cells reproduce by dividing. Decomposers can make their own food. Plants don't need oxygen from the air.**

EXTRA ACTIVITIES

- Use the internet to show pupils the amazing array of different cell types: red blood cells, white blood cells, muscle cells, nerve cells and plant cells. Point out that most have a nucleus which is the control centre of the cell. (Red blood cells don't have a nucleus.) The nucleus divides when the cell is reproducing.

ANSWERS AT A GLANCE

1. Cells – tissue – organ – system – organism.
2. Circulatory – heart; Digestive – stomach, liver, pancreas, intestines; Respiratory – lungs, mouth, nose
3. Plants reproduce by seeds or spores. Plants make their own food. Plants can't move around. Plants never stop growing. Plants excrete oxygen. They both breathe in oxygen but plants only do so at night.

PAGES 40–41 How are living things classified?

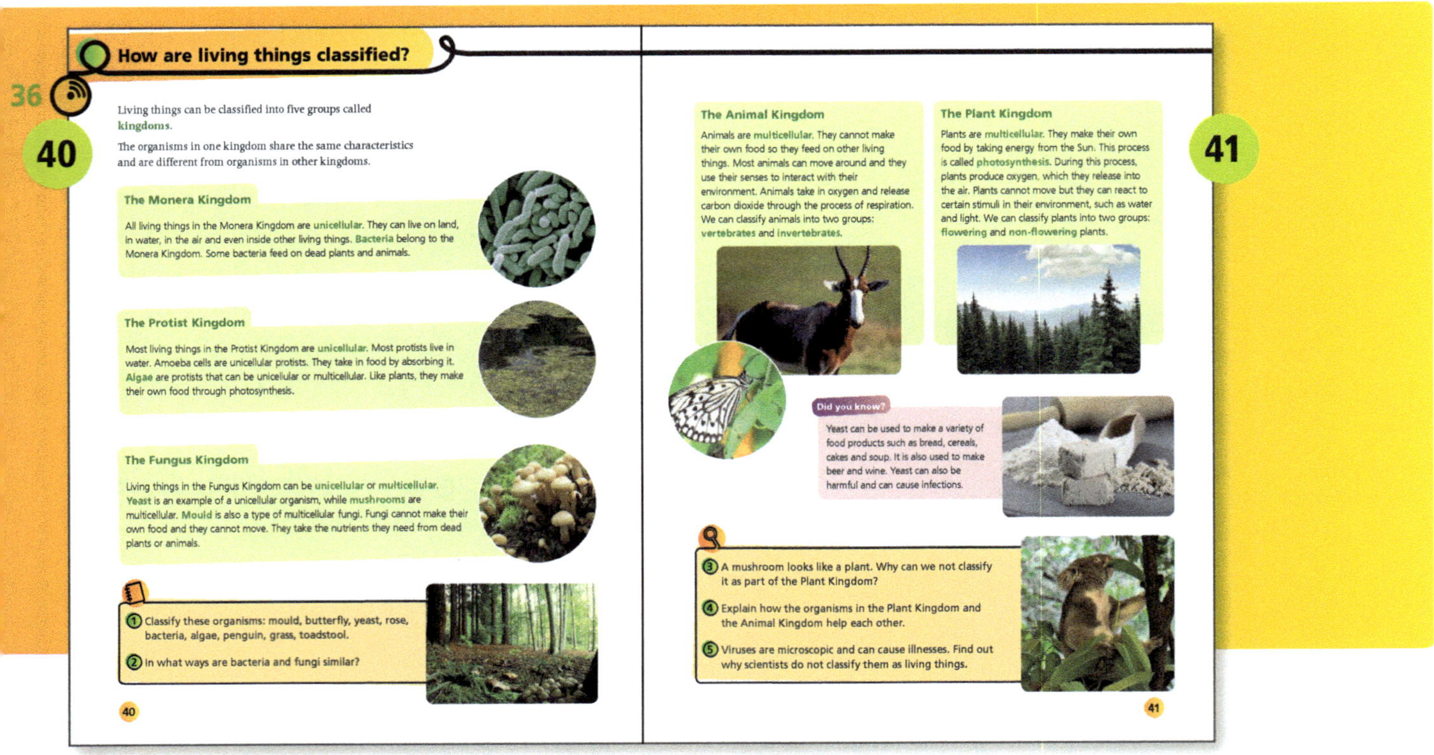

36

40

How are living things classified?

Living things can be classified into five groups called **kingdoms**.

The organisms in one kingdom share the same characteristics and are different from organisms in other kingdoms.

The Monera Kingdom

All living things in the Monera Kingdom are **unicellular**. They can live on land, in water, in the air and even inside other living things. **Bacteria** belong to the Monera Kingdom. Some bacteria feed on dead plants and animals.

The Protist Kingdom

Most living things in the Protist Kingdom are **unicellular**. Most protists live in water. Amoeba cells are unicellular protists. They take in food by absorbing it. **Algae** are protists that can be unicellular or multicellular. Like plants, they make their own food through photosynthesis.

The Fungus Kingdom

Living things in the Fungus Kingdom can be **unicellular** or **multicellular**. **Yeast** is an example of a unicellular organism, while **mushrooms** are multicellular. **Mould** is also a type of multicellular fungi. Fungi cannot make their own food and they cannot move. They take the nutrients they need from dead plants or animals.

1. Classify these organisms: mould, butterfly, yeast, rose, bacteria, algae, penguin, grass, toadstool.
2. In what ways are bacteria and fungi similar?

40

41

The Animal Kingdom

Animals are **multicellular**. They cannot make their own food so they feed on other living things. Most animals can move around and they use their senses to interact with their environment. Animals take in oxygen and release carbon dioxide through the process of respiration. We can classify animals into two groups: **vertebrates** and **invertebrates**.

The Plant Kingdom

Plants are **multicellular**. They make their own food by taking energy from the Sun. This process is called **photosynthesis**. During this process, plants produce oxygen, which they release into the air. Plants cannot move but they can react to certain stimuli in their environment, such as water and light. We can classify plants into two groups: **flowering** and **non-flowering** plants.

Did you know?

Yeast can be used to make a variety of food products such as bread, cereals, cakes and soup. It is also used to make beer and wine. Yeast can also be harmful and can cause infections.

3. A mushroom looks like a plant. Why can we not classify it as part of the Plant Kingdom?
4. Explain how the organisms in the Plant Kingdom and the Animal Kingdom help each other.
5. Viruses are microscopic and can cause illnesses. Find out why scientists do not classify them as living things.

41

PAGE SUMMARY

This double-page spread introduces pupils to the subject of classifying living things. They are already familiar with the fact that animals and plants are living things but this is the first time they will study algae, fungi and bacteria as groups of living things. At this stage, this is just an introduction to a subject area they will study in greater detail over the following years. The main learning aim is to understand that not all living things are plants or animals. They will also practise their classification and study skills.

LANGUAGE

- Questions words: *where, what, why,* etc.
- Short answers: *Yes, it is; No, it doesn't.*
- Vocabulary: *Monera Kingdom, Protist Kingdom, Fungus Kingdom, Plant Kingdom, Animal Kingdom, bacteria, amoeba, algae, yeast, mould, mushroom, toadstool, butterfly, penguin*

ADDITIONAL MATERIALS

- Digital flashcards
- Digital wordcards
- Extra classroom materials: photos of mushrooms, seaweed, an anemone and e.coli or other bacteria

OPENING ACTIVITIES

- Place the wordcards *Plant Kingdom* and *Animal Kingdom* on the board. Explain that these are two very big groups and that we can make smaller groups inside each kingdom. Say **In the Animal Kingdom we can classify animals as vertebrates and invertebrates**. Ask pupils to work in small groups to find other ways of classifying plants and animals. Encourage them to think about: *mammals, birds, fish, reptiles, amphibians, insects, herbivores, carnivores, omnivores, oviparous, viviparous, flowering, non-flowering, trees, bushes, grasses,* etc. You may like to record their information as a spider diagram and ask them to copy it into their notebooks.

MAIN ACTIVITIES

Pages 40, How are living things classified? (CD1 track 36)

- Ask pupils to open their books on page 40 and read the introduction text. Tell them that they are going to learn more about the five groups of living things. Play the audio **(CD1 track 36)** and ask pupils to listen and read. Stop after each text to check understanding and clarify new vocabulary. **Where can bacteria live? How do algae get their food? How do plants get their food? What is mould?**

1 Classify these organisms: mould, butterfly, yeast, rose, bacteria, algae, penguin, grass, toadstool.

- Ask pupils to work individually to answer this question on a piece of rough paper. Check answers by inviting volunteers to come to the board to write the organisms under the correct wordcard. Ask them to copy the chart into their notebooks. *Monera – bacteria; Protist – algae; Fungus – yeast, toadstool, mould; Animal – butterfly, penguin; Plant – rose, grass*

2 In what ways are bacteria and fungi similiar?

- Ask pupils to use the information on page 40 to answer this question. *Bacteria are unicellular and some fungi are unicellular. Fungi feed on dead plants and animal. Some bacteria feed on dead plants and animals too.*

3 A mushroom looks like a plant. Why can we not classify it as part of the Plant Kingdom?

- Ask pupils to think about the characteristics of plants. **How do plants make their food?** (*They make their own food through the process of photosynthesis.*) **Do mushrooms get food the same way?** (*They don't. They take the nutrients they need from dead plants or animals.*)

4 Explain how the organisms in the Plant Kingdom an the Animal Kingdom help each other.

- Organise the class into small groups to discuss this question. Guide them to a variety of answers by asking the groups questions: **How can plants help animals? What can they give them? How can animals help plants? Think about insects. How can animals help distribute the plants seeds?** *See Answers at a glance*

5 Viruses are microscopic and can cause illnesses. Find out why scientist do not classify them as living things.

- This activity can be done at home with the help of parents or in small study groups on a computer or in the library. *Viruses do not perform the life processes of nutrition or interaction. As they only reproduce, they cannot be considered a living thing.*

CLOSING ACTIVITIES

- Divide the class into five groups and give each group a wordcard with the name of a kingdom. Make statements and if the statement coincides with the wordcard, the group stands up and says the name, e.g. **They can make their own food.** (The group with the *Plant Kingdom* card stands up and says *Plants!*)
- Ask pupils to work with a partner to talk about the differences between the kingdoms. Pupil 1 makes a sentence about a kingdom and pupil 2 must make a statement about a different kingdom, but it must be connected to the first statement. *Pupil 1: Monera Kingdom organisms are unicellular. Pupil 2: Animals are multicellular.* Ask pupils to share examples with the rest of the class.

EXTRA IDEAS

- Ask pupils to bring in a photo of themselves taken in a place they like. Tell them they must identify the living things and non-living things in the photo and write a text about these living and non-living things. Ask them to explain how the living things are interacting. You may like to prepare a sample text as a guide.

ANSWERS AT A GLANCE

1 Monera - bacteria; Protist - algae; Fungus - yeast, toadstool, mould; Animal - butterfly, penguin; Plant - rose, grass.

2 Bacterie are unicellular and some fungi are unicellular. Fungi feed on dead plants and animal. Some bacteria feed on dead plants and animals too.

3 A mushroom can't make its own food. It takes nutrients from dead plants or aminals.

4 Plants provide animals with oxygen, which they make through the process of photosynthesis. Animals help the process of pollination. Insects, such as bees, carry pollen to the stigma of plants.

5 Viruses do not perform the life processes of nutrition or interaction. As they only reproduce, the cannot be considered a living thing.

UNIT 3

PAGES 42–43 Find out / Think about it

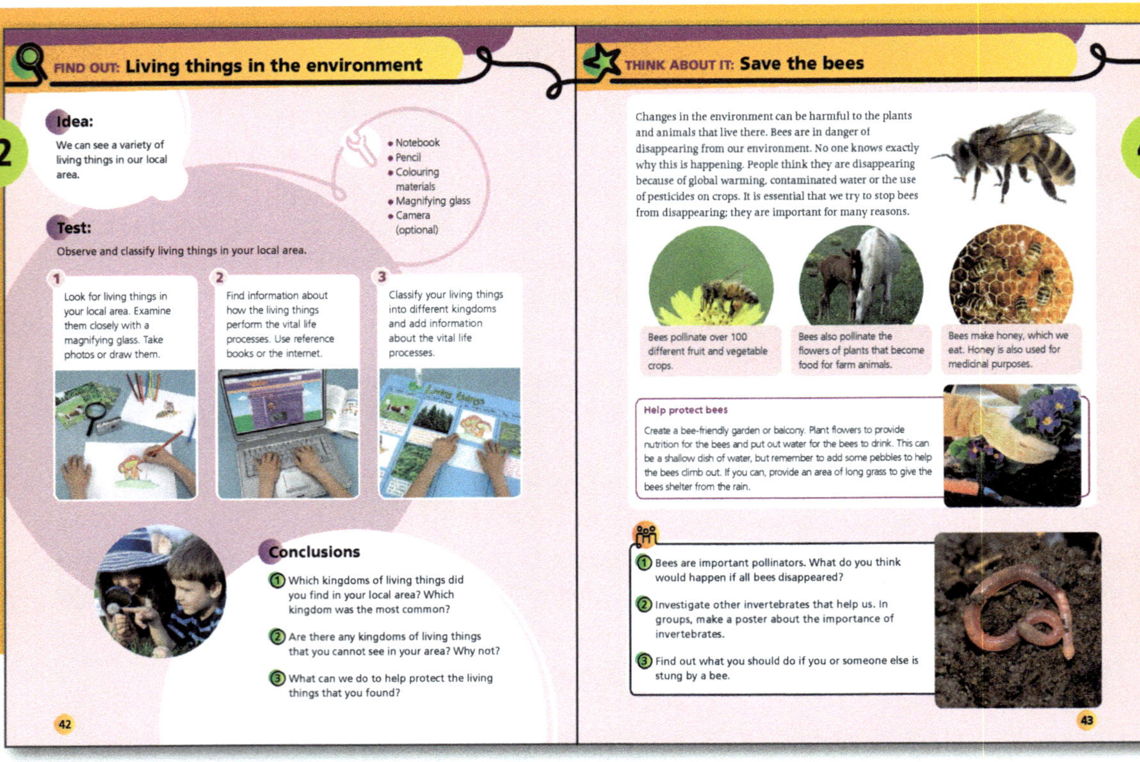
42

FIND OUT: Living things in the environment

Idea:

We can see a variety of living things in our local area.

- Notebook
- Pencil
- Colouring materials
- Magnifying glass
- Camera (optional)

Test:

Observe and classify living things in your local area.

1 Look for living things in your local area. Examine them closely with a magnifying glass. Take photos or draw them.

2 Find information about how the living things perform the vital life processes. Use reference books or the internet.

3 Classify your living things into different kingdoms and add information about the vital life processes.

Conclusions

1 Which kingdoms of living things did you find in your local area? Which kingdom was the most common?

2 Are there any kingdoms of living things that you cannot see in your area? Why not?

3 What can we do to help protect the living things that you found?

42

43

THINK ABOUT IT: Save the bees

Changes in the environment can be harmful to the plants and animals that live there. Bees are in danger of disappearing from our environment. No one knows exactly why this is happening. People think they are disappearing because of global warming, contaminated water or the use of pesticides on crops. It is essential that we try to stop bees from disappearing; they are important for many reasons.

Bees pollinate over 100 different fruit and vegetable crops.

Bees also pollinate the flowers of plants that become food for farm animals.

Bees make honey, which we eat. Honey is also used for medicinal purposes.

Help protect bees

Create a bee-friendly garden or balcony. Plant flowers to provide nutrition for the bees and put out water for the bees to drink. This can be a shallow dish of water, but remember to add some pebbles to help the bees climb out. If you can, provide an area of long grass to give the bees shelter from the rain.

1 Bees are important pollinators. What do you think would happen if all bees disappeared?

2 Investigate other invertebrates that help us. In groups, make a poster about the importance of invertebrates.

3 Find out what you should do if you or someone else is stung by a bee.

43

PAGE SUMMARY

In the first of these two pages (*Find out*), pupils practise their observation, research and classification skills by studying the living things found in their local area. This activity requires some time as it involves field work, research, making a poster and giving a presentation. The second page (*Think about it*), provides your pupils with the opportunity to learn about the worrying situation of bees today. They will read about the importance of bees and will also be given practical ideas about protecting these insects.

LANGUAGE

- Imperatives: *look, examine, draw, observe, take, find, use, classify, add, observe*
- Vocabulary: *local, area, harmful, global, warming, contamitnated, pesticide, crops, honey, dish, shallow, pebbles, shelter, pollinate, disappear*

ADDITIONAL MATERIALS

- Digital flashcards

FIND OUT

OPENING ACTIVITIES

- Organise the class into groups. Give each group a card with the name of an ecosystem. Ask them to work together to make a list of the different living things that we can find in these places. As pupils haven't studied ecosystems in detail yet, choose well known and general places. (Ocean, pond, forest, rainforest, park, Arctic / Polar regions, beach, etc.)
- Place the wordcards *Monera Kingdom, Protist Kingdom, Fungus Kingdom, Plant Kingdom* and *Animal Kingdom* on the board. Invite the groups to classify their lists into kingdoms. Invite each group to share their lists with the rest of the class.

MAIN ACTIVITIES

- Explain to pupils that it isn't necessary to travel to faraway places to investigate living things. Tell them that they will be carrying out an investigation about living things that are found in their local area. This investigation will have to be carried out partly at home so you may prefer to ask pupils to investigate at the weekend. The research and preparation of the presentation can be done at home or at school.

- Ask pupils to open their books and read the steps on page 42. Then, tell them to write the materials and the three steps in their notebook. If you are using the book on the interactive whiteboard, you can play the audio of the steps. You may choose to do this investigation in small groups or in pairs.

⊕ CLOSING ACTIVITIES

- Allow pupils time to make their poster and decide on a time for them give their presentation to the rest of the class. After the presentation, they can display their posters around the school or in the classroom for other children to enjoy.

1 Which kingdoms of living things did you find in your local area? Which kingdom was the most common?

- Pupils can compare their findings in small groups or with a partner.

2 Are there any kingdoms of living things that you cannot see in your area? Why not?

- Discuss why they didn't find any examples of certain kingdoms. For example, perhaps there was no water and so they couldn't find protists. All pupils should say that they didn't see any examples of the Monera Kingdom, as you would need a microscope.

3 What can we do to help protect the living things that you found?

- Encourage them to think about ways to help protect their local environment. Elicit the need to respect all living things and to look after habitats.

THINK ABOUT IT

⊕ OPENING ACTIVITIES

- Brainstorm names of invertebrates with the class. Write the names that they call out and count how many invertebratesbthey say. Ask them how they feel about invertebrates. Ask **Do you like them? Which ones do you like? Which ones don't you like? Why don't you like them?**

MAIN ACTIVITIES

- Ask pupils to open their books on page 43 and say **Let's read about bees.** If you are using the interactive whiteboard, you can play the audio and encourage pupils to read along in their books. Then, ask pupils to look at the pictures and describe what they can see in pairs. Ask **What are the photos telling us?** (*Bees pollinate the plants we eat. They pollinate plants that other animals eat and we eat some of these animals too. Bees make honey which is used in medicines.*)

⊕ CLOSING ACTIVITIES

- Encourage pupils to talk to their parents about making a bee friendly area at home. Why not set one up at school?

1 Bees are important pollinators. What do you think would happen if all bees disappeared?

- Ask pupils to discuss this question in small groups. Invite volunteers to share their ideas. *Plants wouldn't be pollinated so the plants that rely on insect pollination would die out. This would affect the herbivores and then the omnivores and carnivores. Their food chains would be broken.*

2 Investigate other invertebrates that help us. In groups, make a poster about the importance of invertebrates.

- Ask pupils to identify the invertebrate in the photo. Ask if they know how the earthworm helps us. (*It breaks down dead organic matter and creates tunnels in the soil which allow air and water to pass through.*) Ask if they can name any other helpful invertebrates.

3 Find out what you should do if you or someone else is stung by a bee.

- This activity can be done at home with the help of parents or in small study groups on a computer or in the library. *The sting should be removed if it is still in the skin. Ice will help stop the pain but don't put it directly on the skin. Wrap the ice in a towel before putting it on the sting. Check for an allergic reaction. If the person is allergic to bee stings, get medical help immediately.*

PAGES 44–45 Look back: Living things

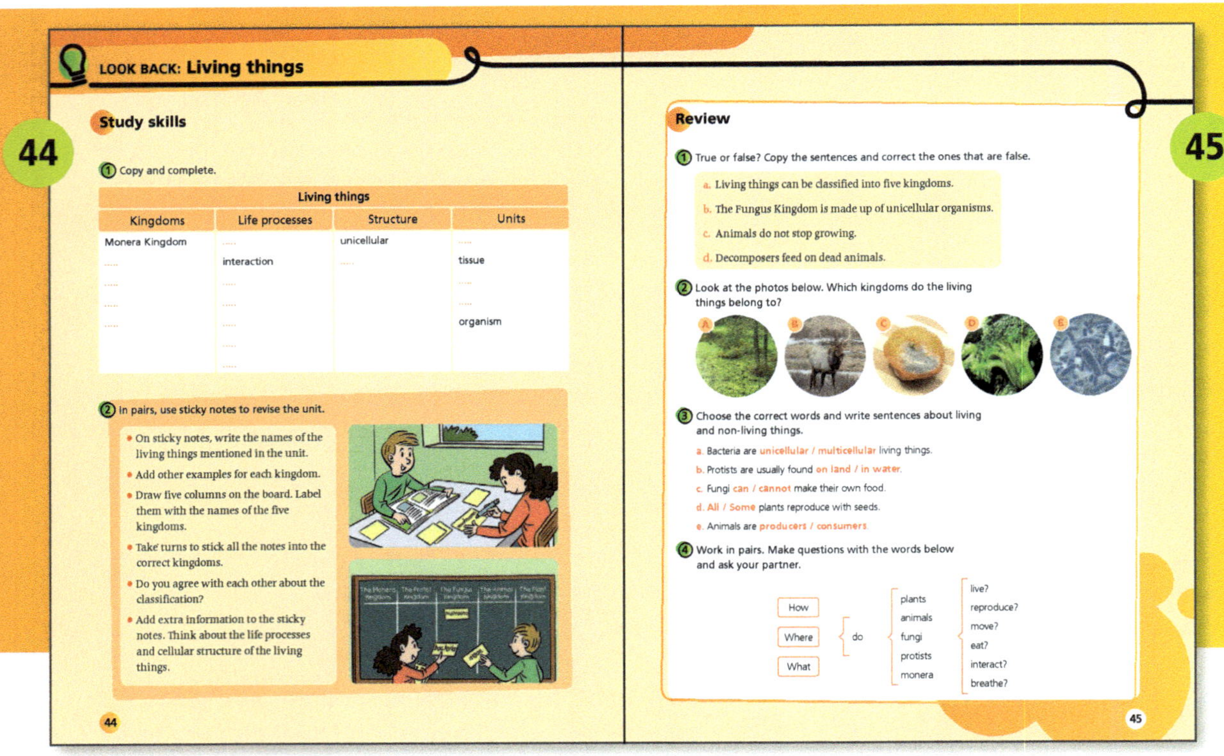

44

LOOK BACK: Living things

Study skills

1 Copy and complete.

Living things			
Kingdoms	Life processes	Structure	Units
Monera Kingdom	.....	unicellular	.....
.....	interaction	.....	tissue
.....	.....		.....
.....	.....		.....
.....	.....		organism
	.....		
	.....		

2 In pairs, use sticky notes to revise the unit.

- On sticky notes, write the names of the living things mentioned in the unit.
- Add other examples for each kingdom.
- Draw five columns on the board. Label them with the names of the five kingdoms.
- Take turns to stick all the notes into the correct kingdoms.
- Do you agree with each other about the classification?
- Add extra information to the sticky notes. Think about the life processes and cellular structure of the living things.

44

45

Review

1 True or false? Copy the sentences and correct the ones that are false.

a. Living things can be classified into five kingdoms.
b. The Fungus Kingdom is made up of unicellular organisms.
c. Animals do not stop growing.
d. Decomposers feed on dead animals.

2 Look at the photos below. Which kingdoms do the living things belong to?

A B C D E

3 Choose the correct words and write sentences about living and non-living things.

a. Bacteria are unicellular / multicellular living things.
b. Protists are usually found on land / in water.
c. Fungi can / cannot make their own food.
d. All / Some plants reproduce with seeds.
e. Animals are producers / consumers.

4 Work in pairs. Make questions with the words below and ask your partner.

How / Where / What — do — plants / animals / fungi / protists / monera — live? / reproduce? / move? / eat? / interact? / breathe?

45

PAGE SUMMARY

This double-page spread allows pupils the opportunity to organise what they've learned in the unit by means of a classification table. They can also work collaboratively to make a classification chart to help them summarise what they have learned in the unit. On the *Review* page, pupils complete activities individually to check their understanding of material covered in this unit. Activity 4 is a pairwork speaking activity to encourage them to form correct questions as they revise content. It is also a peer evaluation opportunity.

LANGUAGE

- Imperatives: *write, copy, correct, use, complete, add, drag, label, think, look, choose, work, make, ask, answer*
- Question words: *how, where, what*, etc.
- Forming questions
- Quantifiers: *some, all*, etc.

ADDITIONAL MATERIALS

- Digital flashcards
- Digital wordcards
- Extra classroom materials: sticky notes

OPENING ACTIVITIES

- *What am I?* Describe the characteristics of the different kingdoms and ask pupils to identify the them. **I'm unicellular and I can be harmful. I can live everywhere, even inside other organisms.** (*Monera kingdom*)
- Choose words from the unit to give the class a spelling quiz. Explain that you are going to spell out words letter by letter. When you stop they should recognise the word. Tell them not to anticipate the word and call it out. Ask them to exchange papers to correct each other's work. Invite volunteers to write the words on the board.
- Ask pupils to look through the unit and write one statement which can be true or false. Each pupil reads their sentence and the rest of the class have to respond. If the statement is correct they clap once. If the statement is false they must stamp their foot once.

MAIN ACTIVITIES

Page 44, Study skills

1 Copy and complete.

- Remind pupils that when we organise new information, it is easier to understand and remember it. Focus the pupils' attention on the concept map and ask them to tell you what the missing words are. Encourage them to make full sentences, such as *Living things can be unicellular or multicellular.* Tell them to copy and complete the concept map in their notebooks.

Living things			
Kingdoms	Life processes	Structure	Units
Monera Kingdom Protist Kingdom Fungus Kingdom Plant Kingdom Animal Kingdom	nutrition interaction reproduction respiration excretion growth movement	unicellular multicellular	cells tissue organs systems organism

2 In pairs, use sticky notes to revise the unit.

- You will need the following materials: sticky notes and a pen. This activity requires pupils to look for names of living things mentioned in this unit. If there is a problem of space you may prefer to give each set of partners a large piece of card for their chart. You may decide to divide up the task and have the pairs concentrate on different kingdoms.

Page 45, Review

1 True or false? Copy the sentences and correct the ones that are false.

a. True

b. False. The Fungus Kingdom is made up of unicellular and multicellular organisms.

c. False. Animals stop growing when they become mature.

d. False. Decomposers feed on dead animals and dead plants.

2 Look at the photos below. Which kingdoms do the living things belong to?

a. Protist Kingdom

b. Animal Kingdom

c. Fungus Kingdom

d. Plant Kingdom

e. Monera Kingdom

3 Choose the correct words and write sentences about living and non-living things.

a. unicellular

b. in water

c. cannot

d. Some

e. consumers

4 Work in pairs. Make questions with the words below and ask your partner.

- Pupils can formulate many different questions with the words provided in this activity. Before they start, make sure they understand the difference between how, where and what. You can read out questions and ask the pupils if they are correct or not. **How do plants live? Is this a possible question?** (*No, it isn't.*) Some examples are:

- How do plants reproduce?

  They reproduce using seeds or spores.

- Where do protists live?

  Protists live on land and in water.

- What do fungi eat?

  They feed on the remains of dead animals and plants.

- How do plants breathe?

  They breathe through holes in their leaves called stomata.

- How do animals interact?

  They use their sense organs.

Activity Book answers / Audio CD1 track list

14

UNIT 3 Living things

1 Read the sentences. Write *living things* or *non-living things.*

a. They are made up of cells. *living things*
b. They have tissues and organs. living things
c. They can be natural parts of an environment, like water. non-living things
d. They grow and reproduce. living things
e. They interact with their environment. living things
f. They can be man-made/artificial. non-living things
g. They carry out the process of nutrition. living things

2 Look at the photos below. Write the characteristics from Activity 1. Add extra information.

a

Plants interact with their environment. They react to water and light. They grow throughout their lives. They reproduce using seeds, spores or stolons. They make their own food using photosynthesis

b

Humans are made up cells. They have tissues, organs and body systems. They grow until they become mature. They interact with their environment. They eat other living things for energy.

c

Mushrooms are a type of fungi. They grow and reproduce. They feed on dead plants animals. They cannot move.

14

15

3 Look at the pictures. Unscramble the words.

a
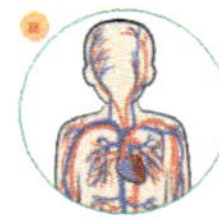
dboy ysstme — body system

b
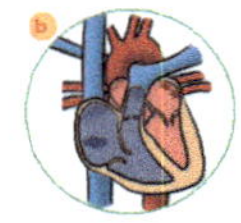
ognar — organ

c
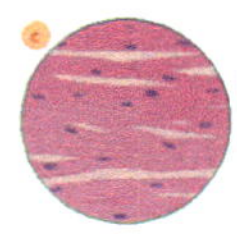
sstieu — tissue

d
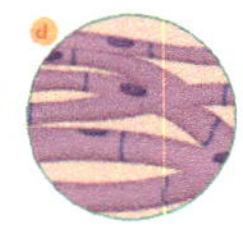
ecll — cell

4 Answer the questions below using the words from Activity 3.

a. Which structure is the smallest living unit?
A cell is the smallest living unit.

b. What do cells form when they work together?
Cells form tissue when they work together.

c. When tissues work together, what do they form?
Tissues form organs when they work together.

d. When organs work together, what do they form?
Organs form body systems when they work together.

5 Order the structures from Activity 3, from the simplest to the most complex.

cell → tissue → organ → body system → living thing or organism

15

16

UNIT 3

6 Find the seven vital life processes in the crossword below.

N	U	T	R	I	T	I	O	N	E	S	I	M	
G	Y	U	E	Y	B	N	N	A	S	I	N	A	
H	J	R	P	T	M	B	Y	M	D	N	A	G	
R	O	F	R	W	D	O	S	R	K	T	S	R	
P	F	D	O	U	E	S	E		R	E		O	
A	S	P	D	G	T	Y	A	O	T	R	I	W	
I	I	F	U	R	D	S	W	E	H	A	N	T	
L	E	X	C	R	E	T	I	O	N	C	G	H	
A	F	C	T	A	I	S	B	O	T	T	W	I	
L	H	I	I	K	C	T	O	N	T	I	T	M	
Y	S	M	O	V	E	M	E	N	T	O	N	A	
E	B	F	N	F	N	O	C	P	G	N	U	S	
E	R	E	S	P	I	R	A	T	I	O	N	C	

7 Cross out the mistake in each sentence. Write the correct word or words.

a. Plants make their own food using the process of ~~metamorphosis~~. *photosynthesis*
b. All living things eat with their environment. interact
c. Most animals are viviparous, which means they lay eggs. oviparous
d. Animals take in carbon dioxide from the air or water. oxygen
e. Animals expel harmful substances such as sweat, urine and oxygen. carbon dioxide
f. Animals cannot move from place to place, but they can move towards light or water. plants

16

17

8 Write and draw the missing information about the different kingdoms.

	Monera Kingdom	Protist Kingdom	Fungus Kingdom
Cells:	*unicellular*	unicellular multicellular	unicellular multicellular
Where:	on land, in water, in the air or inside other living things	*mostly in water*	on land
Examples:	bacteria	*amoeba* algae	yeast mould
Appearance:	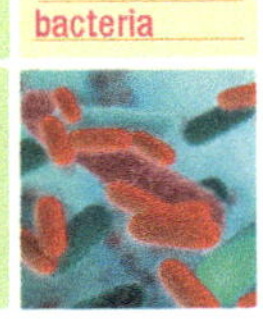		

9 Write full sentences about the Animal Kingdom and the Plant Kingdom.

Classifications:	*The Animal Kingdom can be divided into vertebrates and invertebrates. The Plant Kingdom can be* divided into flowering and non-flowering plants
Cellular structure:	The Animal Kingdom and the Plant Kingdom are made up of multicellular organisms.
Where they can be found:	Plants and animals live on land and in water
Nutrition:	Plants make their own food using photosynthesis. Animals consume other living things.

17

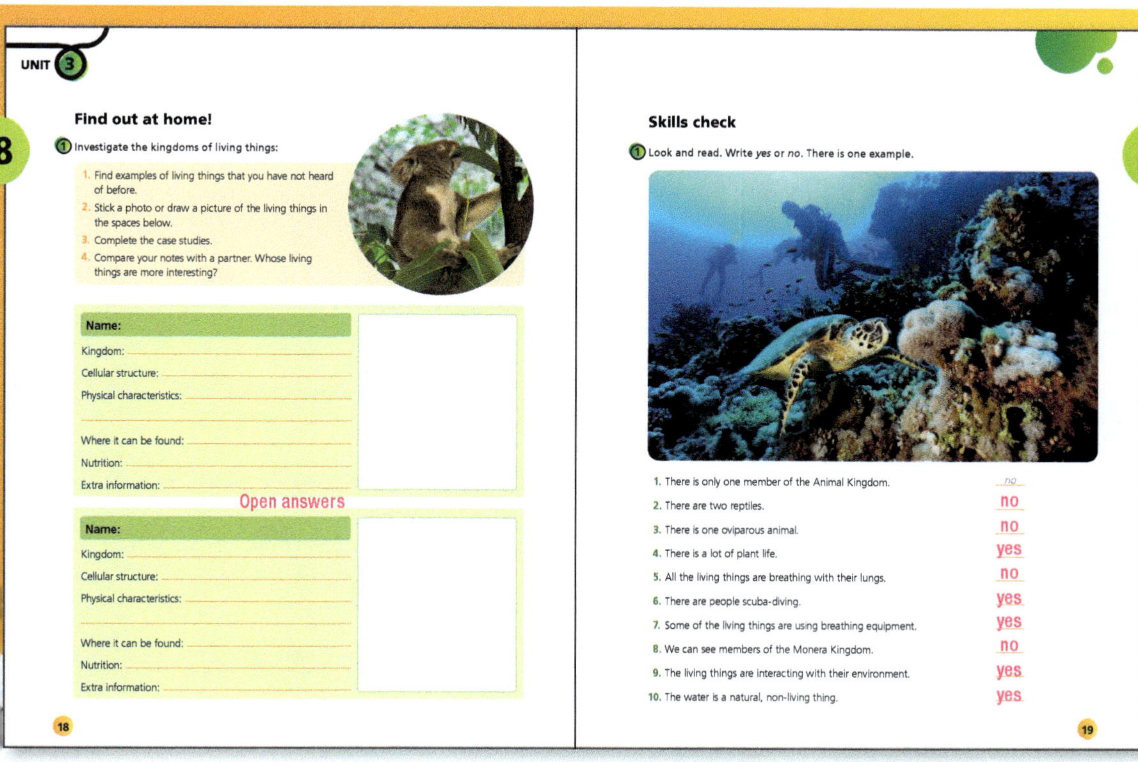

UNIT 3

Find out at home!

1 Investigate the kingdoms of living things:

1. Find examples of living things that you have not heard of before.
2. Stick a photo or draw a picture of the living things in the spaces below.
3. Complete the case studies.
4. Compare your notes with a partner. Whose living things are more interesting?

Name:
Kingdom:
Cellular structure:
Physical characteristics:
Where it can be found:
Nutrition:
Extra information:

Open answers

Name:
Kingdom:
Cellular structure:
Physical characteristics:
Where it can be found:
Nutrition:
Extra information:

18

Skills check

1 Look and read. Write *yes* or *no*. There is one example.

1. There is only one member of the Animal Kingdom. *no*
2. There are two reptiles. no
3. There is one oviparous animal. no
4. There is a lot of plant life. yes
5. All the living things are breathing with their lungs. no
6. There are people scuba-diving. yes
7. Some of the living things are using breathing equipment. yes
8. We can see members of the Monera Kingdom. no
9. The living things are interacting with their environment. yes
10. The water is a natural, non-living thing. yes

19

UNIT 3 Audio CD1 track list

TRACK	ACTIVITY
30	**Pupil's Book page 35,** Unit introduction
31	**Pupil's Book page 35,** Song *Living things*
32	**Pupil's Book page 36,** Story: *A trip to the science lab*
33	**Pupil's Book page 38,** What do living things have in common?
34	**Pupil's Book page 38,** How are living things organised?
35	**Pupil's Book page 39,** The life processes of living things
36	**Pupil's Book page 40,** How are living things classified?

TERM 1 Think together

CONTENT	EVALUATION CRITERIA
First approaches to scientific activity and the scientific method. Use of different information sources (direct and indirect). Use ICTs.	Obtain relevant information about specific phenomena, make predictions, integrate information from direct and indirect observation and communicate the results.
First approaches to simple experiments and investigations.	Conjecture as to the results of natural occurrences and of simple experiments and investigations.
Individual and group work.	Work independently and proactively and develop strategies for working in a group.
Planning a project and presenting a report.	Carry out a project and present a report.

LEARNING STANDARDS	KEY COMPETENCES	PAGES
With help, selects and organises specific and relevant information; analyses it and draws conclusions; reflects on the experience and the process; presents the results.	MST, LTL	46, 47
Use books, libraries, etc. and collaborate in the care and maintenance of all the materials available in the school and the classroom.	MST, LTL	46, 47
Shows autonomy in the planning of activities and tasks and shows initiative in decision taking.	LTL, AUT	46, 47
With help, carries out simple experiments or investigations, and conjectures as to the results.	MST, LTL, AUT	46, 47
Uses strategies to help their own learning, as well as asking for help and information.	LTL, AUT	46, 47
First approaches to Cooperative Learning.	SOC, LTL	46, 47
Begins observation, using relevant instruments and consulting written documents and images.	LTL, AUT	46, 47
Shows autonomy and proactiveness in the planning of and carrying out of actions.	AUT	46, 47
Presents work clearly and in an organised fashion.	LIN, LTL, AUT	46, 47
With help, carries out a project and presents a report, using paper and/or digital means, collecting information from different sources, presenting the results orally and with the support of images and short texts.	LIN, LTL, AUT, DIG	46, 47

PAGES 46-47 Think together: Organise your time

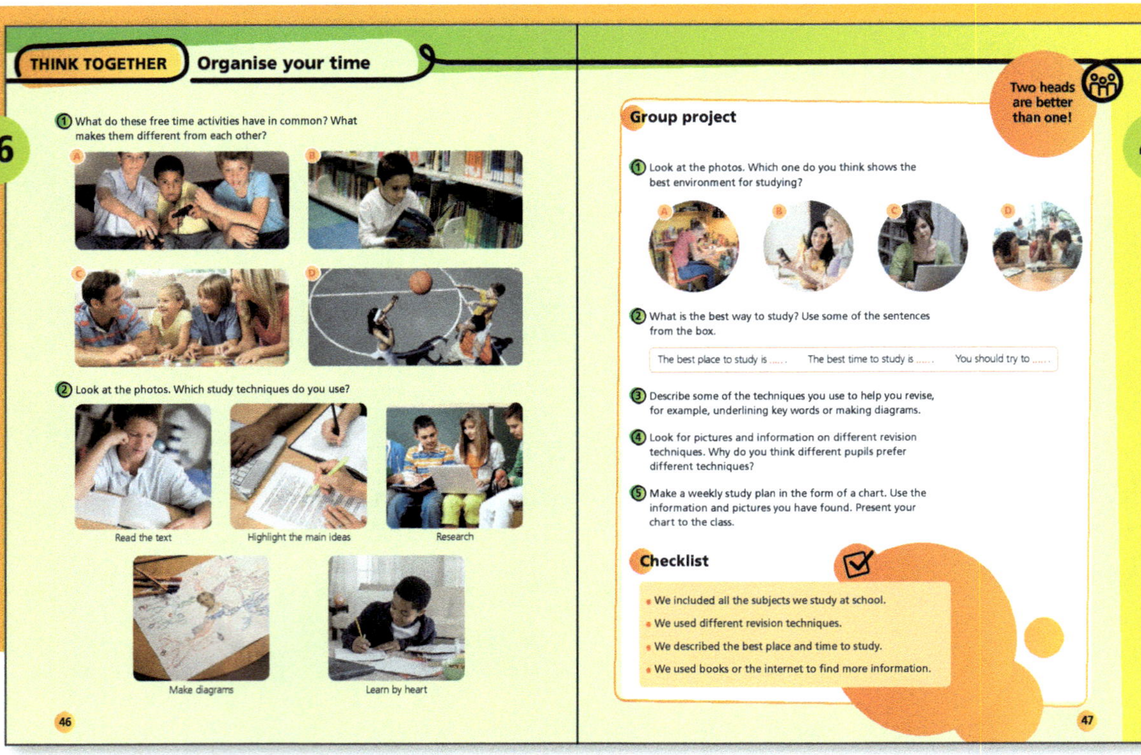
THINK TOGETHER Organise your time

46

1 What do these free time activities have in common? What makes them different from each other?

A B C D

2 Look at the photos. Which study techniques do you use?

Read the text

Highlight the main ideas

Research

Make diagrams

Learn by heart

46

Group project

Two heads are better than one!

47

1 Look at the photos. Which one do you think shows the best environment for studying?

A B C D

2 What is the best way to study? Use some of the sentences from the box.

The best place to study is ...... The best time to study is ...... You should try to ......

3 Describe some of the techniques you use to help you revise, for example, underlining key words or making diagrams.

4 Look for pictures and information on different revision techniques. Why do you think different pupils prefer different techniques?

5 Make a weekly study plan in the form of a chart. Use the information and pictures you have found. Present your chart to the class.

Checklist

- We included all the subjects we study at school.
- We used different revision techniques.
- We described the best place and time to study.
- We used books or the internet to find more information.

47

PAGE SUMMARY

On these pages, pupils will revise the importance of organising their free time. By working in cooperative groups, the activities become much more dynamic and interactive. The different activities will be done following different cooperative learning structures that will provide the optimal learning experience for the pupil and will guarantee the involvement of all the members of the group.

LANGUAGE

- Question words: *what, how*, etc.
- Making comparisons: *In Picture A they are staring at a screen, but in Picture D they are exercising.*
- Vocabulary: *video games, board games, exercise, highlight, research, diagram, silence, technique, revision*

ADDITIONAL MATERIALS

- Digital flashcards
- Digital wordcards

OPENING ACTIVITIES

- Before doing these activities using different cooperative learning structures, you should form the groups. Teachers should form the groups rather than letting the pupils choose their own group members. Remember to form heterogeneous groups of three or four students.
- Tell the pupils what they will be doing in their groups, what procedures you will follow, and what your expectations are. If during these activities any group is having difficulty, spend some time in class on the relevant team skills.

MAIN ACTIVITIES

1 What do these free time activities have in common? What makes them different from each other?

- This is a *Think-pair check* activity. Focus your pupils' attention on the four photos at the top of page 46.
- Ask your pupils to look at the photos and think independently about the questions: what do all of them have in common? How are they different?
- Tell them to discuss their answers in pairs. Ensure that each pupil shares something with their partner.
- Then, ask the pairs to share their answers with the rest of the class.

(2) Look at the photos. Which study techniques do you use?

- This is a *Think-pair check* activity. Focus your pupils' attention on the five photos at the bottom of page 46.
- Ask your pupils to look at the photos and think independently about the question: which study technique do they use? Why?
- Tell them to discuss their answers in pairs. Ensure that each pupil shares something with their partner.

GROUP PROJECT

(1) Look at the photos. Which one do you think shows the best environment for studying?

- Ask pairs to compare the photos from activity 1. Ask them what the advantages and disadvantages of each situation are.

(2) What is the best way to study? Use some of the sentences from the box.

- This is a *Think-write-pair check* activity.
- Ask your pupils to look at the model sentences in the box. Then, ask your pupils to think about the question in relation to the model sentences in the box.
- Ask your pupils to write their ideas.
- Once they have finished, ask them to pair up and discuss their ideas.

(3) Describe some of the techniques you use to help you study, for example, underlining key words or making diagrams.

- This is a *Group members* consult activity.
- Ask your pupils to put their pencils down in the middle of the table.
- All members of the team should contribute in answering the question, but they don't all have to suggest the same thing.
- When everyone in the group has decided on their answer (they can borrow suggestions from their group members), ask them to pick up their pencils and write it down.

(4) Look for pictures and information on different study techniques. Why do you think some pupils prefer different techniques?

- Pupils can look for pictures and more information in reference books, higher-level school books or on the internet.

(5) Make a weekly study plan in the form of a chart. Use the information and pictures you have found. Present your chart to the class.

- This is a *Group project* activity.
- Clearly explain the project the groups are going to do and the amount of time they have to complete it.
- Assign roles:
  - captain (in charge of managing the group and assigning the different roles)
  - materials manager
  - spokesperson
  - timekeeper
- After distributing the materials, ask your pupils to work to complete the task.
- Monitor your pupils.
- Ask the groups to share their project with the class.

CHECKLIST

- Group assessment is essential in cooperative learning to ensure that there is analysis of interactions and promotion of teamwork. Pupils should understand that how they work together affects the quality and quantity of concepts that they learn and understand.
- Ask pupils to discuss and reflect on how the group worked together and identify ideas and actions that helped the group achieve its goals.
- Once they have shared their results, ask them to reflect on how the project could be done better next time.
- Invite your pupils to share their conclusions with the class.

PAGES 48-49 Review pages

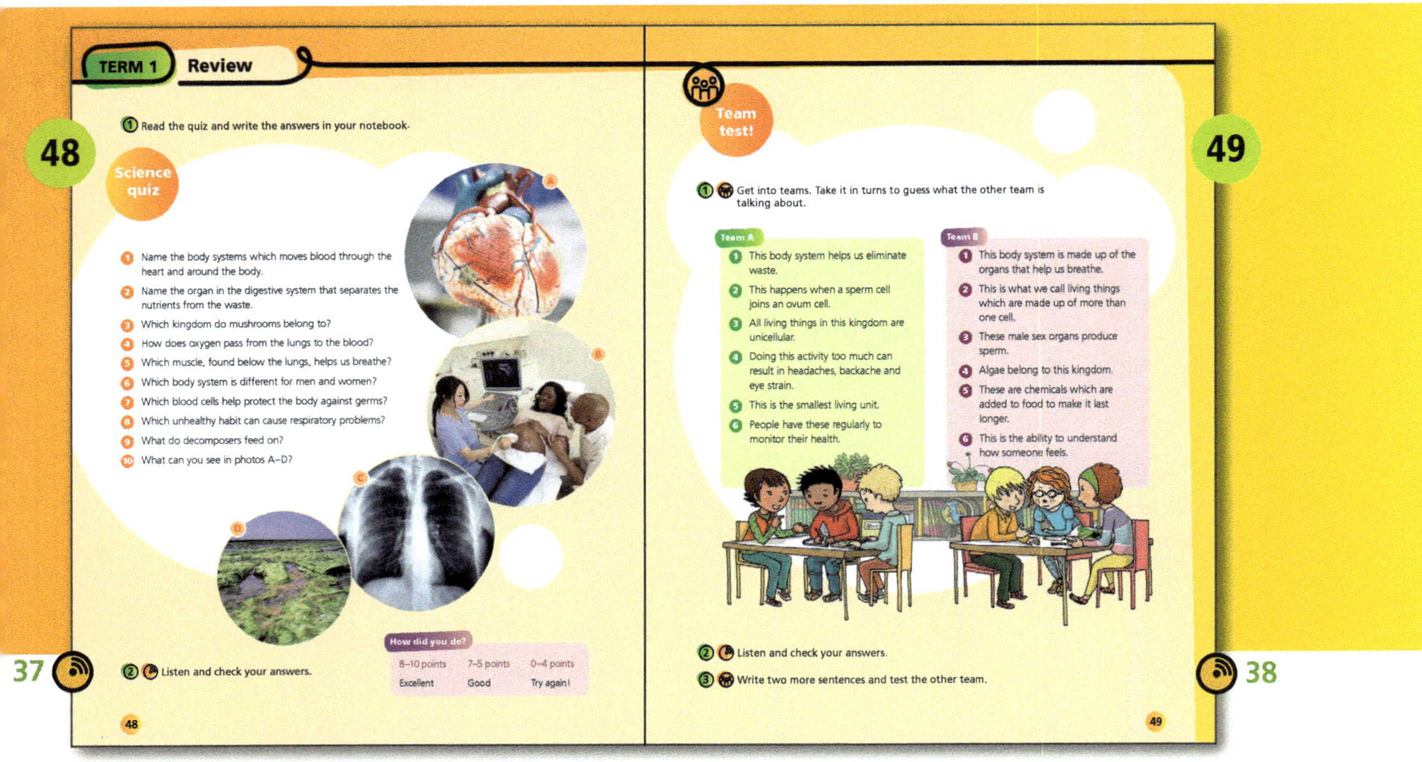

PAGE SUMMARY

The aim of the *Term Review* is to review and recycle what pupils have learned over the term and encourage a positive attitude towards revision as a group and as individuals. Before you begin the *Science quiz*, decide if you prefer this to be an individual or collaborative revision activity and if you want pupils to use what they know or to look back for the answers. The Team test can be done in two teams or in small groups of two teams. Pupils should be encouraged to correct their own work, or peer correct. You can check the answers to both activities using the audio.

LANGUAGE

- Vocabulary: *heart, body system, digestive system, nutrients, waste, oxygen, lungs, muscle, germs, respiratory problems, decomposer, ovum, unicellular, algae*

ADDITIONAL MATERIALS

- A clock for visual time keeping

SCIENCE QUIZ

1 Read the quiz and write the answers in your notebooks.

1. Name the body system which moves blood through the heart and around the body.

The circulatory system moves blood through the heart and around the body.

2. Name the organ in the digestive system that separates the nutrients from the waste.

In the digestive system, the small intestine separates the nutrients from the waste.

3. Which kingdom do mushrooms belong to?

Mushrooms belong to the Fungus Kingdom.

4. How does oxygen pass from the lungs to the blood?

Oxygen passes from the lungs and into our blood through the alveoli.

5. Which muscle, found below the lungs, helps us breathe?

The diaphragm is a strong muscle, below the lungs, which helps us breathe.

6. Which body system is different for men and women?

The reproductive system is different for men and women.

7. Which blood cells help protect the body against germs?

White blood cells help protect the body against germs.

8. Which unhealthy habit can cause respiratory problems?

Smoking can cause respiratory problems.

9. What do decomposers feed on?

Decomposers feed on dead plants and animals.

10. What can you see in photos A–D?

Photo A shows a model heart. The heart is the organ that pumps blood around the body.

Photo B shows a woman having an ultrasound scan. Ultrasound machines allow doctors to monitor the foetus inside the mother.

Photo C shows an X-ray. X-rays help doctors diagnose illnesses.

Photo D shows algae. Algae belong to the Protist Kingdom and can be unicellular or multicellular.

2 Listen and check your answers. (CD 1. Track 37)

- Pupils can check their own answers or check a partner's or another group's answers.

TEAM TEST!

1 Get into teams. Take it in turns to guess what the other team is talking about.

1. Team A: This body system helps us eliminate waste. Answer: *the excretory system*

1. Team B: This body system is made up of the organs that help us breathe. Answer: *the respiratory system*

2. Team A: This happens when a sperm cell joins an ovum cell. Answer: *fertilisation*

2. Team B: This is what we call living things which are made up of more than one cell. Answer: *multicellular*

3. Team A: All living things in this kingdom are unicellular. Answer: *the Monera Kingdom*

3. These male sex organs produce sperm. Answer: *testicles*

4. Team A: Doing this activity too much can result in headaches, backache and eye strain: Answer: *playing video games*

4. Team B: Algae belong to this kingdom. Answer: *the Protist Kingdom*

5. Team A: This is the smallest living unit. Answer: *a cell*

5. These are chemicals which are added to food to make it last longer. Answer: *additives*

6. Team A: People have these regularly to monitor their health. Answer: *medical check-ups*

6. Team B: This is the ability to understand how someone feels. Answer: *empathy*

2 Listen and check your answers. (CD 1. Track 38)

- Pupils can check the other group's answers.

3 Write two more sentences and test the other team.

- Give pupils a limited amount of time to go through the units and make up two more sentences to test their classmates. Circulate and check accuracy and suitability.
- At the end of the test, the winning team can choose either a video link or song from the unit, or request a particular game you play in class to close the lesson.

UNIT 4 Animals

CONTENT	EVALUATION CRITERIA
Vertebrates.	Know the characteristics of and classify vertebrates.
Invertebrates.	Know the characteristics of and classify invertebrates.
Interest in and respect for animals.	Show interest in the study of animals and in their care and protection.
First approaches to scientific activity and the scientific method. Use of different information sources (direct and indirect). Use ICTs.	Obtain relevant information about specific phenomena, make predictions, integrate information from direct and indirect observation and communicate the results.
First approaches to simple experiments and investigations.	Conjecture as to the results of natural occurrences and of simple experiments and investigations.
Individual and group work.	Work independently and proactively and develop strategies for working in a group.
Planning a project and presenting a report.	Carry out a project and present a report.

LEARNING STANDARDS	KEY COMPETENCES	PAGES
Observes, directly and indirectly, knows the characteristics of and classifies vertebrates.	MST, LTL	52-57
Observes, directly and indirectly, knows the characteristics of and classifies invertebrates.	MST, LTL	56, 57
Shows interest in the study of animals and in their care and protection.	MST, SOC	60, 61
With help, selects and organises specific and relevant information; analyses it and draws conclusions; reflects on the experience and the process; presents the results.	MST, LTL	53, 60, 61
Use books, libraries, etc. and collaborate in the care and maintenance of all the materials available in the school and the classroom.	MST, LTL	50-63
Shows autonomy in the planning of activities and tasks and shows initiative in decision taking.	LTL, AUT	53, 60, 61
With help, carries out simple experiments or investigations, and conjectures as to the results.	MST, LTL, AUT	60
Uses strategies to help their own learning, as well as asking for help and information.	LTL, AUT	53, 62
First approaches to cooperative learning.	SOC, LTL	51, 61
Begins observation, using relevant instruments and consulting written documents and images.	LTL, AUT	53, 60
Shows autonomy and proactiveness in the planning of and carrying out of actions.	AUT	60, 61
Presents work clearly and in an organised fashion.	LIN, LTL, AUT	60, 61
With help, carries out a project and presents a report, using paper and/or digital means, collecting information from different sources, presenting the results orally and with the support of images and short texts.	LIN, LTL, AUT, DIG	60, 61

UNIT INFORMATION

UNIT SUMMARY

In this unit, pupils will review and extend their knowledge of the Animal Kingdom

At the beginning of the unit, pupils review the characteristics of vertebrates. This subject area is covered in the opening illustration with the help of the course characters, Carla and Alex, who are on a school trip to the Natural Science Museum. The school trip continues in the story and, on their return to school, Alex and Carla carry out a *School trip project* to review the characteristics that they have learned.

These opening pages are designed to test pupils' prior knowledge and ease them into the subject matter of the unit, provoking interest and participation.

They will move on to study vertebrate nutrition, respiration and reproduction in detail. This is a new area of study for pupils and one that requires a high level of language and knowledge acquisition. The aim of this lesson focuses on the comparison of how different animal groups perform these life processes. Finally, pupils will study the six invertebrate groups.

EXPERIMENT

Find out

In the *Find out* activity on page 60, your pupils will prepare a working model to observe how the shape of a bird's wing can help it fly.

Pupils will need:

- paper
- scissors
- glue
- ruler
- string

Further ideas

Pupils can use reference books or the internet to research how the wings of different birds are specifically adapted to help them survive. They can also research the adaptations of other types of animals.

VALUES AND ATTITUDES

In this unit, your pupils will learn to appreciate the variety and diversity of animals that belong to the Animal Kingdom. They will practise their classification skills and observe similarities and differences between the animal groups. Encourage pupils to think about how varied and interesting life on Earth is and how fascinating it is discover how different living things carry out the life processes.

Think about it

The *Think about it* page in this unit focuses on an endangered animal. The intention of this section is to encourage pupils to think about how we need to preserve and protect the animals that share our planet. They should also think about how animals depend on their natural environment and be aware of our responsibility to respect and preserve these habitats.

EVALUATION MATERIAL

These documents can be downloaded from the Teachers section of the digital component and printed.

The materials include:

- **Unit diagnostic test:** provides an overview of the unit and allows you to assess the pupils' prior knowledge.
- **End-of-unit test:** in addition to the Review section at the end of each unit, this summative test can be used to evaluate pupils' progress after studying the unit content.
- **Class unit evaluation grid:** based on the evaluation criteria and learning standards of the unit.

DIGITAL RESOURCES

Presentations

- **Unit summary**: a simple slide presentation with text, images and audio to review the main ideas of the unit. It can be used at the beginning of the unit to test pupils' prior knowledge of the unit content or at the end of the unit as a revision tool.
- **Find out:** a slide presentation of the unit's *Find out page* with text, photos and audio. The slide presentation is perfect for a heads-up class, showing the steps one by one. Use this tool to get the pupils to predict the next steps (with their books closed) or to focus their attention on each step as they carry out the project themselves.

Activities

Activities vary per unit and include the following:

- **Memory game:** useful activity for reviewing key vocabulary and modelling pronunciation.
- **Labelling:** pupils label a diagram by dragging and dropping key terms.
- **Spelling:** pupils drag and drop letters to spell key terms.
- **Read and reveal:** pupils read sentences and guess the missing words, which are revealed by clicking the spaces.
- **Classification:** pupils drag and drop concepts and key terms in a simple classification table.
- **Wordsearch:** pupils find key terms hidden in the wordsearch.
- **Definitions:** pupils drag and drop words to complete definitions.

Song lyrics

Listen to the song *Animals reproduce* and follow the lyrics line by line.

Posters

Attractive and informative posters to display in class. You can use them to review key concepts and vocabulary.

Videos

Use the video links in this unit to present content in a dynamic, real-life context while reinforcing the pupils' listening skills.

Teachers

Digital flashcards and wordcards: topics include *Vertebrate nutrition, Vertebrate respiration, Vertebrate reproduction and Invertebrates.*

Downloadable pdfs: evaluation tests, evaluation grids, templates, useful links and further information.

PAGES 50–51 Animals

PAGE SUMMARY

The aim of the unit opener is to develop your pupils' observation skills and to find out what they already know about the topic of the unit. Use the picture to elicit vocabulary related to vertebrate animals, as well as action verbs that describe what is going on in the scene and words which describe the various characters and objects. Get your pupils to work in groups to complete activities 1–4 and to have fun listening to the song and completing activity 5.

LANGUAGE

- Question forms: *Is it …? Can it …? Does it …? Has it got …?*
- Vocabulary: *vertebrates, invertebrates, backbone, skeleton, mammals, birds, fish, reptiles, amphibians, herbivores, carnivores, omnivores, viviparous, oviparous*

ADDITIONAL MATERIALS

- Digital flashcards
- Digital wordcards
- Extra materials: picture of a mammal, a bird, a fish, a reptile and an amphibian

(+) OPENING ACTIVITIES

- Place pictures of a mammal, a bird, a fish, a reptile and an amphibian on the board and label them 1 – 5. Organise the class into five groups and give each group a number which corresponds to one of the pictures. Tell pupils to work together to write as many facts as they can about their animal group.
- If you are using an interactive whiteboard, focus only on the illustration, not the questions. Either elicit ideas (*There's a whale jumping out of the water; Carla is holding a fish*, etc.) or ask questions indicating each part of the picture: **What's Alex doing? What can you see in the pool?**
- Alternatively, use the interactive whiteboard writing tools. Ask pupils to come up to the board, mark an area of the picture and describe what they can see. Help them to produce full, correct sentences.

MAIN ACTIVITIES

Page 51, Unit introduction (CD1 track 39)

- Play the audio of the unit introduction and tell pupils to listen and read. Then ask one or two pupils to read out loud. This way, pupils will feel more self-confident when it comes to pronouncing new words.

- Ask pupils to close their books. Ask: **What are the two main groups of animals?** *(Vertebrates and invertebrates.)* **What do all vertebrates have?** *(A backbone and internal skeleton.)* **What are the five classes of vertebrates?** *(Mammals, birds, fish, reptiles, amphibians.)* Place the corresponding wordcards on the board.

1 Can you name the animals in the picture?

- When pupils name *dolphin and orca* (killer whale) encourage them to name other marine animals (animals that live in the sea). Pupils may notice that Carla is holding a *fish* and they may point out that the humans are animals too.

2 Which vertebrate groups do these animals belong to?

- Extend the question by asking: **How are marine mammals different from land mammals?** *(They have flippers not legs, they are streamlined and some have a blowhole.)* **How are they similar?** *(They have warm blood. They breathe with lungs. They are viviparous. The babies drink their mother's milk.) See Answers at a glance.*

3 Are the animals in the picture in their natural habitat?

- Encourage pupils to talk about whether wild animals should be kept in captivity. Ask them if they think the animals are happy in zoos or confined spaces. Try to get them to find positive and negative things. *(The animals are safe from sea pollution and predators in a zoo. Zoos help protect endangered animals. The animals aren't free. They need more space, etc.) No they are not.*

4 Are these animals herbivores, carnivores or omnivores?

- Ask pupils to explain the difference between carnivores, herbivores and omnivores. Ask them how we know what an animal eats. Say **Which part of the body tells us what animals eat?** *(The teeth or the beak.) See Answers at a glance.*

5 Listen to the song. Point to the vertebrate groups you hear.

- Focus pupils' attention on the five photos. Ask them to read and repeat the words. Check for understanding.

CD1 • track 40

Animals reproduce
Animals create offspring
Oviparous and viviparous
This stops them becoming extinct
Oviparous animals lay eggs
These eggs hatch into new offspring
Parrots, frogs and crocodiles
Are oviparous living things
[chorus]Animals reproduce…
Viviparous animals give birth
They give birth to live offspring
Humans, monkeys and dolphins
Are viviparous living things
[chorus]Animals reproduce…
'Stops them becoming extinct'

- Play the song *Animals reproduce* **(CD1 track 40)** and ask pupils to point to the vertebrate group that they hear. Then play the song a second time and encourage pupils to sing along (you can use the Song lyrics section on the digital component to display the song line by line while you listen). *Mammal, bird, reptile, amphibian.*

ANSWERS AT A GLANCE

1. Dolphin, killer whale, fish, humans.
2. Mammals (dolphin, killer whale and humans) and fish.
3. No, they aren't.
4. Carnivores. Killer whales and dolpins are carnivores. Humans can be omnivores or herbivores. Fish can be carnivores, herbivores or omnivores.
5. Mammal, bird, reptile, amphibian.

PAGES 52–53 A trip to the Natural Science Museum

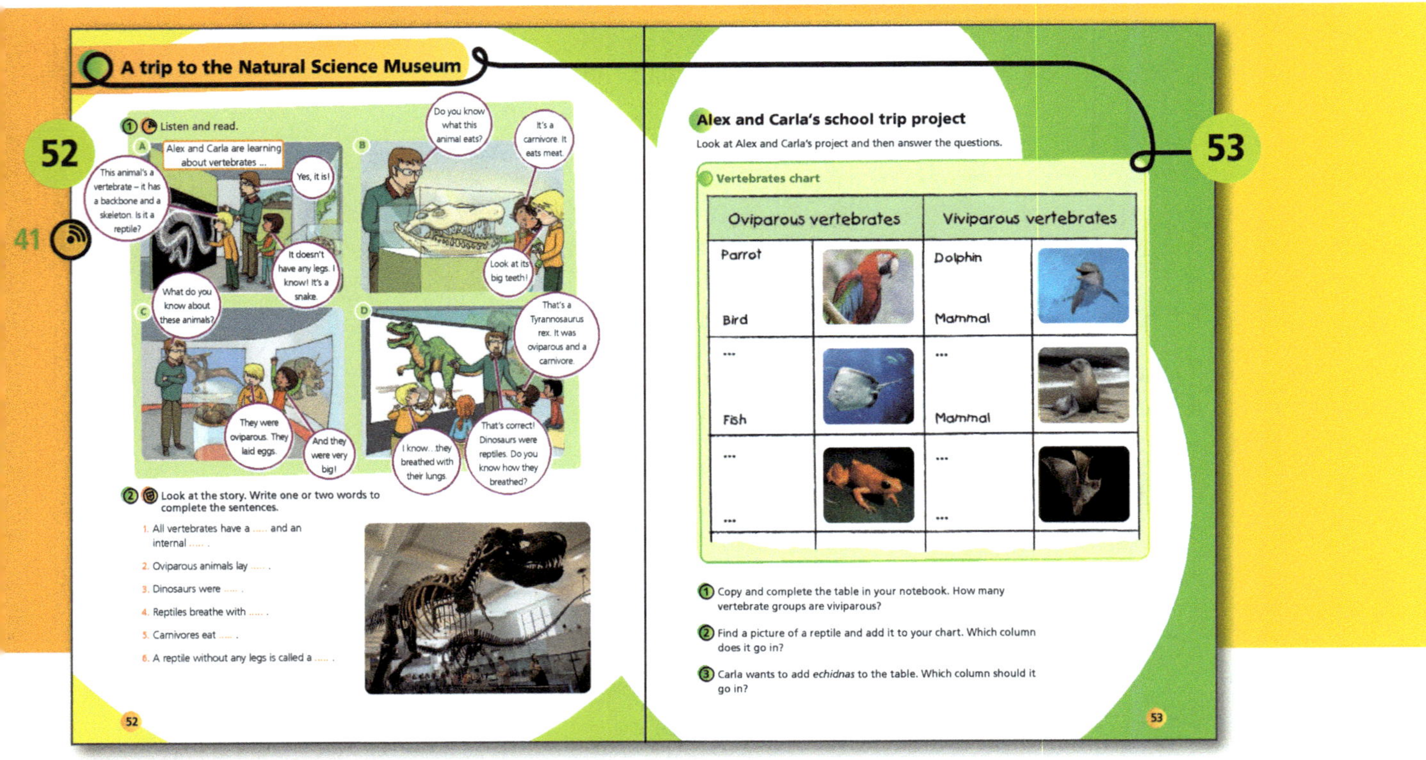
52
41

A trip to the Natural Science Museum

1 Listen and read.

2 Look at the story. Write one or two words to complete the sentences.

1. All vertebrates have a ..... and an internal ..... .
2. Oviparous animals lay ..... .
3. Dinosaurs were ..... .
4. Reptiles breathe with ..... .
5. Carnivores eat ..... .
6. A reptile without any legs is called a ..... .

52

53

Alex and Carla's school trip project

Look at Alex and Carla's project and then answer the questions.

Vertebrates chart

Oviparous vertebrates		Viviparous vertebrates	
Parrot Bird		Dolphin Mammal	
... Fish		... Mammal	
... ...		... ...	

1 Copy and complete the table in your notebook. How many vertebrate groups are viviparous?

2 Find a picture of a reptile and add it to your chart. Which column does it go in?

3 Carla wants to add *echidnas* to the table. Which column should it go in?

53

PAGE SUMMARY

This double-page spread opens with a story in which your pupils have the opportunity to see Carla and Alex on their school trip to the Natural Science Museum. Carla and Alex are talking to the guide and showing their knowledge of vertebrates. The story is reinforced with an exam style sentence completion activity that is related to both the story and the opening double page spread. On page 53, pupils can study Carla and Alex's school trip project about viviparous and oviparous animals.

LANGUAGE

- Present simple
- Past simple: *was / were*
- Past tense: *laid, breathed*
- Vocabulary: *vertebrate, carnivore, oviparous, reptiles, lungs, dinosaur, Tyrannosaurus rex*

ADDITIONAL MATERIALS

- Digital flashcards
- Digital wordcards
- School project: photos of an echidna and a duckbilled platypus

OPENING ACTIVITIES

- Write the following words on the board, jumbled up in circles: *carnivore, oviparous, Tyrannosaurus rex, vertebrate, skeleton* and *reptile*. Explain that the words are associated to something you might see in a natural science museum. Ask for volunteers to come to the board and unjumble the words. Now ask if anyone can make sentences using the unjumbled words. *The Tyrannosaurus was a reptile. It was oviparous*, etc.

MAIN ACTIVITIES

1 Listen and read. (CD1 track 41)

- Draw pupils' attention to the story at the top of page 52 and explain to them that they are going to listen to a story about Alex and Carla's trip to the Natural Science Museum. Say **Let's listen and read**. Play the audio.
- Ask pupils to look at the illustrations and describe what is happening in each one using their own words. For example, *Alex is looking at a skeleton of a snake; there is a skull in a glass case; they are talking about dinosaurs*.
- Divide pupils into groups of three and ask them to choose a character from the story – Alex, Carla or the guide. Pupils should then read their part of the story aloud in their small group. Invite a group to the front of the class to act the story out.

(2) Look at the story. Write one or two words to complete the sentences.

- This activity aims to revise vocabulary, reinforce what pupils have learned in the story and refresh concepts studied in previous levels. Ask pupils to work with a partner to complete the sentences. Correct as a class and then tell pupils to copy the completed sentences into their notebook.

1. All vertebrates have a **backbone** and an **internal skeleton**.
2. Oviparous animals lay **eggs**.
3. Dinosaurs were **reptiles**.
4. Reptiles breathe with their **lungs**.
5. Carnivores eat **meat**.
6. A reptile without any legs is called a **snake**.

SCHOOL TRIP PROJECT

- Before pupils open their books, elicit the names of the different animal groups. Place the following wordcards on the board: *mammals, birds, fish, reptiles* and *amphibians*.
- Explain to pupils that following their trip to the Natural Science Museum, Alex and Carla have done a project to illustrate what they have learned about animal reproduction.
- Tell pupils to look at the photo on page 53 and ask for volunteers to read the two headings: *Oviparous vertebrates* and *Viviparous vertebrates*. Invite volunteers to explain what oviparous and viviparous mean. *(Oviparous vertebrates lay eggs. Viviparous vertebrates are born alive.)* Invite volunteers to arrange the vertebrate groups on the board into oviparous or viviparous columns.

(1) Copy and complete the table in your notebook. How many vertebrate groups are viviparous?

- Ask pupils to work with a partner to decide which words are missing from the chart. Ask: **What are the names of these animals? Which animal group do they belong to?** Invite a volunteer to read question one. Elicit that only one vertebrate group is viviparous – mammals.

(2) Find a picture of a reptile and add it to your chart. Which column does it go in?

- Invite a pupil to read question 2. Ask pupils to name as many reptiles as they can. Write the names on the board and invite volunteers to name the characteristics these animals share. Elicit that *reptiles should be included in the oviparous vertebrates column.*

(3) Carla wants to add *echidnas* to the table. Which column should it go in?

- Remind pupils that they read about echidnas the previous year. Ask **Who can tell me something about them?** Place photos of an echidna and a duckbilled platypus on the board. Elicit that they are mammals but that they are oviparous. These mammals are called monotremes. Elicit that *echidnas should be in the oviparous vertebrate column.*

(+) CLOSING ACTIVITIES

- Use the information on pages 52 and 53 to invent true and false statements. *Dinosaurs were mammals. A manta ray is a fish.* Ask pupils to repeat the true statements and correct the false ones.

(+) EXTRA IDEAS

- Ask the class to investigate the monotreme group of vertebrates. Ask them to choose one example and find out the following information: a physical description of the animal, which part of the world they live in, their habitat and what they eat. Encourage pupils to find pictures of the animal too.

ANSWERS AT A GLANCE

Page 52

1 backbone, skeleton; 2 eggs; 3 reptiles; 4 lungs; 5 meat; 6 snake

Page 53

(1) Manta ray; Frog – Amphibian; Sea lion; Bat – mammal. One vertebrate group is viviparous – mammals.

(2) Oviparous vertebrate.

(3) Oviparous vertebrate.

PAGES 54–55 Vertebrate nutrition and Vertebrate respiration

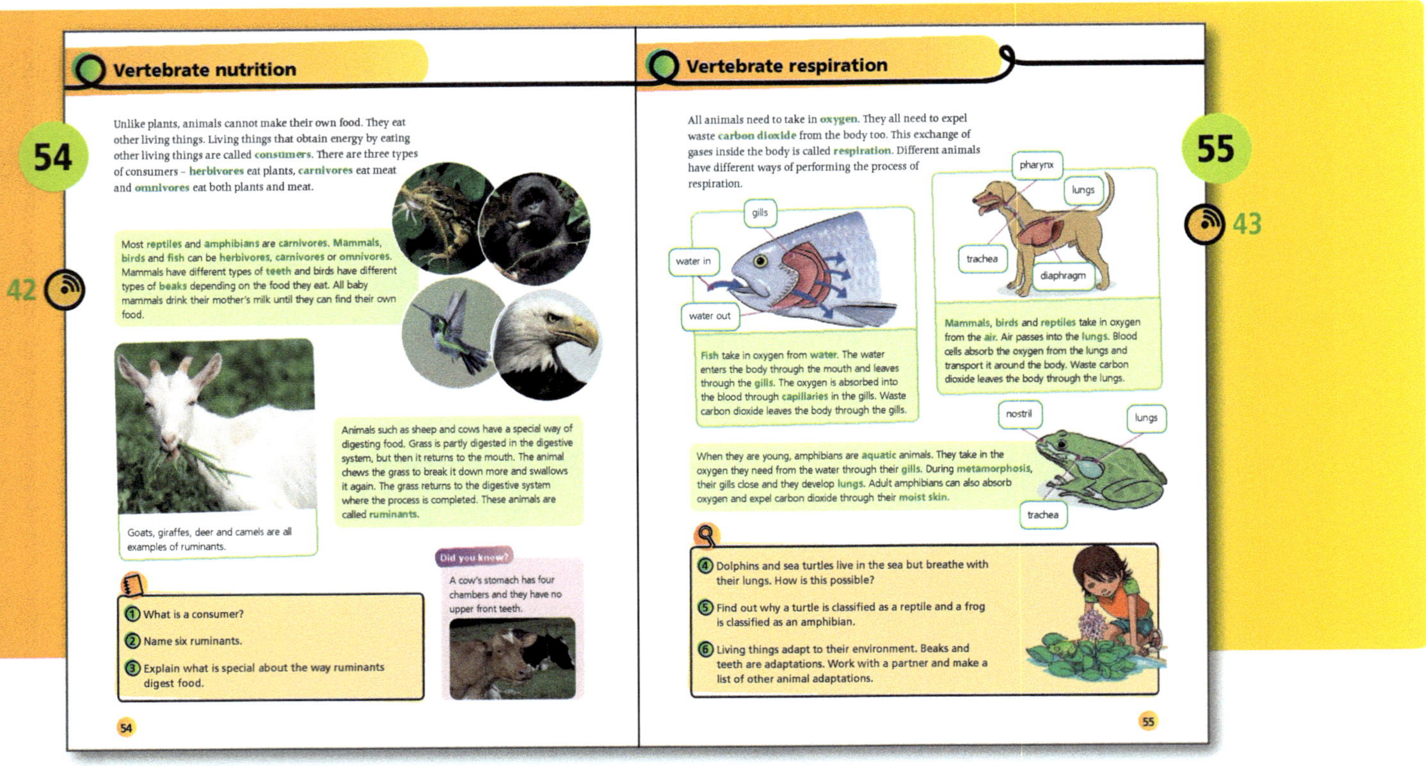

54

42

Vertebrate nutrition

Unlike plants, animals cannot make their own food. They eat other living things. Living things that obtain energy by eating other living things are called **consumers**. There are three types of consumers – **herbivores** eat plants, **carnivores** eat meat and **omnivores** eat both plants and meat.

Most **reptiles** and **amphibians** are **carnivores. Mammals, birds** and **fish** can be **herbivores, carnivores** or **omnivores**. Mammals have different types of **teeth** and birds have different types of **beaks** depending on the food they eat. All baby mammals drink their mother's milk until they can find their own food.

Goats, giraffes, deer and camels are all examples of ruminants.

Animals such as sheep and cows have a special way of digesting food. Grass is partly digested in the digestive system, but then it returns to the mouth. The animal chews the grass to break it down more and swallows it again. The grass returns to the digestive system where the process is completed. These animals are called **ruminants**.

Did you know?

A cow's stomach has four chambers and they have no upper front teeth.

1. What is a consumer?
2. Name six ruminants.
3. Explain what is special about the way ruminants digest food.

54

55

43

Vertebrate respiration

All animals need to take in **oxygen**. They all need to expel waste **carbon dioxide** from the body too. This exchange of gases inside the body is called **respiration**. Different animals have different ways of performing the process of respiration.

Fish take in oxygen from **water**. The water enters the body through the mouth and leaves through the **gills**. The oxygen is absorbed into the blood through **capillaries** in the gills. Waste carbon dioxide leaves the body through the gills.

Mammals, birds and **reptiles** take in oxygen from the **air**. Air passes into the **lungs**. Blood cells absorb the oxygen from the lungs and transport it around the body. Waste carbon dioxide leaves the body through the lungs.

When they are young, amphibians are **aquatic** animals. They take in the oxygen they need from the water through their **gills**. During **metamorphosis**, their gills close and they develop **lungs**. Adult amphibians can also absorb oxygen and expel carbon dioxide through their **moist skin**.

4. Dolphins and sea turtles live in the sea but breathe with their lungs. How is this possible?
5. Find out why a turtle is classified as a reptile and a frog is classified as an amphibian.
6. Living things adapt to their environment. Beaks and teeth are adaptations. Work with a partner and make a list of other animal adaptations.

55

PAGE SUMMARY

This double-page spread introduces pupils to vertebrate nutrition and respiration. There is a lot of new vocabulary and concepts on this double page. Pupils should focus first on nutrition and then on respiration. The main learning aim is to understand how adaptations help the organism to carry out vital functions and how organisms are adapted to their environment.

LANGUAGE

- Quantifiers: *most, all*
- Present tense
- Linking words: *first, then, next, after that, finally*
- Vocabulary: *nutrition, respiration, mammals, birds, fish, reptiles, amphibians, consumers, herbivores, carnivores, omnivores, ruminants, goats, giraffes, deer, teeth, beak, stomach, lungs, gills, moist skin, blood, capillaries, oxygen, carbon dioxide, metamorphosis, aquatic, obtain, absorb, expel, digest*

ADDITIONAL MATERIALS

- Digital flashcards
- Digital wordcards

OPENING ACTIVITIES

- If you are using an interactive whiteboard, click on the opening text on page 54 and highlight the first two sentences: *Unlike plants, animals cannot make their own food. They eat other living things*. Alternatively, ask pupils to open their books on page 54 and read the first two sentences to the class. Ask: **What living things do consumers eat?** *(Other animals, plants or both animals and plants.)*

MAIN ACTIVITIES

Page 54, Vertebrate nutrition (CD1 track 42)

- Before reading the text, draw pupils' attention to the photos on page 54. Ask them to identify the animals *(frog, gorilla, humming bird, eagle, goat and cows)* Play the audio of the introductory text and ask pupils to listen and read. Ask **What are the three types of consumers?** *(herbivores, carnivores and omnivores.)* Ask **Which animals in the photos are herbivores?** *Note: Gorillas are mainly herbivores but they will eat ants and termites. (Humming birds, goats and cows.)*
- Place the wordcards: *herbivore, carnivore* and *omnivore* on the board. Play CD1 track 42. Pupils should listen and read. Ask pupils to complete the sentences: **Most reptiles and amphibians are** ________. *(carnivores);* **Mammals, birds and fish can be** ________. *(carnivores, herbivores or omnivores)*

- Point out that some herbivore mammals have a special digestive system. Draw their attention to the photo of the goat and say **Let's find out about the goats' digestive system**. Ask them to read the *Did you know?* box. Ask **Why do ruminants have this complex digestive system?** *(Their food is difficult to digest.)*

1 What is a consumer?

- Encourage pupils to answer using full sentences. *A consumer is a living thing that obtains energy by eating other living things.*

2 Name six ruminants.

- Pupils can find the answer to this question within the text on page 54. *Goats, giraffes, deer, camels, sheep and cows.*

3 Explain what is special about the way ruminants digest food.

- Pupils can find the answer to this question within the text on page 54. They can write their answer down, in pairs of small groups. *See Answers at a glance*

Page 55, Vertebrate respiration (CD1 track 43)

- Before reading, ask pupils to stand up and slowly breathe in and out. Ask **What are you taking in from the air?** (*Oxygen*); **What are you expelling into the air?** (*Carbon dioxide*); **Do all animals breathe this way?** (*No, they don't*); **Which animals breathe differently?** (*Fish and young amphibians*); **Why do they breathe differently?** (*They take oxygen from the water.*)
- Read the introductory text to the class. Pause at the key words and encourage pupils to supply the missing words. Play **CD1 track 43** and ask pupils to listen and read.
- Now organise the class into groups of three. Assign one information box to each member of the group. Tell them to read their box several times. When they are sure they understand the text, they must close their book. Ask them to explain their information to the other members of their group.

4 Dolphins and sea turtles live in the sea but breathe with their lungs. How is this possible?

- Elicit that *they can stay under water without breathing longer than humans but they have to come up to the surface to breathe.*

5 Find out why a turtle is classified as a reptile and a frog is classified as an amphibian.

- Elicit that *amphibians lay eggs in water and reptiles lay eggs on land.*

6 Living things adapt to their environment. Beaks and teeth are adaptations. Work with a partner and make a list of other animal adaptations.

- Focus pupils' attention on the photos on page 54. Point out the difference between the hummingbird's beak and the eagle's beak. Ask **What do eagles eat?** (*They eat meat.*) **Why do humming birds have such long thin beaks?** (*To reach the nectar inside the flower.*) Ask pupils to work with a partner to list more adaptations for survival. *Open answer*

+ CLOSING ACTIVITIES

- Play *Correct me, please* to test pupils on a few concepts from pages 54 and 55. Replace correct words with words which are incorrect and funny. *Birds have different glasses depending on the type of food they eat,, etc.*

+ EXTRA IDEAS

- Show animal wordcards and ask pupils to say describe the animals' nutrition and respiration..

ANSWERS AT A GLANCE

1. A consumer is a living thing that obtains energy by eating other living things.
2. Goats, giraffes, deer, camels, sheep and cows.
3. First, grass is digested in the digestive system. Then it returns to the mouth. The animal chews it again to break it down more and swallows it again. The grass returns to the digestive system where the process is completed.
4. Dolphins and turtles have to come up to the surface to breathe.
5. Amphibians lay eggs in water and reptiles lay eggs on land.
6. Open answer.

PAGES 56–57 Vertebrate reproduction

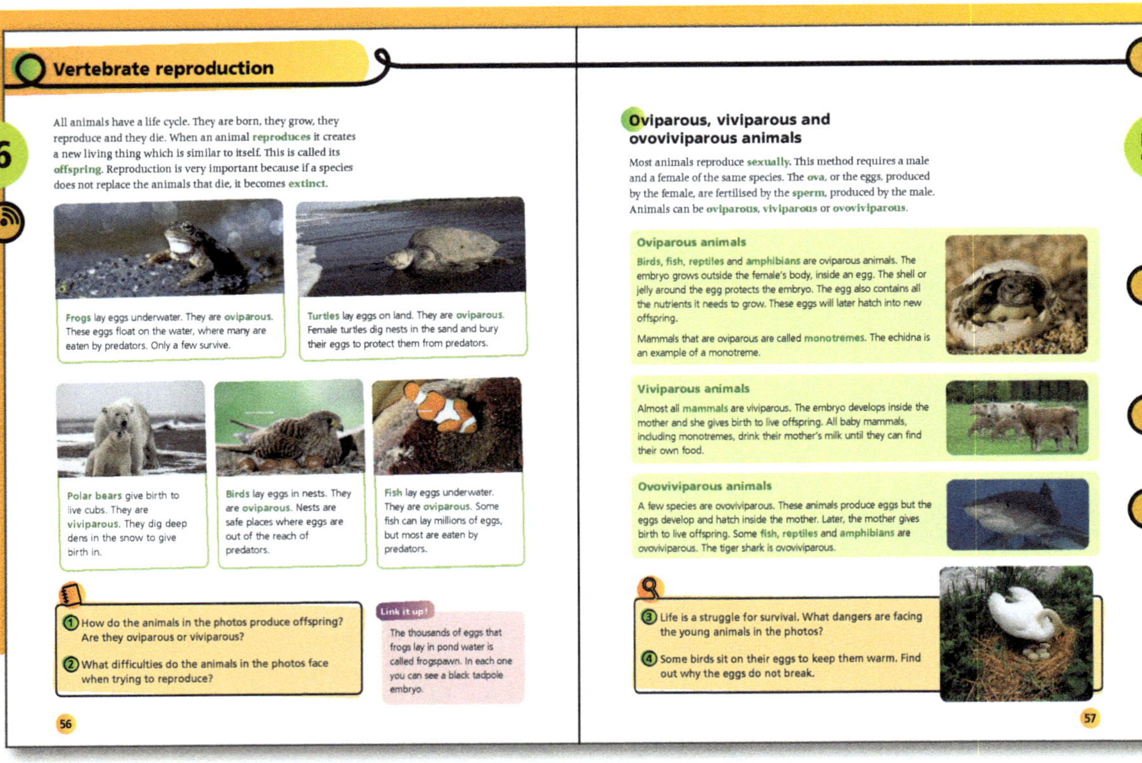
56
44

Vertebrate reproduction

All animals have a life cycle. They are born, they grow, they reproduce and they die. When an animal **reproduces** it creates a new living thing which is similar to itself. This is called its **offspring**. Reproduction is very important because if a species does not replace the animals that die, it becomes **extinct**.

Frogs lay eggs underwater. They are **oviparous**. These eggs float on the water, where many are eaten by predators. Only a few survive.

Turtles lay eggs on land. They are **oviparous**. Female turtles dig nests in the sand and bury their eggs to protect them from predators.

Polar bears give birth to live cubs. They are **viviparous**. They dig deep dens in the snow to give birth in.

Birds lay eggs in nests. They are **oviparous**. Nests are safe places where eggs are out of the reach of predators.

Fish lay eggs underwater. They are **oviparous**. Some fish can lay millions of eggs, but most are eaten by predators.

1. How do the animals in the photos produce offspring? Are they oviparous or viviparous?
2. What difficulties do the animals in the photos face when trying to reproduce?

Link it up!

The thousands of eggs that frogs lay in pond water is called frogspawn. In each one you can see a black tadpole embryo.

56

45
57

Oviparous, viviparous and ovoviviparous animals

Most animals reproduce **sexually**. This method requires a male and a female of the same species. The **ova**, or the eggs, produced by the female, are fertilised by the **sperm**, produced by the male. Animals can be **oviparous**, **viviparous** or **ovoviviparous**.

Oviparous animals

Birds, **fish**, **reptiles** and **amphibians** are oviparous animals. The embryo grows outside the female's body, inside an egg. The shell or jelly around the egg protects the embryo. The egg also contains all the nutrients it needs to grow. These eggs will later hatch into new offspring.

Mammals that are oviparous are called **monotremes**. The echidna is an example of a monotreme.

46

Viviparous animals

Almost all **mammals** are viviparous. The embryo develops inside the mother and she gives birth to live offspring. All baby mammals, including monotremes, drink their mother's milk until they can find their own food.

47

Ovoviviparous animals

A few species are ovoviviparous. These animals produce eggs but the eggs develop and hatch inside the mother. Later, the mother gives birth to live offspring. Some **fish**, **reptiles** and **amphibians** are ovoviviparous. The tiger shark is ovoviviparous.

48

3. Life is a struggle for survival. What dangers are facing the young animals in the photos?
4. Some birds sit on their eggs to keep them warm. Find out why the eggs do not break.

57

PAGE SUMMARY

On this double-page spread, pupils revise vertebrate reproduction by looking at oviparous and viviparous vertebrates. This subject matter will be familiar to them by now. However, pupils will now look at the problems animals have surviving in the wild and will understand the importance of reproduction. Page 45 gives pupils a detailed explanation of the differences between oviparous, viviparous and ovoviviparous animals.

LANGUAGE

- Questions words: *where, what, why, how, etc.*
- Quantifiers: *some, most, all, almost all, many, a few*
- Vocabulary: *oviparous, viviparous, ovoviviparous, monotremes, life cycle, offspring, predator, species*

ADDITIONAL MATERIALS

- Digital flashcards
- Digital wordcards
- Extra materials: photos of a baby, a very young child, adolescents, adults and an elderly person

OPENING ACTIVITIES

- Place photos of the stages of life on the board and ask pupils to guess the ages of the people in them. Remind pupils that there are different age groups. Ask them if they can name the age groups they can see in the photos. *(Babies, children, adolescents, adults and elderly people.)* Point out that all living things have a life cycle– they are born, they grow, they reproduce and they die.
- Invite volunteers to come to the board to draw the life cycle of a butterfly. Encourage them to explain the different stages as they draw. *(Eggs, caterpillar, chrysalis, adult butterfly.)* Ask **What is the name of this process?** *(Metamorphosis)*

MAIN ACTIVITIES

Page 56, Vertebrate reproduction (CD1 track 44)

- Ask pupils to open their books at page 56 and read the introduction text. Ask **What happens when an animal reproduces?** *(It creates a new living thing similar to itself.)* **What happens if a species doesn't replace the animals that die?** *(It becomes extinct.)* **Why are animals that perform the process of metamorphosis different from other animals?** *(The young don't look like the parents.)*

- Write these questions on the board: **Are the animals in the photos viviparous or oviparous? Where do they have their babies?** Tell pupils to read the information boxes and answer the questions individually. Suggest they write their answers in note form.

① How do the animals in the photos produce offspring? Are they oviparous or viviparous?

- Write the words *frogs, turtles, polar bears, birds and fish* on the board. Invite pupils to come to the board and write oviparous or viviparous next to each animal name. Then invite other pupils to write where they lay their eggs or have their cubs. *See Answer at a glance.*

② What difficulties do the animals in the photos face when trying to reproduce?

- Ask pupils to read the text boxes again. Ask **What is the problem for most of these animals?** (*They are hunted by predators.*) Make sure they understand the word predator. Ask **Which animal doesn't have this problem?** Elicit that the polar bear does not have predators because it is at the top of the food chain.

Page 57, Oviparous, viviparous and ovoviviparous animals (CD1 track 45)

- Ask pupils to look at the photos on page 57. Point out that the turtle is oviparous and the cow is viviparous. Tell them to look at the photo of the tiger shark. Explain that the tiger shark is neither oviparous nor viviparous. Ask them to read the introductory text to find out what type of animal it is. (*It's ovoviviparous.*) Invite pupils to guess what ovoviviparous means.
- Play and ask pupils to listen and read the three information boxes **(CD1 tracks 46-48)**. Organise the class into small groups and ask them to work together to write one question about each text box for the class to answer. Model the activity first. **What protects the egg?** (*The shell or jelly.*) **Do monotremes drink their mother's milk?** (*Yes, they do.*)

③ Life is a struggle for survival. What dangers are facing the young animals in the photos?

- Organise the class into small groups to talk about this question. Ask them to look at the photo of the polar bears on page 56. Remind them that polar bears have no predators but that they are endangered. Elicit the reason for this. (*Ice is melting at the Poles because of global warming and so they are losing their habitat.*) Encourage pupils to discuss the dangers that the animals in the photos could face. *See Answers at a glance*

④ Some birds sit on their eggs to keep them warm. Find out why the eggs do not break.

- This activity can be done at home with help from pupils' parents or in small study groups on the computer or in the library. *The rounded shape of the eggs makes them very strong at the sides.*

⊕ CLOSING ACTIVITIES

- Play the *Alphabet game* to list vertebrates. Pupils have to suggest a vertebrate for each letter of the alphabet.
- Divide the class into two teams. Explain that each team has to take turns to call out the name of an oviparous animal. Team members must call out in order and must not repeat a name. They score a point for each correct name. If a team member cannot name an animal, the turn passes to the other team. To ensure careful listening, tell pupils that the repetition of a name means losing a point.

ANSWERS AT A GLANCE

① Frogs, turtles, birds and fish lay eggs. Animals that lay eggs are oviparous. Polar bears give birth to live offsprong. They are viviparous.

② They are hunted by predators.

③ Predators, humans, habitat loss, pollution, etc.

④ The rounded shape of the eggs makes them very strong at the sides.

PAGES 58–59 Invertebrates

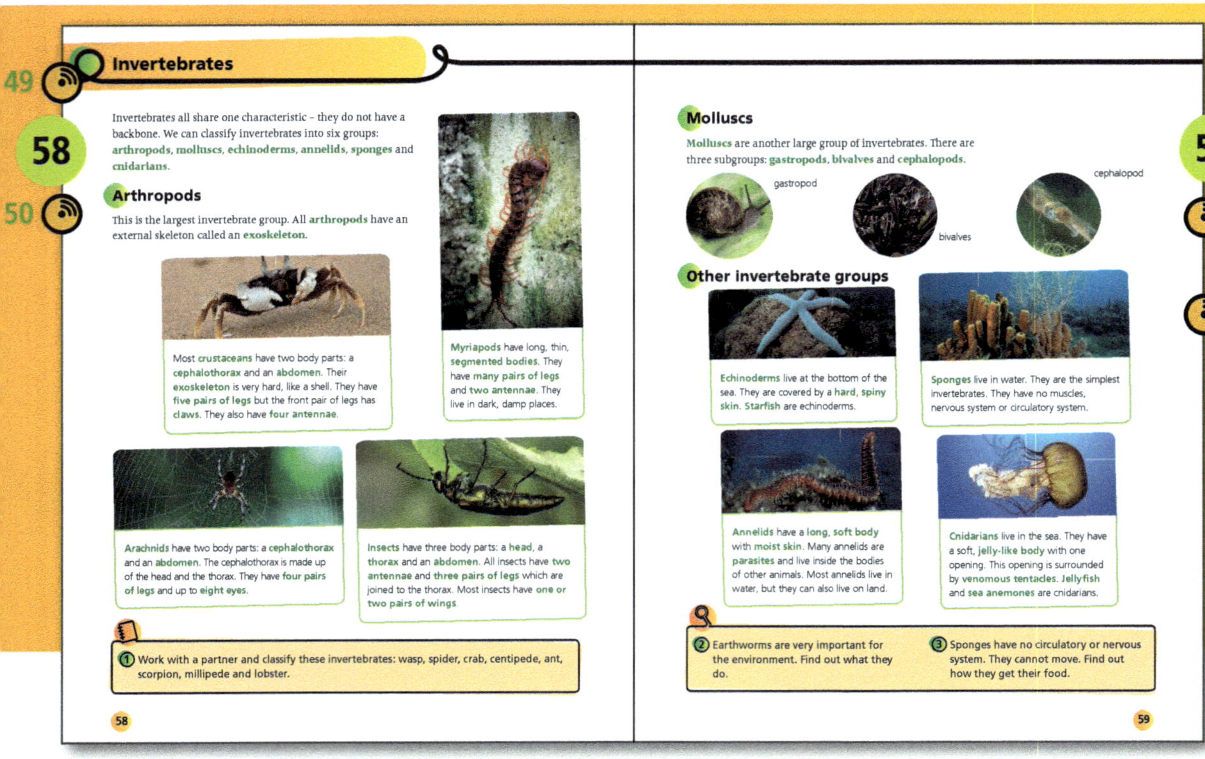

49

58

50

Invertebrates

Invertebrates all share one characteristic - they do not have a backbone. We can classify invertebrates into six groups: **arthropods, molluscs, echinoderms, annelids, sponges** and **cnidarians**.

Arthropods

This is the largest invertebrate group. All **arthropods** have an external skeleton called an **exoskeleton**.

Most **crustaceans** have two body parts: a **cephalothorax** and an **abdomen**. Their **exoskeleton** is very hard, like a shell. They have **five pairs of legs** but the front pair of legs has **claws**. They also have **four antennae**.

Myriapods have long, thin, **segmented bodies**. They have **many pairs of legs** and **two antennae**. They live in dark, damp places.

Arachnids have two body parts: a **cephalothorax** and an **abdomen**. The cephalothorax is made up of the head and the thorax. They have **four pairs of legs** and up to **eight eyes**.

Insects have three body parts: a **head**, a **thorax** and an **abdomen**. All insects have **two antennae** and **three pairs of legs** which are joined to the thorax. Most insects have **one or two pairs of wings**.

1. Work with a partner and classify these invertebrates: wasp, spider, crab, centipede, ant, scorpion, millipede and lobster.

58

59

51

52

Molluscs

Molluscs are another large group of invertebrates. There are three subgroups: **gastropods, bivalves** and **cephalopods**.

gastropod

bivalves

cephalopod

Other invertebrate groups

Echinoderms live at the bottom of the sea. They are covered by a **hard, spiny skin. Starfish** are echinoderms.

Sponges live in water. They are the simplest invertebrates. They have no muscles, nervous system or circulatory system.

Annelids have a **long, soft body** with **moist skin**. Many annelids are **parasites** and live inside the bodies of other animals. Most annelids live in water, but they can also live on land.

Cnidarians live in the sea. They have a soft, **jelly-like body** with one opening. This opening is surrounded by **venomous tentacles. Jellyfish** and **sea anemones** are cnidarians.

2. Earthworms are very important for the environment. Find out what they do.
3. Sponges have no circulatory or nervous system. They cannot move. Find out how they get their food.

59

PAGE SUMMARY

On this double-page spread, pupils will begin by reviewing what they learned in previous years about invertebrates. They will look in detail at the main invertebrate groups (arthropods and molluscs) and will also be introduced to four other groups which contain well known animals. Pupils will develop skills in observation and classification.

LANGUAGE

- Quantifiers: *most, all, some, many, etc.*
- Superlative adjectives: *largest, simplest*
- Vocabulary: *invertebrates, arthropods, crustaceans, myriapods, arachnids, insects, molluscs, gastropod, bivalves, cephalopod, echinoderms, annelids, sponges, cnidarians*

ADDITIONAL MATERIALS

- Digital flashcards
- Digital wordcards
- Extra material: a clear container, sand, soil, compost, leaves, water, earthworms

OPENING ACTIVITIES

- Activate knowledge from previous years by brainstorming the names of invertebrates. Write the names on the board. Count how many different vertebrates pupils can name.
- Now write the words *walk, swim* and *fly* on the board. Ask two pupils to come to the board and give each one a ruler. Say the name of an invertebrate. Ask pupils to hit the correct circle to say how it moves. They may have to hit more than one circle. The first pupil to hit the correct word, or words, wins the game. Change pairs.

Page 58, Invertebrates (CD1 track 49)

- Ask pupils to open their books at page 58. Say **Let's read the introductory text** (see Helpful tips, pages 20 -23). Read the names of the six invertebrate groups and ask pupils to repeat the names after you.

Page 58, Arthropods (CD1 track 50)

- Ask pupils to read the texts about arthropods (you can also listen to the audio). Drill pronunciation and check understanding of new vocabulary. Ask **What do all arthropods have in common?** (*They don't have a backbone or internal skeleton. They have an external skeleton called an exoskeleton.*) Ask pupils to identify the subgroups the animals belong to.

Page 59, Molluscs (CD1 track 51)

- Ask pupils to open their books at page 59. You can play the audio and encourage pupils to read along in their books or use one of the reading activities from pages 20-23. Practise the pronunciation of the sub-groups. Remind pupils that they studied molluscs last year. Say: **What are the names of the animals in the photos?** (*Snail, mussels, octopus.*) **What do they have in common?** (*They all have a soft body.*)

Page 59, Other invertebrate groups (CD1 track 52)

- Play the audio and ask pupils to listen and read. Help pupils to identify the animals in the photos and ask them to describe them. Help pupils to understand why they cannot be classified as arthropods or molluscs.

1 Work with a partner and classify these invertebrates: wasp, spider, crab, centipede, ant, scorpion, millipede and lobster.

- Ask pupils to work with a partner to classify these invertebrates. Suggest they draw a chart with the headings *insects, arachnids, crustaceans* and *myriapods* and that they should decide where to classify the invertebrates. See *Answers at a glance*

2 Earthworms are very important for the environment. Find out what they do.

- This activity can either be done as a project in pairs or groups, or for homework with the help of pupils' parents. Encourage pupils to find images of earthworms to illustrate their work. You could also set up a wormery (worm farm) in class for a few weeks so that pupils can observe the earthworms at work. You will need: a clear container, sand, soil, compost, leaves, water and worms. See *Answers at a glance.*

3 Sponges have no circulatory or nervous system. They cannot move. Find out how they get their food.

- Ask pupils to look at the photo of sponges on page 59. Encourage them to describe what they can see. Point out that sponges cannot hunt for food because they are unable to move. As they have no nervous system, they do not know when food is near them. Encourage pupils to think of ways in which the sponge can get food. Elicit that *sponges filter food from the water that passes through them.*

+ CLOSING ACTIVITIES

- Hand out the wordcards with the names of the invertebrate sub-groups to your pupils. Explain that they have to say three sentences about the group on the card. The rest of the class has to guess which group it is. **It has a soft body. It lives in water. It has two shells. What is it?** (*A bivalve or a mussel.*)

+ EXTRA IDEAS

- Invertebrates such as the earthworm are very important for the environment. Explain that today, bees are in danger. Thousands are dying. Ask pupils to find out why bees are so important for life on this planet and what we can do to help them survive. This activity can be done at home with the help of pupils' parents.

ANSWERS AT A GLANCE

1. Insects – wasp, ant; Arachnids – spider, scorpion; Crustaceans – crab, lobster; Myriapods – centipede, millipede
2. Earthworms improve the soil by creating pores, through which oxygen and water can enter and carbon dioxide can leave.
3. They filter food from the water as it passes through them.

PAGES 60–61 Find out / Think about it

60

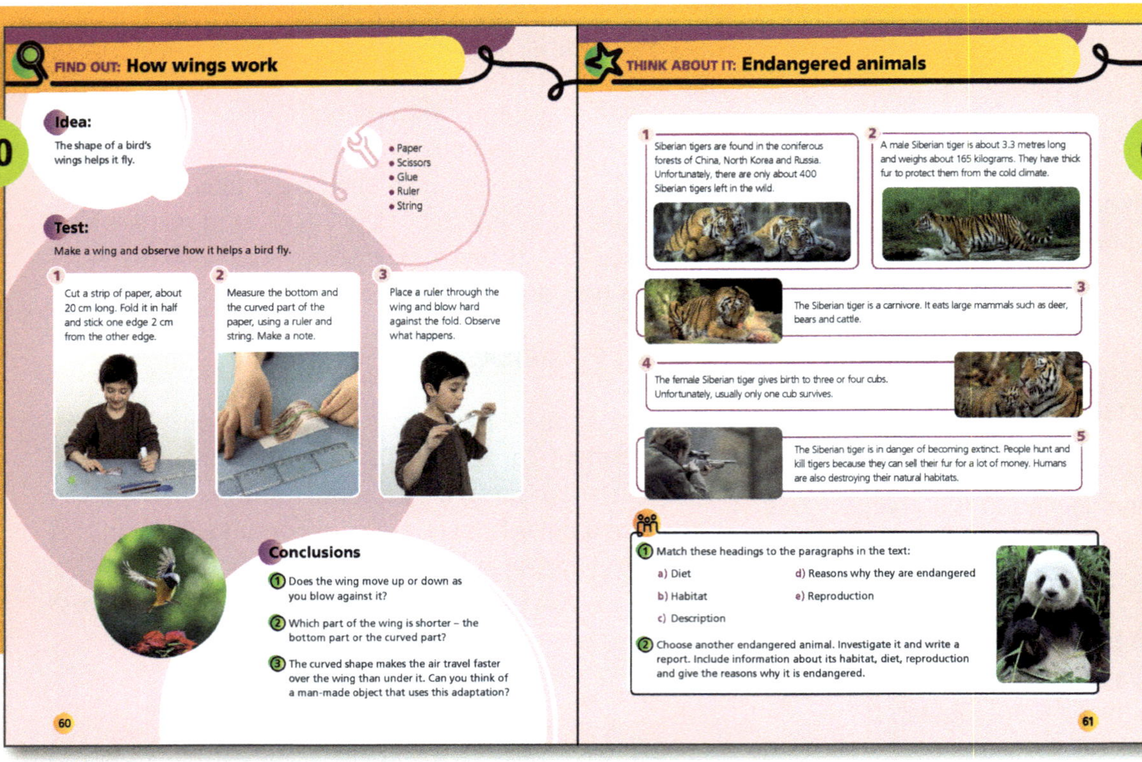
FIND OUT: How wings work

Idea:

The shape of a bird's wings helps it fly.

• Paper
• Scissors
• Glue
• Ruler
• String

Test:

Make a wing and observe how it helps a bird fly.

1 Cut a strip of paper, about 20 cm long. Fold it in half and stick one edge 2 cm from the other edge.

2 Measure the bottom and the curved part of the paper, using a ruler and string. Make a note.

3 Place a ruler through the wing and blow hard against the fold. Observe what happens.

Conclusions

1 Does the wing move up or down as you blow against it?

2 Which part of the wing is shorter – the bottom part or the curved part?

3 The curved shape makes the air travel faster over the wing than under it. Can you think of a man-made object that uses this adaptation?

60

THINK ABOUT IT: Endangered animals

1 Siberian tigers are found in the coniferous forests of China, North Korea and Russia. Unfortunately, there are only about 400 Siberian tigers left in the wild.

2 A male Siberian tiger is about 3.3 metres long and weighs about 165 kilograms. They have thick fur to protect them from the cold climate.

3 The Siberian tiger is a carnivore. It eats large mammals such as deer, bears and cattle.

4 The female Siberian tiger gives birth to three or four cubs. Unfortunately, usually only one cub survives.

5 The Siberian tiger is in danger of becoming extinct. People hunt and kill tigers because they can sell their fur for a lot of money. Humans are also destroying their natural habitats.

1 Match these headings to the paragraphs in the text:

a) Diet
b) Habitat
c) Description
d) Reasons why they are endangered
e) Reproduction

2 Choose another endangered animal. Investigate it and write a report. Include information about its habitat, diet, reproduction and give the reasons why it is endangered.

61

61

PAGE SUMMARY

In the first of these two pages (*Find out*), pupils make a working model to investigate how the shape of a bird's wing can help it fly. The second page (*Think about it*) provides your pupils with the opportunity to read and learn about an endangered animal– the Siberian tiger. They will then do their own investigation about another endangered animal, leading to individual class presentations and a heightened awareness of the seriousness of this situation.

LANGUAGE

- Imperatives: *cut, fold, stick, measure, make, place, blow, observe*
- Vocabulary: *strip, edge, curved, coniferous, cattle, cub, unfortunately, endangered, extinct*

MATERIALS

- Digital flashcards
- Digital wordcards
- Extra materials: card for each pupil for *Think about it* presentation

FIND OUT

OPENING ACTIVITIES

- Ask **Why can birds fly but we can't?** Ask pupils to work with a partner to discuss this this question. Point out that are many reasons why birds can fly and we cannot. Invite the pairs to share their ideas with the class. (*Birds have wings and feathers, their bones are hollow and their body is streamlined*).

MAIN ACTIVITIES

- Explain to pupils that they will be making a working model to see how the shape of a bird's wing can help it fly. Ask pupils to read the steps on page 60. Then, tell them to write the materials and the three steps in their notebook. Point out that they need to use the string to measure the curved part of the paper. Demonstrate this step if necessary. If you are using the book on the interactive whiteboard, you can play the audio recording of the steps. You may choose to do this investigation together as a class or allow small groups to go through the steps independently.

⊕ CLOSING ACTIVITIES

- Give pupils time to enjoy blowing against the fold in the wing and watching the wing move upwards. Ask pupils to work with a partner to answer the three questions. Correct answers as a class.

1 Does the wing move up or down as you blow against it?

- Encourage pupils to answer in full sentences. *The wing moves up.*

2 Which part of the wing is shorter – the bottom part or the curved part?

- Encourage pupils to answer in full sentences. *The bottom part is shorter.*

3 The curved shape makes the air travel faster over the wing than under it. Can you think of a man-made object that uses this design?

- Encourage pupils to think of a man-made object that can fly. *An airplane wing uses the same curved shape.*

THINK ABOUT IT

⊕ OPENING ACTIVITIES

- Write these names on the board: *giant panda, African elephant, snow leopard, black rhinoceros, mountain gorilla, polar bear, Mediterranean Monk seal, Iberian lynx, Cantabrian bear and Iberian wolf.* You may wish to show images of these animals as a slide show on the interactive whiteboard. Point out that all these animals are mammals but they also have another characteristic in common. Elicit that they are endangered animals.
- Invite volunteers to explain the word 'endangered' *There are not many of this species left and they may become extinct. When a species is extinct there are no more on the planet.*
- Organise the class into groups of four. Ask them to work together to decide where the endangered animals are from and also to talk about the reasons why they are in danger. Allow pupils time to talk about this question. Monitor groups to give ideas and help with vocabulary if necessary. Possible answers: *hunting, habitat loss, pollution, global warming*, etc.

MAIN ACTIVITIES

- Ask pupils to open their books at page 61. Say **Let's read about the Siberian tiger, another endangered animal.** If you are using the interactive whiteboard, you can play the audio and encourage pupils to read along in their books.
- Ask pupils to silently read the information again. Invite volunteers to choose a sentence but change a key word in order to make the sentence incorrect. *The Siberian tiger is a herbivore. The Siberian tiger gives birth to one cub. They are found in rainforests.* The volunteer can then choose a person to correct them.
- Alternatively you could ask the pupils to make up questions about the texts. **What does the Siberian tiger eat? Where does it live? How many cubs do they have?** Again, pupils can choose a classmate to answer the question.

⊕ CLOSING ACTIVITIES

1 Match these headings to the paragraphs in the text:

a) Diet b) Habitat c) Description d) Reasons why they are endangered e) Reproduction

- Ask pupils to look at the pictures and describe what they can see in each photo. Ask pupils to read and identify the information box which corresponds to the headings. *1-b, 2-c, 3-a, 4-e, 5-d*

2 Choose another endangered animal. Investigate it and write a report. Include information about its habitat, diet, reproduction and give the reasons why it is endangered.

- Tell pupils to find out about their chosen animal using the internet or other reference material. They should include the information listed in activity one. Pupils can do this research at home for homework and bring the information to class. Ask them to look for photos of their animal and also to find a map showing where the animal comes from. Suggest that pupils use the text on page 61 as a guide when they begin writing. Give each pupil a piece of card to prepare their information for the presentation.

PAGES 62–63 Look back: Animals

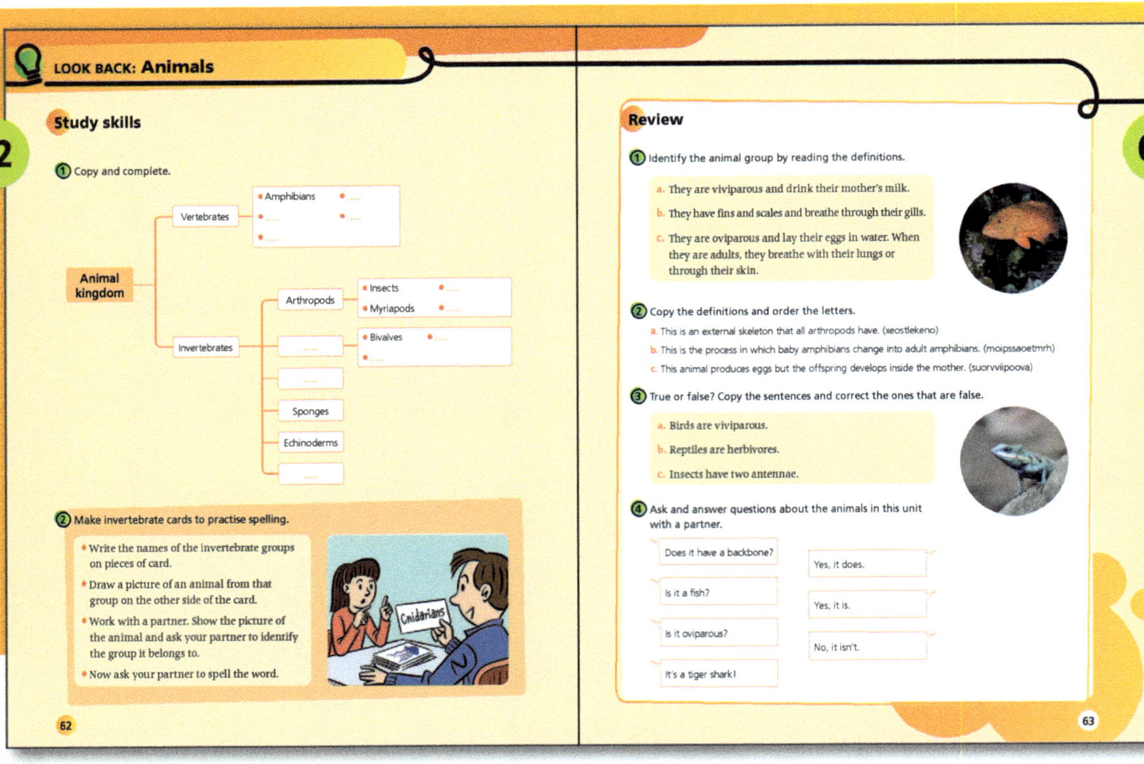

62

LOOK BACK: Animals

Study skills

1 Copy and complete.

Animal kingdom
Vertebrates
• Amphibians •.....
•..... •.....
•.....
Invertebrates
Arthropods
• Insects •.....
• Myriapods •.....
.....
• Bivalves •.....
•.....
.....
Sponges
Echinoderms
.....

2 Make invertebrate cards to practise spelling.

- Write the names of the invertebrate groups on pieces of card.
- Draw a picture of an animal from that group on the other side of the card.
- Work with a partner. Show the picture of the animal and ask your partner to identify the group it belongs to.
- Now ask your partner to spell the word.

Cnidarians

62

63

Review

1 Identify the animal group by reading the definitions.

a. They are viviparous and drink their mother's milk.
b. They have fins and scales and breathe through their gills.
c. They are oviparous and lay their eggs in water. When they are adults, they breathe with their lungs or through their skin.

2 Copy the definitions and order the letters.

a. This is an external skeleton that all arthropods have. (xeostlekeno)
b. This is the process in which baby amphibians change into adult amphibians. (moipssaoetmrh)
c. This animal produces eggs but the offspring develops inside the mother. (suorvviipoova)

3 True or false? Copy the sentences and correct the ones that are false.

a. Birds are viviparous.
b. Reptiles are herbivores.
c. Insects have two antennae.

4 Ask and answer questions about the animals in this unit with a partner.

Does it have a backbone?
Yes, it does.
Is it a fish?
Yes, it is.
Is it oviparous?
No, it isn't.
It's a tiger shark!

63

PAGE SUMMARY

This double-page spread allows pupils the opportunity to organise what they have learned in the unit by means of a concept map. They can also learn a new study skill: using illustrated wordcards to help memorise words that are difficult to spell. On the *Review* page, pupils complete activities individually to check their understanding of material covered in this unit. Activity 4 is a pairwork speaking activity to encourage them to create accurate questions and to give grammatically correct short answers. It is also a peer evaluation opportunity.

LANGUAGE

- Imperatives: *match, write, copy, complete, write, draw, work, show, identify, order, correct*
- Encourage pupils to speak and write in complete sentences.

ADDITIONAL MATERIALS

- Digital flashcards
- Digital wordcards
- Extra classroom materials: magazines to cut out pictures of people of different ages

FIND OUT

OPENING ACTIVITIES

- Draw the outline of a spider diagram on the board. In the centre, draw a large circle for the name of a vertebrate group. Around the circle have smaller circles labelled: *Respiration, Nutrition, Reproduction, Movement, Protective covering* and *Body parts.* Divide the class into five groups. Assign each of them a vertebrate group. Tell pupils to work together to fill in the spider diagram with the details of their particular group. Say **What can we put for in the reproduction circle for mammals?** (*Viviparous*) **What about protective covering for amphibians?** (*Moist skin*) When the groups have completed their spider diagrams, invite them to use it to explain the characteristics to the rest of the class.
- Revise key points of the invertebrate lesson by playing *Simon says.* Tell pupils to listen carefully because if they make a mistake they are out of the game. The winner is the one who stays in the game the longest. Suggestions: *Simon says put your hands on your head if a snail has a shell. Simon says stand up if myriapods have lots of legs. Simon says cross your arms if molluscs have an exoskeleton. Sit down!*

MAIN ACTIVITIES

Page 62, Study skills

1 Copy and complete

- Remind pupils that when we organise new information, it is easier to understand and remember it.
- Focus pupils' attention on the concept map and ask them to tell you what the missing words are. Encourage them to make full sentences, such as *The vertebrate group is made up of amphibians, reptiles, fish, birds and mammals*. Tell pupils to copy and complete the concept map in their notebooks.

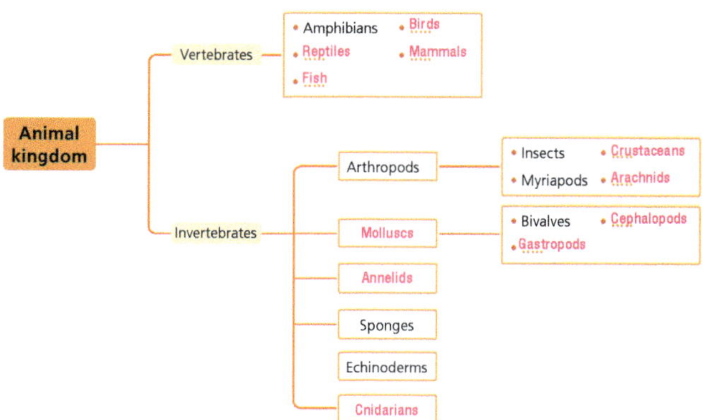

2 Make invertebrate cards to practise spelling.

- Pupils already know how to cut the card to make the wordcards. Explain that invertebrate names are difficult to learn and remember so these cards will help them memorise words which are difficult to spell.
- Explain that pupils should write the name on one side of the card and draw a picture on the other side. Encourage pupils to take their time when drawing the invertebrates, as the illustrations can help them to remember the words. Check that they have spelt the words on their cards correctly.
- When the activity is completed, ask pupils to work with a partner. Tell pupils to take it in turns to show the picture and to identify and spell the name.

Page 63, Review

Note: This part of the review can be done with minimal teacher guidance. You may wish to work through the activities as a class or in small groups or partners. Alternatively, you can ask pupils to do them individually as self-evaluation. This review could also be done as homework.

1 Identify the animal group by reading the definitions.

a. Mammals

b. Fish

c. Amphibians

2 Copy the definitions and order the letters.

a. Exoskeleton

b. Metamorphosis

c. Ovoviviparous

3 True or false? Copy the sentences and correct the ones that are false.

a. False. Birds are oviparous.

b. False. Most reptiles are carnivores.

c . True.

4 Ask and answer questions about the animals in this unit with a partner.

- Before pupils start this activity, make sure they understand that they can ask other questions apart from *Is it …?* and *Does it …?* Explain that pupils can also use other structures such as *Can it …? Has it got …?*
- Ask pupils to write the names of the animals they have chosen on a piece of paper before they begin the activity. This will prevent pupils from changing the animal in the middle of the activity.

Activity Book answers / Audio CD1 track list

20

UNIT 4 Animals

1 Tick (✓) the correct option.

	vertebrates	vertebrates and invertebrates	invertebrates
a. They have a life cycle: they are born, they grow, they reproduce and they die.		✓	
b. They do not have a backbone.			✓
c. They have a backbone and an internal skeleton.	✓		
d. They are consumers.		✓	
e. If they do not reproduce, their species will die and become extinct.		✓	

2 Write the correct vertebrate group and match the sentences to the photos.

a. Birds are warm-blooded. They have wings, feathers and beaks.
b. Amphibians are cold-blooded. They are born in water, with gills, and move to land when they grow lungs and legs.
c. Mammals are warm-blooded and have fur or hair. Their babies drink their mother's milk until they can find their own food.
d. Reptiles are cold-blooded and their bodies are covered in scales.
e. Fish are cold-blooded. They live in water and breathe with gills.

b frog — e manta ray — c gorilla — d turtle — a goldfinch

3 Rewrite the sentences with the correct information.

a. Herbivores eat meat and carnivores eat plants. — Herbivores eat plants and carnivores eat meat.
b. Consumers produce their own food. — Animals are consumers.
c. Mammals, birds and fish are carnivores. — Mammals, birds and fish can be carnivores, herbivores or omnivores.
d. Most amphibians and reptiles are herbivores. — Most amphibians and reptiles are carnivores.

20

21

4 Complete the texts about how animals eat. Match the texts to the pictures.

~~chew~~ ~~short~~ ~~flat~~ ~~hooked~~ ~~digested~~ ~~thin~~ ~~sharp~~ ~~chambers~~ ~~nuts~~

d — a — e

a. Carnivores have long, sharp teeth to help them catch and eat other animals.
b. Herbivores have lots of flat teeth for grinding plants.
c. Ruminants have four chambers in their stomachs. When they eat, their food goes to the first chamber and is partly digested. Then, the food returns to their mouth and the ruminants chew it again before swallowing it and finishing the digestion process.
d. Birds like eagles have sharp, hooked beaks for eating meat.
e. Birds like sparrows have short beaks for eating seeds and nuts.
f. Birds like hummingbirds have long, thin beaks for drinking nectar from flowers.

f — b — c

5 Choose the correct option and order the stages of respiration.

Respiration in fish

1 Water enters the body through the *gills* / (*mouth*).
3 Waste (*carbon dioxide*) / *oxygen* leaves the body through the gills.
2 The oxygen is absorbed into the blood through *veins* / (*capillaries*) in the gills.

Respiration in reptiles, birds and mammals

2 Blood cells absorb the *carbon dioxide* / (*oxygen*) from the lungs and transport it around the body.
3 Waste carbon dioxide leaves the body through the *diaphragm* / (*lungs*).
1 Air passes into the (*lungs*) / *gills*.

21

UNIT 4

22

6 Complete the sentences about respiration in amphibians.

a. When they are young, amphibians are aquatic animals. They take in the oxygen they need from the water through their gills.
b. During metamorphosis, their gills close and they develop lungs.
c. Adult amphibians can absorb oxygen and expel carbon dioxide through their moist skin.

7 Complete the texts about different types of reproduction.

~~egg~~ ~~birth~~ ~~embryo~~ ~~viviparous~~ ~~inside~~ ~~live~~ ~~ovoviviparous~~ ~~offspring~~ ~~oviparous~~

a. Most mammals are viviparous. The embryo develops inside the mother and she gives birth to live offspring.
b. Birds, fish, reptiles and amphibians are oviparous animals. The embryo grows outside the female's body inside an egg, which hatches into new offspring.
c. A few species are ovoviviparous. These animals produce eggs but the eggs develop and hatch inside the mother. Later the mother gives birth to live offspring.

8 Identify the parts of these invertebrates.

1. claws
2. antennae
3. cephalothorax
4. abdomen
5. wings
6. thorax

22

23

9 Complete the chart about invertebrates.

Arthropods

~~tarantula~~ ~~crustacean~~ ~~arachnid~~ ~~centipede~~ ~~beetle~~ ~~myriapod~~ ~~crab~~ ~~insect~~

crustacean	arachnid	insect	myriapod
crab	tarantula	beetle	centipede

Molluscs

~~cephalopod~~ ~~mussels~~ ~~gastropod~~ ~~squid~~ ~~bivalve~~ ~~snail~~

gastropod	cephalopod	bivalve
snail	squid	mussels

Other invertebrates

starfish cnidarian jellyfish annelid fireworm echinoderm ~~sponges~~

sponges	annelid	cnidarian	echinoderm
	fireworm	jellyfish	starfish

10 Choose the correct word.

a. (*Myriapods*) / *Arachnids* / *Gastropods* have long, thin, segmented bodies. They live in dark, damp places.
b. *Insects* / *Echinoderms* / (*Cephalopods*) have large heads and tentacles. They live in water.
c. *Arachnids* / (*Insects*) / *Starfish* have three body parts: a head, a thorax and an abdomen. They have two antennae, three pairs of legs and usually have wings.

23

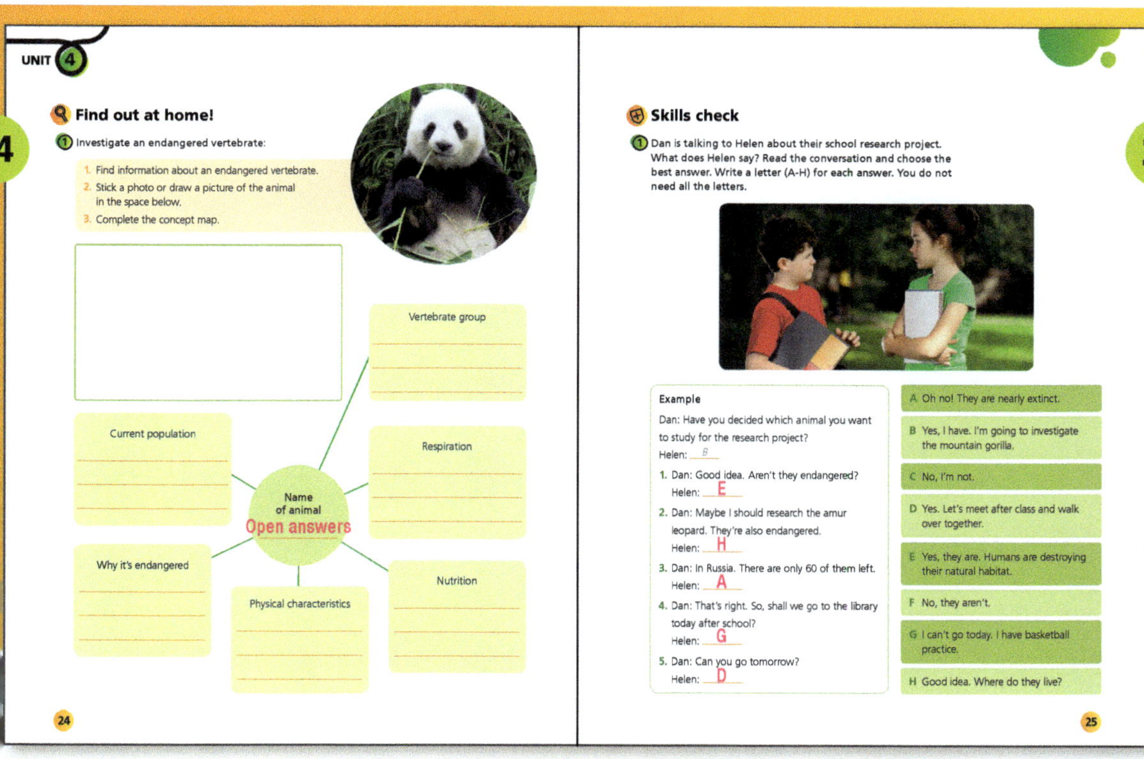
UNIT 4

4

Find out at home!

1 Investigate an endangered vertebrate:

1. Find information about an endangered vertebrate.
2. Stick a photo or draw a picture of the animal in the space below.
3. Complete the concept map.

Vertebrate group

Current population

Respiration

Name of animal

Open answers

Why it's endangered

Nutrition

Physical characteristics

24

25

Skills check

1 Dan is talking to Helen about their school research project. What does Helen say? Read the conversation and choose the best answer. Write a letter (A-H) for each answer. You do not need all the letters.

Example

Dan: Have you decided which animal you want to study for the research project?

Helen: B

1. Dan: Good idea. Aren't they endangered?
   Helen: E
2. Dan: Maybe I should research the amur leopard. They're also endangered.
   Helen: H
3. Dan: In Russia. There are only 60 of them left.
   Helen: A
4. Dan: That's right. So, shall we go to the library today after school?
   Helen: G
5. Dan: Can you go tomorrow?
   Helen: D

A Oh no! They are nearly extinct.

B Yes, I have. I'm going to investigate the mountain gorilla.

C No, I'm not.

D Yes. Let's meet after class and walk over together.

E Yes, they are. Humans are destroying their natural habitat.

F No, they aren't.

G I can't go today. I have basketball practice.

H Good idea. Where do they live?

25

Unit 4 Audio CD1 track list

TRACK	ACTIVITY
39	**Pupil's Book page 51,** Unit introduction
40	**Pupil's Book page 51,** Song *Animals reproduce*
41	**Pupil's Book page 52,** Story: *A trip to the Natural Science Museum*
42	**Pupil's Book page 54,** Vertebrate nutrition
43	**Pupil's Book page 55,** Vertebrate respiration
44	**Pupil's Book page 56,** Vertebrate reproduction
45	**Pupil's Book page 57,** Oviparous, viviparous and ovoviviparous animals

TRACK	ACTIVITY
46	**Pupil's Book page 57,** Oviparous animals
47	**Pupil's Book page 57,** Viviparous animals
48	**Pupil's Book page 57,** Ovoviviparous animals
49	**Pupil's Book page 58,** Invertebrates
50	**Pupil's Book page 59,** Arthropods
51	**Pupil's Book page 59,** Molluscs
52	**Pupil's Book page 59,** Other invertebrate groups

UNIT 5 Plants

CONTENT	EVALUATION CRITERIA
Plants.	Know the characteristics of and classify plants.
Agriculture.	Observe and identify the principal characteristics of agriculture.
First approaches to scientific activity and the scientific method. Use of different information sources (direct and indirect). Use ICTs.	Obtain relevant information about specific phenomena, make predictions, integrate information from direct and indirect observation and communicate the results.
First approaches to simple experiments and investigations.	Conjecture as to the results of natural occurrences and of simple experiments and investigations.
Individual and group work.	Work independently and proactively and develop strategies for working in a group.
Planning a project and presenting a report.	Carry out a project and present a report.

LEARNING STANDARDS	KEY COMPETENCES	PAGES
Observes, directly and indirectly, knows the characteristics of and classifies plants.	MST, LTL	66-73
Observes and identifies the principal characteristics of agriculture.	MST	75
With help, selects and organises specific and relevant information; analyses it and draws conclusions; reflects on the experience and the process; presents the results.	MST, LTL	67, 74, 75
Use books, libraries, etc. and collaborate in the care and maintenance of all the materials available in the school and the classroom.	MST, LTL	64-77
Shows autonomy in the planning of activities and tasks and shows initiative in decision taking.	LTL, AUT	67, 74, 75
With help, carries out simple experiments or investigations, and conjectures as to the results.	MST, LTL, AUT	74, 75
Uses strategies to help their own learning, as well as asking for help and information.	LTL, AUT	67, 74-76
First approaches to cooperative learning.	SOC, LTL	65, 75
Begins observation, using relevant instruments and consulting written documents and images.	LTL, AUT	67, 74
Shows autonomy and proactiveness in the planning of and carrying out of actions.	AUT	74, 75
Presents work clearly and in an organised fashion.	LIN, LTL, AUT	74, 75
With help, carries out a project and presents a report, using paper and/or digital means, collecting information from different sources, presenting the results orally and with the support of images and short texts.	LIN, LTL, AUT, DIG	74, 75

UNIT INFORMATION

UNIT SUMMARY

In this unit, pupils will review and extend their knowledge of plants. They will learn how the parts of the plant help it perform the life processes of nutrition, respiration and reproduction. At the beginning of the unit, pupils will revise parts of a plant and simple classification. This subject area is covered in the opening illustration with the help of the course characters, Carla and Alex, who are on a school trip to the botanical gardens. The school trip continues in the story and, on their return to school, Alex and Carla carry out a *School trip project* to review the parts of the plants they have learned. These opening pages are designed to test pupils' prior knowledge and ease them into the subject matter of the unit, provoking interest and participation. They will move on to study photosynthesis and compare it to respiration. Pupils will study reproduction in flowering plants and learn about pollination. They will also be introduced to reproduction in non-flowering plants. This is a new area of study for the pupils and one that requires a high level of language and knowledge acquisition. Therefore, the aim of this unit should be to *introduce* pupils to the subject matter, encouraging the pupils to compare and contrast plants and processes.

EXPERIMENT

Find out

In the *Find out* activity on page 74, your pupils will prepare a field log about the plants in their neighbourhood.

The pupils will need:

- scrap paper
- drawing materials
- glue
- camera (optional)

Further ideas

The pupils could also include samples of leaves, seeds, flowers, bark rubbings, etc. to illustrate their log.

VALUES AND ATTITUDES

In this unit, your pupils will learn to appreciate that plants are living things and how important they are for the planet. Throughout the unit, try to encourage pupils to think not only about how we need plants for food, medicine and clothes but also the importance of the production of oxygen through photosynthesis.

Think about it

The *Think about it* page in this unit focuses on rainforests. The intention of this section is to focus on the importance of rainforests and to make the pupils aware of the consequences for the planet should they disappear. A link can be made to Social Science by including map work and physical geography. The pupils are also encouraged to research further information.

EVALUATION MATERIAL

These documents can be downloaded from the *Teachers* section of the digital component and printed.

The materials include:

- **Unit diagnostic test:** provides an overview of the unit and allows you to assess the pupils' prior knowledge.
- **End-of-unit test:** in addition to the *Review* section at the end of each unit, this summative test can be used to evaluate pupils' progress after studying the unit content.
- **Class unit evaluation grid:** based on the evaluation criteria and learning standards of the unit.

DIGITAL RESOURCES

Presentations

- **Unit summary**: a simple slide presentation with text, images and audio to review the main ideas of the unit. It can be used at the beginning of the unit to test pupils' prior knowledge of the unit content or at the end of the unit as a revision tool.
- **Find out:** a slide presentation of the unit's Find out page with text, photos and audio. The slide presentation is perfect for a heads-up class, showing the steps one by one. Use this tool to get the pupils to predict the next steps (with their books closed) or to focus their attention on each step as they carry out the project themselves.

Activities

Activities vary per unit and include the following:

- **Memory game:** useful activity for reviewing key vocabulary and modelling pronunciation.
- **Labelling:** pupils label a diagram by dragging and dropping key terms.
- **Spelling:** pupils drag and drop letters to spell key terms.
- **Read and reveal:** pupils read sentences and guess the missing words, which are revealed by clicking the spaces.
- **Classification:** pupils drag and drop concepts and key terms in a simple classification table.
- **Wordsearch:** pupils find key terms hidden in the wordsearch.
- **Definitions:** pupils drag and drop words to complete definitions.
- **Song lyrics:** Listen to the song *Plants* and follow the lyrics line by line.
- **Posters** Attractive and informative posters to display in class. You can use them to review key concepts and vocabulary.
- **Videos** Use the video links in this unit to present content in a dynamic, real-life context while reinforcing the pupils' listening skills.
- **Teachers**
- **Digital flashcards and wordcards:** topics include *Plant nutrition, Plant reproduction* and *Plant classification*.
- **Downloadable pdfs:** evaluation tests, evaluation grids, templates, useful links and further information.

PAGES 64–65 Plants

PAGE SUMMARY

The aim of the unit opener is to develop your pupils' observation skills and find out what they already know about the topic of the unit. Use the picture to elicit vocabulary related to plants, parts of plants and what things they need to grow. Encourage the pupils to describe what is going on in the scene and to describe the various characters and objects. Get your pupils to work in groups to complete activities 1–4 and to have fun listening to the song and completing activity 5.

LANGUAGE

- Question words: *who, how many, which, where, etc.*
- Prepositions of place: *in, on, under, next to, behind, in front of*
- *There is / are*
- Present continuous: *She is running*
- Vocabulary: *roots, stem, leaves, flowers, trunk, branches, tree, bush, grass, fruit*

ADDITIONAL MATERIALS

- Digital flashcards
- Digital wordcards

OPENING ACTIVITIES

- Write the word *Plants* on the board and ask the pupils to tell you all the words they can remember related to plants. Write the words randomly on the board as they call them out. Focus the pupils' attention on the board. Point out that the words they have given can be organised into different groups. Ask **Which words can be put with the word 'roots'?** (*Stem leaves, flower, seed and fruit*) Encourage pupils to classify the words into groups such as *parts of the plant, types of plants, what plants need and what plants give us.*
- Alternatively, use the interactive whiteboard writing tools and ask pupils to come up to the board, mark an area of the picture and describe what they can see. Help them to produce full, correct sentences.

MAIN ACTIVITIES

Page 65, Unit introduction (CD1 track 53)

- Read the unit introduction at the top of page 65. Pupils can do a choral reading of the text (see *Helpful tips*, pages 20–23).

- You can play the audio of the unit introduction first, with the pupils reading along with it, and then ask one or two pupils to read out loud. This way, pupils will feel more self-assured when it comes to pronouncing new words.
- Divide pupils into small groups to answer the questions on page 65. Then invite different groups to compare their answers with each other.

1 How can we classify the different plants in the picture?

- Elicit the types of plants the pupils studied in the previous year. They should know the words trees, bushes and grasses. Place these wordcards on the board. Extend the question by asking the pupils to explain how these plants are different from each other. (*A tree is bigger. A tree has a trunk, etc.*) *Trees and grasses*

2 Which different plant parts can you identify in the picture?

- Elicit the words *roots, stem, trunk, flower, leaves* and *fruit*. Encourage pupils to describe where they can see them in the picture. You may wish to extend this activity by asking the pupils to name the plants they can see in the picture. *Roots, stem, trunk, flower, and leaves.*

3 How do the plants absorb water from the soil?

- Ask pupils to say which of their answers from question 3 absorb water from the soil? (*The roots.*) Ask them to look at the picture on pages 64 and 65 and to point at some roots. *We can see the roots of the plant that Alex has in his hands.*

4 How do plants produce energy?

- Ask pupils **Do plants eat like animals?** (*No, the majority of plants do not consumer other living things.*) Explain that plants make their own food and produce their own energy. Tell them that they do this using a process called *photosynthesis*. Pupils can use reference books or the internet to find which elements are involved in this process.

5 Listen and say which word is not in the song.

- Focus the pupils' attention on the six photos. Ask them to read and repeat the words. Check for understanding.

CD1 • track 54

Plants can be grasses, bushes or even trees
Plants have roots, a stem and leaves
Some plants even have flowers
Trees have a trunk and branches
Bushes have branches too
But grasses never do
Plants can be grasses, bushes or even trees
Plants have fruits, a stem and leaves
Some plants even have flowers
Trees have a trunk and branches
Bushes have branches too
But grasses never do

- Play the song *Plants* **(CD1 track 54)** and ask pupils to point to the words that they hear. Then play the song a second time and encourage pupils to sing along (you can use the *Song lyrics* section on the digital component to display the song line by line and listen to the song). *Fruit*

+ CLOSING ACTIVITIES

- Choose a plant in the picture and describe it for the class. The pupil who guesses the plant correctly either by name or by pointing to it, then chooses another plant to describe.

+ CLOSING ACTIVITIES

- Show images of different types of plants (water lilies, deciduous and evergreen trees, cacti, roses, ivy, etc.) and encourage the pupils to talk about the different adaptations they can see.

ANSWERS AT A GLANCE

1. Trees and grasses.
2. Roots, stem, trunk, flower and leaves.
3. Plants absorb water with their roots.
4. Plants produce energy through the process of photosynthesis.
5. Fruit.

PAGES 66–67 A trip to the botanical gardens

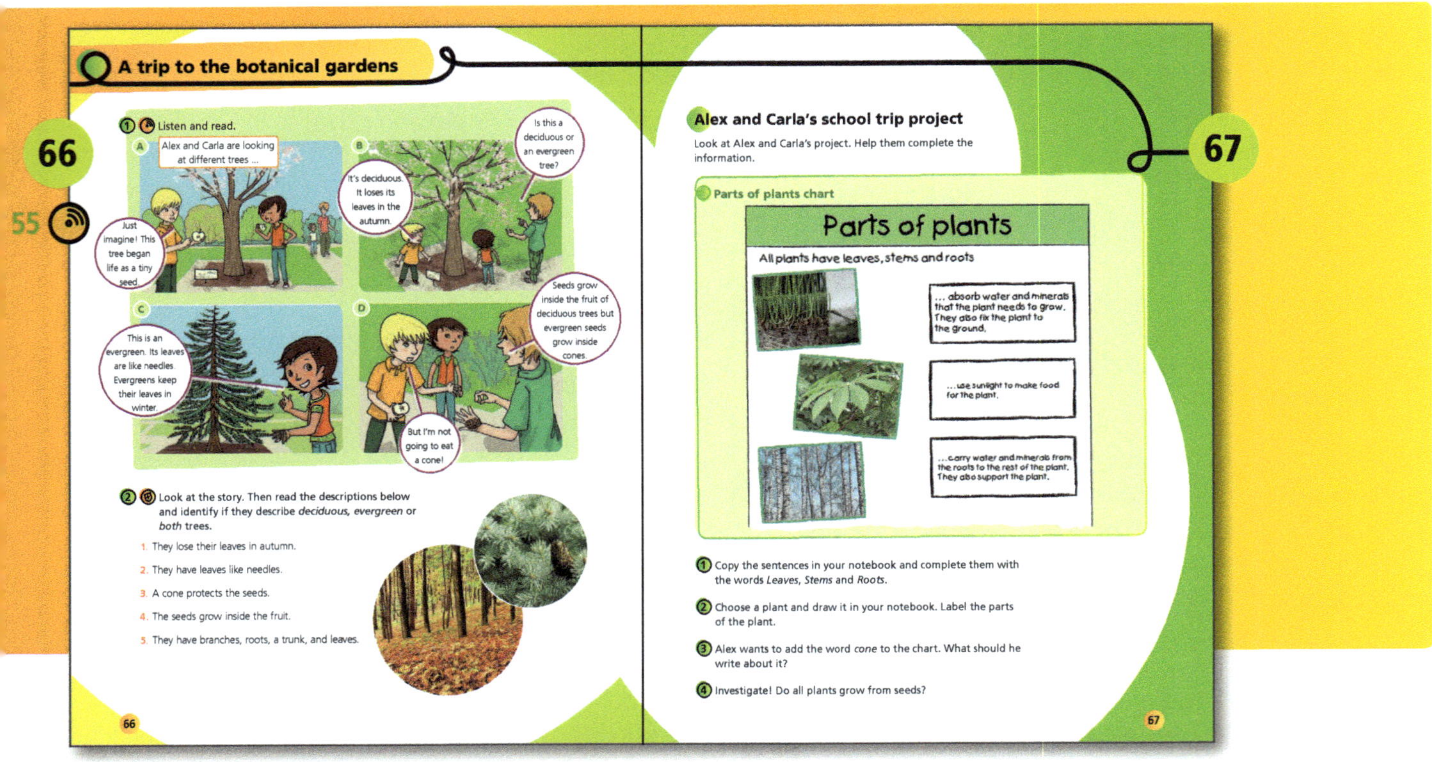

PAGE SUMMARY

This double-page spread opens with a story in which your pupils have the opportunity to see Carla and Alex at a particular moment of their school trip to the botanical gardens. Carla and Alex are talking to a gardener and showing their knowledge of deciduous and evergreen trees. The story is reinforced with an exam style matching activity that is related to the story. On page 67, the pupils can study Carla and Alex's school trip project about the functions of the parts of a plant.

LANGUAGE

- Present simple
- Comparative adjectives: *taller, shorter*, etc.
- Vocabulary: *deciduous, evergreen, fruit, cone, seed, leaves, needles, trunk, branches, roots, stem*

ADDITIONAL MATERIALS

- Digital flashcards
- Digital wordcards
- Extra classroom materials: magazines for cutting out pictures of plants

OPENING ACTIVITIES

- Play the *Plants* song **(CD1 track 54)** and encourage pupils to sing along.
- Draw a picture of a flower and a tree on the board. Invite pupils to label the pictures with the word cards. (*Stem, roots, leaves, flower, trunk and branches.*)
- Write the following words on the board: **Grasses/ Bushes/ Trees are taller than/shorter than grasses/ bushes/trees**. Encourage the pupils to make sentences using the structures on the board. For example, *Trees are taller than bushes.*

MAIN ACTIVITIES

1 Listen and read. (CD1 track 55)

- Draw the pupils' attention to the story at the top of page 66 and explain to them that they are going to listen to a story about Alex and Carla's trip to the botanical gardens. Say **Let's listen and read**. Play the audio.
- Ask pupils to look at each of the illustrations and describe what is happening in each one using their own words. For example, *Carla is eating an apple*; *Alex is looking at the seeds inside his apple.*

- Divide pupils into groups of three and ask them to choose a character from the story – Alex, Carla or the gardener. Pupils then read their part of the story aloud in their small group. You can invite a group to the front of the class to act the story out.

2 Look at the story. Then read the descriptions below and identify if they describe *deciduous, evergreen* or *both* trees.

- This activity aims to introduce some new vocabulary, reinforce what pupils have learned in the story and refresh concepts studied in previous levels. Before asking pupils to do the activity individually, go through the sentences as a class activity. Draw the outline of a deciduous tree and an evergreen tree on the board. Tell pupils to put their hands on their heads if the sentence is about deciduous trees, to stand up for evergreen and to clap once for both types of trees. *1-Deciduous 2-Evergreen 3-Evergreen 4 -Deciduous 5-Both*

SCHOOL TRIP PROJECT

- Before the pupils open their books, elicit the different parts of the plant included in the photos on page 67. Ask a volunteer to come to the board and draw the roots. Ask another volunteer to draw the stem. Finally ask a volunteer to draw the leaves. Invite the pupils to add other parts to the plant. Ask other pupils to label the pictures with the wordcards.
- Explain to pupils that following their trip to the botanical gardens, Alex and Carla have done a project to summarise what they have learned about parts of the plant.
- Tell pupils to look at the photos on page 67. Ask for volunteers to identify the photos and to read the descriptions.

1 Copy the sentences in your notebook and complete them with the words *Leaves, Stems* and *Roots*.

- Elicit the answers and ask pupils to put up their hand if they agree with the answer. Now tell them to do activity 1 in their notebooks. *Answers at a glance*

2 Choose a plant and draw it in your notebook. Label the parts of the plant.

- This can be a free activity or you could prepare an outline drawing of a plant for the pupils. You could also project an image for them to copy. *Open answer*

3 Alex wants to add the word *cone* to the chart. What should he write about it?

- Pupils can refer to the comic to answer this question. Invite volunteers to write definitions on the board. (*Evergreen seeds grow inside a cone. Deciduous seeds grow inside a fruit*). Encourage peer correction of spelling if appropriate. *Open answer*

4 Investigate! Do all plants grow from seeds?

- Not all plants produce seeds. Flowering plants and evergreen trees produce seeds. *Ferns and mosses produce spores. Others grow from stolons*

+ CLOSING ACTIVITIES

- Hand out the wordcards for *tree, grass, leaves, roots, stem, branches, trunk, evergreen* and *deciduous* to different pupils in the class. Give definitions and ask the pupils who have the correct wordcard to stand up and read it. Ask pupils if they are right or not. Collect in the cards and hand them out again. This time encourage pupils to give a definition for their word.

+ EXTRA IDEAS

- Pupils find pictures of different plants at home and make a display. They then label the parts they can see.

ANSWERS AT A GLANCE

Page 66

2 1-Deciduous 2-Evergreen 3-Evergreen 4 -Deciduous 5-Both

Page 67

1 First paragraph – roots.
Second paragraph – leaves.
Third paragraph – stem.

2 Open answer.

3 Open answer.

4 Ferns and mosses produce spores. Others grow from stolons.

PAGES 68–69 Plant nutrition

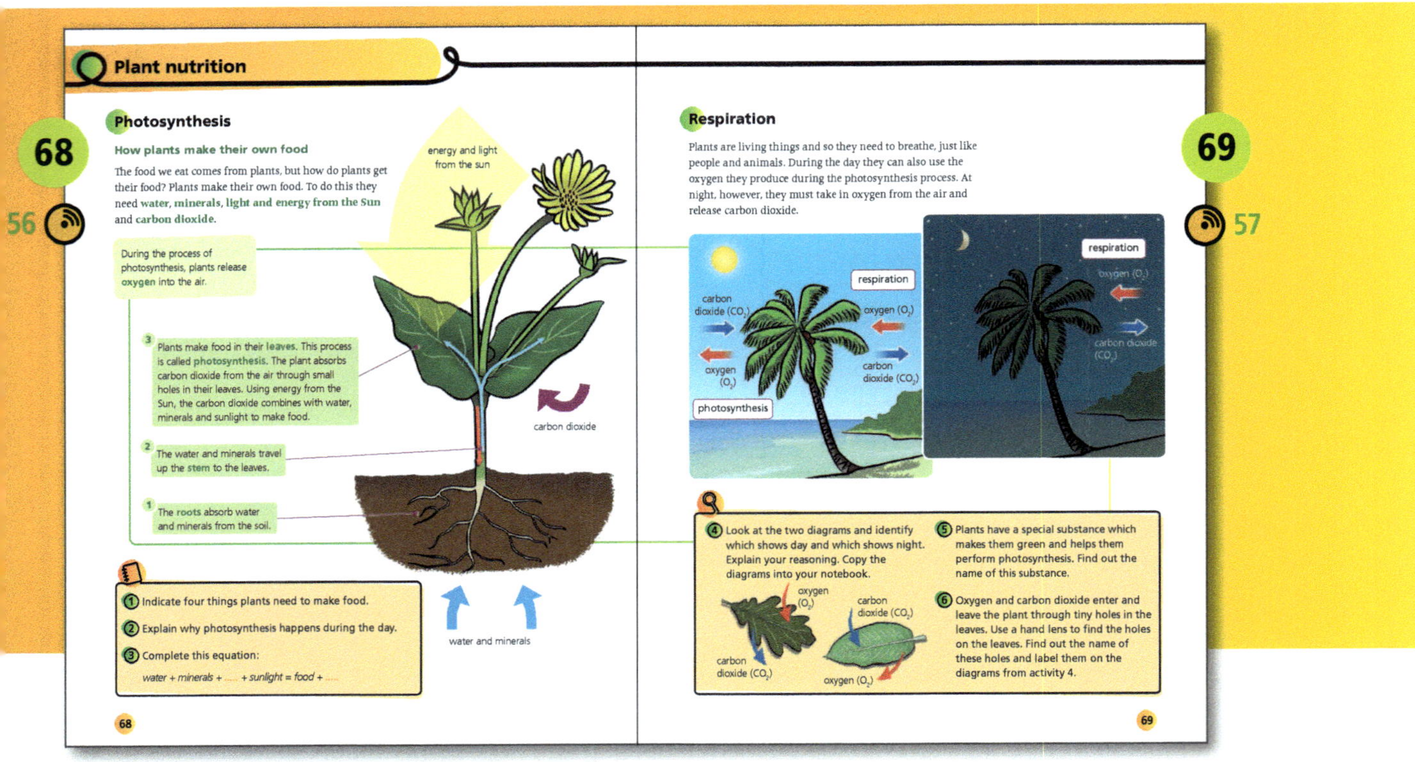

PAGE SUMMARY

This double-page spread introduces pupils to the processes of nutrition and respiration in plants. There is a lot of new vocabulary and concepts on this double page. Do not expect pupils at this stage to absorb all of the information; the main learning aim is to understand how plants make their own food and how this process is related to the process of respiration. The pups will learn the particular roles that different parts of the plant have in these processes.

LANGUAGE

- Questions words: *where, what, why, etc*
- Present tense for processes
- Linking words: *first, next, then, after that, finally*
- Vocabulary: *nutrition, respiration, photosynthesis, light, energy, sunlight, minerals, water, oxygen*

ADDITIONAL MATERIALS

- Digital flashcards
- Digital wordcards
- Extra materials: scrap paper for diagrams, hand lenses, leaves, white flower or celery, water, food colouring

OPENING ACTIVITIES

- If you are using an interactive whiteboard, click on the opening text on page 54 and highlight the first two sentences: *Unlike plants, animals cannot make their own food. They eat other living things*. Alternatively, ask pupils to open their books on page 54 and read the first two sentences to the class. Ask: **What living things do consumers eat?** *(Other animals, plants or both animals and plants.)*

MAIN ACTIVITIES

Page 68, Photosynthesis (CD1 track 56)

- Before you read the text, ask pupils to look at the illustration of the plant. Tell them to trace the path of the elements with their finger as you read. Read the text boxes on page 68 and check understanding. **What do the roots absorb? How can the water and minerals travel to the leaves?**

1 Indicate four things plants need to make food.

- Read a list of elements and ask the pupils to stand up when they hear something that the plant needs to make food. For example, say ***Sunlight, snow, oxygen, carbon dioxide, plant pot, butter, minerals, water, sand***. *Water, minerals, sunlight and carbon dioxide*

2 Explain why photosynthesis happens during the day.

- Ask the pupils to repeat the things necessary for photosynthesis. Ask **Which one isn't present at night?** (*Sunlight*) You can give scaffolding to help pupils construct their answer. (Photosynthesis happens during the day and not at night because the plant needs______ .) *Sunlight is necessary for photosynthesis and there is no sunlight at night.*

3 Complete this equation: water + minerals +..... + sunlight = food +.....

- Ask pupils to place the wordcards *water, minerals, sunlight* and *food* on the board. Add the + and the = signs. Invite volunteers to add the missing words. *Carbon dioxide and oxygen*

Page 69, Respiration (CD1 track 57)

- Before you read the text, ask pupils to look at the two illustrations. Ask **Which gases is the plant absorbing in the first picture? Why does the plant need carbon dioxide?**
- Now focus their attention on the second illustration. **Which process can you see in the second picture? Why isn't the plant making its own food now?**
- Ask pupils to take turns to read the text to their partner.

4 Look at the two diagrams and identify which shows day and which shows night. Explain your reasoning. Copy the diagrams into your notebook.

- Ask pupils to draw one of the leaves on a piece of scrap paper and to pass it to their partner. Their partner says whether it shows day or night. Now ask them to complete the activity in their notebooks. *The diagram on the left shows night. The diagram on the right shows day.*

5 Plants have a special substance which makes them green and helps them perform photosynthesis. Find out the name of this substance.

- This activity can be done at home with the help of parents or in small study groups on a computer or in the library. *Chlorophyll*

6 Oxygen and carbon dioxide enter and leave the plant through tiny holes in the leaves. Use a magnifying glass to find the holes on the leaves. Find out the name of these holes and label them on the diagrams from activity 4.

- Ask pupils how oxygen and carbon dioxide enter the plant. Arrange the class into small groups and hand out a hand lens and various leaves to each group. Make sure the pupils are looking on the underside of the leaf. Ask them to label them on the diagrams from activity 4. *Stomata are found on the underside of the leaves.*

CLOSING ACTIVITIES

- Write the words *first, next, then, after that* and *finally* on the board. Organise the class into small groups. Tell pupils to look at page 60 and to make a chant describing photosynthesis.

EXTRA IDEAS

- Place a white flower or a stick of celery in a clear container of water. Add a few drops of food colouring to the water. Tell the pupils to observe the plant during the day. They will see the plant change colour as the water travels through it.

ANSWERS AT A GLANCE

1. Water, minerals, sunlight and carbon dioxide
2. Sunlight is necessary for photosynthesis and there is no sunlight at night.
3. Water + minerals + sunlight + carbon dioxide = food + oxygen
4. The diagram on the left shows night. The diagram on the right shows day.
5. Chlorophyll.
6. Stomata are found on the underside of the leaves.

PAGES 70-71 Plant reproduction

70 58

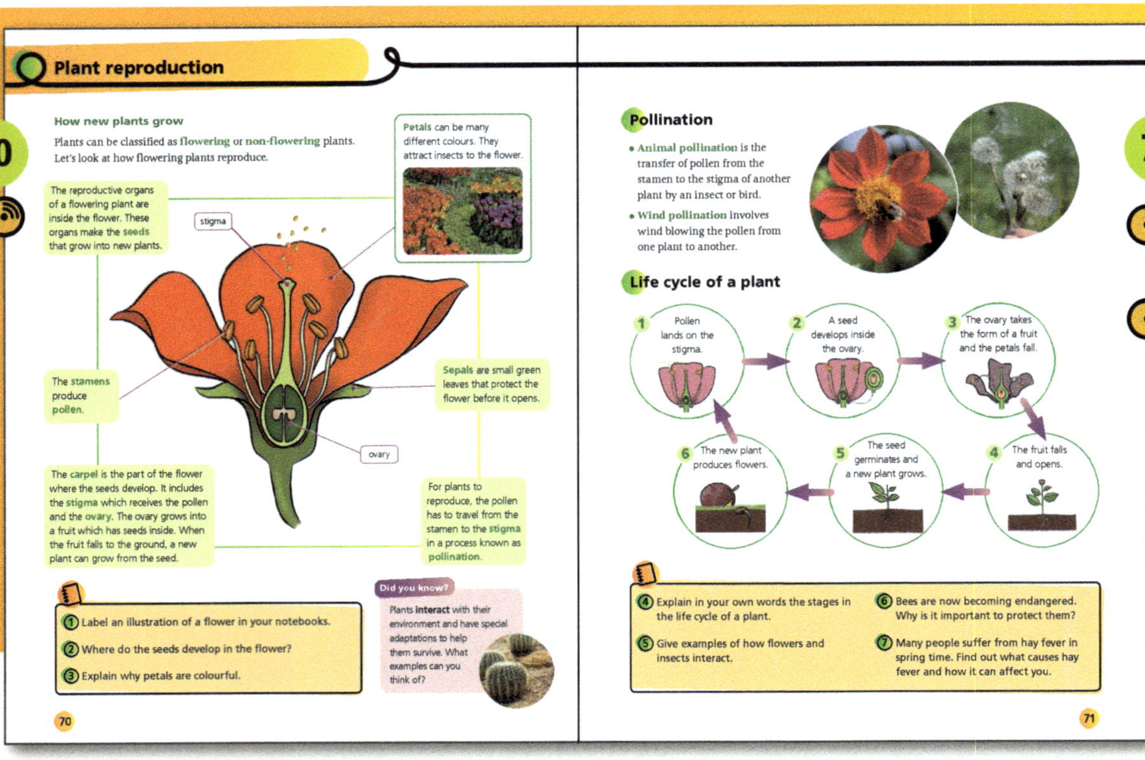

Plant reproduction

How new plants grow

Plants can be classified as **flowering** or **non-flowering** plants. Let's look at how flowering plants reproduce.

The reproductive organs of a flowering plant are inside the flower. These organs make the **seeds** that grow into new plants.

Petals can be many different colours. They attract insects to the flower.

stigma

The **stamens** produce **pollen**.

Sepals are small green leaves that protect the flower before it opens.

ovary

The **carpel** is the part of the flower where the seeds develop. It includes the **stigma** which receives the pollen and the **ovary**. The ovary grows into a fruit which has seeds inside. When the fruit falls to the ground, a new plant can grow from the seed.

For plants to reproduce, the pollen has to travel from the stamen to the **stigma** in a process known as **pollination**.

1. Label an illustration of a flower in your notebooks.
2. Where do the seeds develop in the flower?
3. Explain why petals are colourful.

Did you know?

Plants **interact** with their environment and have special adaptations to help them survive. What examples can you think of?

70

Pollination

- **Animal pollination** is the transfer of pollen from the stamen to the stigma of another plant by an insect or bird.
- **Wind pollination** involves wind blowing the pollen from one plant to another.

Life cycle of a plant

1 Pollen lands on the stigma.

2 A seed develops inside the ovary.

3 The ovary takes the form of a fruit and the petals fall.

4 The fruit falls and opens.

5 The seed germinates and a new plant grows.

6 The new plant produces flowers.

4. Explain in your own words the stages in the life cycle of a plant.
5. Give examples of how flowers and insects interact.
6. Bees are now becoming endangered. Why is it important to protect them?
7. Many people suffer from hay fever in spring time. Find out what causes hay fever and how it can affect you.

71

71 59 60

PAGE SUMMARY

On this double-page spread pupils learn about flowering plant reproduction on page 70 and pollination and revision of the life cycle of a plant on page 71. This subject matter will be quite familiar to them by now. The different parts of the flower, however, will be new vocabulary and should be the focus. Page 71 compares animal and wind pollination before reviewing the life cycle of a plant. The extra activity will give pupils the opportunity to observe and record the plant's life cycle.

LANGUAGE

- Questions words: *where, what, why, etc.*
- Sequence words: *then, next, after that, etc.*
- Present simple
- Vocabulary: *petals, sepals, stamen, carpel, stigma, ovary, fruit, seed, pollen, pollination, transfer*

ADDITIONAL MATERIALS

- Digital flashcards
- Digital wordcards
- Extra activity: beans, plastic cups, cotton wool, water

OPENING ACTIVITIES

- Review the previous lesson about photosynthesis by asking the pupils to describe how a plant makes its food. Point out that nutrition is one of the life processes that living things perform. Ask **What are the other life processes?** (*Reproduction and interaction*) Ask the pupils to talk to their partners about how plants reproduce and interact with the environment.

MAIN ACTIVITIES

Page 70, How new plants grow (CD1 track 58)

- Tell pupils to point to the different parts of the flower in the picture. **Point to the stamens. Point to the sepals.**Now invite volunteers to read the different information boxes to the class. Check understanding. **Where are the reproductive organs of a plant?** (*In the flower*) **What do the stamens produce?** (*Pollen*)

Page 71, Pollination (CD1 track 59)

- Read the text about pollination and ask the pupils to identify the two types of pollination in the photos. Ask pupils to name other animals that help with pollination. (*Bees, butterflies, wasps, birds, etc.*). Elicit from pupils that plants such as grasses use wind pollination because they don't have colourful petals to attract insects.

Page 71, Life cycle of a plant (CD1 track 60)

- Use this activity to encourage pupils to think about how a seed germinates and a plant grows. Invite pupils to read the sentences and copy them on the board. Ask the class to decide how the seed germinates and begins to grow. Guide their discussions by asking questions. **What does a seed need to germinate? Which part grows first? What happens next?**

1 Label an illustration of a flower in your notebooks.

- Copy the diagram of the flower onto the board. Invite pupils to come and label the different parts of the flower with the wordcards. As the pupils place the cards, ask the others to explain the role of each part of the plant. **What do the stamens do?** (*They produce pollen.*) **Why are the sepals important?** (*They protect the flower.*) Now ask the pupils to copy the illustration into their notebook.

2 Where do the seeds develop in the flower?

- Ask the pupils to point to where the seeds develop in the picture on page 70. *In the ovary*

3 Explain why petals are colourful.

- In pairs, ask them to explain in their own words why petals are colourful. *The colourful petals attract the insects.*

4 Explain in your own words the stages in the life cycle of a plant.

- Encourage pupils to draw very simple diagrams in their notebooks. In pairs, ask them to explain in their own words the life cycle of a plant. Ask them to use the linking words: *first, next, then, after that* and *finally* when explaining the cycle. *Open answer*

5 Give examples of how flowers and insects interact.

- Ask pupils for their ideas and record them on the board. See *Answers at a glance*

6 Bees are now becoming endangered. Why is it important to protect them?

- This activity can be done at home with the help of parents or in small study groups on a computer or in the library. *See Answers at a glance*

7 Many people suffer from hay fever in spring time. Find out what causes hay fever and how it can affect you.

- Find out how many pupils suffer from hay fever in the class and which plants cause them problems. Invite them to talk about the effects of this allergy. *Respiratory problems, itching, coughing and sneezing. People are affected by different plants: grasses, olive trees, etc.*

CLOSING ACTIVITIES

- Test pupils on a few basic concepts from pages 70 and 71 using error correction. Ask pupils to correct your mistakes. **The stigma produces pollen. The ovary grows into a seed.**

EXTRA IDEAS

- Give each pupil a transparent plastic cup, some cotton wool and a seed. Tell them to place the seed between the cotton wool and the side of the cup and to water the seed. Place the seeds in a light part of the classroom. Encourage the pupils to observe the germination of their seeds.

ANSWERS AT A GLANCE

1. Diagram in notebooks.
2. In the ovary.
3. The colourful petals attract the insects.
4. Open answer.
5. Possible answers: animals live in and on plants. Animals eat plants. Animals need the oxygen produced by plants. Plants need the carbon dioxide produced by animals. Dead animals make soil fertile.
6. We need bees to pollinate our plant s so that plants reproduce. Most of the plants we use for food are pollinated by bees. Honey is used in medicines.
7. Respiratory problems, itching, coughing and sneezing. People are affected by different plants: grasses, olive trees, etc.

PAGES 72-73 Plant classification

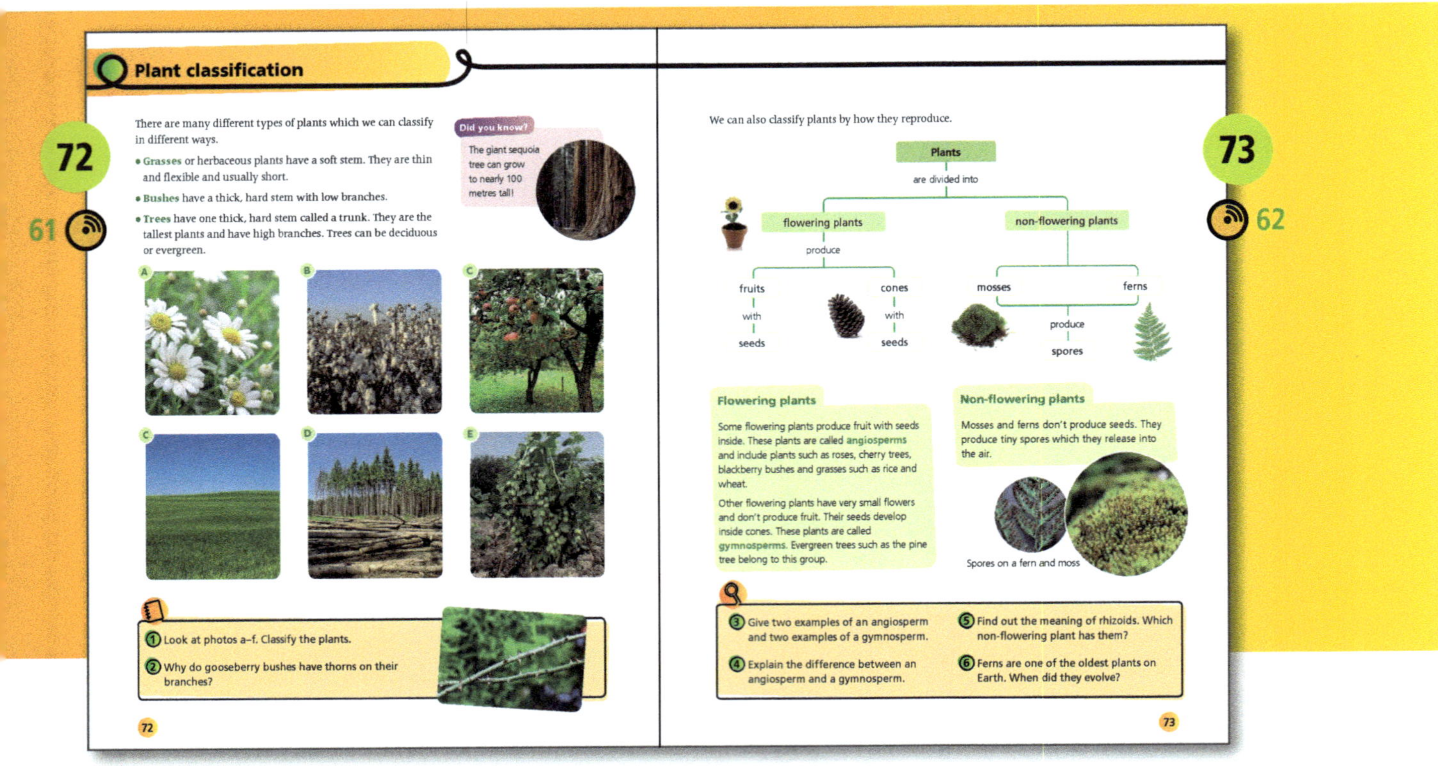

PAGE SUMMARY

On this double-page spread pupils revise how plants are classified. At first they will revise classification by stems. This subject matter will be familiar to them by now. The main learning aim is to further their knowledge of how we classify plants by the way they reproduce. They will be introduced to more advanced vocabulary and they will also be introduced to plants that don't produce seeds, such as ferns and mosses.

LANGUAGE

- Adjectives: *soft, hard, thin, thick, low, high, flexible, herbaceous*
- *Have got / has got*
- Vocabulary: *grasses, bushes, trees, deciduous, evergreen, angiosperm, gymnosperm, mosses, ferns, stem, trunk, branches, fruits, cones, seeds, spores, thorns, soft, hard, thin, thick, low, high, flexible, herbaceous*

ADDITIONAL MATERIALS

- Digital flashcards
- Digital wordcards

OPENING ACTIVITIES

- Hand out a piece of A4 paper to the pupils. Say **I'm thinking of a flower. I'm going to describe it. Can you draw it?** Describe a flower to the pupils. **It's got six, big, red petals. It's got five small sepals. It's got a green carpel and six long stamens.**
- Divide pupils into pairs and ask them to do a picture dictation.
- Ask pupils to think about the parks and gardens in their local area. Ask **What plants are there? Are all the plants the same?** Divide the class into small groups and ask them to talk about the different types of plants they know. When the groups give the names of the plants classify them into groups of grasses, bushes and trees on the board.

MAIN ACTIVITIES

Page 72, Plant classification (CD1 track 61)

- Ask pupils to open their books on page 72 and ask them to cover the text. Invite volunteers to describe a photo and ask the rest of the class to identify the correct photo. Ask the pupils if they know the names of the plants.

- If you are using an interactive whiteboard, click on the opening text on page 72 and highlight the first sentence. *There are many different types of plants which we can classify in different ways*. Ask **How can we classify plants?** (*Grasses, bushes and trees*) Ask pupils to read the texts with their partner. Check understanding and vocabulary.

1 Look at photos a–f. Classify the plants

- Ask the pupils to classify the plants into grasses, bushes and trees with their partner. Record the answers on the board as a chart. *a-grass b-bush c-tree d-grass e-tree f-bush*

2 Why do gooseberry bushes have thorns on their branches?

- Use the photo of the gooseberry bush to explain the meaning of thorns. Encourage pupils to think of other plants that have thorns. (*Roses, blackberries, etc.*)Elicit that *thorns are adaptations to protect the fruit from animals*.

Page 73, We can also classify plants by how they reproduce. (CD1 track 62)

- Focus pupils' attention on the Flowering plants part of the chart and the text underneath. Ask pupils to listen and read. Write the word *angiosperm* on the board and ask for examples of this type of plant. Repeat with *gymnosperm*.
- Now focus their attention on the non-flowering plant text. Ask pupils to listen and read. Ask **Can you name two non-flowering plants?**(*Ferns and mosses*) **What do they produce?** (*Spores*) Explain that spores are tiny cells, much smaller than seeds, which are carried by the wind.

3 Give two examples of an angiosperm and two examples of a gymnosperm.

- Write the pupils' suggestions on the board. *Angiosperms: roses, cherry trees, blackberry bushes, gooseberry bushes, rice and wheat. Gymnosperm: pine trees, fir trees*

4 Explain the difference between an angiosperm and a gymnosperm.

- Write the beginning of the sentences on the board and invite pupils to come up to complete them. **Angiosperms produce ______________ inside ______________. Gymnosperms ______________ inside ______________.** *Angiosperms produce seeds inside fruit. Gymnosperms produce seeds inside cones.*

5 Find out the meaning of rhizoids. Which non-flowering plant has them?

- This activity can be done at home with the help of parents or in small study groups on a computer or in the library. *Mosses have rhizoids. They function like roots but aren't roots.*

6 Ferns are one of the oldest plants on Earth. When did they evolve?

- This activity can also be done at home with the help of parents or in small study groups on a computer or in the library. *During the Devonian Era (345 – 435 million years ago).*

CLOSING ACTIVITIES

- Play *Repeat if true*. Pupils listen to your statements. If they think the statement is true, they repeat it. If they think the statement is false, they shake their heads and remain silent. Invite a pupil to correct the false statement.

ANSWERS AT A GLANCE

1. a-grass b-bush c-trees d-grass e-trees f-bush
2. Thorns are adaptations to protect the fruit from animals.
3. Angiosperms: Roses, cherry trees, blackberry bushes, gooseberry bushes, rice and wheat. Gymnosperm: Evergreens – pine trees, fir trees
4. Angiosperms produce seeds inside fruit. Gymnosperms produce seeds inside cones.
5. 5 Mosses have rhizoids. They function like roots but aren't roots.
6. 6 During the Devonian Era (345 – 435 million years ago).

PAGES 74-75 Find out / Think about it

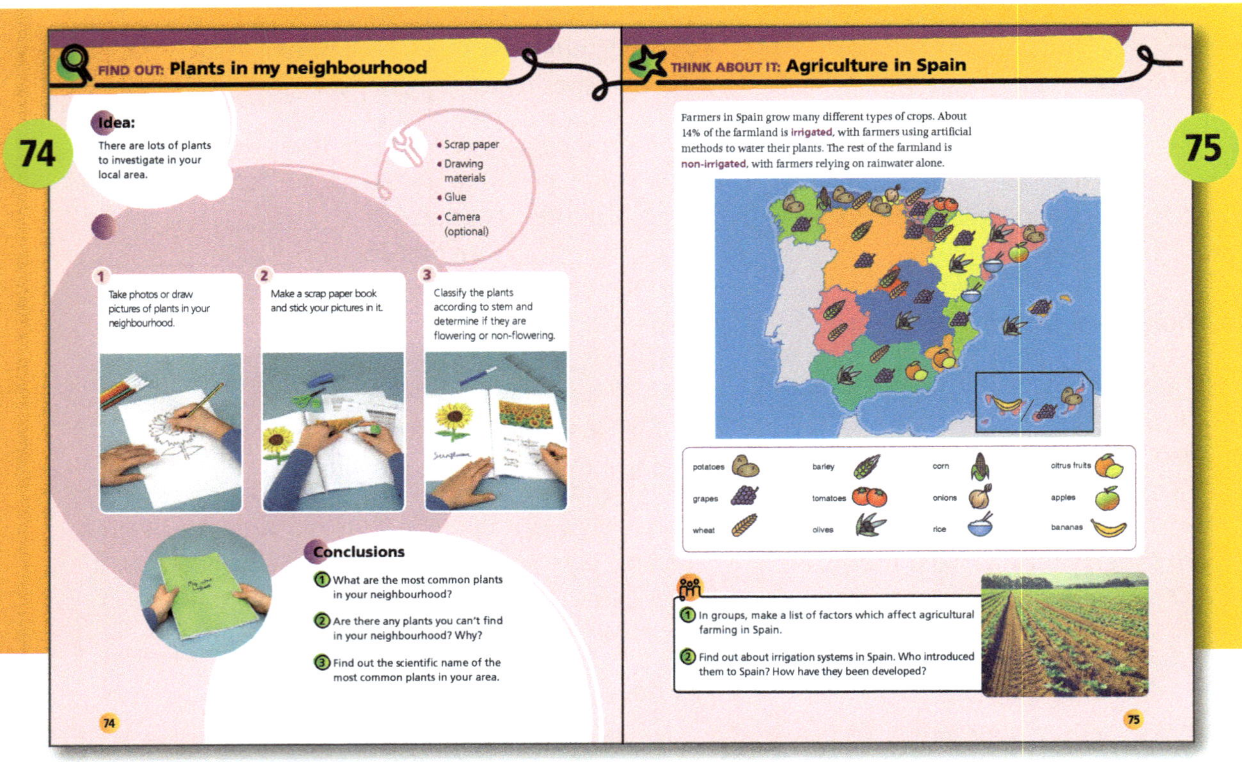

PAGE SUMMARY

In the first of these two pages (*Find out*), pupils make a field log about the plants in their neighbourhood. This task will practise their classification skills. The second page *(Think about it)* provides your pupils with the opportunity to learn about living agriculture in Spain and to investigate the factures which affect it.

LANGUAGE

- Imperatives: *take, draw, make, stick, classify, determine*
- Vocabulary: *neighbourhood, scrap paper*

ADDITIONAL MATERIALS

- Digital flashcards
- Extra materials: a physical and political map of South America, photos of daisies, dog roses and apple trees

FIND OUT

OPENING ACTIVITIES

- Pupils fold a piece of A4 paper in half, in half again and in half one more time. When they open the paper up they should have a grid with eight squares. Pupils write eight words connected to plants (parts of a plant, types of plants, etc.) Draw a similar grid on the board. Say a word and write it in a square on the grid. If pupils have the same word, the cross it out. When a pupil has crossed out all the words in their grid, they can shout out *Bingo*!

MAIN ACTIVITIES

- Explain to pupils that they will be making a log about the plants that grow in the neighbourhood. Brainstorm the names of plants that grow where you live and make a list on the board. Explain that they need to think about the type of plants they will choose and also to be able to classify them. Ask questions to help pupils organise their work. **Is it a flowering plant? Does it have fruit?** When the pupils have the necessary information and photos, the log can be made in class.
- Ask pupils to read the steps on page 74. Then, tell them to write the materials and the three steps in their notebook. If you are using the book on the interactive whiteboard, you can play the audio of the steps.

⊕ CLOSING ACTIVITIES

1 What are the most common plants in your neighbourhood?

- Invite pupils to show each other their logs. As a class activity decide which plants are the most common in the neighbourhood. *Open answer*

2 Are there any plants you can't find in your neighbourhood? Why?

- Remind pupils that plants adapt to their environment, just as animals do. In the same way that a giraffe couldn't live in a desert, certain plants can't live in a different environment. Ask pupils to think about factors which affect plant life. (*Climate, relief, altitude, soil, etc.*) *Open answer*

3 Find out the scientific name of the most common plants in your area.

- Write the names *Bellis perennis*, *Rosa canina* and *Malus domestica* on the board and explain that these are the scientific names for three well known plants. Invite the pupils to guess the common names. Place a photo of a daisy, a dog rose and an apple tree on the board and ask the class to match the name to the picture. *Bellis perennis - daisy, Rosa canina – dog rose and Malus domestica – apple tree.*
- Put pupils in groups to investigate in class on the computer, or ask them to investigate with their parents at home. *Open answer*

THINK ABOUT IT

⊕ OPENING ACTIVITIES

- Display a map of the autonomous communities of Spain and a relief map of the Iberian Peninsula on the board. Identify the communities and talk about the communities they have visited. Take the opportunity to revise the cardinal points. Ask: **Is Galicia in the north or south?** (*North*); **Which communities are on the Mediterranean coast?** (*Andalucía, Murcia, Valencia, Cataluña*); **Where is Madrid?** (*In the centre*)
- Now focus their attention on the relief map of Spain. Say: **Spain has a very varied relief. Which landforms can you see on the map?** (*Mountain ranges and chains, plateau, plains, valleys, coast line, bays*, etc.) Point out that the relief of an area affects the climate and this affects the type of plants that can grow there.
- Ask the pupils to work with a partner to make a list of the plants or crops that farmers grow in Spain. Write their suggestions on the board.

MAIN ACTIVITIES

- Ask pupils to open their books on page 75 and say: **Let's read about agriculture in Spain**. If you are using the interactive whiteboard, you can play the audio and encourage pupils to read along in their books. Ask: **Why do farmers have to use artificial methods to water their crops?** (*There isn't enough rain.*) Invite the pupils to name the different crops that they can see on the map. Ask: **Where do they grow potatoes? Do they grow in the north or the south?** (*In the north*)
- Then, ask pupils to look at the map and describe what they can see in pairs. *Bananas grow in the Canary Islands. Wheat and barley are important in Madrid and Extremadura. Rice grows on the Mediterranean coast*, etc.

⊕ CLOSING ACTIVITIES

1 In groups, make a list of factors which affect agricultural farming in Spain.

- Organise the class into small groups and invite a pupil to read the question for the class. Elicit that climate and relief affect agriculture. Ask them to study the map on page 75 and discuss the reasons why certain crops grow in certain places. *Open answer*

2 Find out about irrigation systems in Spain. Who introduced them to Spain? How have they been developed?

- This activity can be done at home with the help of parents or in small study groups on a computer or in the library. You may like to ask the pupils to also investigate the plastic greenhouse cultivations in the south of Spain. *The Romans used irrigation methods but they were reintroduced and improved by the Muslims in Al-Andalus.*

PAGES 76-77 Look back: Plants

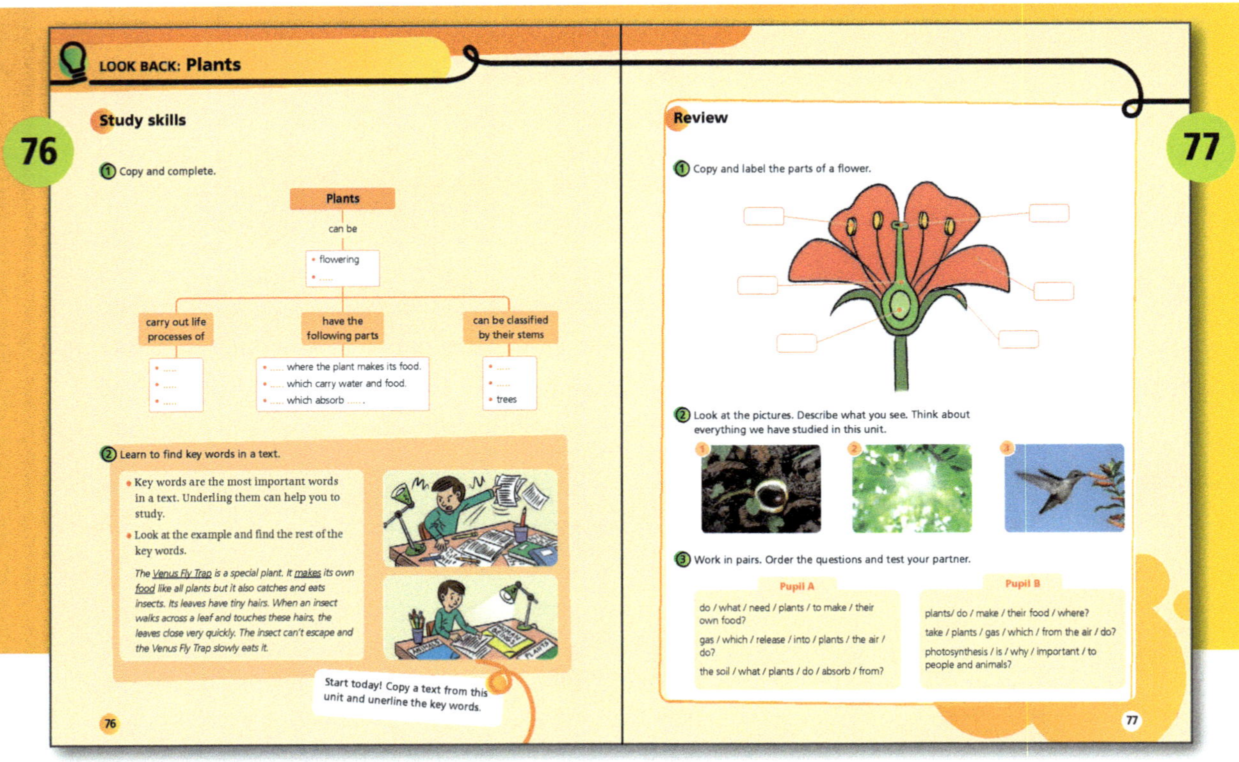

PAGE SUMMARY

This double-page spread allows pupils the opportunity to organise what they've learned in the unit by means of a concept map. They can also learn a new study skill – pupils find key words in a text to help them summarise what they have learned and to revise. On the *Review page*, pupils complete activities individually to check their understanding of material covered in this unit. Activity 3 is a pairwork speaking activity to encourage them to construct simple questions and to create complete, accurate sentences. It is also a peer evaluation opportunity.

LANGUAGE

- Imperatives: *match, write, copy, correct, talk, use, work*
- Question words: *what, which, why, where*
- Forming questions
- Encourage pupils to speak and write in complete sentences

ADDITIONAL MATERIALS

- Digital flashcards
- Digital wordcards

OPENING ACTIVITIES

- Play a game with the opening illustration on pages 64 and 65. Pupils look at the illustration and point to what you describe. This works well on the interactive whiteboard as you can ask two pupils or teams to come to the board and use the writing tools to mark their answers. It can be a race.
- Review vocabulary by playing the *Definitions* game with wordcards from this unit (see *Helpful tips*, pages 20-23). Divide the class into two teams. Place two chairs at the front of the class, each chair facing a team. Ask one pupil from each team to sit on the chair, facing their team. Stick a wordcard on the board between the two pupils. The teams take turns to give definitions for the word on the board. **This plant is a non-flowering plant that has rhizoids** (*Mosses*). The team member who guesses first gains a point for their team. Two new team members come to the chairs.
- Draw a plant on the board showing the parts of a plant and the parts of a flower. Invite pupils to come up to the board to label the picture. Encourage peer correction.

MAIN ACTIVITIES

Page 76, Study skills

① Copy and complete.

- Remind pupils that when we organise new information, it is easier to understand and remember it. Focus the pupils' attention on the concept map and ask them to tell you what the missing words are. Encourage them to make full sentences, such as Plants can be flowering or non-flowering. Tell them to copy and complete the concept map in their notebooks.

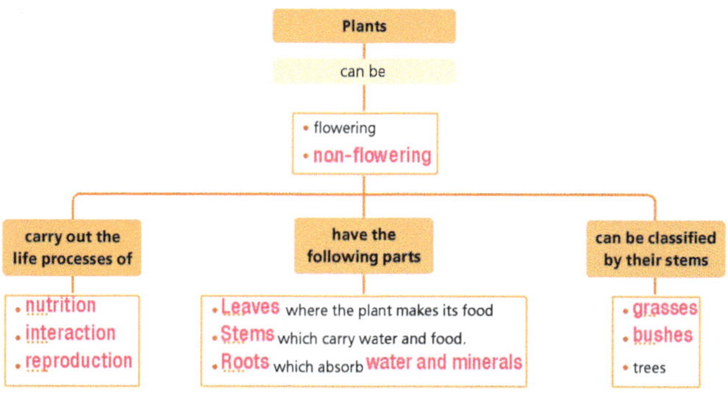

② Learn to find key words in a text.

- Explain that key words are the most important words in a text and that underling them can help you to study.
- Focus the pupils' attention on the text about the Venus Fly trap on page 76. Read the text to the class and tell them to follow in their books. Check for understanding by asking questions. **Does it make its own food? What else does it eat? How does it catch the insects?** Now ask pupils to work with a partner to find the key words in the text. If you have an interactive board highlight the words the pupils suggest. If not write the text on the board and underline the words. Pupils copy the text in their notebooks and underline the key words with a coloured pencil.

Page 77, Review

Note: This part of the review can be done with minimal teacher guidance. You may wish to work through the activities as a class or in small groups or partners. Alternatively, you can ask pupils to do them individually as self-evaluation. This review could also be done as homework.

① Copy and label the parts of a flower

- Anticlockwise from the top left: stamen, carpel, ovary, sepal, petal, stigma

② Look at the pictures. Describe what you see. Think about everything we have studied in this unit.

- The first picture shows a seed. The seed is protected by sharp spikes.
- The second picture shows sunlight which the plant uses to make food using the process of photosynthesis.
- The third picture shows hummingbird collecting nectar from a flower. The bird will also pollinate the flower.

③ Work in pairs. Order the questions and test your partner.

Pupil A

What do plants need to make their own food? *Water, minerals, sunlight and carbon dioxide*

Which gas do plants release into the air? *Oxygen*

What do plants absorb from the soil? *Water and minerals*

Pupil B

Where do plants make their food? *In their leaves*

Which gas do plants take from the air? *Carbon dioxide*

Why is photosynthesis important to people and animals? *It provides oxygen*

Activity Book answers / Audio CD1 track list

26

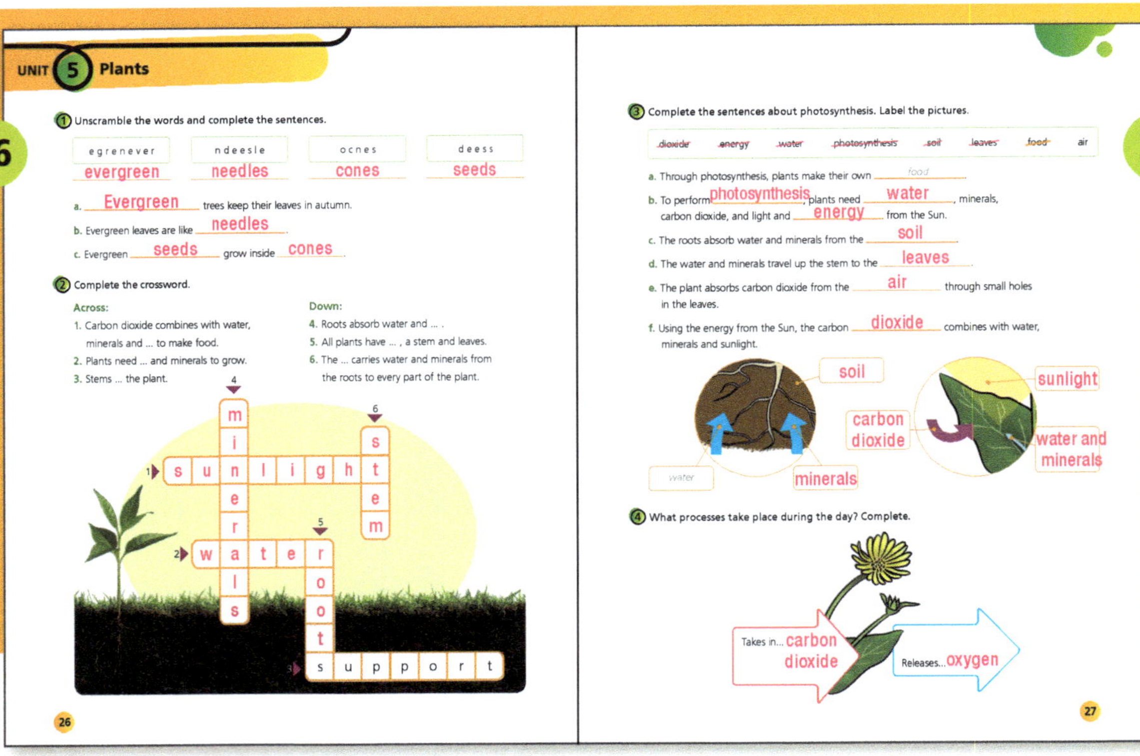

UNIT 5 Plants

1 Unscramble the words and complete the sentences.

egrenever	ndeesle	ocnes	deess
evergreen	needles	cones	seeds

a. Evergreen trees keep their leaves in autumn.

b. Evergreen leaves are like needles.

c. Evergreen seeds grow inside cones.

2 Complete the crossword.

Across:
1. Carbon dioxide combines with water, minerals and ... to make food.
2. Plants need ... and minerals to grow.
3. Stems ... the plant.

Down:
4. Roots absorb water and ... .
5. All plants have ... , a stem and leaves.
6. The ... carries water and minerals from the roots to every part of the plant.

26

3 Complete the sentences about photosynthesis. Label the pictures.

dioxide energy water photosynthesis soil leaves food air

a. Through photosynthesis, plants make their own food.

b. To perform photosynthesis, plants need water, minerals, carbon dioxide, and light and energy from the Sun.

c. The roots absorb water and minerals from the soil.

d. The water and minerals travel up the stem to the leaves.

e. The plant absorbs carbon dioxide from the air through small holes in the leaves.

f. Using the energy from the Sun, the carbon dioxide combines with water, minerals and sunlight.

4 What processes take place during the day? Complete.

27

27

28

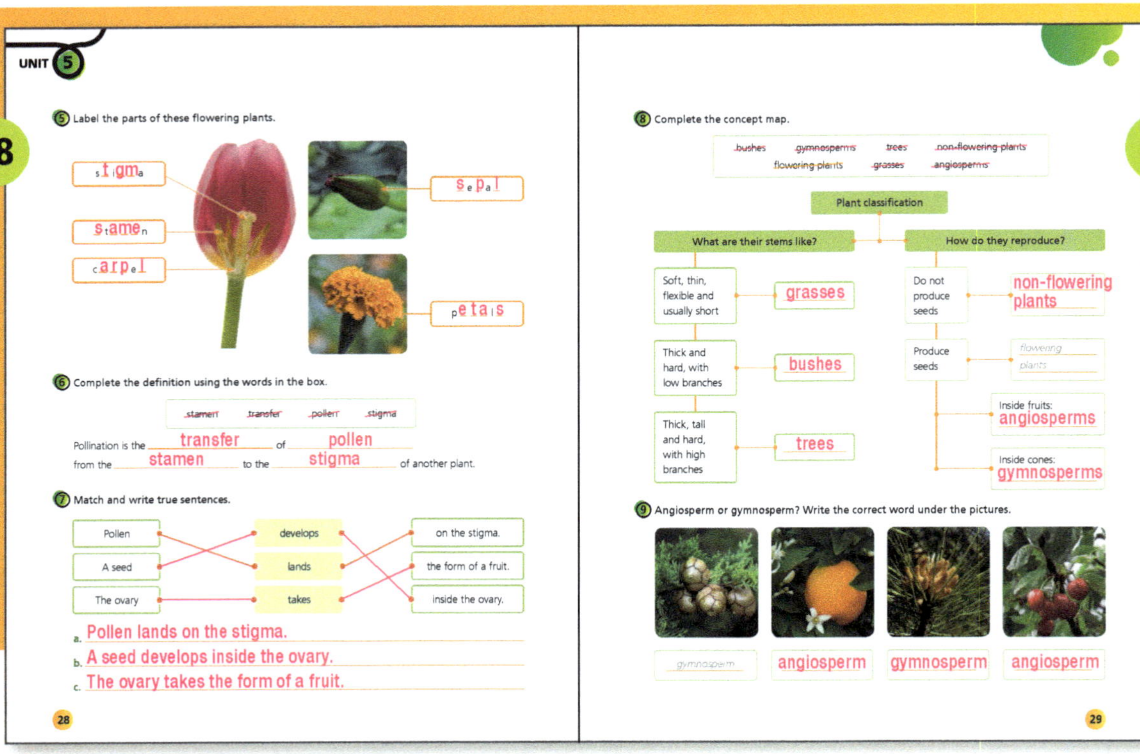

UNIT 5

5 Label the parts of these flowering plants.

6 Complete the definition using the words in the box.

stamen transfer pollen stigma

Pollination is the transfer of pollen from the stamen to the stigma of another plant.

7 Match and write true sentences.

Pollen	develops	on the stigma.
A seed	lands	the form of a fruit.
The ovary	takes	inside the ovary.

a. Pollen lands on the stigma.

b. A seed develops inside the ovary.

c. The ovary takes the form of a fruit.

28

8 Complete the concept map.

bushes gymnosperms trees non-flowering plants flowering plants grasses angiosperms

9 Angiosperm or gymnosperm? Write the correct word under the pictures.

gymnosperm angiosperm gymnosperm angiosperm

29

28

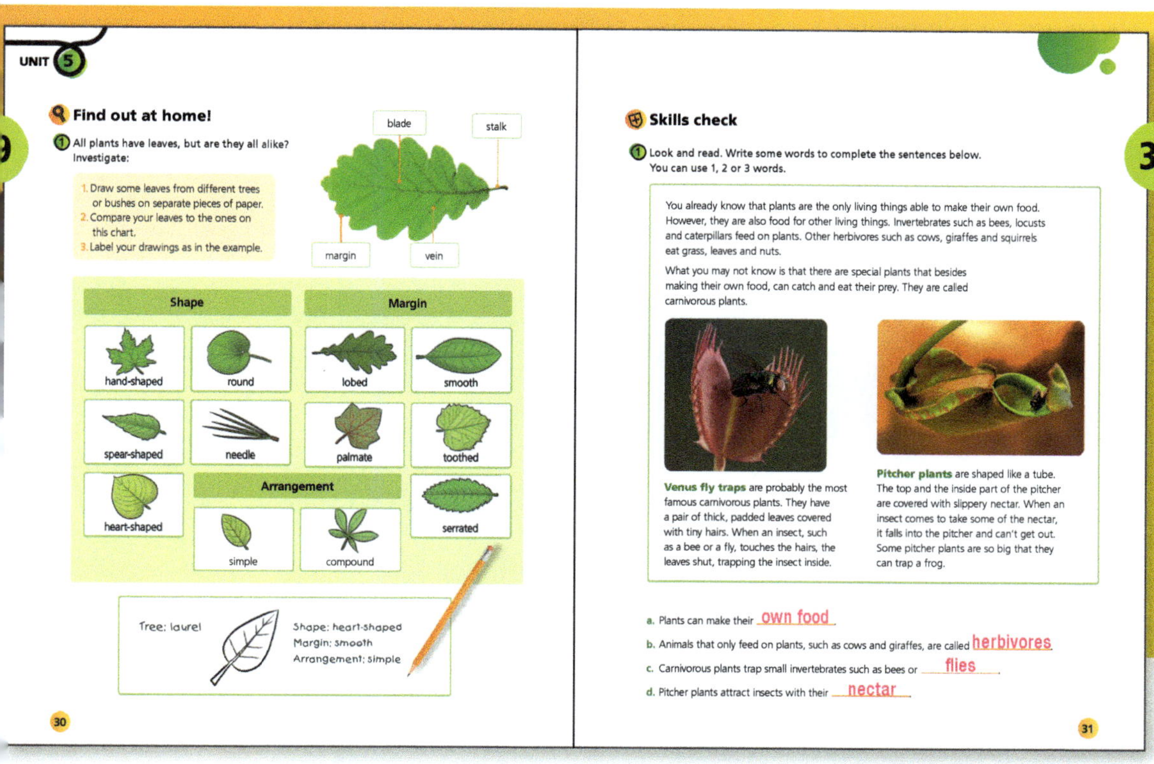
UNIT 5

Find out at home!

1 All plants have leaves, but are they all alike? Investigate:

1. Draw some leaves from different trees or bushes on separate pieces of paper.
2. Compare your leaves to the ones on this chart.
3. Label your drawings as in the example.

30

Skills check

1 Look and read. Write some words to complete the sentences below. You can use 1, 2 or 3 words.

You already know that plants are the only living things able to make their own food. However, they are also food for other living things. Invertebrates such as bees, locusts and caterpillars feed on plants. Other herbivores such as cows, giraffes and squirrels eat grass, leaves and nuts.

What you may not know is that there are special plants that besides making their own food, can catch and eat their prey. They are called carnivorous plants.

Venus fly traps are probably the most famous carnivorous plants. They have a pair of thick, padded leaves covered with tiny hairs. When an insect, such as a bee or a fly, touches the hairs, the leaves shut, trapping the insect inside.

Pitcher plants are shaped like a tube. The top and the inside part of the pitcher are covered with slippery nectar. When an insect comes to take some of the nectar, it falls into the pitcher and can't get out. Some pitcher plants are so big that they can trap a frog.

a. Plants can make their own food.
b. Animals that only feed on plants, such as cows and giraffes, are called herbivores.
c. Carnivorous plants trap small invertebrates such as bees or flies.
d. Pitcher plants attract insects with their nectar.

31

30

Unit 5 Audio CD1 track list

TRACK	ACTIVITY
53	**Pupil's Book page 65,** Unit introduction
54	**Pupil's Book page 65,** Song *Plants*
55	**Pupil's Book page 66,** Story: *A trip to the botanical gardens*
56	**Pupil's Book page 68,** Photosynthesis
57	**Pupil's Book page 69,** Respiration

TRACK	ACTIVITY
58	**Pupil's Book page 70,** How new plants grow
59	**Pupil's Book page 71,** Pollination
60	**Pupil's Book page 72,** Life cycle of a plant
61	**Pupil's Book page 73,** Plant classification
62	**Pupil's Book page 74,** We can also classify plants by how they reproduce

UNIT 6 Ecosystems

CONTENT	EVALUATION CRITERIA
Ecosystems.	Identify and explain the relationships between living things: ecosystems.
Food chains and webs.	Identify and explain the relationships between living things: food chains and webs.
Extinction of species.	Recognise and describe some of the reasons for extinction of species.
First approaches to scientific activity and the scientific method. Use of different information sources (direct and indirect). Use ICTs.	Obtain relevant information about specific phenomena, make predictions, integrate information from direct and indirect observation and communicate the results.
First approaches to simple experiments and investigations.	Conjecture as to the results of natural occurrences and of simple experiments and investigations.
Individual and group work.	Work independently and proactively and develop strategies for working in a group.
Planning a project and presenting a report.	Carry out a project and present a report.

LEARNING STANDARDS	KEY COMPETENCES	PAGES
Identifies and explains the elements of ecosystems.	MST, LIN	79-83
Identifies and describes different types of ecosystems.	MST, LIN	86, 87
Recognises the concept of habitat and gives some examples.	MST	82, 86, 87
Identifies and explains the relationships between living things: food chains and webs.	MST, LIN	84, 85, 88
Recognises and describes some of the reasons for the extinction of species.	MST, LIN	89
Helps actively in the conservation of the environment.	MST, SOC	89
With help, selects and organises specific and relevant information; analyses it and draws conclusions; reflects on the experience and the process; presents the results.	MST, LTL	81, 88, 89
Use books, libraries, etc. and collaborate in the care and maintenance of all the materials available in the school and the classroom.	MST, LTL	78-91
Shows autonomy in the planning of activities and tasks and shows initiative in decision taking.	LTL, AUT	81, 88, 89
With help, carries out simple experiments or investigations, and conjectures as to the results.	MST, LTL, AUT	88, 89
Uses strategies to help their own learning, as well as asking for help and information.	LTL, AUT	81, 88-90
First approaches to cooperative learning.	SOC, LTL	79, 89
Begins observation, using relevant instruments and consulting written documents and images.	LTL, AUT	88
Shows autonomy and proactiveness in the planning of and carrying out of actions.	AUT	88, 89
Presents work clearly and in an organised fashion.	LIN, LTL, AUT	88, 89
With help, carries out a project and presents a report, using paper and/or digital means, collecting information from different sources, presenting the results orally and with the support of images and short texts.	LIN, LTL, AUT, DIG	88,89

UNIT INFORMATION

UNIT SUMMARY

In this unit, pupils will learn about the different components that make up an ecosystem. They will study the different relationships between living things and also the relationship between organisms and the non-living elements found in an ecosystem. They should become aware of the delicate balance of nature and the importance of each living and non-living thing.

At the beginning of the unit, pupils will review living and non-living things. This subject area is covered in the opening illustration with the help of the course characters, Carla and Alex, who are on a school trip to a salt water marsh. The school trip continues in the story and, on their return to school, Alex and Carla carry out a *School trip project* to classify the living and non-living things they saw in the nature reserve. These opening pages are designed to test pupils' prior knowledge.

They will move on to study the components of an ecosystem looking at the relationships between the living and non-living elements. Food chains and food webs are important relationships so the pupils will study them in detail. Finally they will learn about different ecosystems and will learn how climate, location and relief affect them. Throughout this unit, encourage the pupils to think about our responsibility to protect the planet's diversity

EXPERIMENT

Find out

IIn the *Find out* activity on page 88, your pupils will prepare a poster to show how various food chains are connected and form a food web.

The pupils will need:

- coloured card
- colouring materials
- tape or glue
- coloured wool

Further ideas

Pupils can continue their investigation of ecosystems by researching different ecosystems that have extreme environments, such as Antarctica or Death Valley. They can do this at home with their parents and use reference books and/or the internet

VALUES AND ATTITUDES

In this unit, the pupils will learn to appreciate the variety of ecosystems and the diversity of life found on this planet. Encourage them to think about the need to protect the environment and respect the habitats of living things. It is important that they are aware of the delicate balance of the food chain and how the loss of one link can affect the entire chain. They should also reflect on how human actions can affect the environment. Try to focus on the fact that many organisations and individuals are working hard to protect the environment:

Think about it

The *Think about it* page in this unit focuses on extinction and endangered living things. The intention of this section is to appreciate that many natural extinctions have taken place throughout history but also to be aware of how modern life is affecting the Earth and endangering many organisms that share this planet with us.

EVALUATION MATERIAL

These documents can be downloaded from the *Teachers* section of the digital component and printed .

The materials include:

- **Unit diagnostic test**: provides an overview of the unit and allows you to assess the pupils' prior knowledge.
- **End-of-unit test**: in addition to the *Review* section at the end of each unit, this summative test can be used to evaluate pupils' progress after studying the unit content.
- **Class unit evaluation grid**: based on the evaluation criteria and learning standards of the unit.

DIGITAL RESOURCES

Presentations

- **Unit summary**: a simple slide presentation with text, images and audio to review the main ideas of the unit. It can be used at the beginning of the unit to test pupils' prior knowledge of the unit content or at the end of the unit as a revision tool.
- **Find out**: a slide presentation of the unit's *Find out* page with text, photos and audio. The slide presentation is perfect for a heads-up class, showing the steps one by one. Use this tool to get the pupils to predict the next steps (with their books closed) or to focus their attention on each step as they carry out the project themselves.

Activities

Activities vary per unit and include the following:

- **Memory game**: useful activity for reviewing key vocabulary and modelling pronunciation.
- **Labelling**: pupils label a diagram by dragging and dropping key terms.
- **Spelling**: pupils drag and drop letters to spell key terms.
- **Read and reveal**: pupils read sentences and guess the missing words, which are revealed by clicking the spaces.
- **Classification:** pupils drag and drop concepts and key terms in a simple classification table.
- **Wordsearch:** pupils find key terms hidden in the wordsearch.
- **Definitions:** pupils drag and drop words to complete definitions.

Song lyrics

Listen to the song *Ecosystems* and follow the lyrics line by line.

Posters

Attractive and informative posters to display in class. You can use them to review key concepts and vocabulary.

Videos

Use the video links in this unit to present content in a dynamic, real-life context while reinforcing the pupils' listening skills.

Teachers

Digital flashcards and wordcards: topics include *Elements of ecosystems, Food chains and food webs* and *Different types of ecosystems*

Downloadable PDFs: evaluation tests, evaluation grids, templates, useful links and further information.

PAGES 78–79 Ecosystems

PAGE SUMMARY

The aim of the unit opener is to develop your pupils' observation skills and find out what they already know about the topic of the unit. Use the picture to elicit vocabulary related to living and non-living things, as well as action verbs that describe what is going on in the scene and elements to describe the various characters and objects. Get your pupils to work in groups to complete activities 1–4 and to have fun listening to the song and completing activity 5.

LANGUAGE

- Question words: *who, how many, what, where,* etc.
- Prepositions of place: *in, on, under, next to, behind*
- Speculation: *might / might not*
- Comparative adjectives: *as small as …*
- Vocabulary: *ecosystem, living things, non-living things, community, interaction, binoculars, interact, marsh, desert, mountain, forest, grassland, ocean, polar*

ADDITIONAL MATERIALS

- Digital flashcards
- Digital wordcards

OPENING ACTIVITIES

- Begin by asking the pupils what they can remember about habitats from the previous year. They should be able to tell you about the well-known habitats and that there are water and land habitats. Ask them to give examples of animals that live in each one named.
- If you are using an interactive whiteboard, focus only on the illustration of the salt water marsh, not the questions. Either elicit ideas (*Some flamingos are eating; Carla is drawing the flamingos,* etc.) or ask questions indicating each part of the picture: *What's Alex doing? What can you see in the background?.*

MAIN ACTIVITIES

Page 79, Unit introduction (CD2 track 02)

- You can play the audio of the unit introduction first, with pupils reading along. Ask questions to check understanding. **What is an ecosystem?** (*All the living and non-living things in a specific area and the interaction that occurs between them.*) **How big is an ecosystem?** (*As small as a leaf or as large as a forest.*) Divide the pupils into small groups to answer the questions at the top of page 79. Then invite different groups to compare their answers with each other.

1 What living and non-living things can you see in the picture?

- Pupils may need some help with vocabulary but encourage them to try to describe the things instead of using Spanish. *See Answers at a glance*

2 Make a list of other living things that might live in this ecosystem.

- Before starting the list, review the five kingdoms of living things. **What are the five kingdoms of living things?** (*Monera, Protist, Fungus, Plant and Animal*) Write the names on the board. Ask **Do you think there will be any protists in this ecosystem?** (*Yes, algae.*) **What about fungi?** (*Yes, there might be some mushrooms.*) Allow pupils time to make their lists and invite volunteers to give their ideas. *Open answer*

3 In the picture you can see a marsh. Make a list of other large ecosystems.

- If you have done the opening activity, pupils will have no problem making the list. For a greater challenge ask them to spell out their suggestions for you to write them on the board.*See Answers at a glance*

4 Find out why flamingos are pink.

- This activity can be done at home with the help of parents or in small study groups on a computer or in the library. *See Answers at a glance*

5 Listen to the song. Point to and name the ecosystems you hear.

- Focus the pupils' attention on the six photos. Ask them if they can identify the ecosystems.
- Play the song *Ecosystems* **(CD2 track 03)** and ask pupils to point to the photo of the ecosystem that they hear. Then play the song a second time and encourage pupils to sing along (you can use the *Song lyrics* section on the digital component to display the song line by line and listen to the song.) *Desert, Polar regions, rainforest, grasslands and ocean*

CD2 • track 03

Ecosystems
Living things interact with their homes
Ecosystems
Where the place provides their needs
It's cold in the Arctic
There are no trees
And only a few plants in summer
But it's home for the polar bear and arctic fox
[chorus]Ecosystems …
Living things interact with their homes
Ecosystems
Where the place provides their needs
Deserts are hot and dry
Perfect for the cactus
They are home for nocturnal animals
Like the desert fox and hare
[chorus]Ecosystems …
Tropical rainforests are hot and humid
They have a lot of rain
So many different plants grow there
Giving shelter to parrots, monkeys and frogs
[chorus]Ecosystems …
Oceans are salt water
Home to so many living things
Jellyfish, crabs and whales
Dolphins, seaweed and plankton too
Ecosystems
Sand, soil, rock and water
Ecosystems
Interaction is survival

ANSWERS AT A GLANCE

1 Living things: flamingos, trees, bushes, grass, rushes and people. Non-living things: water, air, mud, soil, sand, clothes, notebook, pencil and binoculars.

2 Open answer.

3 Ocean, rainforest, desert, polar regions, grassland, mountain, shoreline, coral reef, forest, river, etc.

4 Flamingos eat tiny crustaceans (shrimps) that live under the water. This gives the flamingos their pink colour. However depending on their diet, flamingos can also be a pale orange colour.

5 Desert, Polar Regions, rainforest, grasslands and ocean.

PAGES 80-81 A trip to the salt marshes nature reserve

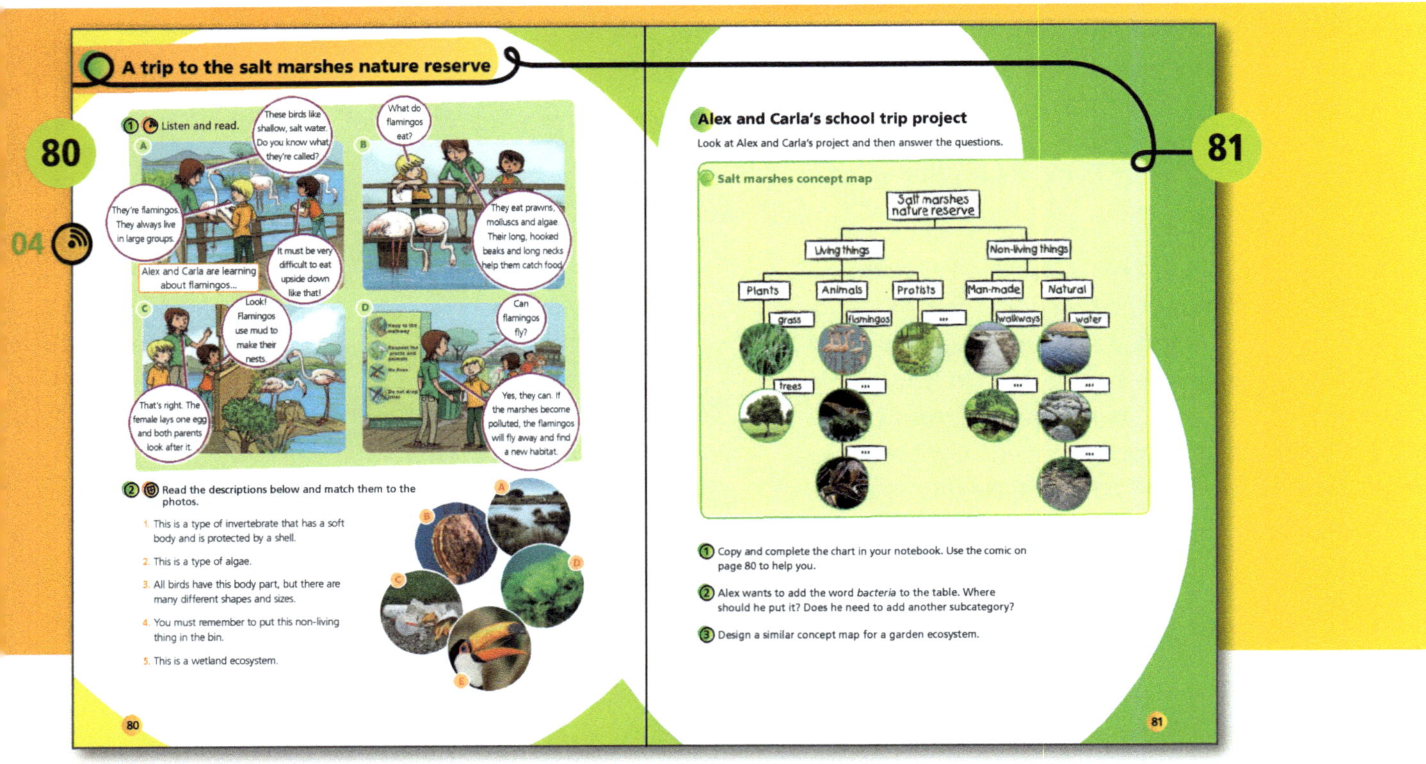

PAGE SUMMARY

This double-page spread opens with a story in which your pupils have the opportunity to see Carla and Alex at a particular moment of their school trip to the salt marshes nature reserve. Carla and Alex are talking to the guide and learning about the flamingos that live there. The story is reinforced with an exam style matching activity that is related to the story and opening double page spread. On page 81, the pupils can study Carla and Alex's school trip project about the marshes.

LANGUAGE

- First conditional: *If the marshes become polluted, the flamingos will fly away.*
- Vocabulary: *habitat, marsh, prawns, molluscs, algae, invertebrate, beak, shell, mud, nest, litter, bin, fire, walkway, upside down, soft, lay*

ADDITIONAL MATERIALS

- Digital flashcards
- Digital wordcards
- Extra classroom materials: A4 cards cut into two pieces, drawing materials

OPENING ACTIVITIES

- Play *Odd one out*. Choose three words from one kingdom and a distractor, e.g. mushrooms, toadstools, algae and yeast. Write them on the board in a random order and ask **Which is the odd one out?** (*Algae is because it belongs to the Protist kingdom, while the others belong to the Fungus kingdom.*)
- Use the sentences in activity 2 to play *True or False*. Explain that if the sentence is true they must repeat it but if it is false they are to remain silent and shake their heads. **A marsh is a wetland ecosystem.** (*True*); **Birds' beaks are always the same shape.** (*False*); **You must put your litter in a bin.** (*True*); **All molluscs have a shell.** (*False*); **Algae live in water.** (*True*)

MAIN ACTIVITIES

1 Listen and read. (CD2 track 04)

- Draw the pupils' attention to the story at the top of page 80 and explain to them that they are going to listen to a story about Alex and Carla's trip to the salt marshes nature reserve. Say **Let's listen and read**. Play the audio.
- Ask pupils to look at each of the illustrations and describe what is happening in each one using their own words. For example, *Carla is looking at the flamingos' nest. The flamingos are eating.*

- Divide pupils into groups of three and ask them to choose a character from the story – Alex, Carla or the guide. Pupils then read their part of the story aloud in their small group. You can invite a group to the front of the class to act the story out.

② Read the descriptions below and match them to the photos.

- This activity aims to introduce some new vocabulary, reinforce what pupils have learned in the story and refresh concepts studied in previous levels. This activity provides some extra exam-style reading and writing practice. Pupils complete the activity in their notebooks and check their answers in pairs. *1 - B; 2 – D; 3 – E; 4 – C; 5 - A*

SCHOOL TRIP PROJECT

- Explain to the pupils that following their trip to the salt marshes, Alex and Carla have done a project to summarise what they have learned about the living and non-living things they have seen there. Tell pupils to look at the photos on page 81 and ask for volunteers to read the words. Ask the pupils to work with a partner to decide on the missing words and to answer question 2. Suggest they use a double page to draw the chart and to draw it softly first in case they need to adjust the size. Check answers as a class activity before they begin to draw the chart.

① Copy and complete the chart in your notebook. Use the comic on page 80 to help you

- Pupils can work in pairs or in small groups. Encourage them to say the answers using full sentences, before copying the concept map in their notebooks. *Animals: prawns and molluscs; Man-made: bridges; Natural: rocks and mud.*

② Alex wants to add the word *bacteria* to the table. Where should he put it? Does he need to add another subcategory?

- Encourage pupils to think of which kingdom bacteria belong to. Ask them whether this category appears in the table. *He must add Monera kingdom as a subcategory of living things in order to include bacteria.*

③ Design a similar concept map for a garden ecosystem.

- This activity can take up a lot of time so you may prefer to ask the pupils to work with a partner to list the living and non-living things they can find in a garden ecosystem. Tell them to classify their ideas following the example on page 81. *Open answer*

⊕ CLOSING ACTIVITIES

- *Play Secret countdown.* Whisper a sentence from the lesson, e.g. *Flamingos eat prawns, molluscs and algae* to one of the pupils. That pupil then whispers it to the person on their left. As the pupils are passing on the message, countdown from ten to zero quietly. When you reach zero, the last person to hear the message should say it out loud.

⊕ EXTRA IDEAS

- Draw the pupils' attention to the notice in the final scene of the story on page 80. Invite volunteers to read the rules of the nature reserve: *Keep to the walkways; Respect the plants and animals; No fires; Do not drop litter.* Ask them to think of other possible rules. Give each pupil half a sheet of A4 card. Ask the pupils to make notices for a nature reserve.

ANSWERS AT A GLANCE

Page 80

② 1 - B; 2 – D; 3 – E; 4 – C; 5 – A

Page 81

① Animals: prawns and molluscs; Man-made: bridges; Natural: rocks and mud.

② He must add Monera kingdom as a subcategory of living things in order to include bacteria..

③ Open answer.

PAGES 82–83 Elements of ecosystems

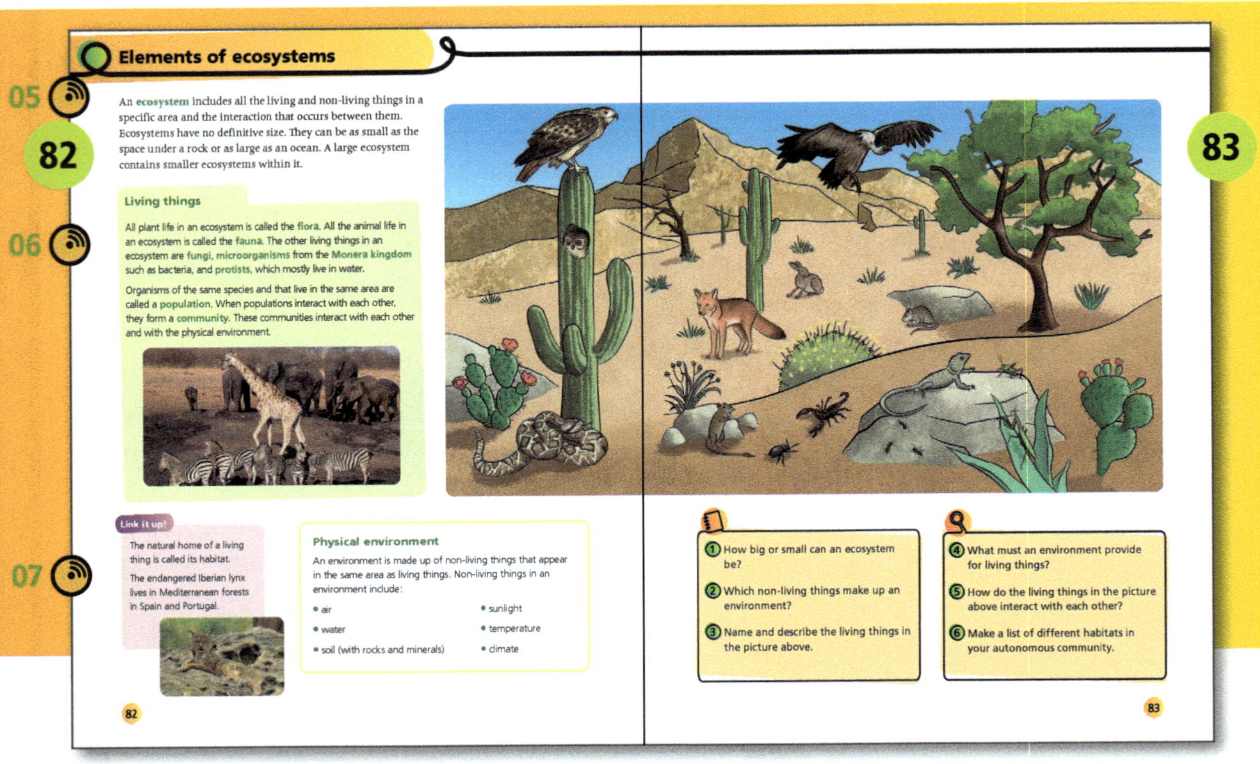

PAGE SUMMARY

This double-page spread introduces pupils to the elements that make up an ecosystem. They will learn about the relationships between populations and communities of living things and become aware of the importance of the physical environment. There is a lot of new vocabulary and concepts on this double page. Do not expect pupils at this stage to absorb all of the information; the main learning aim is to understand how an ecosystem includes all the living and non-living things in a specific area and the interaction that occurs between them.

LANGUAGE

- Questions words: *where, what, why, etc.*
- Comparative adjectives: *smaller than, as small as*
- Vocabulary: *ecosystem, flora, fauna, fungi, microorganisms, population, community, habitat, environment, shelter, air, water, soil, rock, sunlight, temperature, climate, species, interaction*

ADDITIONAL MATERIALS

- Digital flashcards
- Digital wordcards

OPENING ACTIVITIES

- If you are using an interactive whiteboard, click on the opening text on page 82 and highlight the first sentence: *An ecosystem includes all the living and non-living things in a specific area and the interaction that occurs between them.*

MAIN ACTIVITIES

Pages 82, Elements of an ecosystem (CD2 track 05)

- Read the introduction text with the class. Ask: **What makes up an ecosystem?** (*All the living and non-living things in a specific area.*) **How big is an ecosystem?** (*Ecosystems have no definite size.*)

Pages 82, Living things (CD2 track 06)

- Say **Let's find out about living things**. Play the audio **(CD2 track 06)**. Pupils listen and read. Check for understanding. Ask pupils for examples of flora and fauna. Ask **What other living things can we find in an ecosystem?** (*Fungi, microorganisms such as bacteria from the Monera Kingdom and protists.*)
- Ask pupils to look at the photo of the grassland. Ask **Can you see any populations?** (*Yes, the zebras and elephants*); **What do the populations form when they interact?** (*A community*)

Pages 82, Physical environment (CD2 track 07)

- Invite a pupil too read the Physical environment box or play the audio **(CD2 track 07)**
- Draw the pupils' attention to the *Link it up* box. Read the text and explain that the habitat must supply all the things an organism needs to survive. Ask **What do you think the lynx needs to survive?** (*Water, air, food and shelter.*) Point out that water and air are part of the physical environment. Lynxes also make dens in rocky crevices.

1 How big or small can an ecosystem be?

- Invite a pupil to read the question and ask the class to look for the answer on page 82. *Ecosystems have no definitive size. They can be as small as the space under a rock or as large as an ocean.*

2 Which non-living things make up an environment?

- Ask the question and tell pupils to find the answer on page 82. Ask the class to copy the question and answer into their notebook. They can check their answers in pairs. *Water, air, soil, sunlight, temperature and climate*

3 Name and describe the living things in the picture above.

- Divide the class into two teams. If you have an interactive whiteboard focus on the illustration on pages 82 and 83. The teams take turns to name and describe a living thing in the picture. The team wins a point for each correct sentence. *There is a small owl in the cactus,* etc. *Open answer*

4 Name and describe the living things in the picture above.

- Invite a pupil to read the question. Say: **Imagine that you are a pirate and the other pirates have left you alone on an island. What must you look for if you are going to survive? Air isn't a problem as it's all around you but what else do you need?** Elicit that you will need fresh water, food and a place to live (shelter). If it is cold you will need something to keep you warm. *Water, air, shelter, sunlight, correct temperature.*

5 How do the living things in the picture above interact with each other?

- Organise the class into small groups and ask them to discuss this question. Point out that an owl is living inside a cactus. Allow the groups time to look for different examples of interaction. Invite volunteers to share their group's ideas with the rest of the class. *See Answers at a glance*

6 Make a list of different habitats in your autonomous community.

- This activity can be done at home with the help of parents or in small study groups on a computer or in the library. *Open answer*

+ CLOSING ACTIVITIES

- Place the wordcards *air, water, soil, rock, sunlight, temperature, climate, flora, fauna, microorganisms* and *fungi* in a random order on the board. Write two heading: *living things* and *physical environment.* Invite the pupils to come to the board and classify the wordcards into the two groups. You may like to ask pupils to copy the chart into their notebook.

ANSWERS AT A GLANCE

1. Ecosystems have no definitive size.
2. Water, air, soil, sunlight, temperature and climate.
3. Open answer.
4. Water, air, shelter, sunlight, correct temperature
5. (Example answer) Many eat each other. The plants provide food and oxygen. The animals provide carbon dioxide for the plants. The cactus stores water. The insects help plants pollinate.
6. Open answer.

PAGES 84–85 Food chains and food webs

08 84 10 85 09

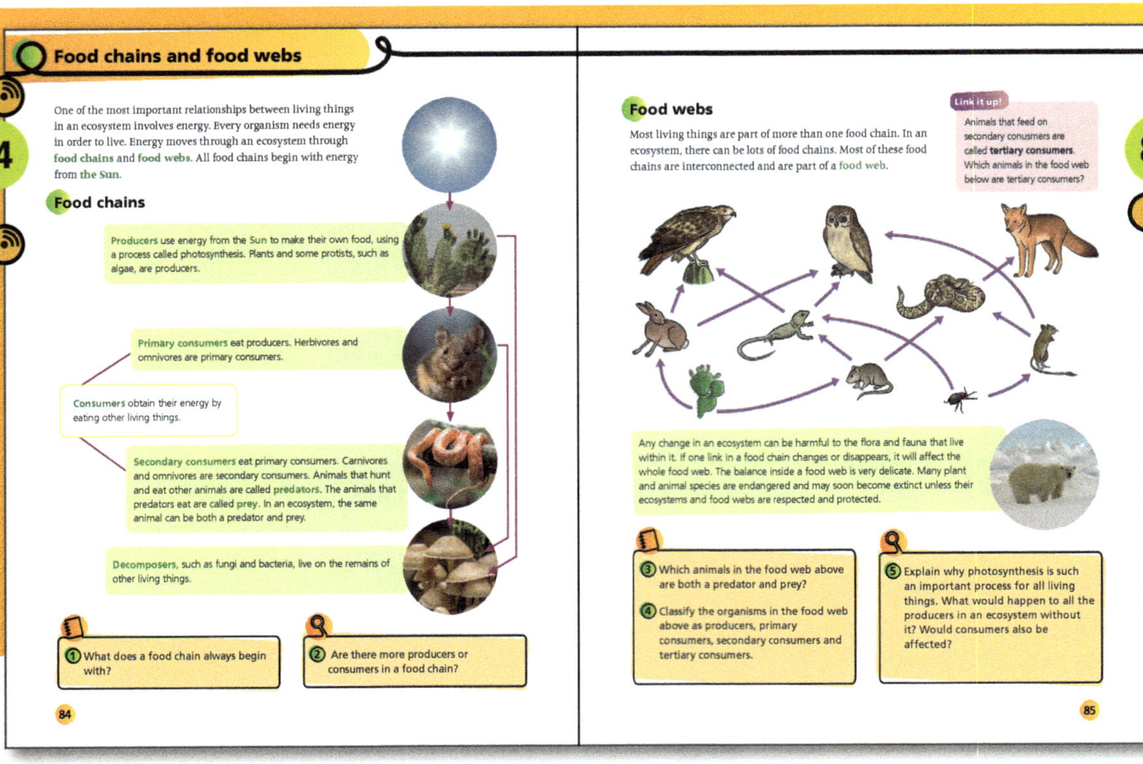
Food chains and food webs

One of the most important relationships between living things in an ecosystem involves energy. Every organism needs energy in order to live. Energy moves through an ecosystem through food chains and food webs. All food chains begin with energy from the Sun.

Food chains

Producers use energy from the Sun to make their own food, using a process called photosynthesis. Plants and some protists, such as algae, are producers.

Primary consumers eat producers. Herbivores and omnivores are primary consumers.

Consumers obtain their energy by eating other living things.

Secondary consumers eat primary consumers. Carnivores and omnivores are secondary consumers. Animals that hunt and eat other animals are called predators. The animals that predators eat are called prey. In an ecosystem, the same animal can be both a predator and prey.

Decomposers, such as fungi and bacteria, live on the remains of other living things.

1 What does a food chain always begin with?

2 Are there more producers or consumers in a food chain?

84

Food webs

Most living things are part of more than one food chain. In an ecosystem, there can be lots of food chains. Most of these food chains are interconnected and are part of a food web.

Link it up!

Animals that feed on secondary conusmers are called **tertiary consumers**. Which animals in the food web below are tertiary consumers?

Any change in an ecosystem can be harmful to the flora and fauna that live within it. If one link in a food chain changes or disappears, it will affect the whole food web. The balance inside a food web is very delicate. Many plant and animal species are endangered and may soon become extinct unless their ecosystems and food webs are respected and protected.

3 Which animals in the food web above are both a predator and prey?

4 Classify the organisms in the food web above as producers, primary consumers, secondary consumers and tertiary consumers.

5 Explain why photosynthesis is such an important process for all living things. What would happen to all the producers in an ecosystem without it? Would consumers also be affected?

85

PAGE SUMMARY

On this double-page spread pupils study the most important relationship between living things in an ecosystem. They will learn how energy moves through an ecosystem through food chains and food webs. They will understand that all food chains begin with the Sun and will realise the importance of plants in the food chain. In this lesson the pupils practise their classification and sequencing skills and will be asked to predict the consequences of any changes that may affect an ecosystem.

LANGUAGE

- Questions words: *where, what, why,* etc.
- Sequence words: *first, then, next, after that, finally*
- Possibility: *can /may*
- Second conditional: *What would happen if…..*
- Vocabulary: *food chain, food web, producers, primary consumer, secondary consumer*

ADDITIONAL MATERIALS

- Digital flashcards **and** wordcards
- Extra classroom materials: sticky notes, paper plates, drawing material, string

OPENING ACTIVITIES

- Organise the class into groups of four. Give each member of the group a sticky note. Ask them to choose an ecosystem and then to each write the name of an organism that lives in that ecosystem on the sticky note. They mustn't look at the other notes or show theirs to anyone at the moment. Ask them to stick the note on their chest and to arrange themselves into a line according to who eats who. Point out that the most important element is missing from all the lines but it isn't a living thing. Ask **Where does the energy on this planet come from?** (*The Sun*)

MAIN ACTIVITIES

Page 84, Food chains and food webs (CD2 track 08)

- Read the introductory text or play the audio **(CD2 track 08)**. Pupils listen and read.

Page 84, Food chains (CD2 track 09)

- Before you read, ask pupils to look at the photos on the right of the page. Ask: **What can you see in the first photo?** (*The Sun*); **What is in the next photo?** (*A cactus, a plant*) When all the photos have been named, focus the pupils' attention on the text. Say **Let's find out about food chains.** Pause after each text and ask questions to check understanding.

(1) What does a food chain always begin with?

- Read question 1 to the class and ask pupils to answer the question in their notebooks. *The Sun*

(2) Are there more producers or consumers in a food chain?

- Ask the class to read question 2 and think about the answer. Ask: **What would happen if there were more animals than plants? What would the animals do? Why would this be a serious situation?** Elicit that the animals would eat all the plants, there would be no food for the herbivores and the Earth would lose the oxygen that the plants produce. *There are more producers than consumers.*

Page 85, Food webs (CD2 track 10)

- Focus the pupils' attention on the diagram showing the food web from the desert ecosystem. Ask volunteers to identify the organisms in the food web. Check they are all familiar with the names. Explain that the arrows on a food web are very important because they show how the energy moves from one organism to another. Ask them to find the animals that aren't eaten by other animals.

(3) Which animals in the food web above are both a predator and prey?

- Ask pupils to work with a partner to answer question 3. *Lizard, snake and rat.*

(4) Classify the organisms in the food web above as producers, primary consumers, secondary consumers and tertiary consumers.

- Allow pupils time to classify the organisms. Draw a chart on the board and correct the activity by asking volunteers to complete the chart. *Producer – cactus; Primary consumer – rabbit, mouse; Secondary consumer – snake, rat, lizard; Tertiary consumer – owl, eagle and fox*

(5) Explain why photosynthesis is such an important process for all living things. What would happen to all the producers in an ecosystem without it? Would consumers also be affected?

- This question can be discussed as a class activity. *See Answers at a glance.*

(+) CLOSING ACTIVITIES

- Ask pupils to choose an ecosystem that they know and to design a food chain which begins with the Sun and includes a producer, a primary consumer, a secondary consumer, a tertiary consumer and a decomposer. Check their lists and then ask them to draw the chain in their note book. Remind them that the arrows show the movement of energy.

(+) EXTRA IDEAS

- For this activity you need six paper plates or six circular cards and string for each pupil. Ask them to draw the links in a food chain on each of the plates. Before starting the activity, ask the class to give examples for each link, especially the decomposers. (*Mushrooms, bacteria, earthworms, lobster, etc.*) The pupils then connect the plates together with the string.

ANSWERS AT A GLANCE

(1) The Sun.

(2) There are more producers than consumers.

(3) Lizard, snake and rat.

(4) Producer – cactus; Primary consumer – rabbit, mouse; Secondary consumer – snake, rat, lizard; Tertiary consumer – owl, eagle and fox.

(5) The producers wouldn't be able to make food and would die out. No oxygen would be produced and carbon dioxide would increase as the plants aren't using it. This will increase, global warming. The herbivores would lose their food source. The carnivores and omnivores would then lose their food source.

PAGES 86-87 Diffrent types of ecosystems

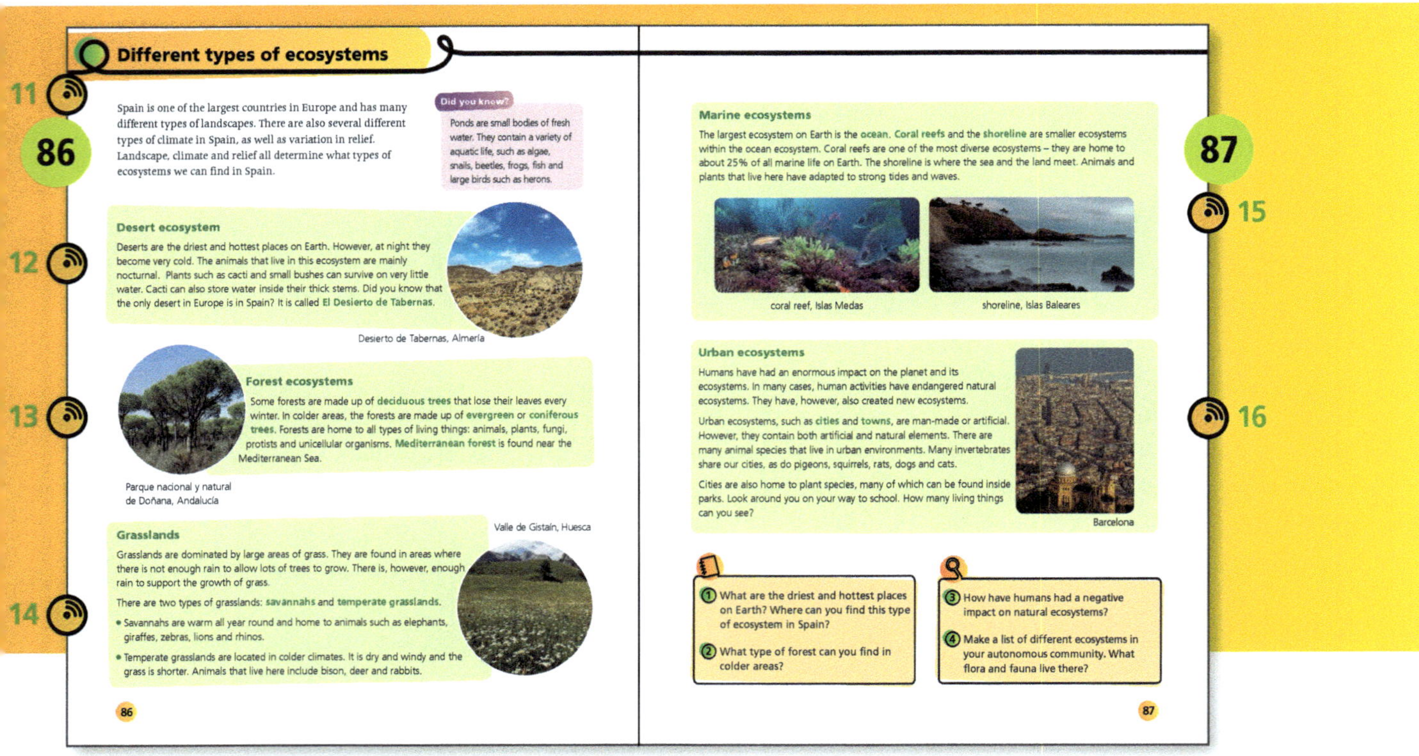

Different types of ecosystems

Spain is one of the largest countries in Europe and has many different types of landscapes. There are also several different types of climate in Spain, as well as variation in relief. Landscape, climate and relief all determine what types of ecosystems we can find in Spain.

Did you know?
Ponds are small bodies of fresh water. They contain a variety of aquatic life, such as algae, snails, beetles, frogs, fish and large birds such as herons.

Desert ecosystem
Deserts are the driest and hottest places on Earth. However, at night they become very cold. The animals that live in this ecosystem are mainly nocturnal. Plants such as cacti and small bushes can survive on very little water. Cacti can also store water inside their thick stems. Did you know that the only desert in Europe is in Spain? It is called El Desierto de Tabernas.

Desierto de Tabernas, Almería

Forest ecosystems
Some forests are made up of deciduous trees that lose their leaves every winter. In colder areas, the forests are made up of evergreen or coniferous trees. Forests are home to all types of living things: animals, plants, fungi, protists and unicellular organisms. Mediterranean forest is found near the Mediterranean Sea.

Parque nacional y natural de Doñana, Andalucía

Grasslands
Grasslands are dominated by large areas of grass. They are found in areas where there is not enough rain to allow lots of trees to grow. There is, however, enough rain to support the growth of grass.
There are two types of grasslands: savannahs and temperate grasslands.
- Savannahs are warm all year round and home to animals such as elephants, giraffes, zebras, lions and rhinos.
- Temperate grasslands are located in colder climates. It is dry and windy and the grass is shorter. Animals that live here include bison, deer and rabbits.

Valle de Gistaín, Huesca

86

Marine ecosystems
The largest ecosystem on Earth is the ocean. Coral reefs and the shoreline are smaller ecosystems within the ocean ecosystem. Coral reefs are one of the most diverse ecosystems – they are home to about 25% of all marine life on Earth. The shoreline is where the sea and the land meet. Animals and plants that live here have adapted to strong tides and waves.

coral reef, Islas Medas

shoreline, Islas Baleares

Urban ecosystems
Humans have had an enormous impact on the planet and its ecosystems. In many cases, human activities have endangered natural ecosystems. They have, however, also created new ecosystems.
Urban ecosystems, such as cities and towns, are man-made or artificial. However, they contain both artificial and natural elements. There are many animal species that live in urban environments. Many invertebrates share our cities, as do pigeons, squirrels, rats, dogs and cats.
Cities are also home to plant species, many of which can be found inside parks. Look around you on your way to school. How many living things can you see?

Barcelona

1. What are the driest and hottest places on Earth? Where can you find this type of ecosystem in Spain?
2. What type of forest can you find in colder areas?
3. How have humans had a negative impact on natural ecosystems?
4. Make a list of different ecosystems in your autonomous community. What flora and fauna live there?

87

PAGE SUMMARY

This double-page spread introduces pupils to different types of ecosystems. The main focus of this lesson is on ecosystems which can be found in Spain and in this way content can be linked to the pupils' Social Science course. They will consider how climate and relief can shape an ecosystem and will reflect on how human activity has affected the ecosystems.

LANGUAGE

- Questions words: *where, what, why, etc.*
- Comparative and superlative adjectives
- Vocabulary: *landscape, climate, relief, desert ecosystem, forest ecosystem, grasslands, marine ecosystem, urban ecosystem, coral reef, shoreline, savannah, temperate*

ADDITIONAL MATERIALS

- Digital flashcards
- Digital wordcards
- Extra classroom materials: physical and political map of Spain

OPENING ACTIVITIES

- Show the class a picture of a whale, a camel and a polar bear. Ask **Can these three animals share the same ecosystem?** Elicit that it would be impossible because a whale is a marine animal and needs the ocean. The polar bear needs a cold climate and the camel needs a hot dry climate. Point out that different ecosystems have different organisms and physical environments.
- Display the political and physical maps of Spain in the classroom. Show pupils where they are at the moment on both maps. Ask: **Tell me about the place where we live. Is it a city? What is the landscape like near us? Are there any mountains? Is there a river nearby? Are we close to the sea or the ocean?**

MAIN ACTIVITIES

Pages 86-87, Different types of ecosystems (CD2 track 11)

- Read the introduction text with the class. Ask pupils to look at the photos on pages 86 and 87 and name the places they see. **Which part of Spain has a desert ecosystem?** (*El desierto de Tabernas in Almeria.*) Show pupils where this is on the map.

- Place the wordcards *Desert Ecosystem, Forest Ecosystem, Grasslands, Marine Ecosystem* and *Urban Ecosystem* on the board in preparation for making a chart. Play the audio **(CD2 tracks 12-16)**. Pupils listen and read. Check for understanding. **Which plants grow in the desert? Which type of tree grows in colder temperatures? What kind of animals do we see in the savannah? Can you name two ecosystems inside the ocean ecosystem? Why is it important to protect the coral reefs? What man-made elements can we find in an urban ecosystem?**
- Invite volunteers to come to place the wordcards *coral reef, shoreline, savannah, temperate, deciduous* and *evergreen* on the board to show the smaller ecosystems. This is a good moment to draw the pupils' attention to the *Did you know?* box. Explain that ponds can be found in many different ecosystems.

1 What are the driest and hottest places on Earth? Where can you find this type of ecosystem in Spain?

- Read the question and ask pupils to find the answer on page 86 with a partner. *Deserts. In Almeria*

2 What type of forest can you find in colder areas?

- Read the question to the class and follow the same procedure as question 1. *Evergreen, forests.*

3 How have humans had a negative impact on natural ecosystems?

- You may like to show the class images of human activity on ecosystems, e.g. images of the rainforest and logging, the Mediterranean coast before the 1960s, a polluted river, a forest fire, etc. Organise the class into groups and ask them to discuss this question. Suggest they think of ways we can protect the natural environment. (Natural reserves, laws, etc.) Invite the groups to share their ideas with the rest of the class. *Open answer*

4 Make a list of different ecosystems in your autonomous community. What flora and fauna live there?

- This activity can be done at home with the help of parents or in small study groups on a computer or in the library. *Open answer.*

+ CLOSING ACTIVITIES

- *Where am I?* Describe different ecosystems and ask the pupils to guess where you are. I **can see lots of deciduous trees. There are a lot of living things here. The Iberian lynx lives here.** (*Mediterranean forest*)
- Organise the class into groups and ask them to read the information on pages 86 and 87 again. Ask them to work together to write ten questions to ask the rest of the class. Remind them to make a note of the answers too. The groups can either take turns to ask the questions or you may prefer to take in their lists and ask the questions yourself.

+ EXTRA IDEAS

- Ask pupils to choose an ecosystem that they would be interested in researching. Explain that it doesn't have to be an ecosystem in Spain. (Rainforests, Arctic / Polar regions, tundra, etc.) Ask them to find out about the plants and animals that live there, the climate and the food chain in this ecosystem. Ask them to include pictures or photos. You may like to use this activity as a presentation.

ANSWERS AT A GLANCE

1. Deserts. In Almeria.
2. Evergreen, forests.
3. Open answer.
4. Open answer.

PAGES 88–89 Find out / Think about it

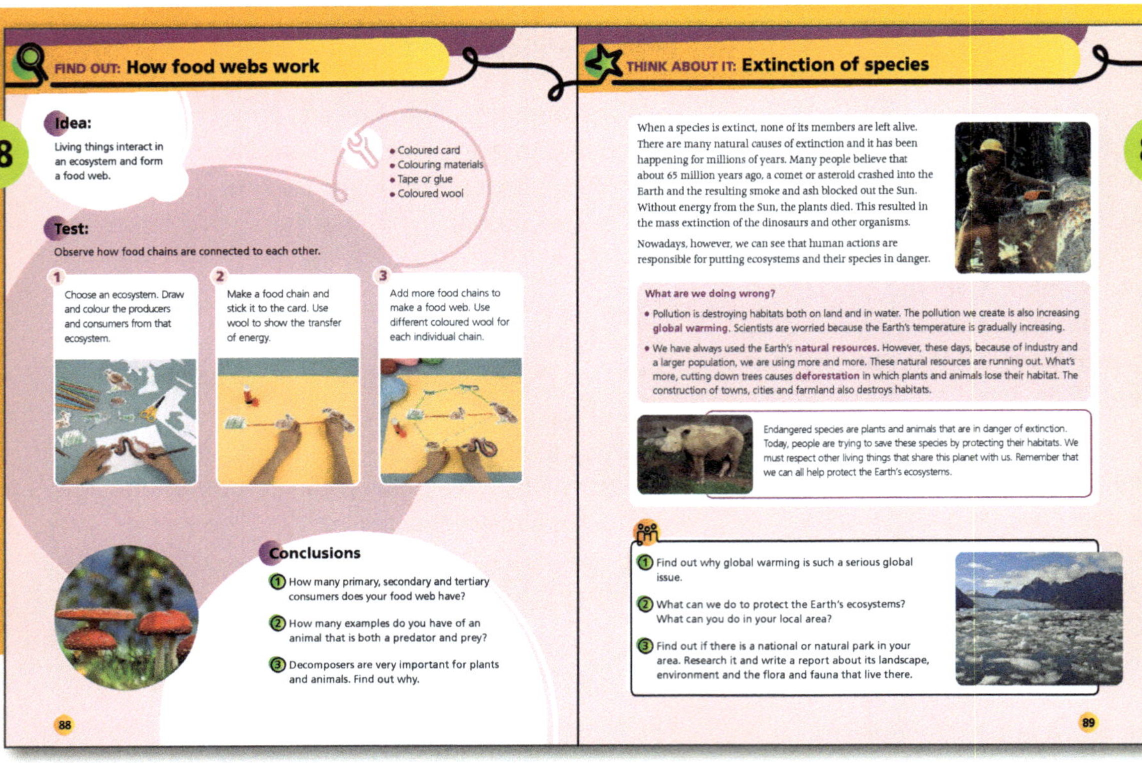
88

FIND OUT: How food webs work

Idea:

Living things interact in an ecosystem and form a food web.

- Coloured card
- Colouring materials
- Tape or glue
- Coloured wool

Test:

Observe how food chains are connected to each other.

1 Choose an ecosystem. Draw and colour the producers and consumers from that ecosystem.

2 Make a food chain and stick it to the card. Use wool to show the transfer of energy.

3 Add more food chains to make a food web. Use different coloured wool for each individual chain.

Conclusions

1. How many primary, secondary and tertiary consumers does your food web have?
2. How many examples do you have of an animal that is both a predator and prey?
3. Decomposers are very important for plants and animals. Find out why.

88

89

THINK ABOUT IT: Extinction of species

When a species is extinct, none of its members are left alive. There are many natural causes of extinction and it has been happening for millions of years. Many people believe that about 65 million years ago, a comet or asteroid crashed into the Earth and the resulting smoke and ash blocked out the Sun. Without energy from the Sun, the plants died. This resulted in the mass extinction of the dinosaurs and other organisms.

Nowadays, however, we can see that human actions are responsible for putting ecosystems and their species in danger.

What are we doing wrong?

- Pollution is destroying habitats both on land and in water. The pollution we create is also increasing **global warming**. Scientists are worried because the Earth's temperature is gradually increasing.
- We have always used the Earth's **natural resources**. However, these days, because of industry and a larger population, we are using more and more. These natural resources are running out. What's more, cutting down trees causes **deforestation** in which plants and animals lose their habitat. The construction of towns, cities and farmland also destroys habitats.

Endangered species are plants and animals that are in danger of extinction. Today, people are trying to save these species by protecting their habitats. We must respect other living things that share this planet with us. Remember that we can all help protect the Earth's ecosystems.

1. Find out why global warming is such a serious global issue.
2. What can we do to protect the Earth's ecosystems? What can you do in your local area?
3. Find out if there is a national or natural park in your area. Research it and write a report about its landscape, environment and the flora and fauna that live there.

89

PAGE SUMMARY

In the first of these two pages (*Find out*), pupils make a poster showing how food chains in an ecosystem are interconnected and form a food web. The second page (*Think about it*) provides your pupils with the opportunity to learn about the harmful affect human activity can have on natural ecosystems.

LANGUAGE

- Imperatives: *choose, draw, colour, make, stick and add*
- Present continuous
- Present simple
- Present perfect
- Vocabulary: *wool, extinct, alive, comet, asteroid, smoke, ash, mass, extinction, pollution, global warming, industry, natural resources, deforestation, farmland, habitat*

ADDITIONAL MATERIALS

- Digital flashcards
- Extra classroom materials: images from the oil spill of The Prestige

FIND OUT

OPENING ACTIVITIES

- Draw simple sketches on the board of the Sun, grass, a rabbit, a snake and an owl. Make sure they aren't in order of the food chain. Invite pupils to the board to draw the arrows to show the movement of energy through the food chain. Ask them to identify each link. *The grass is a producer because it uses energy from the Sun to make its own food*, etc.
- Take the wordcards related to food webs and ask pupils to give you definitions for each one. **What is a predator?** (*It's an animal that hunts and eats other animals.*) **What is a primary consumer?** (*It's an animal that eats plants.*) **What is a carnivore?** (*It's an animal that only eats meat.*)

MAIN ACTIVITIES

- Explain to pupils that they will be making a poster to show how living things interact in an ecosystem and form a food web. They will then be able to follow the movement of energy through the ecosystem.
- Ask pupils to read the steps on page 88. Then, tell them to write the materials and the three steps in their notebook. If you are using the book on the interactive whiteboard, you can play the audio of the steps.

- You may choose to do this investigation in small groups, in pairs or allow the pupils to go through the steps independently.

⊕ CLOSING ACTIVITIES

- Give pupils time to enjoy seeing each other's posters and to compare the different ecosystems. *The producers in my food chain are algae.* Encourage pupils to answer in full sentences. Ask the pupils to answer questions 1 and 2 by using the poster they have made.

1 How many primary, secondary and tertiary consumers does your food web have?

- Encourage pupils to answer using full sentences. *Open answer*

2 How many examples do you have of an animal that is both a predator and prey?

- Encourage pupils to answer using full sentences. *Open answer*

3 Decomposers are very important for plants and animals. Find out why.

- Ask pupils to name some decomposers. (*Fungi – toadstools and mushrooms, bacteria and some invertebrates such as earthworms*). This activity can be done at home in more detail with the help of parents or in small study groups on a computer or in the library. *They break down the remains of dead animals and plants and the nutrients return to the soil. This makes the soil richer and of a better quality. This is beneficial for plants and herbivores.*

THINK ABOUT IT

⊕ OPENING ACTIVITIES

- Ask pupils to name as many ecosystems that they can and write them on the board. Remind them that the balance in an ecosystem is very delicate. Ask them what human actions could damage the ecosystems. For example, forest ecosystems can be damaged by fire. Encourage pupils to give their opinions and to listen to the others when they are speaking.
- You may like to show some images of The Prestige disaster focusing on the volunteers cleaning the beaches and then showing the clean beaches today.

MAIN ACTIVITIES

- Ask pupils to open their books on page 89 and say **Let's read about what is happening to this planet.** If you are using the interactive whiteboard, you can play the audio and encourage pupils to read along in their books. Then, ask pupils to look at the pictures and describe what they can see in pairs.

⊕ CLOSING ACTIVITIES

1 Find out why global warming is such a serious global issue.

- Draw the pupils' attention to the photo of the melting ice caps. Explain that, because the temperature has increased on Earth, the ice at the Poles is melting. Encourage them to talk about the consequences for the animals that live in that area, linking it if possible to food chains. Guide them to think about what will happen to the oceans and seas if the ice melts and how that will affect the land. *Open answer*

2 What can we do to protect the Earth's ecosystems? What can you do in your local area?

- Many pupils become very worried when talking about these problems. Now would be a good time to talk about ecological organisations such as WWF which try to protect the environment.
- You may like to ask the class to look for information about their campaigns. Ask pupils to think about a local park. Ask them if they think it is being looked after and protected. If not, encourage them to talk about the problems. (*There aren't enough bins. It's dirty. Cars can enter.*) *Open answer*

3 Find out if there is a national or natural park in your area. Research it and write a report about its landscape, environment and the flora and fauna that live there.

- This activity can be done at home with the help of parents or in small study groups on a computer or in the library. *Open answer*

PAGES 90–91 Look back: Ecosystems

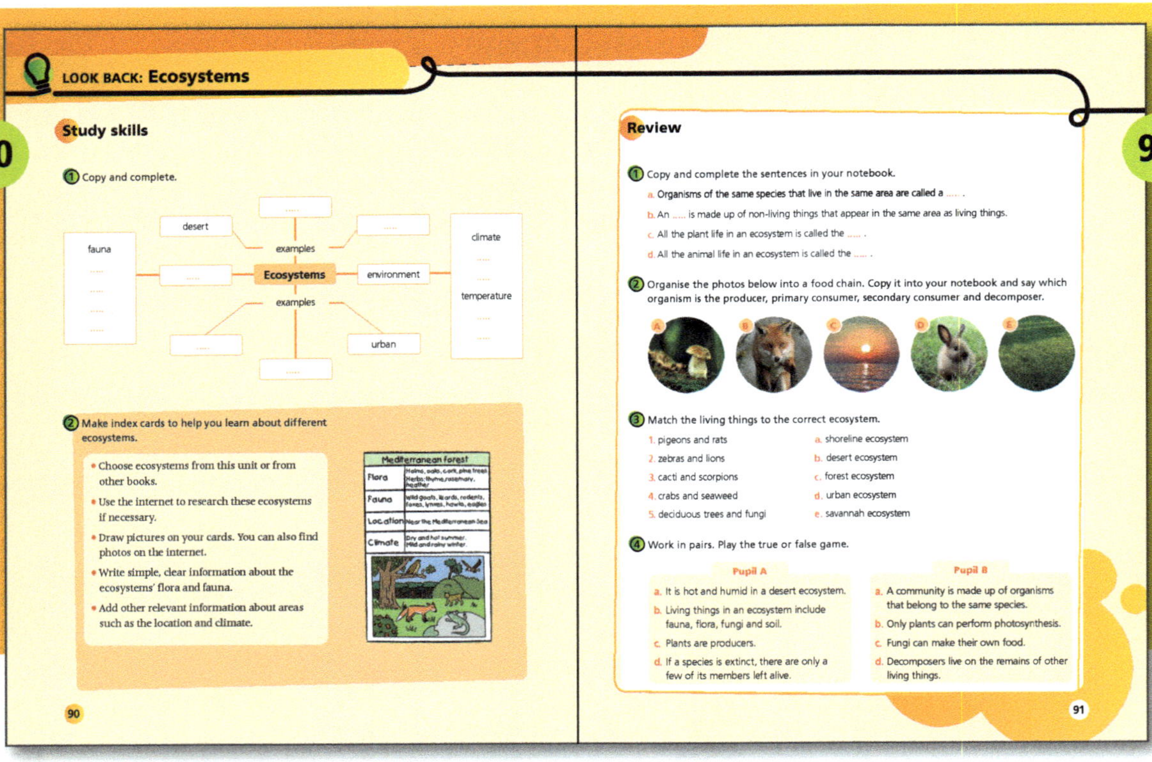

PAGE SUMMARY

This double-page spread allows pupils the opportunity to organise what they've learned in the unit by means of a concept map. They can also learn a new study skill – in this unit pupils explore the type of learner they are. On the *Review* page, pupils complete activities individually to check their understanding of material covered in this unit. Activity 4 is a pairwork speaking activity to encourage them to construct questions with the correct word order and provide accurate responses. It is also a peer evaluation opportunity.

LANGUAGE

- Imperatives: *match, write, copy, use, complete, make, choose, draw, add, organise, work and play*
- Present simple
- Encourage pupils to speak and write in complete sentences.

ADDITIONAL MATERIALS

- Digital flashcards
- Digital wordcards

OPENING ACTIVITIES

- Draw a noughts and crosses grid on the board. Divide the class into two teams. Give a definition of a word from the unit and ask the teams to answer if it's true or false. If their answer is correct, invite them to choose a square on the grid to place their nought or cross.
- Invite two pupils to come to the board. Tell them that you want them to write the word you say on the board. Warn them to keep their word covered so that their opponent can't see it. Ask them to use capital letters to avoid arguments! When both pupils have written the word, the class calls out Let's see. The winner is the pupil who writes the word correctly.
- Play a game of *Hangman* where the pupils have to discover the words *endangered*, *deforestation* and *pollution*.

MAIN ACTIVITIES

Page 90, Study skills

1 Copy and complete.

- Remind pupils that when we organise new information, it is easier to understand and remember it.
- Focus the pupils' attention on the concept map and ask them to tell you what the missing words are. Encourage them to make full sentences, such as *The desert is an ecosystem.*
- Tell them to copy and complete the concept map in their notebooks.

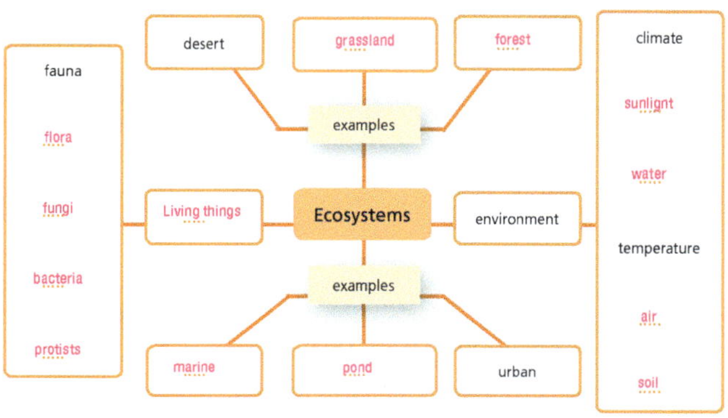

2 Make index cards to help you learn about different ecosystems.

- Pupils can work in groups and make two or three cards per group. Tell the pupils to use the example on page 90 as a guide. Suggest they collect all the information and record it on paper before they begin to make the cards. Pupils can use the cards to test each other and revise in groups.

Page 91, Review

Note: This part of the review can be done with minimal teacher guidance. You may wish to work through the activities as a class or in small groups or partners. Alternatively, you can ask pupils to do them individually as self-evaluation. This review could also be done as homework.

1 Copy and complete the sentences in your notebook.

a. Population

b. Environment

c. Flora

d. Fauna

2 Organise the photos below into a food chain. Copy it into your notebook and say which organism is the producer, primary consumer, secondary consumer and decomposer.

c. the Sun

e. grass – producer

d. rabbit – primary consumer

b. fox – secondary consumer

a. fungi – decomposer

3 Match the living things to the correct ecosystem.

1. d
2. e
3. b
4. a
5. c

4 Work in pairs. Play the true or false game.

Pupil A

a. False (It is hot and dry in a desert ecosystem)

b. False (Living things in an ecosystem include fauna, flora, fungi and microorganisms and/or protists)

c. True.

d. False (If a species is extinct, there are no members left alive)

Pupil B

a. False (A population is made up of organisms that belong to the same species)

b. False (Plants and some Protists can perform photosynthesis)

c. False (Fungi can't make their own food)

d. True.

Activity Book answers / Audio CD2 track list

32 33

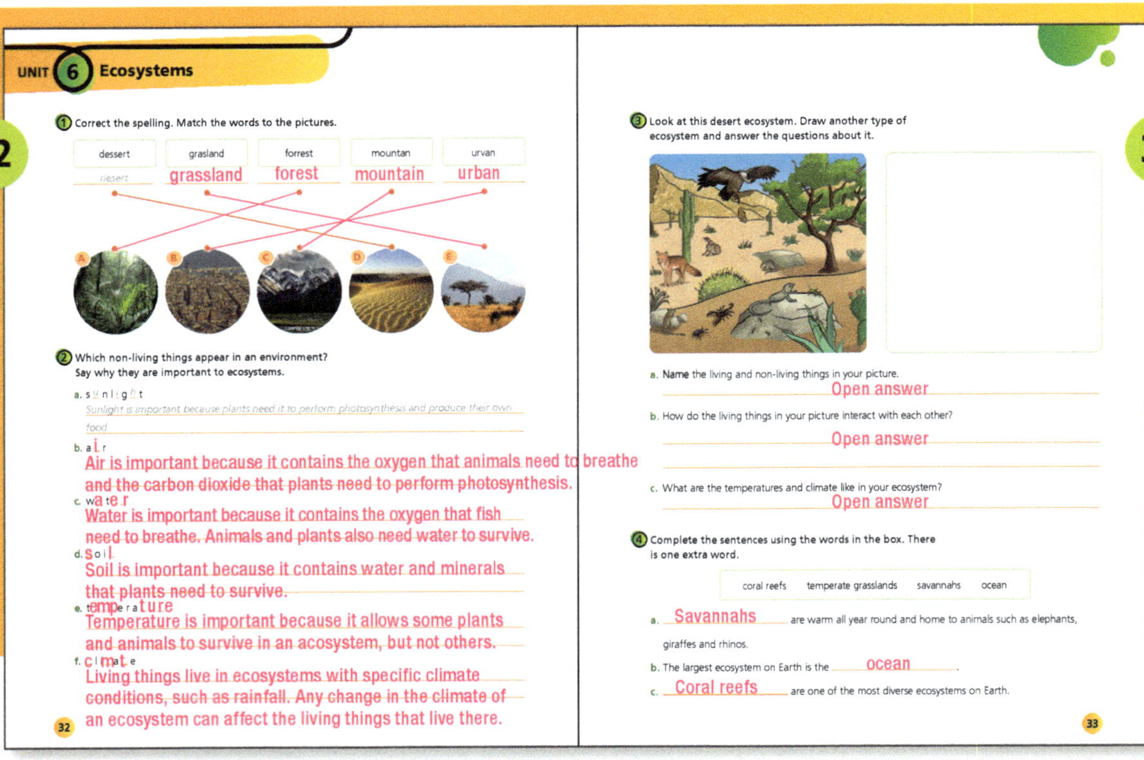

UNIT 6 Ecosystems

1 Correct the spelling. Match the words to the pictures.

dessert	grasland	forrest	mountan	urvan
desert	grassland	forest	mountain	urban

A B C D E

2 Which non-living things appear in an environment? Say why they are important to ecosystems.

a. sunlight
Sunlight is important because plants need it to perform photosynthesis and produce their own food

b. air
Air is important because it contains the oxygen that animals need to breathe and the carbon dioxide that plants need to perform photosynthesis.

c. water
Water is important because it contains the oxygen that fish need to breathe. Animals and plants also need water to survive.

d. soil
Soil is important because it contains water and minerals that plants need to survive.

e. temperature
Temperature is important because it allows some plants and animals to survive in an acosystem, but not others.

f. climate
Living things live in ecosystems with specific climate conditions, such as rainfall. Any change in the climate of an ecosystem can affect the living things that live there.

32

3 Look at this desert ecosystem. Draw another type of ecosystem and answer the questions about it.

a. Name the living and non-living things in your picture.
Open answer

b. How do the living things in your picture interact with each other?
Open answer

c. What are the temperatures and climate like in your ecosystem?
Open answer

4 Complete the sentences using the words in the box. There is one extra word.

coral reefs temperate grasslands savannahs ocean

a. Savannahs are warm all year round and home to animals such as elephants, giraffes and rhinos.

b. The largest ecosystem on Earth is the ocean.

c. Coral reefs are one of the most diverse ecosystems on Earth.

33

34 35

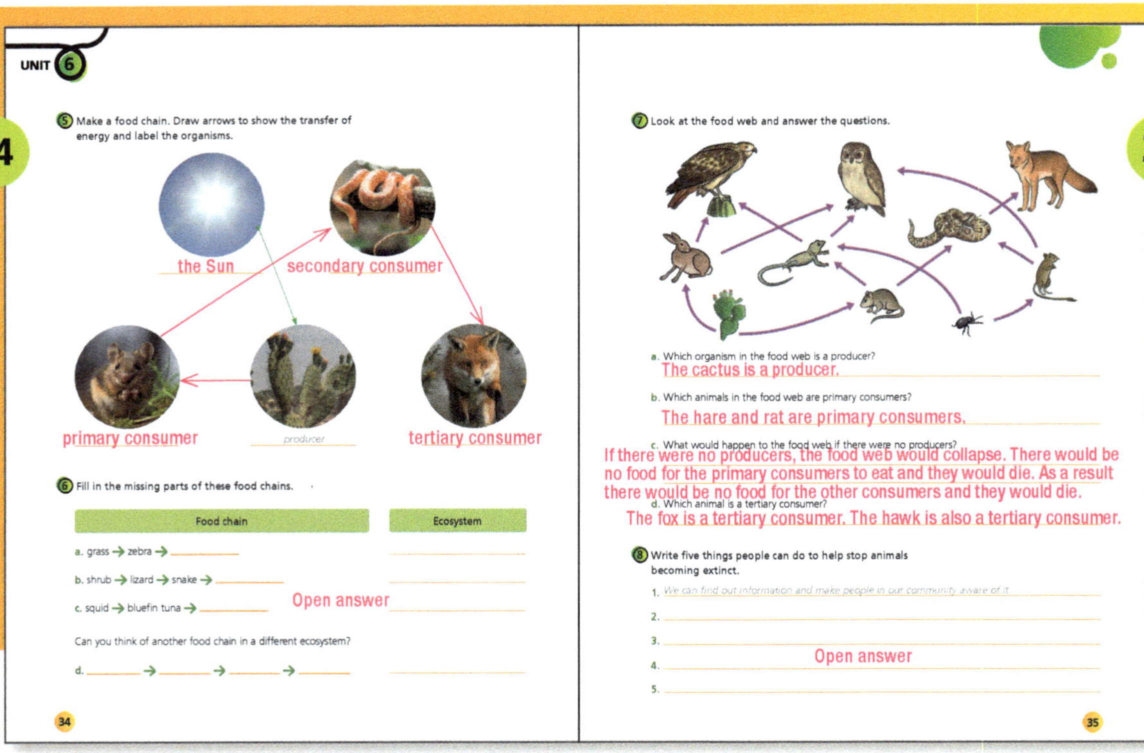

UNIT 6

5 Make a food chain. Draw arrows to show the transfer of energy and label the organisms.

the Sun
secondary consumer
primary consumer
producer
tertiary consumer

6 Fill in the missing parts of these food chains.

Food chain	Ecosystem
a. grass → zebra → ______	
b. shrub → lizard → snake → ______	
c. squid → bluefin tuna → ______	Open answer

Can you think of another food chain in a different ecosystem?

d. ______ → ______ → ______ → ______

34

7 Look at the food web and answer the questions.

a. Which organism in the food web is a producer?
The cactus is a producer.

b. Which animals in the food web are primary consumers?
The hare and rat are primary consumers.

c. What would happen to the food web if there were no producers?
If there were no producers, the food web would collapse. There would be no food for the primary consumers to eat and they would die. As a result there would be no food for the other consumers and they would die.

d. Which animal is a tertiary consumer?
The fox is a tertiary consumer. The hawk is also a tertiary consumer.

8 Write five things people can do to help stop animals becoming extinct.

1. We can find out information and make people in our community aware of it.
2.
3.
4. Open answer
5.

35

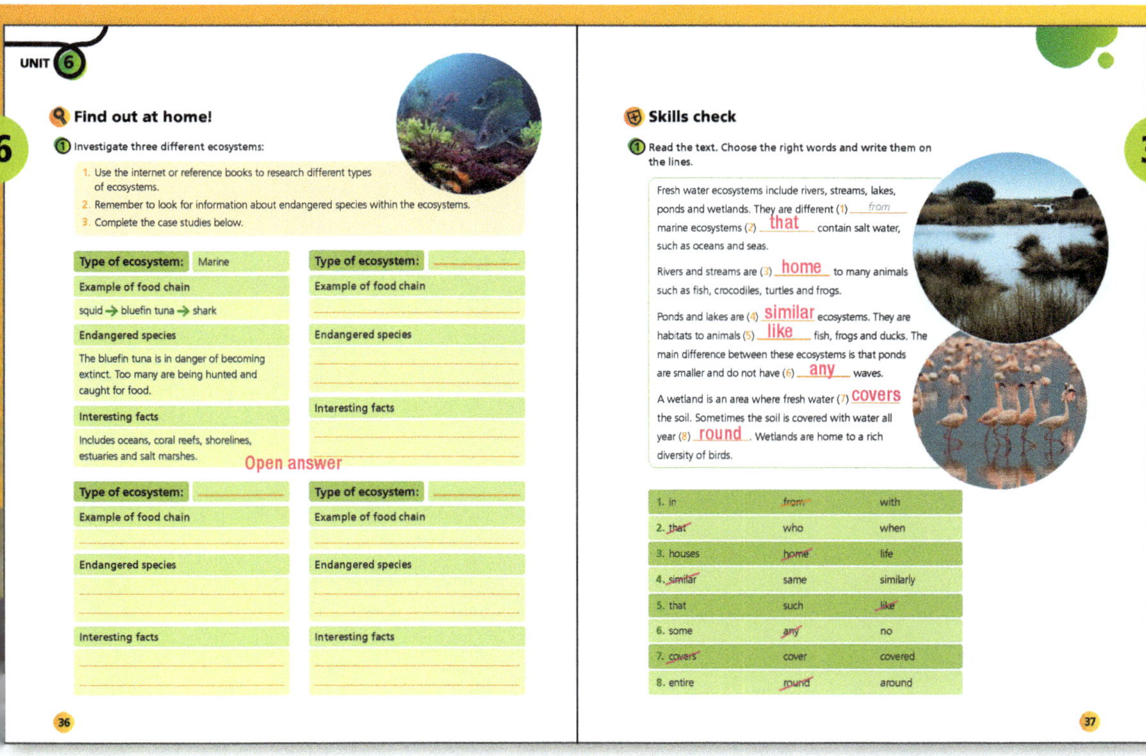

UNIT 6

6

Find out at home!

1 Investigate three different ecosystems:

1. Use the internet or reference books to research different types of ecosystems.
2. Remember to look for information about endangered species within the ecosystems.
3. Complete the case studies below.

Type of ecosystem:	Marine
Example of food chain	
squid → bluefin tuna → shark	
Endangered species	
The bluefin tuna is in danger of becoming extinct. Too many are being hunted and caught for food.	
Interesting facts	
Includes oceans, coral reefs, shorelines, estuaries and salt marshes.	

Type of ecosystem:	______
Example of food chain	
Endangered species	
Interesting facts	

Open answer

Type of ecosystem:	______
Example of food chain	
Endangered species	
Interesting facts	

Type of ecosystem:	______
Example of food chain	
Endangered species	
Interesting facts	

36

37

Skills check

1 Read the text. Choose the right words and write them on the lines.

Fresh water ecosystems include rivers, streams, lakes, ponds and wetlands. They are different (1) *from* marine ecosystems (2) **that** contain salt water, such as oceans and seas.

Rivers and streams are (3) **home** to many animals such as fish, crocodiles, turtles and frogs.

Ponds and lakes are (4) **similar** ecosystems. They are habitats to animals (5) **like** fish, frogs and ducks. The main difference between these ecosystems is that ponds are smaller and do not have (6) **any** waves.

A wetland is an area where fresh water (7) **covers** the soil. Sometimes the soil is covered with water all year (8) **round**. Wetlands are home to a rich diversity of birds.

1. in	~~from~~	with
2. ~~that~~	who	when
3. houses	~~home~~	life
4. ~~similar~~	same	similarly
5. that	such	~~like~~
6. some	~~any~~	no
7. ~~covers~~	cover	covered
8. entire	~~round~~	around

37

Unit 6 Audio CD2 track list

TRACK	ACTIVITY
02	**Pupil's Book page 79,** Unit introduction
03	**Pupil's Book page 79,** Song *Ecosystems*
04	**Pupil's Book page 80,** Story: *A trip to the salt marshes nature reserve*
05	**Pupil's Book page 82,** Elements of ecosystems
06	**Pupil's Book page 82,** Living things
07	**Pupil's Book page 82,** Physical environment
08	**Pupil's Book page 84,** Food chains and food webs
09	**Pupil's Book page 84,** Food chains

TRACK	ACTIVITY
10	**Pupil's Book pages 85,** Food webs
11	**Pupil's Book page 86,** Different types of ecosystems
12	**Pupil's Book pages 86,** Desert ecosystems
13	**Pupil's Book page 86,** Forest ecosystems
14	**Pupil's Book page 86,** Grasslands
15	**Pupil's Book page 87,** Marine ecosystems
16	**Pupil's Book page 87,** Urban systems

CONTENT	EVALUATION CRITERIA
Agriculture.	Observe and identify the principal characteristics of agriculture.
First approaches to scientific activity and the scientific method. Use of different information sources (direct and indirect). Use ICTs.	Obtain relevant information about specific phenomena, make predictions, integrate information from direct and indirect observation and communicate the results.
First approaches to simple experiments and investigations.	Conjecture as to the results of natural occurrences and of simple experiments and investiga
Individual and group work.	Work independently and proactively and develop strategies for working in a group.
Planning a project and presenting a report.	Carry out a project and present a report.

LEARNING STANDARDS	KEY COMPETENCES	PAGES
Observes and identifies the principal characteristics of agriculture.	MST	92, 93
With help, selects and organises specific and relevant information; analyses it and draws conclusions; reflects on the experience and the process; presents the results.	MST, LTL	92, 93
Use books, libraries, etc. and collaborate in the care and maintenance of all the materials available in the school and the classroom.	MST, LTL	92, 93
Shows autonomy in the planning of activities and tasks and shows initiative in decision taking.	LTL, AUT	92, 93
With help, carries out simple experiments or investigations, and conjectures as to the results.	MST, LTL, AUT	92, 93
Uses strategies to help their own learning, as well as asking for help and information.	LTL, AUT	92, 93
First approaches to cooperative learning.	SOC, LTL	92, 93
Begins observation, using relevant instruments and consulting written documents and images.	LTL, AUT	92, 93
Shows autonomy and proactiveness in the planning of and carrying out of actions.	AUT	92, 93
Presents work clearly and in an organised fashion.	LIN, LTL, AUT	92, 93
With help, carries out a project and presents a report, using paper and/or digital means, collecting information from different sources, presenting the results orally and with the support of images and short texts.	LIN, LTL, AUT, DIG	92, 93

PAGES 92-93 Think together: Agriculture

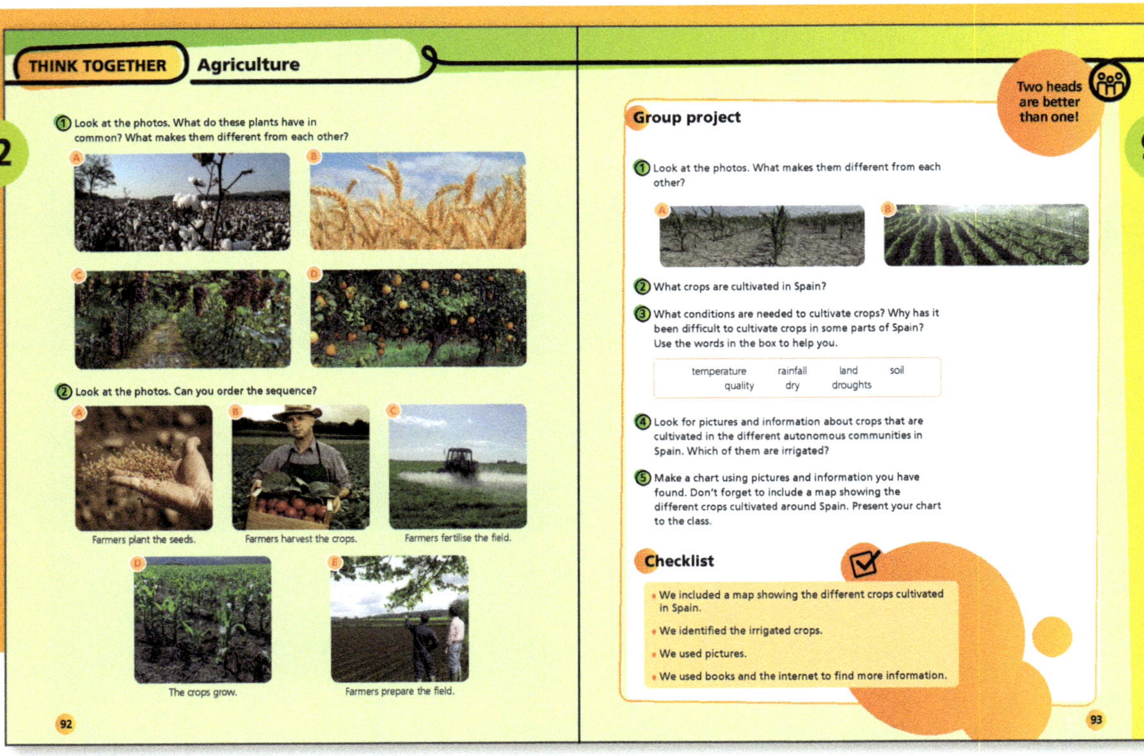

THINK TOGETHER Agriculture

92

1 Look at the photos. What do these plants have in common? What makes them different from each other?

A B C D

2 Look at the photos. Can you order the sequence?

A Farmers plant the seeds.

B Farmers harvest the crops.

C Farmers fertilise the field.

D The crops grow.

E Farmers prepare the field.

92

93

Two heads are better than one!

Group project

1 Look at the photos. What makes them different from each other?

A B

2 What crops are cultivated in Spain?

3 What conditions are needed to cultivate crops? Why has it been difficult to cultivate crops in some parts of Spain? Use the words in the box to help you.

temperature rainfall land soil quality dry droughts

4 Look for pictures and information about crops that are cultivated in the different autonomous communities in Spain. Which of them are irrigated?

5 Make a chart using pictures and information you have found. Don't forget to include a map showing the different crops cultivated around Spain. Present your chart to the class.

Checklist

- We included a map showing the different crops cultivated in Spain.
- We identified the irrigated crops.
- We used pictures.
- We used books and the internet to find more information.

93

PAGE SUMMARY

On these pages, pupils will revise the importance of agriculture and the characteristics of agriculture in Spain. The different activities will be done following different cooperative learning structures that will provide the optimal learning experience for the pupil and will guarantee the involvement of all the members of the group

LANGUAGE

- Question words: *what, how,* etc.
- Making comparisons: *The plant in Picture D has produced fruit, but the plants in Pictures A and B haven't.*
- Vocabulary: *farmer, crops, cultivate, temperature, rainfall, land, soil, drought, fertilise*

ADDITIONAL MATERIALS

- Digital flashcards
- Digital wordcards

OPENING ACTIVITIES

- Before doing these activities using different cooperative learning structures, you should form the groups. Teachers should form the groups rather than letting the pupils choose their own group members. Remember to form heterogeneous groups of three or four students.
- Tell the pupils what they will be doing in their groups, what procedures you will follow, and what your expectations are. If during these activities any group is having difficulty, spend some time in class on the relevant team skills.

MAIN ACTIVITIES

1 Look at the photos. What do these plants have in common? What makes them different from each other?

- This is a *Think-pair check* activity. Focus your pupils' attention on the four photos at the top of page 92.
- Ask your pupils to look at the photos and think independently about the questions: what do all of them have in common? How are they different?
- Tell them to discuss their answers in pairs. Ensure that each pupil shares something with their partner.

Then, ask the pairs to share their answers with the rest of the class.

② Look at the photos. Can you order the sequence?

- This is a *Round robin* activity. Pupils work in groups of five. Focus your pupils' attention on the five photos at the bottom of page 92.
- Using the zoom on the interactive whiteboard, show the pupils each of the five photos. Give each group a sheet of paper and a pencil.
- The first pupil in the group writes the first stage of the sequence, the second pupil writes the second stage, etc.
- When each group has completed the sequence, they can review their answer as a whole and discuss any changes they think are necessary.

GROUP PROJECT

① Look at the photos. What makes them different from each other?

- Ask pairs to compare the photos from activity 1. If they are having difficulty, give them prompts about which photo shows plants being watered.

② What crops are cultivated in Spain?

- This is a *Think-write-pair* check activity.
- Ask your pupils to think about the question. If they are struggling to remember which crops are cultivated in Spain, tell them they can quickly refer to page 75.
- Ask your pupils to write their ideas.
- Once they have finished, ask them to pair up and discuss their ideas.

③ What conditions are needed to cultivate crops? Why has it been difficult to cultivate crops in some parts of Spain? Use the words in the box to help you.

- This is a *Group members consult* activity.
- Ask your pupils to put their pencils down in the middle of the table.
- Ask your pupils to look at the words in the box. All members of the team should contribute in answering the question, but they don't all have to suggest the same thing.
- When everyone in the group has decided on their answer, ask them to pick up their pencils and write it down.

④ Look for pictures and information about crops that are cultivated in the different autonomous communities in Spain. Which of them are irrigated?

- Pupils can look for pictures and more information in reference books, higher-level school books or on the internet.

⑤ Make a chart using pictures and information you have found. Don't forget to include a map showing the different crops cultivated around Spain. Present your chart to the class.

- This is a *Group project* activity.
- Clearly explain the project the groups are going to do and the amount of time they have to complete it.
- Assign roles:
  - captain (in charge of managing the group and assigning the different roles)
  - materials manager
  - spokesperson
  - timekeeper
- After distributing the materials, ask your pupils to work to complete the task.
- Monitor your pupils.
- Ask the groups to share their project with the class.

CHECKLIST

- Group assessment is essential in cooperative learning to ensure that there is analysis of interactions and promotion of teamwork. Pupils should understand that how they work together affects the quality and quantity of concepts that they learn and understand.
- Ask pupils to discuss and reflect on how the group worked together and identify ideas and actions that helped the group achieve its goals.
- Once they have shared their results, ask them to reflect on how the project could be done better next time.
- Invite your pupils to share their conclusions with the class.

PAGES 94-95 Review pages

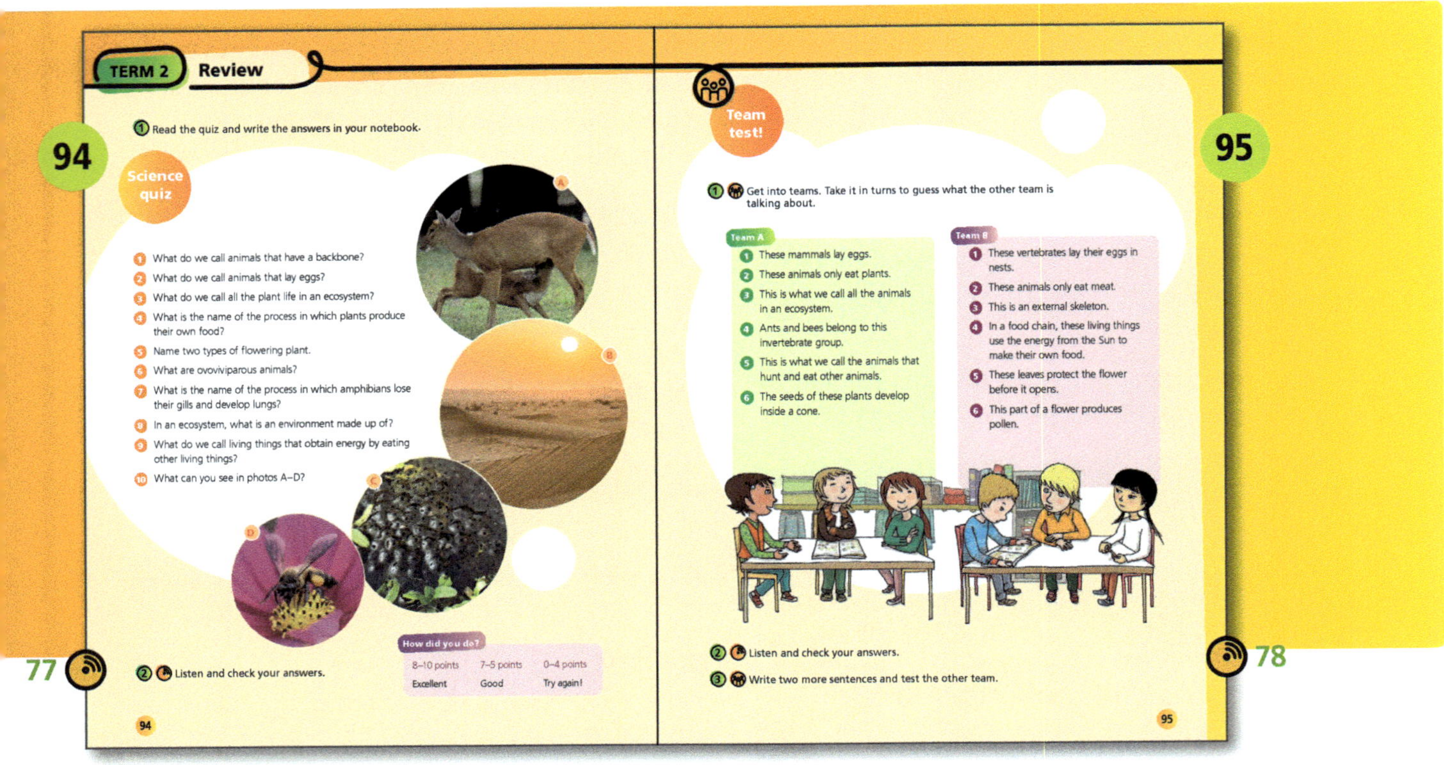
94

TERM 2 Review

① Read the quiz and write the answers in your notebook.

Science quiz

1. What do we call animals that have a backbone?
2. What do we call animals that lay eggs?
3. What do we call all the plant life in an ecosystem?
4. What is the name of the process in which plants produce their own food?
5. Name two types of flowering plant.
6. What are ovoviviparous animals?
7. What is the name of the process in which amphibians lose their gills and develop lungs?
8. In an ecosystem, what is an environment made up of?
9. What do we call living things that obtain energy by eating other living things?
10. What can you see in photos A–D?

77 ② Listen and check your answers.

How did you do?

8–10 points	7–5 points	0–4 points
Excellent	Good	Try again!

94

95

Team test!

① Get into teams. Take it in turns to guess what the other team is talking about.

Team A

1. These mammals lay eggs.
2. These animals only eat plants.
3. This is what we call all the animals in an ecosystem.
4. Ants and bees belong to this invertebrate group.
5. This is what we call the animals that hunt and eat other animals.
6. The seeds of these plants develop inside a cone.

Team B

1. These vertebrates lay their eggs in nests.
2. These animals only eat meat.
3. This is an external skeleton.
4. In a food chain, these living things use the energy from the Sun to make their own food.
5. These leaves protect the flower before it opens.
6. This part of a flower produces pollen.

② Listen and check your answers. 78

③ Write two more sentences and test the other team.

95

PAGE SUMMARY

The aim of the *Term Review* is to review and recycle what pupils have learnt over the term and encourage a positive attitude towards revision as a group and as individuals. Before you begin the Science quiz, decide if you prefer this to be an individual or collaborative revision activity and if you want pupils to use what they know or to look back for the answers. The Team test can be done in two teams or in small groups of two teams. Pupils should be encouraged to correct their own work, or peer correct. You can check the answers to both activities using the audio.

LANGUAGE

- Vocabulary: *backbone, lay, ecosystem, flowering, ovoviviparous, amphibians, gills, mammal, invertebrate, cone, vertebrate, food chain, pollen*

ADDITIONAL MATERIALS

- A clock for visual time keeping

SCIENCE QUIZ

① **Read the quiz and write the answers in your notebooks.**

1. What do we call animals which have a backbone?

Animals that have a backbone are called vertebrates.

2. What do we call animals that lay eggs?

Animals that lay eggs are oviparous.

3. What do we call all the plant life in an ecosystem?

All the plant life in an ecosystem is called the flora.

4. What is the name of the process in which plants produce their own food?

Plants produce their own food through the process of photosynthesis.

5. Name two types of flowering plant.

The two types of flowering plants are angiosperms and gymnosperms.

6. What are ovoviviparous animals?

Ovoviviparous animals produce eggs but the eggs develop and hatch inside the mother. The mother then gives birth to live offspring.

7. What is the name of the process in which amphibians lose their gills and develop lungs?

The process in which amphibians lose their gills and develop lungs is called metamorphosis.

8. In an ecosystem, what is an environment made up of?

In an ecosystem, an environment is made up of non-living things that share the same area as living things. These include air, sunlight, water, temperature, climate and soil.

9. What do we call living things that obtain energy by eating other living things?

Living things that obtain energy by eating other living things are called consumers.

10. What can you see in photos A-D?

Photo A shows a female deer, or a doe, and a young deer, or a fawn. The fawn is drinking its mother's milk. All mammals drink their mother's milk until they can find their own food.

Photo B shows a desert. Deserts are the driest and hottest ecosystems on Earth.

Photo C shows frogspawn. This is the thousands of eggs that frogs lay in pond water.

Photo D shows a wasp feeding on a flower. Pollination occurs when an insect transfers the pollen from the stamen of one plant, to the stigma of another plant.

2 Listen and check your answers. (CD1 Track 77)

- Pupils can check their own answers or check a partner's or another group's answers.

TEAM TEST!

1 Get into teams. Take it in turns to guess what the other team is talking about.

1. Team A: These mammals lay eggs. Answer: *monotremes*

1. Team B: These vertebrates lay their eggs in nests. Answer: *birds*

2. Team A: These animals only eat plants. Answer: *herbivores*

2. Team B: These animals only eat meat. Answer: *carnivores*

3. This is what we call all the animals in an ecosystem. Answer: *fauna*

3. This is an external skeleton. Answer: *exoskeleton*

4. Ants and bees belong to this invertebrate group. Answer: *insects*

4. Team B: In a food chain, these living things use the energy from the Sun to make their own food. Answer: *producers*

5. Team A: This is what we call the animals that hunt and eat other animals. Answer: *predators*

5. These leaves protect the flower before it opens. Answer: *sepals*

6. Team A: The seeds of these plants develop inside a cone. Answer: *gymnosperms*

6. Team B: This part of a flower produces pollen. Answer: *the stamen*

2 Listen and check your answers. (CD1 Track 78)

- Pupils can check the other group's answers.

3 Write two more sentences and test the other team.

- Give pupils a limited amount of time to go through the units and make up two more sentences to test their classmates. Circulate and check accuracy and suitability.
- At the end of the test, the winning team can choose either a video link or song from the unit, or request a particular game you play in class to close the lesson.

CONTENT	EVALUATION CRITERIA
Materials.	Classify materials according to their properties.
Physical and chemical changes.	Identify and explain some physical and chemical changes.
Mixtures.	Understand different types of mixtures and ways of separating them.
Mass and volume.	Define mass and volume and know ways of measuring them.
Density and buoyancy.	Understand the reasons why some things float on water.
Forces.	Know the principal characteristics of different forces and their effects.
First approaches to scientific activity and the scientific method. Use of different information sources (direct and indirect). Use ICTs.	Obtain relevant information about specific phenomena, make predictions, integrate information from direct and indirect observation and communicate the results.
First approaches to simple experiments and investigations.	Conjecture as to the results of natural occurrences and of simple experiments and investigations.
Individual and group work.	Work independently and proactively and develop strategies for working in a group.
Planning a project and presenting a report.	Carry out a project and present a report.

LEARNING STANDARDS	KEY COMPETENCES	PAGES
Classifies materials according to their properties.	MST, LTL	98,99
Identifies and explains the physical changes in form of some materials.	MST, LIN	100
Explains the principal characteristics of some chemical changes: combustion, oxidation and putrefaction.	MST, LIN	101
Knows the difference between different kinds of mixtures.	MST	102, 103
Understands different ways of separating mixtures and carries out simple experiments to test them.	MST, LTL	103
Defines mass and volume and knows different ways of measuring them.	MST, LTL	104
Understands the reasons why some things float on water.	MST	105, 107, 108
Understands the difference between contact and non-contact forces and between attraction and repulsion.	MST	106, 107
Begins to understand the concept of gravity and why it is important.	MST	106, 107
With help, selects and organises specific and relevant information; analyses it and draws conclusions; reflects on the experience and the process; presents the results.	MST, LTL	99, 108, 109
Use books, libraries, etc. and collaborate in the care and maintenance of all the materials available in the school and the classroom.	MST, LTL	96-111
Shows autonomy in the planning of activities and tasks and shows initiative in decision taking.	LTL, AUT	99, 108, 109
With help, carries out simple experiments or investigations, and conjectures as to the results.	MST, LTL, AUT	103, 107, 108
Uses strategies to help their own learning, as well as asking for help and information.	LTL, AUT	99, 108-110
First approaches to cooperative learning.	SOC, LTL	97, 109
Begins observation, using relevant instruments and consulting written documents and images.	LTL, AUT	108, 109
Shows autonomy and proactiveness in the planning of and carrying out of actions.	AUT	108, 109
Presents work clearly and in an organised fashion.	LIN, LTL, AUT	108, 109
With help, carries out a project and presents a report, using paper and/or digital means, collecting information from different sources, presenting the results orally and with the support of images and short texts.	LIN, LTL, AUT, DIG	108, 109

UNIT INFORMATION

UNIT SUMMARY

In this unit, pupils will review and extend their knowledge of materials and matter, reviewing some of their basic properties and the concept that everything is made up of matter. They will also be introduced to the concepts of mass and volume. Pupils will observe contact and non- contact forces: gravity, magnetism, friction and buoyancy, and their effects on objects.

At the beginning of the unit, pupils will refresh their knowledge of common materials and their properties. This subject area is covered in the opening illustration with the help of the course characters, Carla and Alex, who are on a school trip to a materials exhibition. The school trip continues in the story and, on their return to school, Carla and Alex carry out a *School trip project* to review the properties of materials and to associate the properties with the uses of these materials. These opening pages are designed to test pupils' prior knowledge and ease them into the subject matter of the unit, provoking interest and participation.

They will move on to study mass and volume by doing a hands-on investigation. They will also observe the effects of forces. This is a new area of study for pupils and one that requires a high level of language and knowledge acquisition. Therefore, the aim of this unit should be to *introduce* pupils to the subject matter and to give them practical activities to help them understand these new concepts.

EXPERIMENT

Find out

In the *Find out* activity on page 108, your pupils will prepare an investigation to find out how boats can carry objects which would sink in water.

Pupils will need:

- plasticine
- marbles
- container
- water

Further ideas

The pupils could extend this experiment by making boats of different shapes and recording which shapes are more successful at holding the marbles.

VALUES AND ATTITUDES

In this unit, your pupils will learn to recognise different properties of materials and how these properties determine what we can use these materials for. They will also be introduced to force and will be able to see the effects these forces have and appreciate their importance. They will continue to work on important skills such as observation, prediction and forming conclusions.

Throughout this unit encourage pupils to think about how important it is to recycle different materials.

Think about it

The *Think about it* page in this unit focuses on recycling. The intention of this section is to motivate pupils to think of ways to reuse everyday objects in order to reduce the amount of rubbish we generate both at home and at school. You can turn this activity into a practical experience by asking pupils to follow the instructions to make an ecological plant pot.

EVALUATION MATERIAL

These documents can be downloaded from the Teachers section of the digital component and printed.

The materials include:

- **Unit diagnostic test:** provides an overview of the unit and allows you to assess the pupils' prior knowledge.
- **End-of-unit test:** in addition to the Review section at the end of each unit, this summative test can be used to evaluate pupils' progress after studying the unit content.
- **Class unit evaluation grid:** based on the evaluation criteria and learning standards of the unit.

DIGITAL RESOURCES

Presentations

- **Unit summary**: a simple slide presentation with text, images and audio to review the main ideas of the unit. It can be used at the beginning of the unit to test pupils' prior knowledge of the unit content or at the end of the unit as a revision tool.
- **Find out:** a slide presentation of the unit's *Find out* page with text, photos and audio. The slide presentation is perfect for a heads-up class, showing the steps one by one. Use this tool to get the pupils to predict the next steps (with their books closed) or to focus their attention on each step as they carry out the project themselves.

Activities

Activities vary per unit and include the following:

- **Memory game:** useful activity for reviewing key vocabulary and modelling pronunciation.
- **Labelling:** pupils label a diagram by dragging and dropping key terms.
- **Spelling:** pupils drag and drop letters to spell key terms.
- **Read and reveal:** pupils read sentences and guess the missing words, which are revealed by clicking the spaces.
- **Classification:** pupils drag and drop concepts and key terms in a simple classification table.
- **Wordsearch:** pupils find key terms hidden in the wordsearch.
- **Definitions:** pupils drag and drop words to complete definitions.

Song lyrics

Listen to the song *Materials* and follow the lyrics line by line.

Posters

Attractive and informative posters to display in class. You can use them to review key concepts and vocabulary.

Videos

Use the video links in this unit to present content in a dynamic, real-life context while reinforcing the pupils' listening skills.

Teachers

Digital flashcards and wordcards: topics include *Physical and chemical changes, Mixtures, Matter, mass and volume, Why do some objects float on water* and *Forces and their effects*.

Downloadable pdfs: evaluation tests, evaluation grids, templates, useful links and further information.

PAGES 96-97 Matter, materials and forces

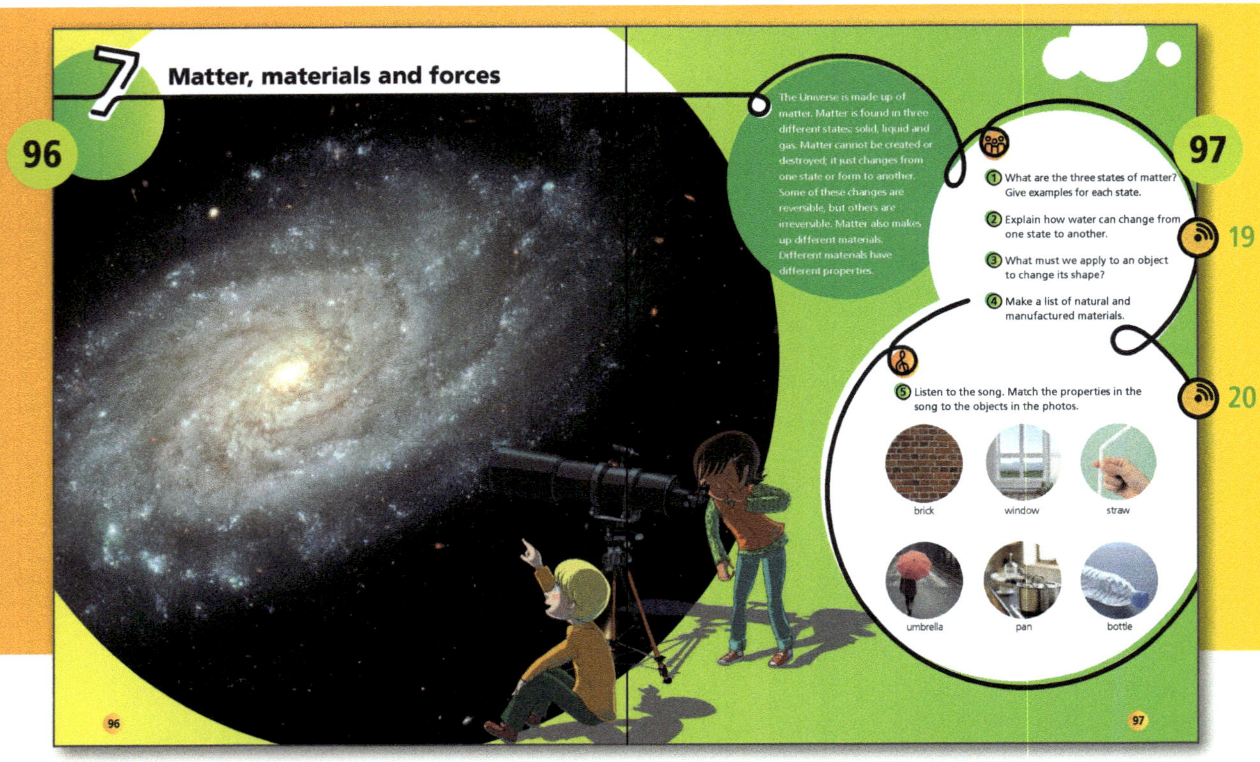

PAGE SUMMARY

The aim of the unit opener is to develop your pupils' observation skills and find out what they already know about the unit topic. Use the picture to elicit vocabulary related to matter, materials and their properties and forces, as well as vocabulary to describe the characters and objects. Get your pupils to work in groups to complete activities 1–4 and to have fun listening to the song and completing activity 5.

LANGUAGE

- Question words: *where, who, how many, etc.*
- Prepositions of place: *in, on, under, next to*
- *There is / are*
- Passive: *It is made of …*
- Vocabulary: *matter, solid, liquid, gas, state, reversible, irreversible, materials, properties, temperature, force, natural materials, manufactured materials*

ADDITIONAL MATERIALS

- Digital flashcards
- Digital wordcards
- Extra materials: a bowl of ice, a bottle of water, a kettle, a spoon, plasticine

OPENING ACTIVITIES

- If you are using an interactive whiteboard, focus only on the illustration, not the questions. Either elicit ideas (*Alex is pointing at a galaxy; Carla is standing next to Alex*, etc.) or ask questions indicating each part of the picture: **What's Alex doing? What can you see between Alex and Carla?**
- Alternatively, use the interactive whiteboard writing tools and ask pupils to come up to the board, mark an area of the picture and describe what they can see. Help them to produce full, correct sentences.

MAIN ACTIVITIES

Page 97, Unit introduction (CD2 track 19)

- Read the unit introduction at the top of page 97 or you can play the audio of the unit introduction first, with pupils reading along, and then ask one or two pupils to read out loud.
- Highlight the sentence *Matter is found in three different states.* Ask pupils to name the three states of matter and place the wordcards on the board. Ask pupils which process depends on matter changing from liquid to gas and to then to solid or liquid again (*the water cycle*). Invite volunteers to come up to the board to draw and explain the water cycle. Ask **Why is this process so important for living things?** (*All living things need water.*)

1 What are the three states of matter? Give examples for each state.

- Pupils should have an understanding of the three states of matter. Point out that air is made up of a mixture of gases: oxygen, nitrogen, carbon dioxide and water vapour. *Solid, liquid and gas. Open answer.*

2 Explain how water can change from one state to another.

- Elicit that thermal energy can make water change from one state to another. *Solid water (ice) will melt and become liquid when heated. Liquid water will become a gas (water vapour) when heated. Water vapour becomes liquid when cooled. Liquid water becomes solid when cooled.*

3 What must we apply to an object to change its shape?

- Hand out a small piece of plasticine to each pupil and ask them to make a ball with it. Then ask them to change the ball into a figure. Let them see each other's models and ask them how they changed its shape. *Force.*

4 Make a list of natural and manufactured materials.

- Ask pupils to name the materials they can see in the classroom first and then to add other materials that they know. Invite pupils to identify if the material is natural or manufactured. *Open answer*

5 Listen to the song. Match the properties in the song to the objects in the photos.

- Before listening to the song ask pupils to name the different properties materials can have. Say **Which properties can you remember from last year? What properties do plastic objects have?** As pupils name the properties, place the corresponding wordcard on the board.
- Focus pupils' attention on the six photos. Ask them to read and repeat the words. Check for understanding. Play the song *Materials* **(CD2 track 20)** and ask pupils to point to the material that has the property they hear. They may have more than one. Then play the song a second time and encourage pupils to sing along (you can use the *Song lyrics* section on the digital component to display the song line by line and listen to the song). See *Answers at a glance*

CD2 • track 60

Resistant, fragile
Rigid, flexible
These are properties of matter
Which material should I choose?
Rough, smooth
Hard and soft
These are properties of matter
Which material should I choose?
Absorbent, waterproof
Transparent, opaque
These are properties of matter
Which material should I choose?
Heat conductors, heat insulators
These are properties of matter
Which material should I choose?

CLOSING ACTIVITIES

- Ask pupils to look around the classroom and identify what materials objects are made of. Draw a chart with two columns on the board. Write the headings *Materials* and *Useful properties*. Give an example to begin the activity: *Wood – hard, rigid and resistant*. Tell pupils to work with a partner to make a chart about the materials in the classroom.

ANSWERS AT A GLANCE

1. Solid, liquid and gas. Open answer.
2. Solid water (ice) will melt and become liquid when heated. Liquid water will become a gas (water vapour) when heated. Water vapour becomes liquid when cooled. Liquid water becomes solid when cooled.
3. Force.
4. Open answer.
5. Brick: resistant, rigid, rough
   Window: transparent, fragile; Straw: flexible
   Umbrella: waterproof
   Pan: heat conductor, resistant, rigid
   Plastic bottle: flexible, waterproof

PAGES 98-99 A trip to the materials exhibition

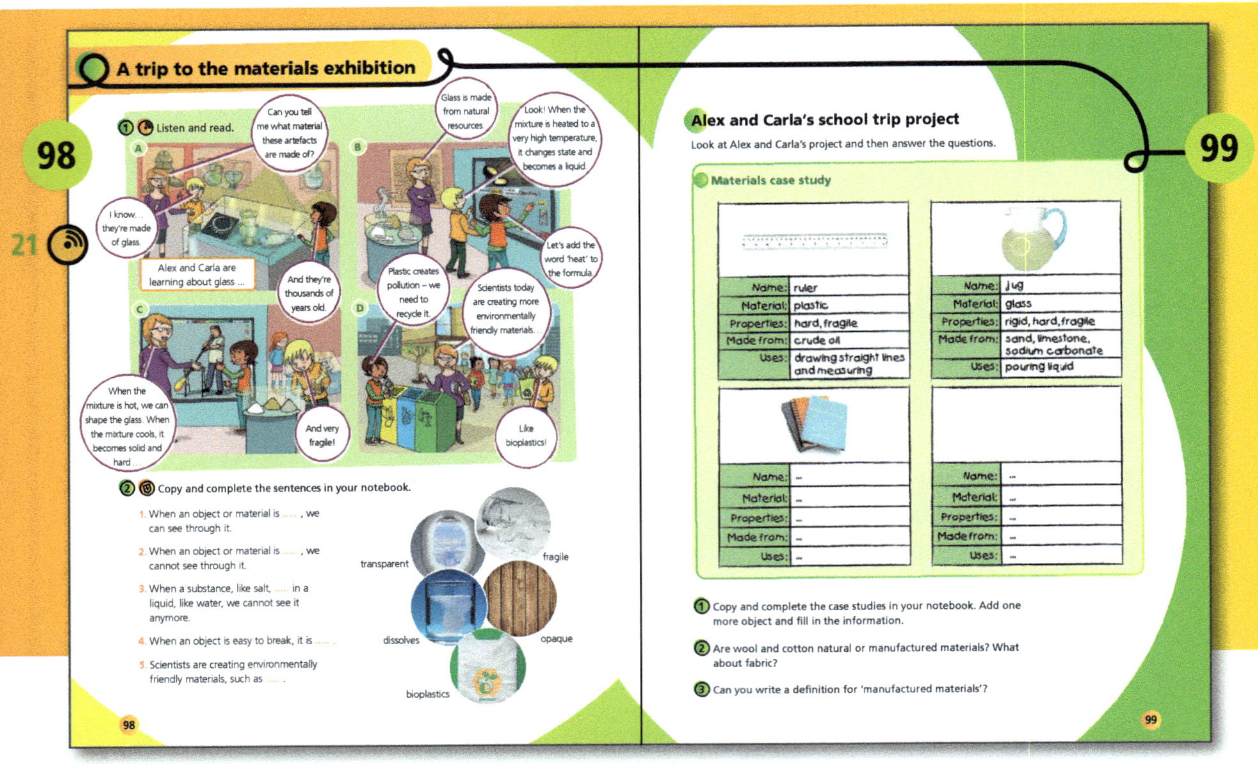

PAGE SUMMARY

This double-page spread opens with a story in which your pupils have the opportunity to see Carla and Alex at a particular moment of their school trip to the materials exhibition. Carla and Alex are talking to their teacher and showing their knowledge of materials. The story is reinforced with an exam-style matching activity that is related to the story and opening double-page spread. On page 99, pupils can study Carla and Alex's school trip project about properties and uses of materials.

LANGUAGE

- Making questions
- Vocabulary: *artefacts, formula, heats, cool, environmentally-friendly, pollution, bioplastics, dissolve, mixture*

ADDITIONAL MATERIALS

- Digital flashcards
- Digital wordcards
- Extra classroom materials: plastic ruler, glass jug, a notebook, cotton, wool, nylon, plastic, paper, metal, water

OPENING ACTIVITIES

- Ask pupils to write down the name of a classroom object on a piece of paper. Play the *Materials* song (CD2 track 20) and ask pupils to stand up if their object has a property from the song.
- Write anagrams on the board and ask pupils to work with a partner to decipher them. Before they begin the activity, tell them that they are all properties of materials.

  aflierg - fragile

  griid - rigid

  icstela - elastic

  tarnisarerptn - transparent

  xfblleei - flexible

  nsiuratlo - insulator

  nudcctoro - conductor

  paeowrtofr - waterproof

MAIN ACTIVITIES

1 Listen and read. (CD2 track 21)

- Draw pupils' attention to the story at the top of page 98 and explain to them that they are going to listen to a story about Carla and Alex's trip to the materials exhibition. Say **Let's listen and read**. Play the audio.

- Ask pupils to look at each of the illustrations and describe what is happening in each one using their own words. For example, *Carla is looking at the artefacts; Alex is going to drop the glass horse.*
- Divide pupils into groups of three and ask them to choose a character from the story – Carla, Alex or the teacher. Pupils then read their part of the story aloud in their small group. You can invite a group to the front of the class to act the story out.

② Copy and complete the sentences in your notebook.

- This activity aims to introduce some new vocabulary, reinforce what pupils have learned in the story and refresh concepts studied in previous levels. Ask pupils to copy the sentences in activity 2. Invite pupils to give definitions for the key words. *1-transparent; 2-opaque; 3-dissolves; 4- fragile; 5- bioplastics*

SCHOOL TRIP PROJECT

- Before pupils open their books, show them a plastic ruler, a glass jug and a notebook. Invite pupils to identify the material and name the properties.
- Explain to pupils that following their trip to the materials exhibition, Carla and Alex have done a project to summarise what they have learned about properties of materials.
- Tell pupils to look at page 99 and ask for volunteers to read the two completed case studies. Encourage them to use complete sentences. *This object is a ruler. It's made of plastic.*
- Draw the case study for the notebooks on the board and invite pupils say the missing information. Ask volunteers to come to complete the information on the board. **What are these?** *(Notebooks);* **What are they made of?** *(Paper);* **Which properties do they have?** *(Opaque, absorbent);* **What is paper made from?** *(Wood);* **What do we use them for?** *(Writing in)*

① Copy and complete the case study in your notebook. Add one more object and fill in the information.

- Ask pupils to do this activity individually and not to show their chosen object to the rest of the class, in order to use it in the closing activities. *Notebooks, paper, opaque, absorbent, flexible, wood, for writing in*

② Are wool and cotton natural or manufactured materials? What about fabric?

- Tell pupils you are going to name different materials. If the material is natural they must raise their right hand and if it is manufactured they must raise their left hand. Make sure to include wool, cotton and fabric. *Cotton and wool are natural but fabric is manufactured.*

③ Can you write a definition for 'manufactured materials'?

- Tell the class: **Natural materials come from living things or from the ground**. Ask them to suggest definitions for manufactured materials. *Manufactured materials are processed from natural materials or chemicals.*

⊕ EXTRA IDEAS

- This investigation can be a class demonstration or done by pupils in small groups. You will need a selection of materials such as cotton, wool, nylon, plastic, paper, metal and a bowl of water.
- **Design a coat:** Ask pupils what properties a coat should have. (*Resistant, flexible, waterproof, heat insulator.*) Write the properties on the board and list the materials pupils will test. Ask pupils to test each material and record the result with a tick or a cross. Using the results of the investigation ask them which material is the best one for a coat.

ANSWERS AT A GLANCE

Page 98

② 1-transparent; 2-opaque; 3-dissolves; 4- fragile; 5- bioplastics

Page 99

① Notebooks, paper, opaque, absorbent, flexible, wood, for writing in.

② Cotton and wool are natural but fabric is manufactured.

③ Manufactured materials are processed from natural materials or chemicals.

PAGES 100-101 Physical and chemical changes

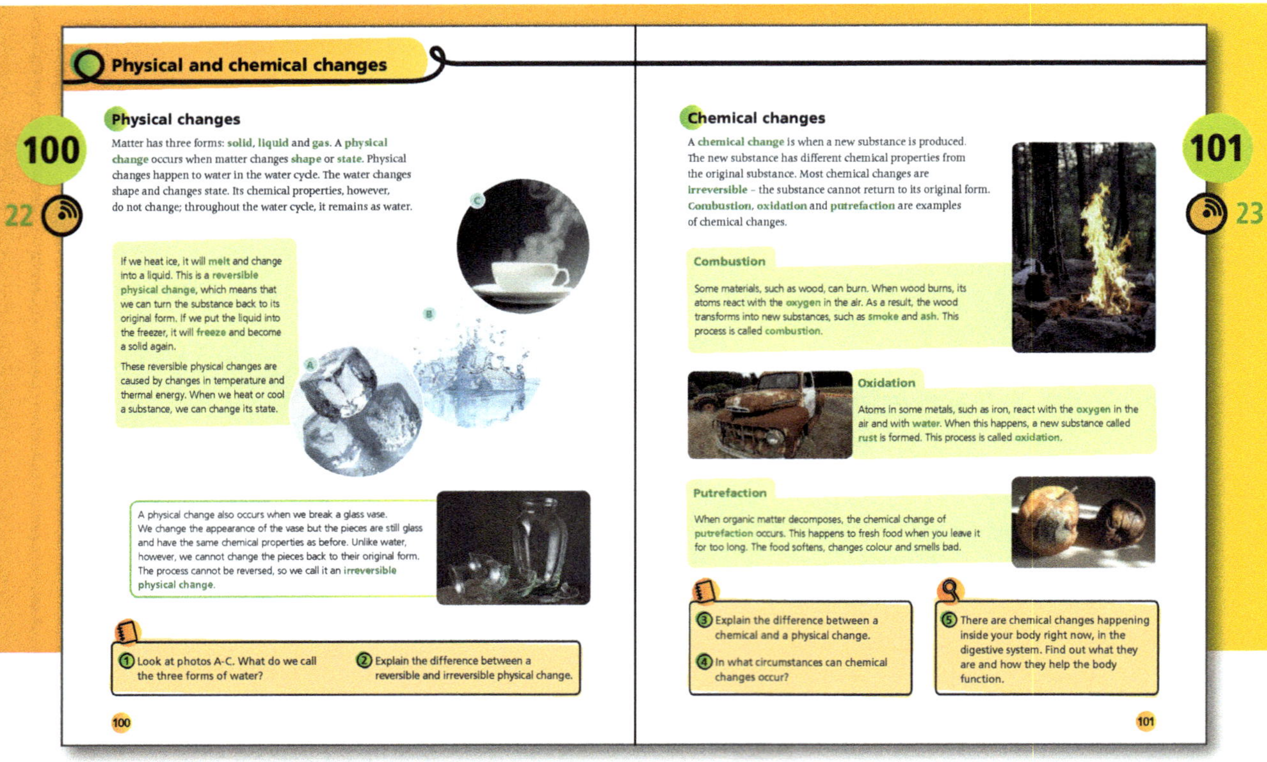
100
22

Physical and chemical changes

Physical changes

Matter has three forms: solid, liquid and gas. A physical change occurs when matter changes shape or state. Physical changes happen to water in the water cycle. The water changes shape and changes state. Its chemical properties, however, do not change; throughout the water cycle, it remains as water.

If we heat ice, it will melt and change into a liquid. This is a reversible physical change, which means that we can turn the substance back to its original form. If we put the liquid into the freezer, it will freeze and become a solid again.

These reversible physical changes are caused by changes in temperature and thermal energy. When we heat or cool a substance, we can change its state.

A physical change also occurs when we break a glass vase. We change the appearance of the vase but the pieces are still glass and have the same chemical properties as before. Unlike water, however, we cannot change the pieces back to their original form. The process cannot be reversed, so we call it an irreversible physical change.

1 Look at photos A-C. What do we call the three forms of water?

2 Explain the difference between a reversible and irreversible physical change.

100

101
23

Chemical changes

A chemical change is when a new substance is produced. The new substance has different chemical properties from the original substance. Most chemical changes are irreversible – the substance cannot return to its original form. Combustion, oxidation and putrefaction are examples of chemical changes.

Combustion

Some materials, such as wood, can burn. When wood burns, its atoms react with the oxygen in the air. As a result, the wood transforms into new substances, such as smoke and ash. This process is called combustion.

Oxidation

Atoms in some metals, such as iron, react with the oxygen in the air and with water. When this happens, a new substance called rust is formed. This process is called oxidation.

Putrefaction

When organic matter decomposes, the chemical change of putrefaction occurs. This happens to fresh food when you leave it for too long. The food softens, changes colour and smells bad.

3 Explain the difference between a chemical and a physical change.

4 In what circumstances can chemical changes occur?

5 There are chemical changes happening inside your body right now, in the digestive system. Find out what they are and how they help the body function.

101

PAGE SUMMARY

On this double-page spread pupils revise and extend their knowledge of physical and chemical changes. The lesson begins with a review of basic physical changes of matter and your pupils will learn about the differences between reversible and irreversible physical changes. Page 101 explores chemical changes: combustion, oxidation and putrefaction. Encourage the pupils to be aware of how matter changes in the world around them.

LANGUAGE

- Questions words: *when, what, why, etc.*
- Passive: *A new substance is formed.*
- Vocabulary: *liquid, solid, gas, physical change, chemical change, reversible, irreversible, shape, state, combustion, oxidation, putrefaction, properties, atoms, organic, fresh, rust, smoke*

ADDITIONAL MATERIALS

- Digital flashcards
- Digital wordcards
- Extra classroom material: scrap paper for each pupil, plasticine, metal paper clips, water, a plastic cup, a banana, paper plate, knife

OPENING ACTIVITIES

- Revise the different states of matter. Draw three columns on the board and write the headings *solid, liquid and gas*. Ask the pupils to give examples of each one.
- Draw the three states of water on the board. Remind the pupils that we can find the three states of water all around us. Ask: **Where can we find water as a solid? Where can we find it in a liquid state? Where can we find it as a gas?** Point out that when matter changes state, it is called a physical change.
- Hand out a piece of scrap paper to each pupil. Tell them to fold the paper three times. Now ask them to open up the paper again. Ask **Is this the same paper as the one I gave you?** Now ask them to tear the same piece of paper into four pieces. Hold up the pieces and ask **Is it still paper?** Explain that some physical changes are reversible and others are irreversible.

MAIN ACTIVITIES

Page 100, Physical changes (CD2 track 22)

- Before you read the text, ask pupils to look at the photos A, B and C. Ask the pupils to identify the three states of matter (*A – solid, B – liquid and C – gas*). Pupils listen and read. Check for understanding. **How can water change state?** *(A change in temperature and thermal energy will make it change state.)* **What happens in the water cycle?** (*Water changes state.*) **Is the water cycle an example of a reversible or irreversible physical change?** (*It's reversible.*)

1 Look at photos A-C. What do we call the three forms of water?

- Ask the pupils to work individually to answer this question in their notebooks. They can then check their answer in pairs. *A – solid/ice; B – liquid; C – gas/water vapour or steam*

2 Explain the difference between a reversible and irreversible physical change.

- Ask the pupils to work individually as they will have just read this information. *See Answers at a glance*

Page 101, Chemical changes (CD2 track 23)

- Before reading the text, fold a piece of paper and elicit that this is a reversible physical change. Tear the paper into four pieces and elicit that it is an irreversible physical change. If you have a safe area, burn one of the pieces of paper inside a metal container. Show the pupils the ash left in the box. Ask **Is this still paper?** (*No, it has changed.*) Place the wordcards *combustion, oxidation* and *putrefaction* on the board and practise the pronunciation.
- Ask the pupils to open their books on page 101 and play the audio **(CD2 track 23)**. The pupils listen and read. Answer any questions they may have and then ask them to read the introductory text as a group (see *Helpful tips*, pages 20-23).

3 Explain the difference between a chemical and a physical change.

- Ask the pupils to work with a partner to answer this question. Suggest they think about folding, tearing and burning the paper. **How is burning paper different? What happens to the paper?** (*When paper burns it changes into different substances.*) Ask the pupils to copy the question and answer into their notebook. *See Answers at a glance*

4 In what circumstances can chemical changes occur?

- Place the wordcards *combustion*, *oxidation* and *putrefaction* on the board. Ask pupils to look at the photos on page 101 and say when combustion, oxidation and putrefaction occur. Write their answers under the wordcards. *See Answers at a glance*

5 There are chemical changes happening inside your body right now, in the digestive system. Find out what they are and how they help the body function.

- This activity can be done at home with the help of parents or in small study groups on a computer or in the library. *See Answers at a glance*

ANSWERS AT A GLANCE

1. A – solid/ice; B – liquid; C – gas/water vapour or steam
2. A reversible physical change means that we can turn the substance back to its original form. An irreversible physical change cannot be reversed.
3. In a physical change, the matter is always the same. In a chemical change, the matter changes.
4. Combustion occurs when we burn something and its atoms react with the oxygen in the air, producing new substances – smoke and ash. Oxidation occurs when metals react with the oxygen in the air and with water. A new substance called rust is produced. Putrefaction occurs when organic matter decomposes.
5. Gastric juices in the stomach and digestive juices in the liver, pancreas and small intestine react with food, breaking it down into nutrients.

PAGES 102-103 Mixtures

24

102

25

26

103

27

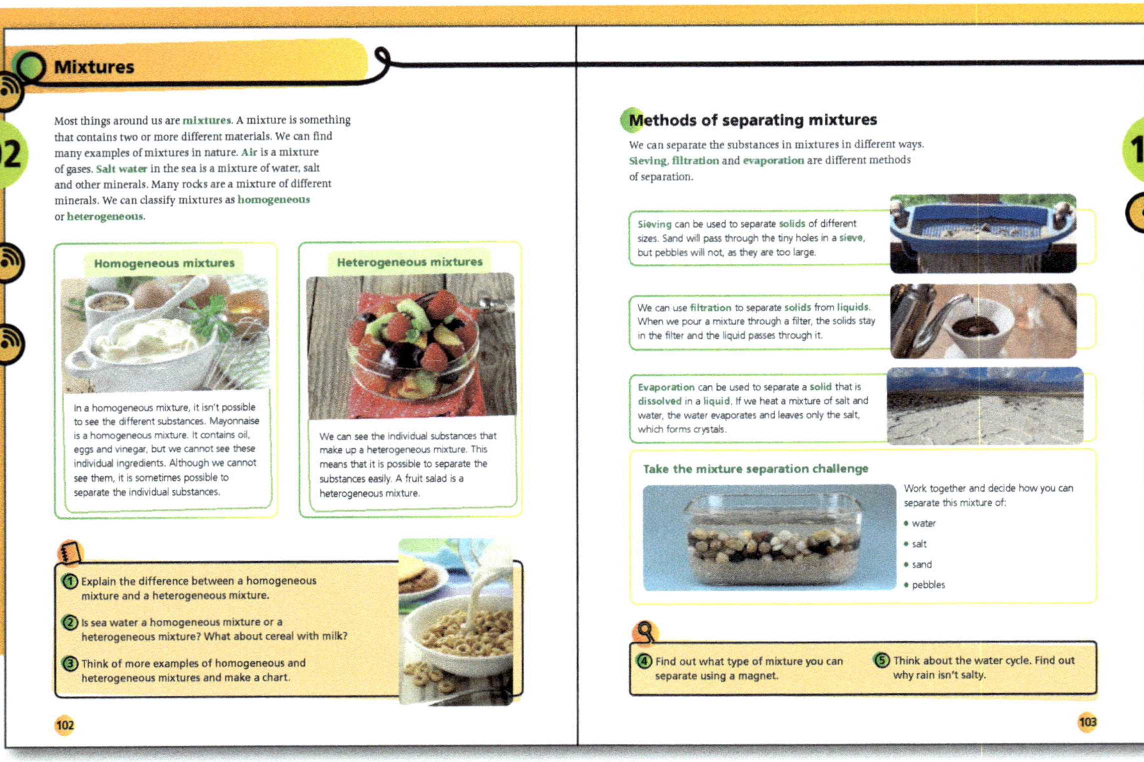

Mixtures

Most things around us are **mixtures**. A mixture is something that contains two or more different materials. We can find many examples of mixtures in nature. **Air** is a mixture of gases. **Salt water** in the sea is a mixture of water, salt and other minerals. Many rocks are a mixture of different minerals. We can classify mixtures as **homogeneous** or **heterogeneous**.

Homogeneous mixtures

In a homogeneous mixture, it isn't possible to see the different substances. Mayonnaise is a homogeneous mixture. It contains oil, eggs and vinegar, but we cannot see these individual ingredients. Although we cannot see them, it is sometimes possible to separate the individual substances.

Heterogeneous mixtures

We can see the individual substances that make up a heterogeneous mixture. This means that it is possible to separate the substances easily. A fruit salad is a heterogeneous mixture.

1. Explain the difference between a homogeneous mixture and a heterogeneous mixture.
2. Is sea water a homogeneous mixture or a heterogeneous mixture? What about cereal with milk?
3. Think of more examples of homogeneous and heterogeneous mixtures and make a chart.

102

Methods of separating mixtures

We can separate the substances in mixtures in different ways. **Sieving**, **filtration** and **evaporation** are different methods of separation.

Sieving can be used to separate **solids** of different sizes. Sand will pass through the tiny holes in a **sieve**, but pebbles will not, as they are too large.

We can use **filtration** to separate **solids** from **liquids**. When we pour a mixture through a filter, the solids stay in the filter and the liquid passes through it.

Evaporation can be used to separate a **solid** that is **dissolved** in a **liquid**. If we heat a mixture of salt and water, the water evaporates and leaves only the salt, which forms crystals.

Take the mixture separation challenge

Work together and decide how you can separate this mixture of:

- water
- salt
- sand
- pebbles

4. Find out what type of mixture you can separate using a magnet.
5. Think about the water cycle. Find out why rain isn't salty.

103

PAGE SUMMARY

On this double-page spread the pupils learn that almost everything around us is a mixture containing two or more different substances. They will observe that there are two types of mixtures: homogeneous and heterogeneous. On page 103 they focus on the process of separating mixtures. The aim of the mixture separation challenge is develop their critical thinking skills and to encourage collaborative learning and team work. If you have time, the mixture separation challenge can be carried out in groups.

LANGUAGE

- Question words: *what, why, which, etc.*
- Express possibility: *can / can't, is possible / is impossible, might / might not*
- Vocabulary: *crystals, dissolve, magnet, homogeneous, heterogeneous, sieving, filtration, evaporation*

ADDITIONAL MATERIALS

- Digital flashcards and wordcards
- Extra classroom materials: rice, lentils, water, salt, clear containers, magnets, flour, sand, pebbles, filters, sieves, plastic plates

OPENING ACTIVITIES

- Ask the pupils to identify physical and chemical changes from your prompts and clues: *The toast is black. There's ice on the pond. A bicycle left in the rain. A broken glass, etc.*
- Pour rice and lentils into a clear container and mix them together. Ask **What's in here?** *(Lentils and rice.)* Pour water into another clear container and mix in some salt. Then ask **What's in here?** (*Water and salt.*) Explain that they are both mixtures but in one mixture we can see the different substances and in the other mixture we can't see the different substances. Place the wordcard mixture on the board.

MAIN ACTIVITIES

Page 102, Mixtures (CD2 track 24)

- Ask pupils to look and listen to you and keep their books closed. Read out the introductory text about mixtures or play the audio. As you read or listen, indicate the two mixtures you made in the opening activities. Place the wordcards *homogeneous* and *heterogeneous* on the board. Ask **Is the rice and lentil mixture homogeneous or heterogeneous?** (*Heterogeneous*) Encourage the class to answer chorally to practise the pronunciation. Ask **Is the mixture of water and salt homogeneous or heterogeneous?** (*Homogeneous*)

- Tell pupils to open their books on page 102 and read the texts as a group **(CD2 tracks 25-26)**. You can use the *Read and repeat* activity (See *Helpful tips*, pages 20-23). Ask pupils which mixture is heterogeneous and which is homogeneous.

① Explain the difference between a homogeneous mixture and a heterogeneous mixture.

- Ask pupils to work with a partner to make a definition for the two types of mixtures. *In a heterogeneous mixture it is easy to see and separate the different substances. In a homogeneous mixture it's impossible to see the different substances.*

② Is sea water a homogeneous mixture or a heterogeneous mixture? What about cereal with milk?

- Write *homogeneous* and *heterogeneous* on the board and draw a chart with two columns. Invite volunteers to write *sea water* and *cereal with milk* in the correct columns. *Homogeneous – sea water. Heterogeneous – cereal with milk*

③ Think of more examples of homogeneous and heterogeneous mixtures and make a chart.

- Ask pupils to work in small groups to think of examples of homogeneous and heterogeneous mixtures. Point out that some are mentioned on page 102: air, rocks, mayonnaise, etc. *Open answers*

Page 103, Methods of separating mixtures (CD2 track 27)

- Ask pupils to open their books on page 103. You can play the audio and encourage the pupils to read along in their books or use one of the reading activities (see *Helpful tips* pages 20 – 23).
- Provide pupils with time to look at the photos of ways of separating mixtures. Show the class a sieve and ask **Which kind of mixtures can I separate using a sieve?** *(Solids of different sizes.)* You may like to demonstrate by separating a mixture of rice and salt. *(The salt will pass through and the rice will stay in the sieve.)* **Which kind of mixtures can I separate using a filter?** (*A solid and a liquid.*) Mix sand into a plastic cup with water and pour the mixture through the filter. (*The sand will stay in the filter and the water will pass through.*) Ask **Which kind of mixtures must we use evaporation to separate them?** (*When the solid is dissolved in a liquid.*)

Page 103, The mixture separation challenge

- Explain to pupils that they are going to get a chance to use what they have learned about mixtures. Ask pupils to open their books on page 103 and read the heading. Alternatively, keep the books closed and present the page on the interactive whiteboard. Tell them to look at the photo and to plan the steps needed to separate the substances.
- You may decide to continue this lesson to provide the pupils with time to do this investigation as a hands-on activity.

④ Find out what type of mixture you can separate using a magnet.

- Pupils should be able to answer these two questions without having to do research. You might like to demonstrate separation using a magnet with metal paper clips. *A mixture with metal pieces*

⑤ Think about the water cycle. Find out why rain isn't salty.

- *The water evaporates but the salt remains in the sea or ocean.*

ANSWERS AT A GLANCE

① In a heterogeneous mixture, it is easy to see and separate the different substances. In a homogeneous mixture, it is impossible to see the different substances.

② Homogeneous – sea water. Heterogeneous – cereal with milk.

③ Open answer.

④ A mixture with metal pieces.

⑤ The water evaporates but the salt remains in the sea or ocean.

PAGES 104-105 Matter, mass and volume

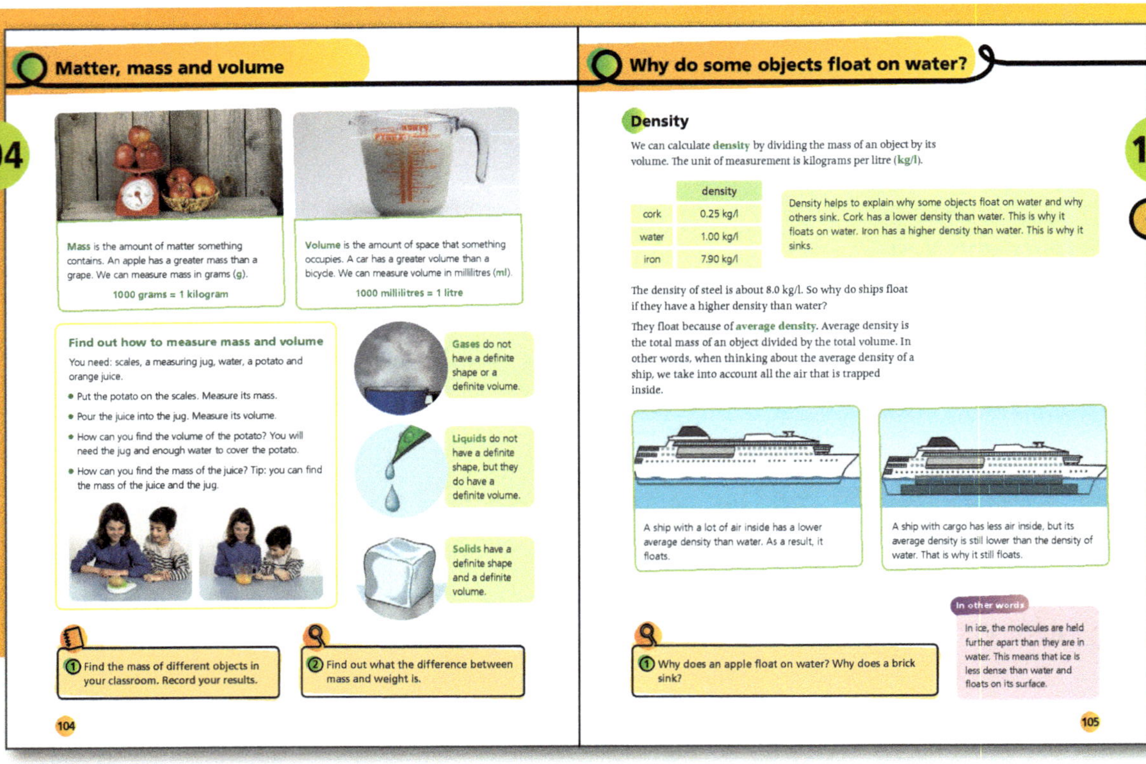

104

Matter, mass and volume

Mass is the amount of matter something contains. An apple has a greater mass than a grape. We can measure mass in grams (g).

1000 grams = 1 kilogram

Volume is the amount of space that something occupies. A car has a greater volume than a bicycle. We can measure volume in millilitres (ml).

1000 millilitres = 1 litre

Find out how to measure mass and volume

You need: scales, a measuring jug, water, a potato and orange juice.

- Put the potato on the scales. Measure its mass.
- Pour the juice into the jug. Measure its volume.
- How can you find the volume of the potato? You will need the jug and enough water to cover the potato.
- How can you find the mass of the juice? Tip: you can find the mass of the juice and the jug.

Gases do not have a definite shape or a definite volume.

Liquids do not have a definite shape, but they do have a definite volume.

Solids have a definite shape and a definite volume.

1 Find the mass of different objects in your classroom. Record your results.

2 Find out what the difference between mass and weight is.

104

Why do some objects float on water?

105

28

Density

We can calculate **density** by dividing the mass of an object by its volume. The unit of measurement is kilograms per litre (**kg/l**).

	density
cork	0.25 kg/l
water	1.00 kg/l
iron	7.90 kg/l

Density helps to explain why some objects float on water and why others sink. Cork has a lower density than water. This is why it floats on water. Iron has a higher density than water. This is why it sinks.

The density of steel is about 8.0 kg/l. So why do ships float if they have a higher density than water?

They float because of **average density**. Average density is the total mass of an object divided by the total volume. In other words, when thinking about the average density of a ship, we take into account all the air that is trapped inside.

A ship with a lot of air inside has a lower average density than water. As a result, it floats.

A ship with cargo has less air inside, but its average density is still lower than the density of water. That is why it still floats.

1 Why does an apple float on water? Why does a brick sink?

In other words

In ice, the molecules are held further apart than they are in water. This means that ice is less dense than water and floats on its surface.

105

PAGE SUMMARY

On this double-page spread pupils investigate the concepts of mass, volume and density. They will also be introduced to the concept of atoms and how the organisation of atoms affects the state of matter. The main learning aim is to recognise the characteristics of the three states of matter and to carry out a practical activity to investigate mass, volume and density.

LANGUAGE

- Comparative adjectives
- Vocabulary: *mass, volume, density, grams, kilograms, litres, millilitres, kilograms per litre*

ADDITIONAL MATERIALS

- Digital flashcards
- Digital wordcards
- Extra classroom materials: a bag of sugar, a litre of orange juice, scales, 2 measuring jugs, a potato, water, three freezer bags, calculator, two balloons, a metre stick, a transparent container, syrup, coloured water, oil

OPENING ACTIVITIES

- Take in to class a carton of juice and a bag of sugar. Ask pupils which units we use to measure sugar and juice. Elicit that we measure sugar in grams and juice in litres. Ask them to name other products that we measure in grams and litres (*salt, apples, biscuits, water, milk, oil*, etc.).

MAIN ACTIVITIES

Page 104, Matter, mass and volume

- Tell pupils to open their books on page 104 and to look at the photos at the top of the page. Ask pupils to read. Check for understanding. **How do we measure mass?** (*In grams and kilograms*); **Which has a greater mass, an apple or a grape?** (*An apple*)

1 Find the mass of different objects in your classroom. Record your results.

- Organise the class into groups of four pupils. Ask them to choose three classroom objects and to write the names on a paper. Tell them to estimate the mass of each object and record it on the paper. Invite the groups to come and weigh the objects on the scales and record the number of grams next to the estimated number.

Page 104, Find out how to measure mass and volume

- Ask pupils to read the instructions for the investigation individually. As they read, you can set up the equipment for the investigation.
- Invite pupils to read out the steps and follow their instructions. Invite other pupils to record the results on the board.
- Ask pupils to talk to their partner to find the answer to point 3. Write the volume of the water on the board to give a clue. Invite pupils who give the correct answer to put the potato in the measuring jug and record the results. (*Volume of water with the potato in it – volume of water without the potato = volume of the potato.*)
- Ask pupils to talk to their partner to find the answer to point 4. Empty out the water from the measuring jug in order find the mass of the juice. Write it on the board as a clue. (*Mass of the jug with the juice in it– mass of the jug = mass of the juice.*)

Page 104, Gases, liquids and solids

- Draw pupils' attention to the three states of matter. Invite a pupil to read the text boxes.
- Draw a chart on the board and invite pupils to complete the chart with ticks and crosses, to check understanding.

	Definite shape	Definite volume
Solid	✓	✓
Liquid	×	✓
Gas	×	×

② Find out what what the difference between mass and weight is.

- This activity can be done at home with the help of parents, in small study groups on a computer or in the library. *See Answers at a glance*

Page 105, Why do some objects float on water? (CD2 track 28)

- Set out a bowl of water, a cork and a metal object which is smaller than the cork. Invite pupils to come to the table to observe an experiment. Point out that they already know that some objects sink and others float. Ask them to predict which object will sink or float. Invite pupils to place the cork and metal object in the water. Ask them to explain why this has happened. Accept all answers and say **Let's find out.**

Density

- Ask **How can we calculate density?** (*By dividing the mass of the object by its volume.*) Invite a pupil to read the information box about density again. Ask **What is the density of water?** (*1.00kg/l*); **Will an object with a density of 0.70 kg/l sink or float?** (*Float*); **Will an object with a density of 1.50 kg/l sink or float?** (*Sink*)
- Ask pupils to read the paragraph about average density again. Ask: **If steel has a density of 8.0 kg/l, how can it float? What affects the average density of a ship made of steel?** (*The air inside it.*) You may wish to show the class how a deflated balloon sinks in water but an inflated one floats.

① Why does an apple float on water? Why does a brick sink?

- Ask pupils to discuss this question with a partner. Invite a volunteer to answer the question and check how many people agree by a show of hands. Point out that an apple is mainly made up of water. *An apple has a lower average density than water. A brick has a higher average density than water.*

ANSWERS AT A GLANCE

Page 104

① Open answer.

② The mass of an object is a measure of the amount of matter in that object. Weight is a measure of the force on the object caused by gravity. If you were on the moon, your weight would change because the pull of gravity is weaker than on Earth but your mass would stay the same because you are still made up of the same amount of matter.

Page 105

① An apple has a lower density than water. A brick has a higher density than water.

PAGES 106-107 Forces and their effects

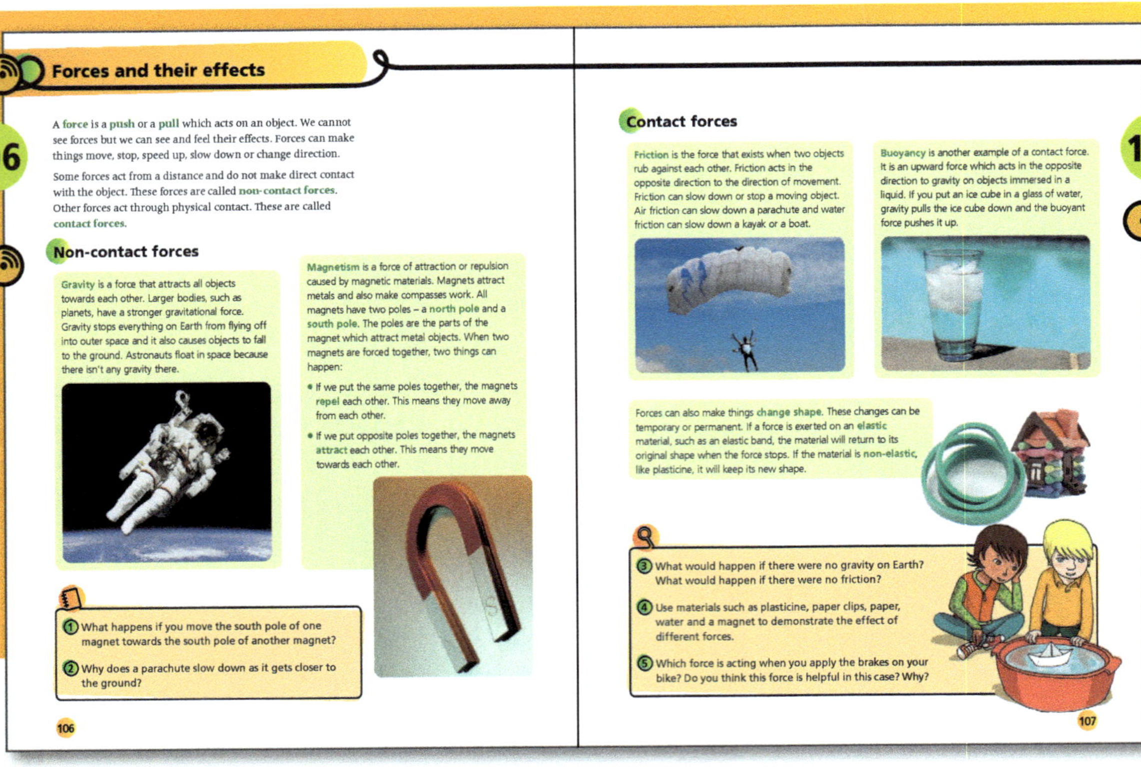

29 **Forces and their effects**

106

A **force** is a **push** or a **pull** which acts on an object. We cannot see forces but we can see and feel their effects. Forces can make things move, stop, speed up, slow down or change direction.

Some forces act from a distance and do not make direct contact with the object. These forces are called **non-contact forces**. Other forces act through physical contact. These are called **contact forces**.

30 **Non-contact forces**

Gravity is a force that attracts all objects towards each other. Larger bodies, such as planets, have a stronger gravitational force. Gravity stops everything on Earth from flying off into outer space and it also causes objects to fall to the ground. Astronauts float in space because there isn't any gravity there.

Magnetism is a force of attraction or repulsion caused by magnetic materials. Magnets attract metals and also make compasses work. All magnets have two poles – a **north pole** and a **south pole**. The poles are the parts of the magnet which attract metal objects. When two magnets are forced together, two things can happen:

- If we put the same poles together, the magnets **repel** each other. This means they move away from each other.
- If we put opposite poles together, the magnets **attract** each other. This means they move towards each other.

1. What happens if you move the south pole of one magnet towards the south pole of another magnet?
2. Why does a parachute slow down as it gets closer to the ground?

106

Contact forces

107 31

Friction is the force that exists when two objects rub against each other. Friction acts in the opposite direction to the direction of movement. Friction can slow down or stop a moving object. Air friction can slow down a parachute and water friction can slow down a kayak or a boat.

Buoyancy is another example of a contact force. It is an upward force which acts in the opposite direction to gravity on objects immersed in a liquid. If you put an ice cube in a glass of water, gravity pulls the ice cube down and the buoyant force pushes it up.

Forces can also make things **change shape**. These changes can be temporary or permanent. If a force is exerted on an **elastic** material, such as an elastic band, the material will return to its original shape when the force stops. If the material is **non-elastic**, like plasticine, it will keep its new shape.

3. What would happen if there were no gravity on Earth? What would happen if there were no friction?
4. Use materials such as plasticine, paper clips, paper, water and a magnet to demonstrate the effect of different forces.
5. Which force is acting when you apply the brakes on your bike? Do you think this force is helpful in this case? Why?

107

PAGE SUMMARY

On this double-page spread pupils will study forces and their effects on objects. This subject matter will not be familiar to them. It is the first time they will reflect on forces so it is important to give them opportunities to investigate and understand this concept with practical activities.

LANGUAGE

- Comparative adjectives
- Present simple
- Vocabulary: *forces, gravity, magnetism, friction, buoyancy, non-contact forces, contact forces, attraction, repulsion, magnetic, north pole, south pole, parachute, kayak, elastic, non-elastic, immersed, attract, repel, rub*

MATERIALS

- Digital flashcards
- Digital wordcards
- Extra classroom materials: *a book, a soft ball, magnets, plasticine, elastic bands, a glass of water, ice cubes, paper clips, paper, bowls*

OPENING ACTIVITIES

- Place the Forces wordcard on the board and give a demonstration of various forces at beginning the lesson. Leave the classroom door open and ask a pupil to close it for you. Explain that they are seeing an example of force. Ask **How did we close the door?** (*By pushing it.*) Now ask a pupil to open the door. Ask **How did we open the door?** (*By pulling it.*) Explain that pushing and pulling are forces. Drop a book on the floor. Ask **Why did the book fall to the floor and not fly around the room?** (*A force acted on the book.*) Roll a soft ball along the floor. Ask **Why did it move and why did it stop?** (*A force made it move and a force made it stop.*)

MAIN ACTIVITIES

Page 106, Forces and their effects (CD2 track 29)

- Tell pupils to open their books on page 106 and read the introductory text with a partner. Suggest the use Order reading (See *Helpful tips*, pages 20-23). The first pupil reads the first sentence aloud and their partner reads the following sentence and so forth. Check for understanding. **What is a force?** *(A push or a pull which acts on an object.)* **How can forces act on an object?** *(They can make things move, slow down, speed up or change direction.)*

- Pupils read Non-contact forces: gravity (CD1 track 30). Ask **Why do astronauts float in space?** *(There isn't any gravity.)* **Why do objects fall to the ground?** *(Gravity pulls the object to the ground.)*
- Now draw pupils' attention to the text about magnetism. Ask **What type of force is magnetism?** *(One of attraction and repulsion.)* **Do magnets attract all materials?** *(No, they only attract metals.)*

1 What happens if you move the south pole of one magnet towards the south pole of another magnet?

- Ask pupils to work with a partner. Hand out two magnets to each pair of pupils and tell them to find out what happens when they move the south pole of a magnet towards the south pole of another magnet. Now ask them to find out what happens when they move the south pole of a magnet towards the north pole of another magnet. *The magnets repel each other. They move apart.*

Page 107, Contact forces (CD2 track 31)

- Draw pupils' attention to the information box about friction. Read the text and pause at key words to have pupils read the missing word or words. (See *Helpful tips*, pages 20-23.) Repeat the procedure with the information box about buoyancy. Gently roll a ball along the table so that it stops. Ask **Which force has stopped the ball?** *(Friction)* Place some ice cubes in a glass of water and invite a pupil to try to push them down. Ask **Which force keeps the ice at the top of the water?** *(Buoyancy)*
- Invite a pupil to read the final information box about changing shape and ask questions to check understanding.

2 Why does a parachute slow down as it gets closer to the ground?

- Draw pupils' attention to question 2 on page 106. Invite a pupil to read the question for the class. *The air friction increases.*

3 What would happen if there were no gravity on Earth? What would happen if there were no friction?

- Ask pupils to work with a partner to talk about the answer to these questions. *See Answers at a glance*

4 Use materials such as plasticine, paper clips, paper, water and a magnet to demonstrate the effect of different forces.

- Place the wordcards *gravity, magnetism, friction* and *buoyancy* on the board. Organise the class into groups of four pupils. Give out the materials to each group and allow them to investigate freely. *Open answer*

5 Which force is acting when you apply the brakes on your bike? Do you think this force is helpful in this case? Why?

- Ask a pupil to read the question for the rest of the class. Invite pupils to give their opinions. *See Answers at a glance*

CLOSING ACTIVITIES

- Play the true or false game using the information from the lesson. Ask pupils to stand up and make a line. If necessary make two lines of pupils but make sure that they have space to move. Explain that if the sentence is true, they must jump to their left. If the sentence is false, they must jump to their right. After each jump, tell them to return to the line. **Magnetism is a contact force.** (*False*); **Force can make on object move.** (*True*); **Force can make an object move.** (*True*)

ANSWERS AT A GLANCE

1. The magnets repel each other. They move apart.
2. The air friction increases.
3. If there were no gravity, everything would float
4. Open investigation.
5. It is friction. It is helpful because the brakes slow down and stop the bike.

PAGES 108-109 Find out / Think about it

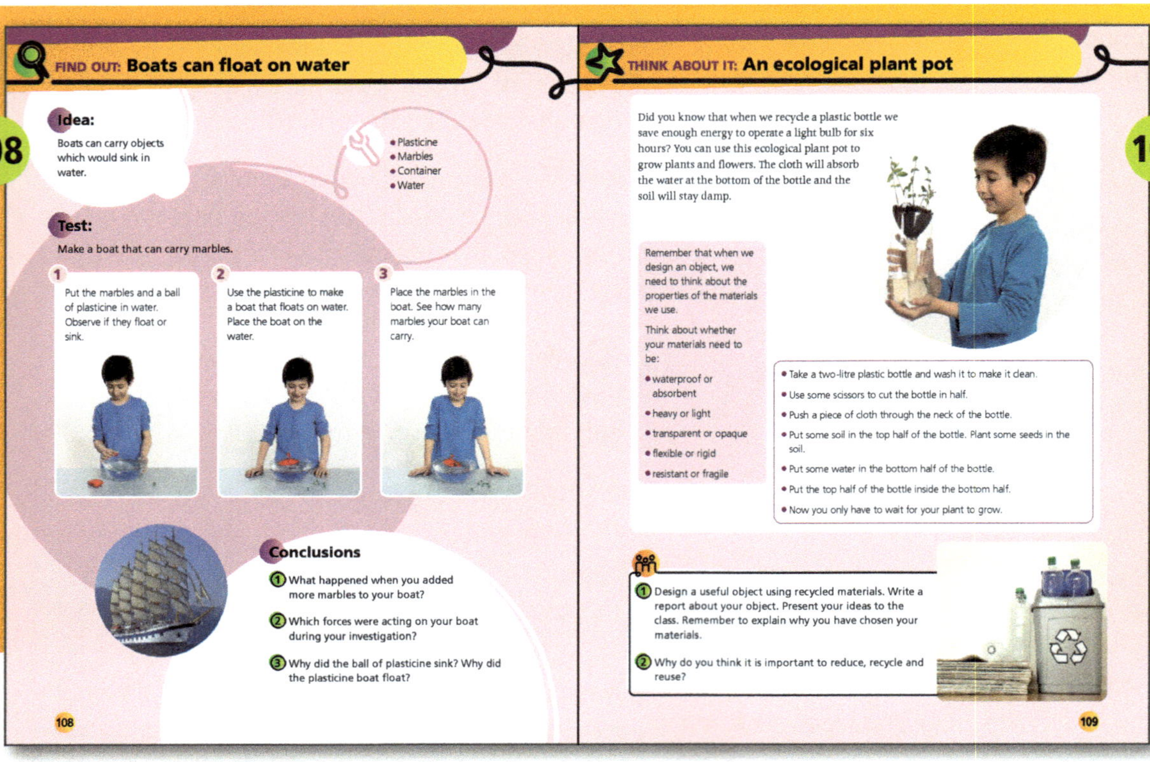
108

FIND OUT: Boats can float on water

Idea:

Boats can carry objects which would sink in water.

- Plasticine
- Marbles
- Container
- Water

Test:

Make a boat that can carry marbles.

1. Put the marbles and a ball of plasticine in water. Observe if they float or sink.
2. Use the plasticine to make a boat that floats on water. Place the boat on the water.
3. Place the marbles in the boat. See how many marbles your boat can carry.

Conclusions

1. What happened when you added more marbles to your boat?
2. Which forces were acting on your boat during your investigation?
3. Why did the ball of plasticine sink? Why did the plasticine boat float?

108

109

THINK ABOUT IT: An ecological plant pot

Did you know that when we recycle a plastic bottle we save enough energy to operate a light bulb for six hours? You can use this ecological plant pot to grow plants and flowers. The cloth will absorb the water at the bottom of the bottle and the soil will stay damp.

Remember that when we design an object, we need to think about the properties of the materials we use.

Think about whether your materials need to be:

- waterproof or absorbent
- heavy or light
- transparent or opaque
- flexible or rigid
- resistant or fragile

- Take a two-litre plastic bottle and wash it to make it clean.
- Use some scissors to cut the bottle in half.
- Push a piece of cloth through the neck of the bottle.
- Put some soil in the top half of the bottle. Plant some seeds in the soil.
- Put some water in the bottom half of the bottle.
- Put the top half of the bottle inside the bottom half.
- Now you only have to wait for your plant to grow.

1. Design a useful object using recycled materials. Write a report about your object. Present your ideas to the class. Remember to explain why you have chosen your materials.
2. Why do you think it is important to reduce, recycle and reuse?

109

PAGE SUMMARY

In the first of these two pages (*Find out*), pupils investigate buoyancy and average density by making a boat to carry objects which would sink. The second page *(Think about it)* provides your pupils with the opportunity to create an object from recycled materials and also to think about ways to reduce waste and reuse materials. You may like to set activity 1 on page 109 as a practical homework and ask pupils to make the object at home.

LANGUAGE

- Imperatives: *put, observe, use, place, see, take, push, plant*
- Vocabulary: *marbles, plasticine, ecological, plant pot, light bulb, damp, cloth, soil, design*

ADDITIONAL MATERIALS

- Digital flashcards
- Digital wordcards
- Extra materials: a sheet of A4 paper for each pupil, 2l plastic bottle, scissors, cloth, soil, grass seeds, water, a can, a tetra pack, a glass bottle, a plastic bottle, plastic wrapping paper, paper, plastic cups

FIND OUT

OPENING ACTIVITIES

- Hand out a sheet of A4 paper to each pupil. Place the wordcards *gravity, magnetism, friction* and *buoyancy* on the board. Ask pupils to fold the paper in half and in half again so that they have four squares marked on the paper. Tell them to draw four simple pictures to represent each force. Explain that they can draw diagrams or pictures but mustn't write any words. At the end of the activity their partner identifies each force.

MAIN ACTIVITIES

- Explain to pupils that they will be investigating how boats can float on water and carry objects that would otherwise sink in water.
- Ask pupils to read the steps on page 108. Then, tell them to write the materials and the three steps in their notebook. If you are using the book on the interactive whiteboard, you can play the audio of the steps. You may choose to do this investigation together as a class or allow small groups to go through the steps independently.

⊕ CLOSING ACTIVITIES

- Give pupils time to enjoy making the boat and adding the marbles. Encourage them to compare boat designs and the number of marbles they can carry. Encourage pupils to answer in full sentences. *My/Our boat can carry five marbles.* Ask pupils if they changed the design of their boat and which design is better – a wide low boat or a narrow high-sided boat.

1 What happened when you added more marbles to your boat?

- Suggest pupils add marbles to the boat slowly. Elicit that *the boat is lower in the water when it is carrying the marbles.*

2 Which forces were acting on your boat during your investigation?

- Elicit from the class that *gravity and buoyancy were acting on the boat during the investigation.*

3 Why did the ball of plasticine sink? Why did the plasticine boat float?

- Elicit that *the ball of plasticine has a higher density than water so it sinks. The model of the boat has air inside it and so the average density is lower than water and it floats.*

THINK ABOUT IT

⊕ OPENING ACTIVITIES

- Show pupils a selection of packaging such as a can, a tetra pack, a glass bottle, a plastic bottle, plastic wrapping paper, paper, etc. Ask **What happens when we have used these things and no longer need them?** Elicit that we recycle them.
- Organise the class into small groups and ask them to talk about two questions. **What do you do at home to reduce waste? What can we do at school to reduce waste?**

MAIN ACTIVITIES

- Ask pupils to open their books on page 109 and say **Let's read about how to make an ecological plant pot**. If you are using the interactive whiteboard, you can play the audio and encourage pupils to read along in their books.
- If you have time, make the plant pots in class. Then, tell them to write the materials and the steps in their notebook. You may choose to do this investigation together as a class demonstration or allow small groups to go through the steps independently. As pupils are working ask: **What are the properties of the plastic bottle?** (*It's resistant, waterproof and transparent.*) **What about the cloth?** (*It's flexible and absorbent.*) **Could we use card instead of plastic for the container?** (*No, card isn't waterproof.*)

⊕ CLOSING ACTIVITIES

1 Design a useful object using recycled materials. Write a report about your object. Present your ideas to the class. Remember to explain why you have chosen your materials.

- Organise the class into small groups and give each group a plastic cup. Ask them to find as many ways as they can of recycling the plastic cup. Ask the groups to present their findings to the rest of the class.
- Now ask a volunteer to read question one. Suggest that they work with a partner or in small groups to design an object from recycled materials. You may like to ask pupils to make their object at home as a practical homework activity or if there is time, ask them to bring in the materials and make it in class.

2 Why do you think it is important to reduce, recycle and reuse?

- Ask pupils to work with a partner to talk about question 2. Elicit that all materials come from nature and if we take too many of them, they will run out. Also, many waste materials cause pollution and harm the environment. You may like to ask pupils to investigate how many years it takes for certain materials to degrade or biodegrade.

PAGES 110-111 Look back: Matter, materials and forces

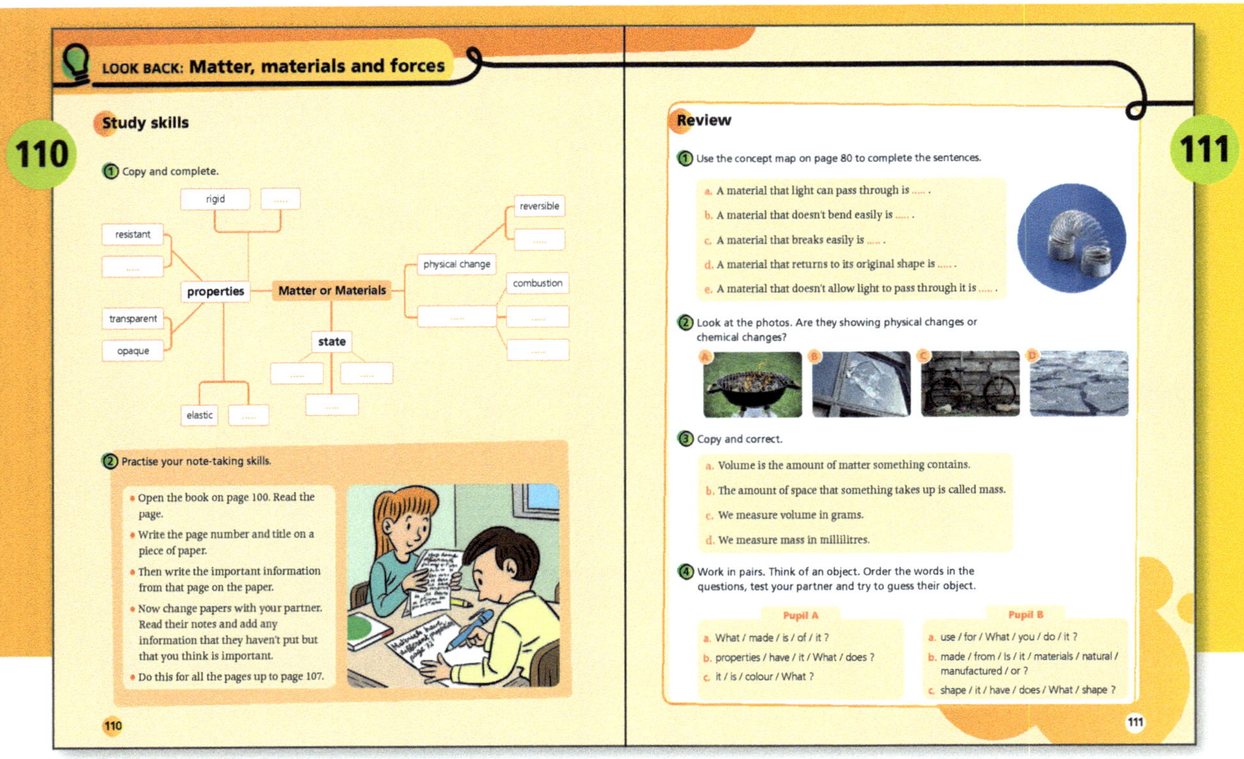

PAGE SUMMARY

This double-page spread allows pupils the opportunity to organise what they've learned in the unit by means of a spider diagram. They can also practise their note-taking skills to help them summarise what they have learned in the unit. On the Review page, pupils complete activities individually to check their understanding of material covered in this unit. Activity 4 is a pair work speaking activity to encourage them to construct accurate questions forms and identify objects described by their partner. It is also a peer evaluation opportunity.

LANGUAGE

- Imperatives: *copy, complete, correct, practise, order, guess, use, write, guess, read*
- Forming questions
- Short answers
- Encourage pupils to speak and write in complete sentences.

ADDITIONAL MATERIALS

- Digital flashcards
- Digital wordcards

OPENING ACTIVITIES

- Tell pupils that you are going to describe different types of materials and that they have to name the property. **It will change shape but then returns to its original state.** (*Elastic*); **Water can't pass through it.** (*Waterproof*)
- Invite a volunteer to come to the board and stand facing the class. Write the name of an object above their head, so that the class can read the name but not the volunteer. The volunteer can then ask questions to find out the name of the object. The class can only answer with short answers: *Yes, it is. No, it doesn't,* etc. You many like to limit the objects to those found in the classroom.
- Organise the class into small groups. Ask them to talk about how forces can help them play sport. Place the wordcards *gravity, magnetism, friction* and *buoyancy* on the board and ask them to think about sports that use these forces. (Basketball: gravity, ice-skating, friction, etc.)

MAIN ACTIVITIES

Page 110, Study skills

1 Copy and complete

- Remind pupils that organising new information makes it easier to understand and remember.
- Focus pupils' attention on the spider diagram and ask them to tell you what the missing words are. Encourage them to make full sentences, such as: *Fragile is the opposite of resistant. Liquid, solid and gas are the three states of matter.*
- Tell them to copy and complete the spider diagram in their notebooks.

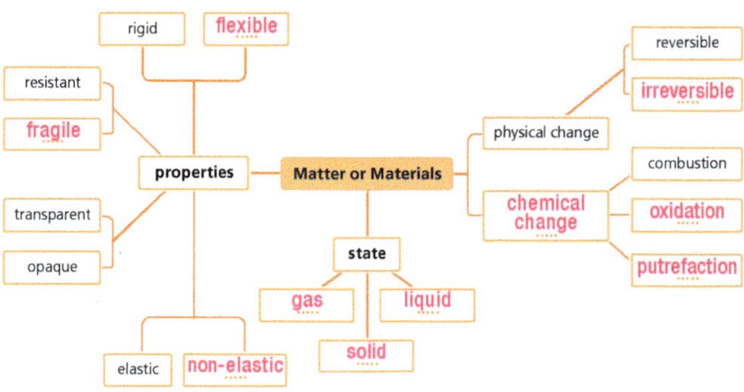

2 Practise your note-taking skills.

- Invite volunteers to read the steps explained on page 110. Hand out a sheet of paper to each pupil. Tell them to open their books on page 110 and read the information. Ask pupils to tell you the important information from that page. Write the suggestions on the board and ask if the rest of the class agree. Tell them to copy the chosen information from the board on to the paper. Now ask them to continue the activity with a partner.

Page 111, Review

Note: This part of the review can be done with minimal teacher guidance. You may wish to work through the activities as a class, in small groups or in pairs. Alternatively, you can ask pupils to do them individually as self-evaluation. This review could also be done as homework.

1 Use the concept map on page 110 to complete the sentences

a. transparent

b. rigid

c. fragile

d. elastic

e. opaque

2 Look at the photos. Are they showing physical changes or chemical changes?

a. Chemical change – combustion

b. Physical change

c. Chemical change – oxidation

d. Physical change

3 True or false? Copy the sentences and correct the ones that are false.

a. *Mass* is the amount of matter something contains.

b. The amount of space that something takes up is called *volume*.

c. We measure volume in *millilitres*.

d. We measure mass in *grams*.

4 Work in pairs. Think of an object. Order the words in the questions ask your partner and try to guess their object.

Pupil A

a. What is it made of?

b. What properties does it have?

c. What colour is it?

Pupil B

a. What do you use it for?

b. Is it made from natural or manufactured materials?

c. What shape does it have?

Activity Book answers / Audio CD2 track list

38

UNIT 7 **Matter, materials and forces**

1 **Complete the concept map using the words in the box.**

~~matter~~ ~~cannot~~ ~~materials~~ ~~gas~~ ~~state~~ ~~solid~~ ~~change~~ ~~liquid~~ ~~destroyed~~

Matter has three states: solid, liquid, gas

The Universe is made up of matter

Matter makes up different ______

Matter cannot be created or destroyed; it can only change from one form or state to another.

2 **Identify the natural and manufactured materials.**

sand: ✓ natural / manufactured
plastic: natural / ✓ manufactured
wood: ✓ natural / manufactured

glass: natural / ✓ manufactured
crude oil: ✓ natural / manufactured
paper: natural / ✓ manufactured

38

39

3 **Find the properties of materials. Use them to complete the sentences.**

N	O	N	E	L	A	S	T	I	C	R
E	E	L	A	R	R	E	S	T	Y	F
L	R	E	S	I	S	T	A	N	T	R
A	I	O	A	G	R	N	T	S	E	A
S	S	P	E	I	R	E	P	S	N	G
T	E	A	R	D	A	E	L	B	I	I
I	R	A	N	S	C	A	R	E	N	L
C	E	O	P	A	Q	U	E	U	A	E
T	R	A	N	S	P	A	R	E	N	T

a. An elastic material will change back to its original shape when the force stops.
b. A non-elastic material will keep its new shape when the force stops.
c. We cannot see through an opaque material.
d. We can see through a transparent material.
e. A resistant material is very strong.
f. A fragile material is easy to break.
g. A rigid material cannot be bent.

4 **Look at the photos below and answer the questions.**

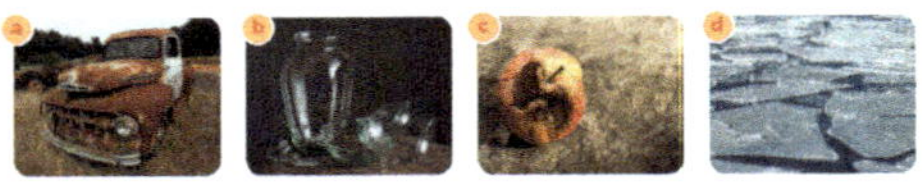

1. Which photo shows a reversible physical change?
Photo d shows a reversible physical change.
2. Which photo shows an irreversible physical change?
Photo b shows an irreversible physical change.
3. Which photo shows the chemical change of putrefaction?
Photo c shows the chemical change of putrefaction.
4. Which photo shows the chemical change when metal reacts with oxygen and water? What is this process called?
Photo a shows the chemical change when metal reacts with oxygen and water. This process is called oxidation.

39

40

UNIT 7

5 **Complete the sentences about mass and volume.**

~~space~~ ~~grams~~ ~~millilitres~~ ~~matter~~

a. Mass is the amount of matter something contains.
b. Mass is measured in grams.
c. Volume is the amount of space something occupies.
d. We can measure volume in millilitres.

6 **Look at the photos and write *mass* or *volume*.**

a. 500 g

b. 500 g

c. 450 g

d. 4 500 g

a. The box of cereal and the ear of corn have the same mass.
b. The box of cereal has a greater volume than the ear of corn.
c. The football has less mass than the bowling ball.
d. The football and the bowling ball have the same volume.

7 **Add a tick (✓) or a cross (✗) for three states of matter.**

States of matter	Have a definite volume	Have a definite shape
Gases	✗	✗
Liquids	✓	✗
Solids	✓	✓

40

41

8 **Complete the sentences about mass and volume.**

a. To calculate the density of an object we divide its *mass* / ~~*volume*~~ by its ~~*mass*~~ / *volume*.
b. Objects that float have a *lower* / ~~*higher*~~ density than water.
c. Objects that sink have a ~~*lower*~~ / *higher* density than water.

9 **Identify the forces. Circle contact or non-contact force.**

~~gravity~~ ~~magnetism~~ ~~buoyancy~~ ~~friction~~

1. buoyancy — (contact force) / non-contact force
2. friction — (contact force) / non-contact force
3. gravity — contact force / (non-contact force)
4. magnetism — contact force / (non-contact force)

10 **Cross out the mistake in each sentence. Write the correct word or words.**

a. Gravity is a force that ~~repels~~ objects towards each other. — attracts
b. ~~Small~~ bodies, such as planets, have a stronger gravitational force. — Large
c. ~~Friction~~ makes objects fall to the ground. — Gravity
d. Magnets have two poles which attract ~~plastic~~ objects. — metal
e. The north poles of two different magnets will ~~attract~~ each other. — repel
f. ~~Magnetism~~ is the force that exists when two objects rub against each other. — Friction
g. Friction acts in the ~~same~~ direction to the direction of movement. — opposite
h. Buoyancy is ~~a downward~~ force which acts in the opposite direction to gravity on objects immersed in a liquid. — an upward

41

UNIT 7

2

Find out at home!

1 Investigate friction:

1. Make a ramp for a toy car. You can use a book or a piece of wood.
2. Let the car roll down the ramp. Observe how fast and far it goes.
3. Put a piece of paper towel on the ramp and let the car roll down. Does the speed change?
4. Put a towel on the ramp and let the car roll down again. Does the car reach the bottom of the ramp? Complete the chart below.

Surface	Observations
	Open answers

2 Answer the questions.

a. On which surface did the car go the fastest and the farthest? the book or piece of wood
b. On which surface did the car travel the shortest distance? the towel
c. Which force makes the car go down the ramp? gravity
d. Which force made the car go slower or travel less distance? friction

42

Skills check

43

1 Look at the signs. Write the correct letter next to each question.

Example: Do not litter. B
1. Be careful when you walk here. G
2. You cannot use your camera. A
3. Remember to wash your hands. F
4. You have to wear a protective hat. E
5. You must not run in this area. H
6. You cannot drink the water here. D

43

Unit 7 Audio CD2 track list

TRACK	ACTIVITY
19	**Pupil's Book page 97,** Unit introduction
20	**Pupil's Book page 97,** Song *Materials*
21	**Pupil's Book page 98,** Story: *A trip to the materials exhibition*
22	**Pupil's Book page 100,** Physical changes
23	**Pupil's Book page 101,** Chemical changes
24	**Pupil's Book page 102,** Mixtures
25	**Pupil's Book page 102,** Homogeneous mixtures
26	**Pupil's Book page 102,** Heterogeneous mixtures
27	**Pupil's Book page 103,** Methods of separating mixtures
28	**Pupil's Book page 105,** Why do some objects float on water?
29	**Pupil's Book page 106,** Forces and their effects
30	**Pupil's Book page 106,** Non-contact forces
31	**Pupil's Book page 107,** Contact forces

UNIT 8 Energy

CONTENT	EVALUATION CRITERIA
Renewable and non-renewable energy.	Differentiate between renewable and non-renewable energy.
Types of energy.	Identify the main characteristics of different types of energy.
Light energy.	Understand the main characteristics of light.
Thermal energy.	Understand the main characteristics of thermal energy.
Sound energy.	Know the main characteristics of sound energy.
First approaches to scientific activity and the scientific method. Use of different information sources (direct and indirect). Use ICTs.	Obtain relevant information about specific phenomena, make predictions, integrate information from direct and indirect observation and communicate the results.
First approaches to simple experiments and investigations.	Conjecture as to the results of natural occurrences and of simple experiments and investigations.
Individual and group work.	Work independently and proactively and develop strategies for working in a group.
Planning a project and presenting a report.	Carry out a project and present a report.

LEARNING STANDARDS	KEY COMPETENCES	PAGES
Differentiates between renewable and non-renewable energy and identifies the different sources of energy and prime materials they come from.	MST, LTL	114,115
Identifies the main characteristics of different types of energy: kinetic, electrical, light, thermal, sound and energy.	MST	116-122
Understands the main characteristicis of light and how it reacts when it comes into contact with different objects: opaque, translucent, transparent, reflection, and refraction.	MST	118
Understands some of the characteristics and effects of thermal energy: change of shape, dilation, transmission of heat, increase in temperature, etc.	MST	119
Knows the main characteristics of sound energy.	MST	120-122
Observes and identifies intensity, sound and pitch.	MST	121
Identifies the principal characteristics of the transmission of sound through different materials.	MST	122
Understands the concept of noise pollution. Proposes ways to avoid it and values the importance of the absence of sound.	MST, SOC	123
With help, selects and organises specific and relevant information; analyses it and draws conclusions; reflects on the experience and the process; presents the results.	MST, LTL	115, 122, 123
Use books, libraries, etc. and collaborate in the care and maintenance of all the materials available in the school and the classroom.	MST, LTL	112-125
Shows autonomy in the planning of activities and tasks and shows initiative in decision taking.	LTL, AUT	115, 122, 123
With help, carries out simple experiments or investigations, and conjectures as to the results.	MST, LTL, AUT	122, 123
Uses strategies to help their own learning, as well as asking for help and information.	LTL, AUT	115, 124
First approaches to cooperative learning.	SOC, LTL	113, 123
Begins observation, using relevant instruments and consulting written documents and images.	LTL, AUT	122, 123
Shows autonomy and proactiveness in the planning of and carrying out of actions.	AUT	122, 123
Presents work clearly and in an organised fashion.	LIN, LTL, AUT	122, 123
With help, carries out a project and presents a report, using paper and/or digital means, collecting information from different sources, presenting the results orally and with the support of images and short texts.	LIN, LTL, AUT, DIG	122, 123

UNIT INFORMATION

UNIT SUMMARY

In this unit, pupils will review and extend their knowledge of energy, looking at different types of energy and the two sources of energy: renewable and non-renewable sources. They will look in detail at light, sound and heat energy.

At the beginning of the unit, pupils will review the types of renewable energy and their advantages. This subject area is covered in the opening illustration with the help of the course characters, Carla and Alex, who are on a school trip to a wind farm. The school trip continues in the story and, on their return to school, Alex and Carla carry out a *School trip project* to review what they have learned. These opening pages are designed to test pupils' prior knowledge.

They will move on to study the types of energy and how energy can be transformed into different types of energy. The unit encourages the pupils to think about the important role energy plays in our lives and the importance of conserving it.

Much of the language in this unit aims to help the pupils develop language and critical thinking skills. They will continue to develop scientific skills through observing, making connections, comparing and contrasting and making predictions.

EXPERIMENT

Find out

IIn the *Find out* activity on page 122, your pupils will carry out an investigation to observe how sound travels through materials by making a paper cup telephone.

The pupils will need:

- two paper cups
- sharp pencil
- long piece of string
- tape or glue
- scissors

Further ideas

The pupils could play a game of trying to identify a classmate when they are speaking through a material, e.g. fabric, paper, a book etc.

VALUES AND ATTITUDES

In this unit, your pupils will learn to appreciate the importance of energy in our lives. They will value energy as an important and necessary resource and explore how renewable energy sources and by conserving energy can help preserve our limited non-renewable energy sources and help protect the environment.

Think about it

The *Think about it* page in this unit focuses noise pollution. The intention of this section is to focus on the dangers of noise and the importance of looking after our hearing.

EVALUATION MATERIAL

These documents can be downloaded from the *Teachers* section of the digital component and printed .

The materials include:

- **Unit diagnostic test**: provides an overview of the unit and allows you to assess the pupils' prior knowledge.
- **End-of-unit test**: in addition to the *Review* section at the end of each unit, this summative test can be used to evaluate pupils' progress after studying the unit content.
- **Class unit evaluation grid**: based on the evaluation criteria and learning standards of the unit.

DIGITAL RESOURCES

Presentations

- **Unit summary**: a simple slide presentation with text, images and audio to review the main ideas of the unit. It can be used at the beginning of the unit to test pupils' prior knowledge of the unit content or at the end of the unit as a revision tool.
- **Find out**: a slide presentation of the unit's *Find out* page with text, photos and audio. The slide presentation is perfect for a heads-up class, showing the steps one by one. Use this tool to get the pupils to predict the next steps (with their books closed) or to focus their attention on each step as they carry out the project themselves.

Activities

Activities vary per unit and include the following:

- **Memory game**: useful activity for reviewing key vocabulary and modelling pronunciation.
- **Labelling**: pupils label a diagram by dragging and dropping key terms.
- **Spelling**: pupils drag and drop letters to spell key terms.
- **Read and reveal**: pupils read sentences and guess the missing words, which are revealed by clicking the spaces.
- **Classification:** pupils drag and drop concepts and key terms in a simple classification table.
- **Wordsearch:** pupils find key terms hidden in the wordsearch.
- **Definitions:** pupils drag and drop words to complete definitions.

Song lyrics

Listen to the song *Energy* and follow the lyrics line by line.

Posters

Attractive and informative posters to display in class. You can use them to review key concepts and vocabulary.

Videos

Use the video links in this unit to present content in a dynamic, real-life context while reinforcing the pupils' listening skills.

Teachers

Digital flashcards and wordcards: topics include *Types of energy, Light energy, Thermal energy* and *Sound energy.*

Downloadable PDFs: evaluation tests, evaluation grids, templates, useful links and further information..

PAGES 112–113 Energy

PAGE SUMMARY

The aim of the unit opener is to develop your pupils' observation skills and find out what they already know about the topic of the unit. Use the picture to elicit vocabulary related to energy, as well as action verbs that describe what is going on in the scene and elements to describe the various characters and objects. Get your pupils to work in groups to complete activities 1– 4 and to have fun listening to the song and completing activity 5.

LANGUAGE

- Question words: *where, what, why, which, how many,* etc.
- Present tense
- Passive
- Vocabulary: *energy, light, sound, thermal, electrical, chemical, kinetic, switch, machine, renewable, non-renewable, wind, the Sun, water, coal, gas, oil, create, destroy, transform*

ADDITIONAL MATERIALS

- Digital flashcards
- Digital wordcards

OPENING ACTIVITIES

- If you are using an interactive whiteboard, focus only on the illustration of the wind farm, not the questions. Either elicit ideas (*There are wind turbines; Carla is wearing shorts, etc.*) or ask questions indicating each part of the picture: *What has Carla got in her hand? What colour is Alex's cap?*
- Alternatively, use the interactive whiteboard writing tools and ask pupils to come up to the board, mark an area of the picture and describe what they can see. Help them to produce full, correct sentences.

MAIN ACTIVITIES

Page 113, Unit introduction (CD2 track 32)

- Play the audio of the unit introduction first, with pupils reading along with it, and then ask one or two pupils to read out loud. This way, pupils will feel more self-assured when it comes to pronouncing new words.
- Check for understanding by asking questions. **Can we create energy?** (*No*); **What happens when we switch on a light?** (*Electrical energy is changed into light and thermal energy*); **Is the picture showing us a renewable or non-renewable source?** (*Renewable*); **What is another word for changed?** (*Transformed*)

1 What types of energy can you see in the picture?

- Point out that in the picture they can a renewable energy source: the wind. Place the following wordcards on the board: *thermal, electrical* and *kinetic*. Give clues and ask pupils to identify the energy. *Thermal and kinetic. (The wind turbines transform kinetic energy into electrical energy).*

2 Which machines in your home need electrical energy to work?

- Pupils will be familiar with this type of question and will have no problem making lists. During feedback, classify the machines into two groups: machines for entertainment and machines to make work easier. *Open answer*

3 Name three renewable and three non-renewable sources of energy.

- To help them remember the names write the first letter of each word on the board: C, G and O. *The Sun, wind and water are renewable. Coal, gas and oil are non-renewable.*

4 Why are wind turbines often placed on high land?

- Pupils should be able to answer this question without research. You may like to draw a sketch on the board to show them that it is windier on high land as there are fewer obstacles to stop the wind. *It is windier on high land.*

5 Listen to the song. What type of energy does each photo represent? There may be more than one.

- Focus the pupils' attention on the six photos. Ask them to tell you what they can see in each photo.
- Play the song *Energy* **(CD2 track 33)** and ask pupils to point to the photo that represents the type of energy that they hear. Then play the song a second time and encourage pupils to sing along (you can use the *Song lyrics* section on the digital component to display the song line by line and listen to the song). *Light, chemical, thermal, electrical, kinetic and sound energy*

CD2 • track 33

Energy, it can't be created
Energy, it can't be destroyed
Energy, it can't be created
Energy, it can't be destroyed
Just look around you energy is everywhere
Light energy
It comes from the Sun
Thermal energy too
And some is stored in fossil fuels
Coal, oil and gas
[chorus]Energy, it can't be created ...
Sound energy is made by vibrations
And kinetic energy is made by motion
Food contains chemical energy
And electrical energy is used in our homes
[chorus]Energy, it can't be created ...
Eat a snack, ride your bike
Switch on a light, sing a song
Feel the Sun on your skin
Or watch a storm
Energy is everywhere

CLOSING ACTIVITIES

- Divide the class into two teams. Place the wordcards *light, thermal, sound, chemical, electrical* and *kinetic* on the board. Call a pupil from each team to come out to the board. Say the name of something that produces each type of energy (e.g. radiator, lamp, etc.) The first pupil to touch the correct card gets a point.

ANSWERS AT A GLANCE

1 Light, thermal and kinetic. (The wind turbines transform kinetic energy into electrical energy.)

2 Open answer.

3 The Sun, wind and water are renewable. Coal, gas and oil are non-renewable.

4 It is windier on high land.

5 Light, chemical, thermal, electrical, kinetic and sound energy.

PAGES 114–115 A trip to a wind farm

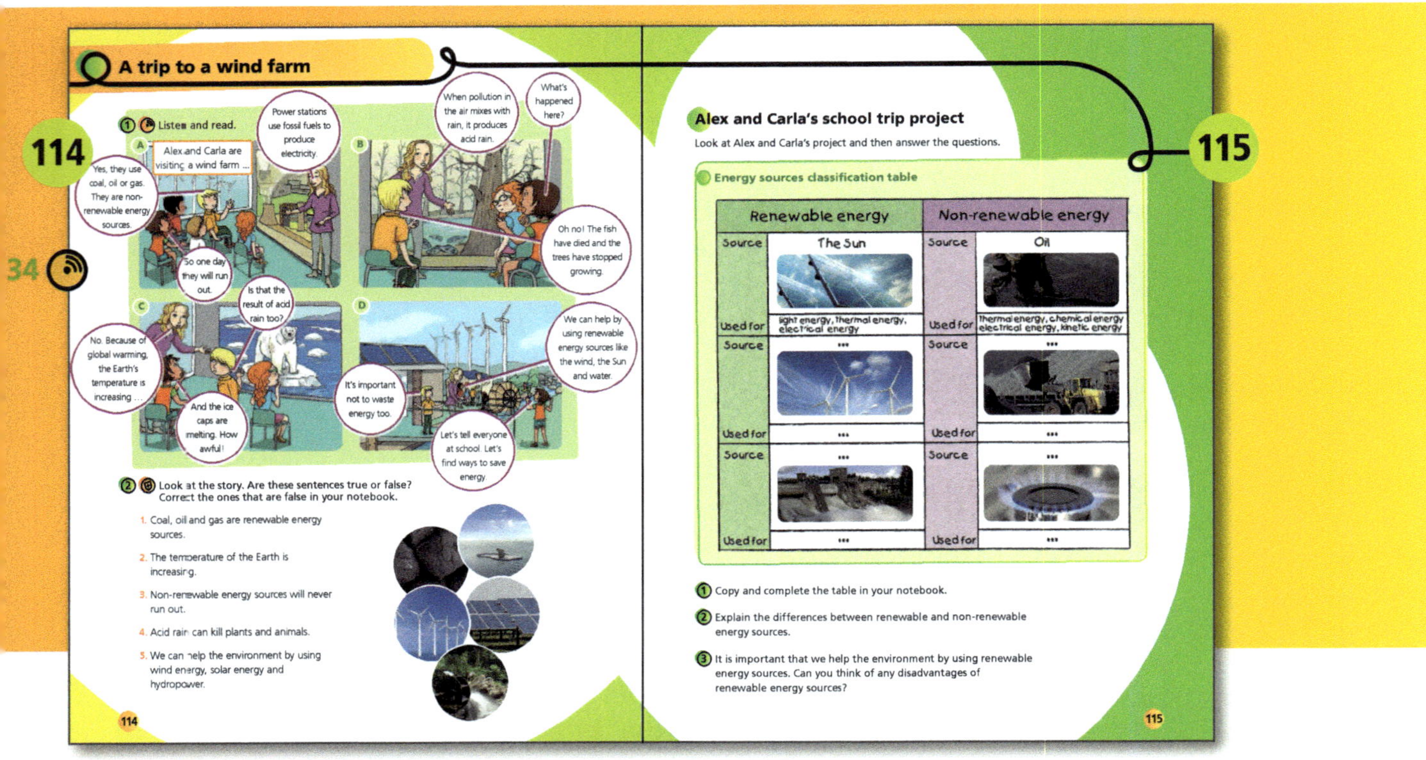

PAGE SUMMARY

This double-page spread opens with a story in which your pupils have the opportunity to see Carla and Alex at a particular moment of their school trip to a wind farm. Carla and Alex are talking to the guide and showing their knowledge of renewable and non-renewable energy sources. The story is reinforced with an exam style true or false activity that is related to the story and opening double page spread. On page 115, the pupils can study Carla and Alex's school trip project about renewable and non-renewable energy sources.

LANGUAGE

- Present continuous
- Present perfect
- Vocabulary: *power station, fossil fuels, electricity, coal, gas, oil, the Sun, wind, water, pollution*

ADDITIONAL MATERIALS

- Digital flashcards
- Digital wordcards
- Extra classroom materials: two plants, water, vinegar, two sprays

OPENING ACTIVITIES

- Play a true or false game about energy. Make statements and tell the pupils to call out if they are true or false. If the sentence is false, invite volunteers to correct it. **Coal is a renewable energy source.** *(False; it's non-renewable.)*
- Ask pupils to look carefully at the last frame of the story. If you are using an interactive whiteboard block out the dialogue so that they focus on the picture. Tell them that there are three different ways of producing electricity in this picture. Elicit that there are wind turbines, solar panels on the roof and a waterwheel.

MAIN ACTIVITIES

1 Listen and read. (CD2 track 34)

- Draw the pupils' attention to the story at the top of page 114 and explain to them that they are going to listen to a story about Alex and Carla's trip to a wind farm. Say**Let's listen and read**. Play the audio.

- Ask pupils to look at each of the illustrations and describe what is happening in each one using their own words. For example, *Carla is is upset about the polar bear. The fish have died.* Ask the pupils what are the two big problems the guide showed the children. *(Acid rain and global warming.)* Ask **What is causing acid rain?** (*Pollution mixes with rain*); **What is causing global warming?** (*Pollution*); Ask **What must we do to protect the planet?** Elicit that we must reduce pollution.

2 Look at the story. Are these sentences true or false? Correct the ones that are false in your notebook.

- This activity aims to introduce some new vocabulary, reinforce what pupils have learned in the story and refresh concepts studied in previous levels. Ask pupils to work with a partner to answer the questions. *1- False: coal, oil and gas are non-renewable energy sources; 2 -True; 3- False: non-renewable energy sources will run out; 4-True; 5- True*

SCHOOL TRIP PROJECT

- Explain to pupils that following their trip to the wind farm, Alex and Carla have done a project to summarise what they have learned about renewable and non-renewable energy sources. Tell pupils to look at the photo on page 115 and ask for volunteers to read the words.

1 Copy and complete the table in your notebook.

- Tell the pupils to copy and complete the table from the book, and then share their ideas with a partner. *Wind – electrical energy; Coal – thermal and electrical energy; Water – electrical energy; Gas – electrical and thermal energy*

2 Explain the differences between renewable and non-renewable energy sources.

- Ask the pupils to talk to their partner to answer this question. Point out that they are both natural but that there are two main differences. *Renewable energy sources will never run out but non-renewable ones will. Renewable energy sources don't cause as much pollution.*

3 It is important that we help the environment by using renewable energy sources. Can you think of any disadvantages of renewable energy sources?

- Pupils will probably need some guidance to answer this question. Suggest they think about what happens when a river is stopped by a dam. (*There is habitat destruction.*) Encourage them to think about which animals could have problems with the wind turbines. (*Birds may be hurt or killed by wind turbines.*) *Open answer*

+ CLOSING ACTIVITIES

- Draw two interconnected circles on the board to make a Venn diagram. Label one circle *renewable*, the other circle *non-renewable*, and the area in the centre *both*. Elicit the information from the pupils and complete the diagram as a class activity. Ask the pupils to copy the diagram into their notebook.

+ EXTRA IDEAS

- Take two plants into class. Tell the class that they are going to observe the consequences of acid rain on plants. Fill one spray with water and the other with a mixture of water and vinegar. Explain that vinegar is an acid. Water and spray one plant, with water. Use the acid mix to water and spray the other plant. Observe the plants for two weeks.

ANSWERS AT A GLANCE

Page 114

2 1- False: coal, oil and gas are non-renewable energy sources; 2 -True; 3- False: non-renewable energy sources will run out; 4-True; 5- True.

Page 115

1 Wind – electrical energy; Coal – thermal and electrical energy; Hydropower – electrical energy; Gas – electrical and thermal energy.

2 Renewable energy sources will never run out but non-renewable ones will. Renewable energy sources don't cause as much pollution.

3 Open answers.

PAGES 116–117 Types of energy

116

35

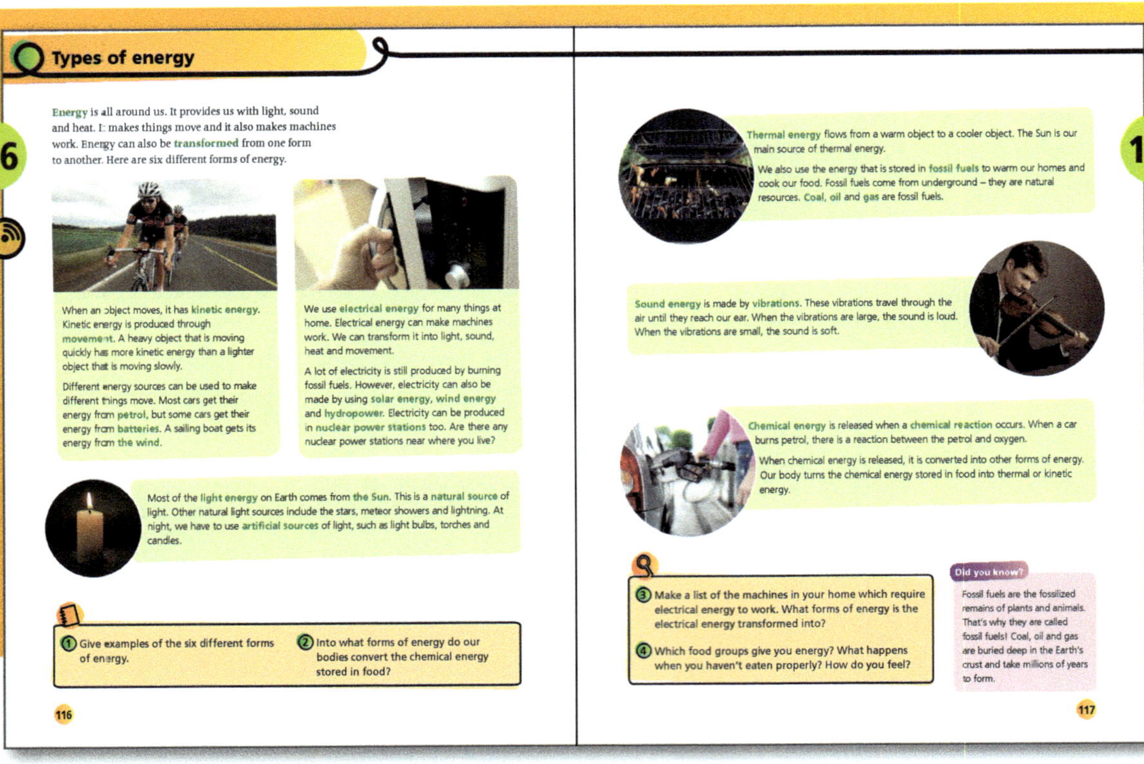

Types of energy

Energy is all around us. It provides us with light, sound and heat. It makes things move and it also makes machines work. Energy can also be **transformed** from one form to another. Here are six different forms of energy.

When an object moves, it has **kinetic energy**. Kinetic energy is produced through **movement**. A heavy object that is moving quickly has more kinetic energy than a lighter object that is moving slowly.

Different energy sources can be used to make different things move. Most cars get their energy from **petrol**, but some cars get their energy from **batteries**. A sailing boat gets its energy from **the wind**.

We use **electrical energy** for many things at home. Electrical energy can make machines work. We can transform it into light, sound, heat and movement.

A lot of electricity is still produced by burning fossil fuels. However, electricity can also be made by using **solar energy**, **wind energy** and **hydropower**. Electricity can be produced in **nuclear power stations** too. Are there any nuclear power stations near where you live?

Most of the **light energy** on Earth comes from **the Sun**. This is a **natural source** of light. Other natural light sources include the stars, meteor showers and lightning. At night, we have to use **artificial sources** of light, such as light bulbs, torches and candles.

1. Give examples of the six different forms of energy.
2. Into what forms of energy do our bodies convert the chemical energy stored in food?

116

117

Thermal energy flows from a warm object to a cooler object. The Sun is our main source of thermal energy.

We also use the energy that is stored in **fossil fuels** to warm our homes and cook our food. Fossil fuels come from underground – they are natural resources. **Coal**, **oil** and **gas** are fossil fuels.

Sound energy is made by **vibrations**. These vibrations travel through the air until they reach our ear. When the vibrations are large, the sound is loud. When the vibrations are small, the sound is soft.

Chemical energy is released when a **chemical reaction** occurs. When a car burns petrol, there is a reaction between the petrol and oxygen.

When chemical energy is released, it is converted into other forms of energy. Our body turns the chemical energy stored in food into thermal or kinetic energy.

3. Make a list of the machines in your home which require electrical energy to work. What forms of energy is the electrical energy transformed into?
4. Which food groups give you energy? What happens when you haven't eaten properly? How do you feel?

Did you know?

Fossil fuels are the fossilized remains of plants and animals. That's why they are called fossil fuels! Coal, oil and gas are buried deep in the Earth's crust and take millions of years to form.

117

PAGE SUMMARY

This double-page spread introduces pupils to the six different types of energy. There is a lot of new vocabulary and concepts on this double page. Do not expect pupils at this stage to absorb all of the information; the main learning aim is to recognise the sources of the types of energy and to understand how energy can change from one type to another. Encourage pupils to think about the importance of energy in their daily lives.

LANGUAGE

- Questions words: *where, what, why, how, etc.*
- Adverbs: *slowly, quickly*
- Vocabulary: *kinetic, chemical, electrical, light, sound, thermal, petrol, batteries, sailing boat, fossil fuels, sailing boat, nuclear power station*

ADDITIONAL MATERIALS

- Digital flashcards
- Digital wordcards

OPENING ACTIVITIES

- Write the word *Energy* on the board and ask for examples of the different types of energy. Place the wordcards on the board when they are named. Write numbers 1 to 6 under the cards.
- Play the *Energy* song **(CD2 track 33)**. Ask the pupils to call out the number of the card when they hear the energy mentioned in the song.
- Ask the pupils to give examples of the different types of energy. (*A bird singing is an example of sound energy. A police siren is sound energy too.*) Encourage all the pupils to participate.

MAIN ACTIVITIES

Pages 116, Types of energy (CD2 track 35)

- If you are using an interactive whiteboard, click on the opening text on page 116 and highlight the introductory text. Alternatively, ask pupils to open their books on page 116 and read the text to the class.

- Read the text boxes as a group or individually (see *Helpful tips* pages 20-23 for reading activities). Ask pupils to work with a partner to ask and answer questions about the energy texts. **Can you name examples of artificial light sources?** (*Light bulbs, candles and torches*); **How does thermal energy move?** (*From warm object to cooler object*) Suggest they each ask one question about each energy type. Invite volunteers to share their questions and answers with the rest of the class.
- Draw the pupils' attention to the *Did you know?* box. Invite a volunteer to read the information.

1 Give examples of the six different forms of energy.

- Read question 1 to the class and ask pupils to copy the question and write the answer in their notebooks. Pupils can check their answer in pairs. *Kinetic, light, sound, thermal, electrical and chemical*

2 Into what forms of energy do our bodies convert the chemical energy stored in food?

- Follow the same procedure as in question 1. *Kinetic and thermal*

3 Make a list of the machines in your home which require electrical energy to work. What forms of energy is the electrical energy transformed into?

- Organise the class into small groups and ask them to make a list of the machines that they have at home and to identify the type of energy that the electrical energy is transformed into. Say **In the toaster, the electrical energy is transformed into thermal energy. What about in the washing machine?** (*Thermal and kinetic*) Feedback as a class activity and write their answers on the board. *Open answers*

4 Which food groups give you energy? What happens when you haven't eaten properly? How do you feel?

- Pupils should know that we get energy from carbohydrates and fats. They will also know that if we don't eat we can feel tired and find it hard to concentrate. Some people suffer from headaches too. *Carbohydrates and fats give us energy. We feel tired and can't concentrate.*

+ CLOSING ACTIVITIES

- Play *Odd one out with* types of energy. Name three items and one distractor. e.g.: coal, gas, wind and oil. *Wind is renewable and the others are non-renewable.* Invite the pupils to make their own examples.

+ EXTRA IDEAS

- Write the word *energy* in the centre of the board and below it write the names of the six types of energy, beginning with kinetic. Draw a box below each word. Draw a running stick figure in the box below the word *kinetic*. Invite pupils to come to the board to draw pictures in the other boxes to represent that type of energy. Ask pupils to copy the chart into their notebooks but explain that they can change the pictures if they want to.

ANSWERS AT A GLANCE

1 Kinetic, light, sound, thermal, electrical and chemical.

2 Kinetic and thermal.

3 Open answer.

4 Carbohydrates and fats give us energy. We feel tired and can't concentrate.

PAGES 118–119 Light energy and Thermal energy

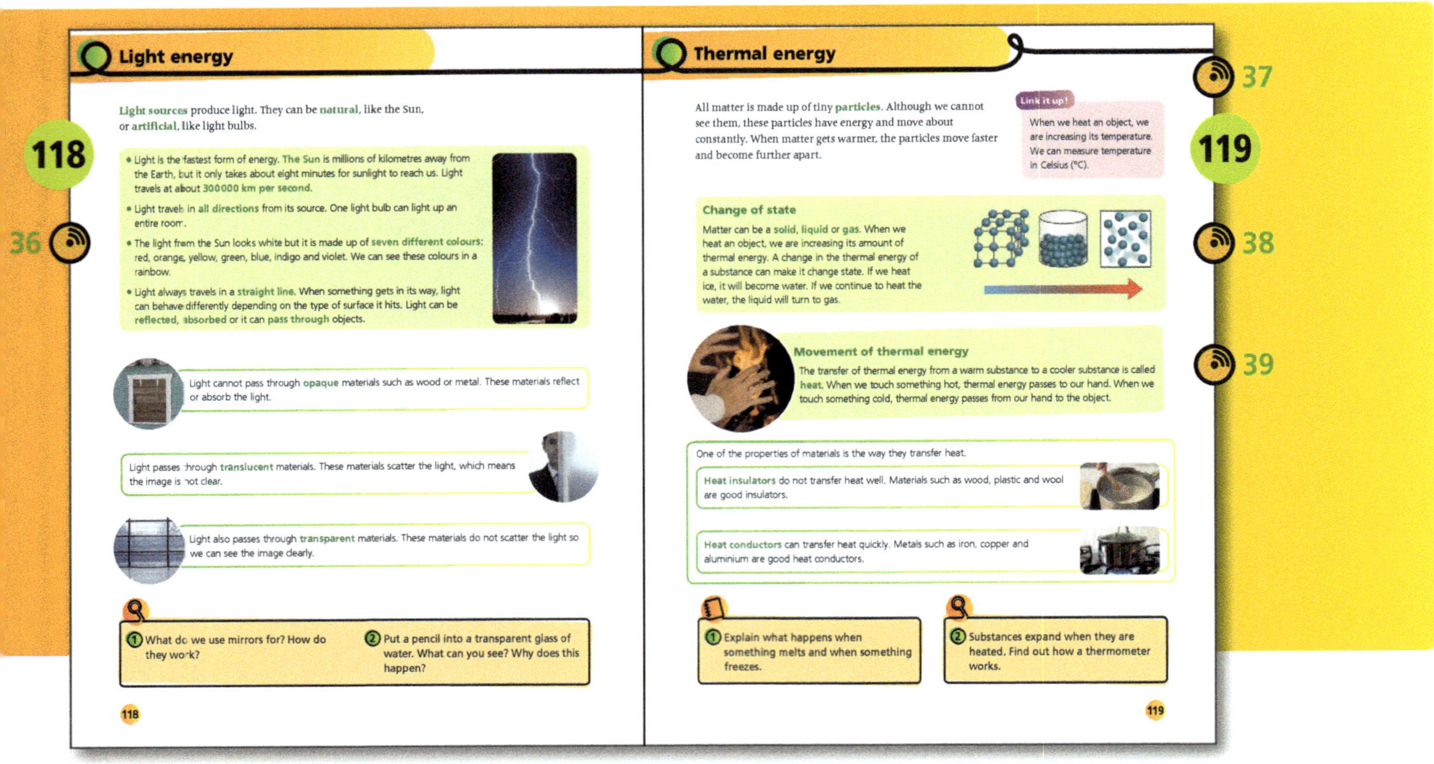

118

36

Light energy

Light sources produce light. They can be **natural**, like the Sun, or **artificial**, like light bulbs.

- Light is the fastest form of energy. **The Sun** is millions of kilometres away from the Earth, but it only takes about eight minutes for sunlight to reach us. Light travels at about **300000 km per second**.
- Light travels in **all directions** from its source. One light bulb can light up an entire room.
- The light from the Sun looks white but it is made up of **seven different colours**: red, orange, yellow, green, blue, indigo and violet. We can see these colours in a rainbow.
- Light always travels in a **straight line**. When something gets in its way, light can behave differently depending on the type of surface it hits. Light can be **reflected**, **absorbed** or it can **pass through** objects.

Light cannot pass through **opaque** materials such as wood or metal. These materials reflect or absorb the light.

Light passes through **translucent** materials. These materials scatter the light, which means the image is not clear.

Light also passes through **transparent** materials. These materials do not scatter the light so we can see the image clearly.

1. What do we use mirrors for? How do they work?
2. Put a pencil into a transparent glass of water. What can you see? Why does this happen?

118

Thermal energy

37

119

All matter is made up of tiny **particles**. Although we cannot see them, these particles have energy and move about constantly. When matter gets warmer, the particles move faster and become further apart.

Link it up!
When we heat an object, we are increasing its temperature. We can measure temperature in Celsius (°C).

38

Change of state
Matter can be a **solid**, **liquid** or **gas**. When we heat an object, we are increasing its amount of thermal energy. A change in the thermal energy of a substance can make it change state. If we heat ice, it will become water. If we continue to heat the water, the liquid will turn to gas.

39

Movement of thermal energy
The transfer of thermal energy from a warm substance to a cooler substance is called **heat**. When we touch something hot, thermal energy passes to our hand. When we touch something cold, thermal energy passes from our hand to the object.

One of the properties of materials is the way they transfer heat.

Heat insulators do not transfer heat well. Materials such as wood, plastic and wool are good insulators.

Heat conductors can transfer heat quickly. Metals such as iron, copper and aluminium are good heat conductors.

1. Explain what happens when something melts and when something freezes.
2. Substances expand when they are heated. Find out how a thermometer works.

119

PAGE SUMMARY

On this double-page spread pupils study in detail the characteristics of light and thermal energy. It is possible to use many hands on activities to aid understanding. Pupils will review the changes of state in matter and are introduced to the concept of particles to prepare them for the concept of atoms and molecules which they will study in later courses. It is also an opportunity to revise the sense of sight and touch. Encourage pupils to compare and contract these two types of energy.

LANGUAGE

- Passive: *It is reflected / absorbed*
- Vocabulary: *natural, artificial, rainbow, source, opaque, translucent, transparent, straight, indigo, violet, solid, liquid, gas, particles, substance, wood*

ADDITIONAL MATERIALS

- Digital flashcards
- Digital wordcards
- Extra classroom materials: old CDs, torch, black card, transparent plastic, mirror

OPENING ACTIVITIES

- Tell pupils to close their eyes and describe what they see. *Nothing, patterns, dots,* etc. Tell them to open their eyes again and describe what they can see. Ask: **What colour is your t-shirt? What shape is your book? Which is the biggest table?** Explain that we see colour, size and shapes. Ask **What must we have so that our eyes can see?** (*Light*)
- Invite the class to tell you what they know about light. Ask **Where does light come from?** Write their suggestions on the board. Say **We can classify these words into two groups.** Elicit that light sources can be natural or artificial.
- Hand out old CDs to the class. This activity works best if there are enough CDs for the pupils to work with a partner. Tell them to hold the shiny side towards the light and tip the disc slowly. Ask them what they can see. Ask: **How can we see these colours? Where do they come from?** Say **Let's find out.**

MAIN ACTIVITIES

Page 118, Light energy (CD2 track 36)

- Ask pupils to open their books on page 116 and read the introduction text. Review natural and artificial light sources by naming sources and asking the pupils to call out *natural* or *artificial*.

- If you are using an interactive whiteboard, click on the main text on page 118 and highlight the points as you read them. Alternatively, ask pupils to open their books on page 118. Check understanding. **What is the fastest form of energy? How long does it take light to reach Earth?**
- Give demonstrations to explain the information points. Switch on the light to demonstrate that light travels in all directions from the source. Darken the room and shine a torch at the board. Ask a pupil to stand between the board and the beam to demonstrate light travels in a straight line. Show the colours on a CD and write the colours in order. Point out that indigo is a dark purple colour and violet is a light purple. Ask the pupils to look out of the window. They can see outside because glass is transparent. Place a card on the window to show the meaning of opaque.

1 What do we use mirrors for? How do they work?

- Pass an unbreakable mirror around the class and let the pupils look at themselves. Point out that light behaves in different ways when it meets an object? Elicit that *the light is reflected.*
- Draw simple diagrams with arrows to show light meeting different objects. Ask pupils to copy them into their notebooks and label them. *The light is reflected and we can see our own image.*

2 Put a pencil into a transparent glass of water. What can you see? Why does this happen?

- Demonstrate this activity for the class. Elicit that the pencil looks broken or bent. Explain that *both the water and air are transparent but they have different densities and the light bends where the two surfaces meet. This is called refraction.*

Page 119, Thermal energy (CD2 track 37)

- Ask pupils to open their books on page 119. Play the audio **(CD2 track 37)** of the introductory text. Ask pupils to look at the three illustrations and identify which one shows a solid, a liquid and a gas. Explain that the arrangement of the particles determines the state of matter.
- Draw the pupils' attention to the *Link it up* box. Invite a pupil to read the information. Write 100°C and 0°C on the board and ask them why these temperatures are important. *(The boiling and freezing points of water.)*
- As the information on this page will be familiar, ask pupils to read the information with a partner (*see Helpful tips*, pages 20 -23 for reading activities). Write the headings *changes of state, movement of thermal energy* and *properties* on the board. Ask pupils to summaries what they have read using their own words.

1 Explain what happens when something melts and when something freezes.

- Ask pupils to work with a partner to answer this question. You may like to put a simple diagram on the board to summarise their answer and get the pupils to copy it into their notebooks. *See Answers at a glance*

2 Substances expand when they are heated. Find out how a thermometer works.

- This activity can be done at home with the help of parents or in small study groups on a computer or in the library. *The mercury expands and is pushed up the tube.*

ANSWERS AT A GLANCE

Page 118

1 The light is reflected and we can see our own image.

2 The pencil looks bent because water and air have different densities.

Page 119

1 When something melts, it changes from a solid to a liquid. When something freezes, it changes from a liquid to a solid.

2 The mercury expands and is pushed up the tube.

PAGES 120-121 Sound energy

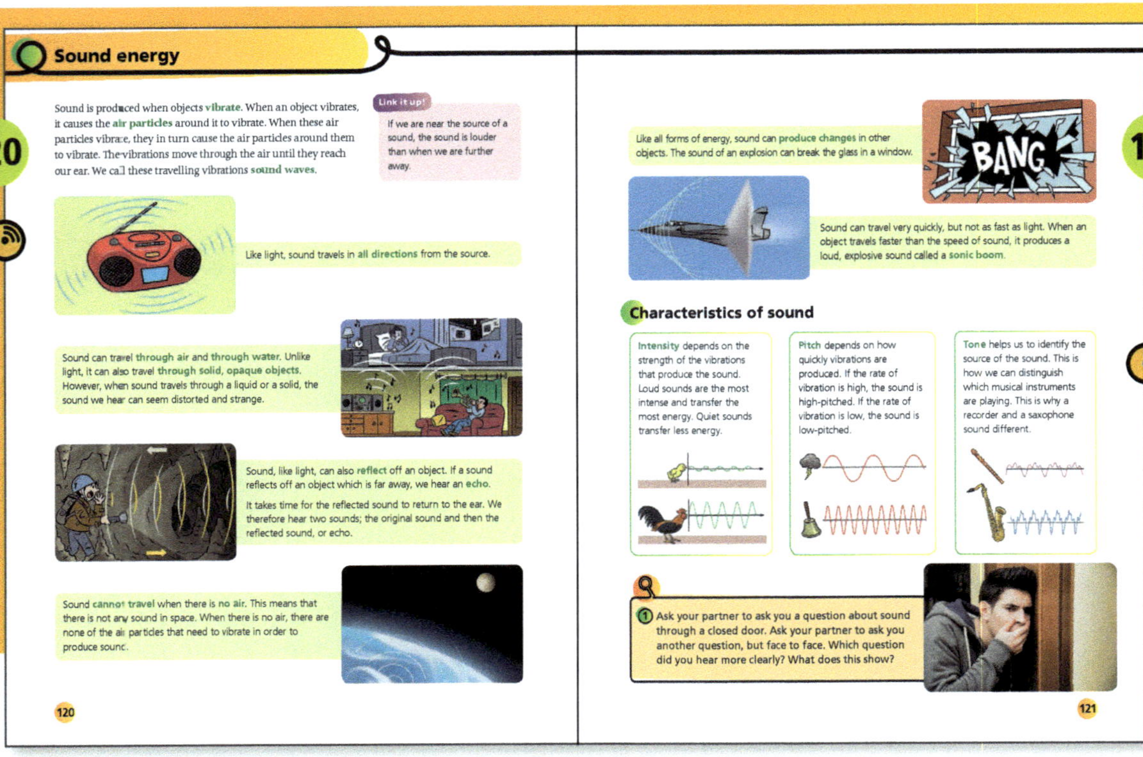
120

40

Sound energy

Sound is produced when objects **vibrate**. When an object vibrates, it causes the **air particles** around it to vibrate. When these air particles vibrate, they in turn cause the air particles around them to vibrate. The vibrations move through the air until they reach our ear. We call these travelling vibrations **sound waves**.

Link it up!

If we are near the source of a sound, the sound is louder than when we are further away.

Like light, sound travels in **all directions** from the source.

Sound can travel **through air** and **through water**. Unlike light, it can also travel **through solid, opaque objects**. However, when sound travels through a liquid or a solid, the sound we hear can seem distorted and strange.

Sound, like light, can also **reflect** off an object. If a sound reflects off an object which is far away, we hear an **echo**.

It takes time for the reflected sound to return to the ear. We therefore hear two sounds; the original sound and then the reflected sound, or echo.

Sound **cannot travel** when there is **no air**. This means that there is not any sound in space. When there is no air, there are none of the air particles that need to vibrate in order to produce sound.

120

121

Like all forms of energy, sound can **produce changes** in other objects. The sound of an explosion can break the glass in a window.

Sound can travel very quickly, but not as fast as light. When an object travels faster than the speed of sound, it produces a loud, explosive sound called a **sonic boom**.

Characteristics of sound

Intensity depends on the strength of the vibrations that produce the sound. Loud sounds are the most intense and transfer the most energy. Quiet sounds transfer less energy.

Pitch depends on how quickly vibrations are produced. If the rate of vibration is high, the sound is high-pitched. If the rate of vibration is low, the sound is low-pitched.

Tone helps us to identify the source of the sound. This is how we can distinguish which musical instruments are playing. This is why a recorder and a saxophone sound different.

41

1 Ask your partner to ask you a question about sound through a closed door. Ask your partner to ask you another question, but face to face. Which question did you hear more clearly? What does this show?

121

PAGE SUMMARY

This double-page spread introduces pupils to the concept of sound energy. This is new content for the class and they will study it in detail as it won't be recycled in the following course. There is a lot of new vocabulary and concepts on this double page.

LANGUAGE

- Questions words: *where, what, why,* etc.
- Negative comparisons: *not as fast as*
- Adverbs: *quickly*
- Vocabulary: *vibration, air particles, sound wave, source, echo, explosion, explosive, intense, space, opaque, solid, liquid, intensity, pitch, tone, high-pitched, low-pitched, strength, vibrate, reflect, produce, transfer, distinguish*

ADDITIONAL MATERIALS

- Digital flashcards
- Digital wordcards

OPENING ACTIVITIES

- At the beginning of the class play the *Energy* song (CD2 track 33). Lower the volume to minimum and slowly increase it, then lower it again. Ask the pupils what they have just heard. Ask **Did anything change?** (*It got louder, then quieter.*) Explain that this is sound energy and that anything that makes a sound produces sound energy.
- Brainstorm things that produce sound energy and write the pupils' suggestions on the board. Point out that some sounds are pleasant. Unpleasant sounds are called noise.

MAIN ACTIVITIES

Pages 120-121, Sound energy (CD2 track 40)

- Before you read the text, ask pupils to look at the illustrations on pages 120 and 121.
- If you are using an interactive whiteboard, block out the texts with the black paint tool. Zoom in on each illustration and ask pupils which properties of sound they think the pictures are showing. Write their suggestions on the board.
- Pupils read the individual text boxes. Pause after each information point to check for understanding. Check that the predictions they made about the texts were correct and tick them on the board.

Pages 121, Characteristics of sound (CD2 track 41)

- Focus the pupils' attention on the three information boxes. Play the audio and ask pupils to listen and read. Ask **What are the three characteristics of sound?** (*Intensity, pitch and tone*); **What does the intensity of sound affect?** (*If the sound is loud or quiet*); **What affects pitch?** (*How quickly the vibrations are produced*); **What does tone help us do?** (*Identify the source*)

1 Ask your partner to ask you a question about sound through a closed door. Ask your partner to ask you another question, but face to face. Which question did you hear more clearly? What does this show?

- Ask pupils to prepare two questions to ask their partner. Explain to the class that they have to take turns to do this activity. Ask the questioner to go outside and ask the question through the door. The partner has to write the question they hear on a piece of paper. The pupil answers the question when they are both back at their places. The second question is then asked and answered. *It's more difficult to hear the question through the door because the sound is distorted.*

+ CLOSING ACTIVITIES

- Ask pupils to work with a partner to compare the properties of sound with the properties of light. Tell them to look back at pages 118 and 119 if necessary. Invite volunteers to feedback the similarities and differences they have found.

+ EXTRA IDEAS

- Write *sound* on the board and invite pupils to come out and build up a spider diagram.
- Type *sound barrier* or *sonic boom* into a search engine together with video and let the pupils watch some videos in order to appreciate this phenomenon.
- Play a game in which pairs of pupils vary intensity and pitch in front of the class. For example, one student could shout (not too loudly!), while the other whispers. The rest of the class then have to write a sentence about each pupil, for example, *Pupil A produced an intense sound; Pupil B's sound wasn't as intense as pupil A's.*
- You could extend this game by bringing in various musical instruments to class. Ask pupils to close their eyes. You could then play two different musical instruments or, alternatively, play the same one twice, but with different intensity or pitch. The class then have to decide whether the variation was in intensity, pitch or timbre.

ANSWERS AT A GLANCE

1 It's more difficult to hear the question through the door because the sound is distorted.

PAGES 122–123 Find out / Think about it

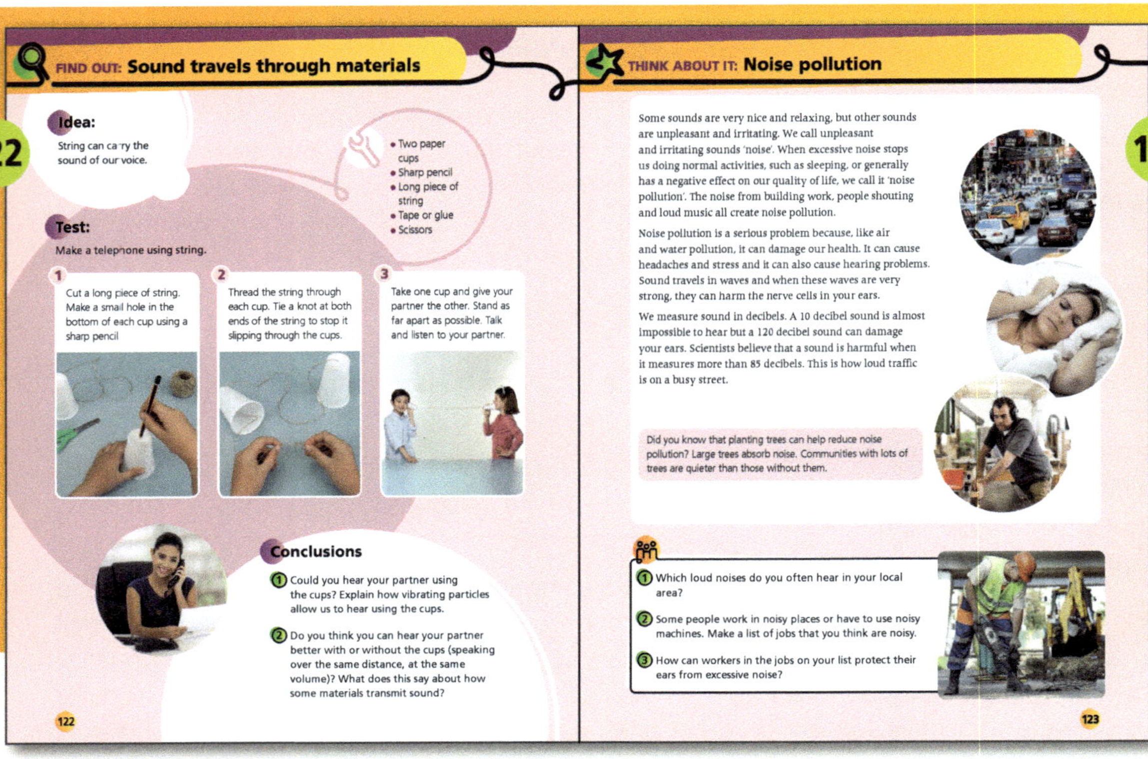
122

FIND OUT: Sound travels through materials

Idea:

String can carry the sound of our voice.

- Two paper cups
- Sharp pencil
- Long piece of string
- Tape or glue
- Scissors

Test:

Make a telephone using string.

1. Cut a long piece of string. Make a small hole in the bottom of each cup using a sharp pencil
2. Thread the string through each cup. Tie a knot at both ends of the string to stop it slipping through the cups.
3. Take one cup and give your partner the other. Stand as far apart as possible. Talk and listen to your partner.

Conclusions

1. Could you hear your partner using the cups? Explain how vibrating particles allow us to hear using the cups.
2. Do you think you can hear your partner better with or without the cups (speaking over the same distance, at the same volume)? What does this say about how some materials transmit sound?

122

123

THINK ABOUT IT: Noise pollution

Some sounds are very nice and relaxing, but other sounds are unpleasant and irritating. We call unpleasant and irritating sounds 'noise'. When excessive noise stops us doing normal activities, such as sleeping, or generally has a negative effect on our quality of life, we call it 'noise pollution'. The noise from building work, people shouting and loud music all create noise pollution.

Noise pollution is a serious problem because, like air and water pollution, it can damage our health. It can cause headaches and stress and it can also cause hearing problems. Sound travels in waves and when these waves are very strong, they can harm the nerve cells in your ears.

We measure sound in decibels. A 10 decibel sound is almost impossible to hear but a 120 decibel sound can damage your ears. Scientists believe that a sound is harmful when it measures more than 85 decibels. This is how loud traffic is on a busy street.

Did you know that planting trees can help reduce noise pollution? Large trees absorb noise. Communities with lots of trees are quieter than those without them.

1. Which loud noises do you often hear in your local area?
2. Some people work in noisy places or have to use noisy machines. Make a list of jobs that you think are noisy.
3. How can workers in the jobs on your list protect their ears from excessive noise?

123

PAGE SUMMARY

In the first of these two pages (*Find out*), pupils make a poster showing how food chains in an ecosystem are interconnected and form a food web. The second page (*Think about it*) provides your pupils with the opportunity to learn about the harmful affect human activity can have on natural ecosystems.

LANGUAGE

- Imperatives: *cut, make, thread, tie, take, give, talk, stand, listen*
- Vocabulary: *string, hole, bottom, knot, negative, quality, decibels, sharp, relaxing, unpleasant, irritating, excessive, harmful, slip, damage, measure, absorb*

ADDITIONAL MATERIALS

- Digital flashcards

FIND OUT

OPENING ACTIVITIES

- Review how sound travels. Read the introductory text on page 120. Pause at key words for pupils to supply the missing word or words in unison. *When an object* ***vibrates****, it causes the* ***air particles*** *around it to* ***vibrate****. When these air particles* ***vibrate****, they in turn cause the air particles around them to vibrate. The vibrations move through the* ***air*** *until they reach our* ***ear****. We call these travelling vibrations* ***sound waves****.*
- Explain that when we talk, our vocal cords make the air particles vibrate. Tell pupils to put their hand against their throat and to read a few lines from the Pupils' Book. Ask them if they can feel the vibrations as they speak. Point out that the vibrations travel through the air and enter our ears. (You may like to review how these vibrations are transformed into signals and arrive at the brain where they are interpreted.)

MAIN ACTIVITIES

- Explain to pupils that they will be making a simple telephone to observe how sound can travel through materials.

- Ask pupils to read the steps on page 122. Then, tell them to write the materials and the three steps in their notebook. If you are using the book on the interactive whiteboard, you can play the audio of the steps. You may choose to do this investigation together as a class or allow small groups to go through the steps independently. When they have made the telephones, tell them to keep the string taut.

⊕ CLOSING ACTIVITIES

- It's a good idea to take pupils outside to the playground to do the speaking part of the activity. Give pupils time to enjoy talking to each other through their homemade phones. Suggest they have a conversation about their plans for the weekend. Encourage pupils to use full sentences.
- Now tell them to have the same conversation without using the telephone. Ask **Can you still hear each other?**
- If you have plenty of space, see how far apart they can get the cup and string telephone to work. What happens when the string goes slack? What happens when someone holds the centre of the string? Will the telephone work around corners?

1 Could you hear your partner using the cups? Explain how vibrating particles allow us to hear using the cups.

- *Your voice vibrates the air inside the cup which makes the bottom of the cup vibrate. The vibrations pass along the string, to the partner's cup which makes the air vibrate and become interpreted as sound by the brain.*

2 Do you think you can hear your partner better with or without the cups (speaking over the same distance, at the same volume)? What does this say about how some materials transmit sound?

- *You hear better with the cups. Air is a gas and the particles are more spread out. This is whay sound vibrations run out before they travel very far.*

THINK ABOUT IT

⊕ OPENING ACTIVITIES

- Organise the class into small groups and ask them to make a list of pleasant sounds and unpleasant sounds. Write their ideas on the board and then ask each pupil to tell the class what their favourite sound is.
- Ask pupils to imagine what it would be like not to be able to hear. Ask them to think about the problems deaf people have to live with.

MAIN ACTIVITIES

- Ask pupils to open their books on page 123 and say **Let's read about noise pollution**. If you are using the interactive whiteboard, you can play the audio and encourage pupils to read along in their books. Then, ask pupils to look at the photos and describe what they can see in pairs. Ask **Why are trees so important?** Elicit that they absorb noise, use carbon dioxide, produce oxygen and give us shade in the summer.
- Ask pupils to talk about their own experiences with loud noise. Encourage all the pupils to participate and also to listen to their classmates' stories.

⊕ CLOSING ACTIVITIES

1 Which loud noises do you often hear in your local area?

- Ask pupils to work with a partner to talk about this question. Answers will vary according to where they live. *Noisy neighbours, traffic, sirens, construction work, airplanes, helicopters, bars and discos. You may like to mention that school playgrounds can be very noisy too!*

2 Some people work in noisy places or have to use noisy machines. Make a list of jobs that you think are noisy.

- Read the question to the class and ask them to suggest work places that are noisy. Write their suggestions on the board. *Factories, building sites, stations and airports, kitchens, road works,* etc.

3 How can workers in the jobs on your list protect their ears from excessive noise?

- Tell the pupils to look at the third photo. Ask **What is the man wearing?** (*Ear protectors*)

PAGES 124–125 Look back: Energy

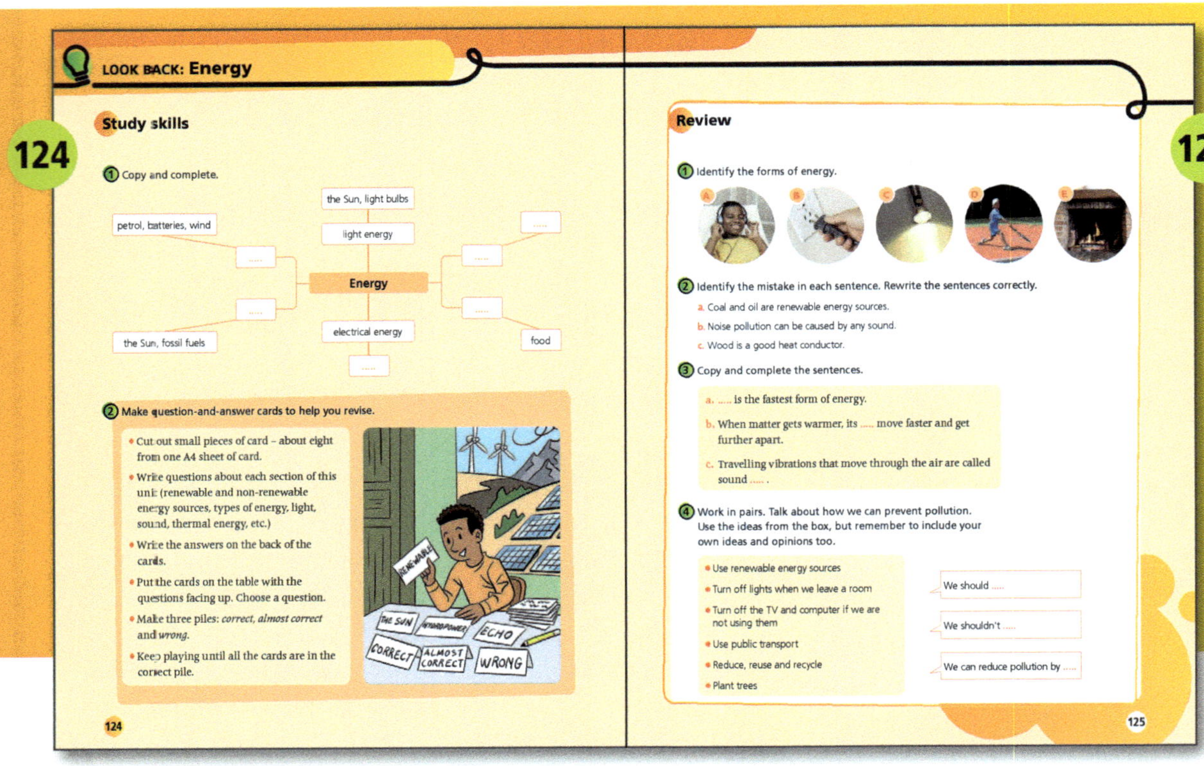

PAGE SUMMARY

This double-page spread allows pupils the opportunity to organise what they've learned in the unit by means of a concept map. They can also learn a new study skill – pupils make question and answer cards to help them revise what they have learned in the unit. On the *Review* page, pupils complete activities individually to check their understanding of material covered in this unit. Activity 4 is a pairwork speaking activity to encourage them to create complete, accurate sentences and identify and use a simple structure (should / shouldn't). It is also a peer evaluation opportunity.

LANGUAGE

- Imperatives: *match, write, copy, correct, talk, use, work, make, cut, choose, identify, rewrite*
- *Should / shouldn't* + infinitive
- By + gerund

ADDITIONAL MATERIALS

- Digital flashcards
- Digital wordcards

OPENING ACTIVITIES

- Display chosen wordcards randomly on the board. Invite volunteers to read the names. Tell the pupils to cover their eyes and remove one or two cards. Ask pupils to look again at the board and identify the missing cards. This activity can be extended by asking pupils to spell the word. Mix up the cards and play again.
- Ask the pupils to look at pages 116 and 117 and to choose three sentences from a text and copy them on a piece of paper. Ask Pupil A to dictate the sentences to Pupil B. Pupil B then dictates their sentences to Pupil A. The dictations are then corrected by the partners. You may like to assign different texts to Pupils A and B.
- Organise the class into small groups. Tell pupils that they are going to design an Eco-school. Explain that they have to think of ways of making the school environmentally friendly. Ask **How are we going to heat the school? How can we generate electricity? How can we reduce, recycle and reuse?** Write their ideas on the board. You may like to make this a writing activity for homework later.

MAIN ACTIVITIES

Page 124, Study skills

1 Copy and complete.

- Remind pupils that when we organise new information, it is easier to understand and remember it. Focus the pupils' attention on the concept map and ask them to tell you what the missing words are. Encourage them to make full sentences: *Food is a source of chemical energy.* Tell them to copy and complete the concept map in their notebooks.

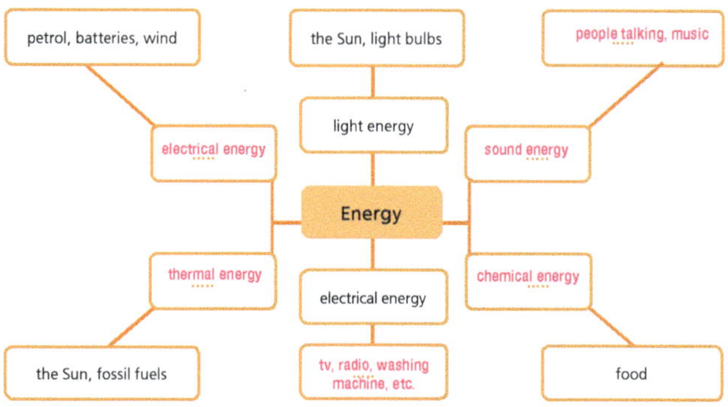

2 Make question-and-answer cards to help you revise.

- Pupils can do this activity in pairs or in small groups. Pupils make their question and answer cards together (writing questions on one side and the answer on the other). In groups or pairs they ask and answer their cards putting them in the correct, almost correct or wrong pile. You may like to demonstrate this activity with one of the groups or pairs.

Page 125, Review

Note: This part of the review can be done with minimal teacher guidance. You may wish to work through the activities as a class or in small groups or partners. Alternatively, you can ask pupils to do them individually as self-evaluation. This review could also be done as homework.

1 Identify the forms of energy.

a. Sound
b. Electrical
c. Light
d. Kinetic
e. Thermal

2 Identify the mistake in each sentence. Rewrite the sentences correctly.

a. Coal and oil *are non-renewable* energy sources.
b. Noise pollution can be caused by *an unpleasant* sound.
c. Wood is a good heat *insulator*

3 Copy and complete the sentences.

a. Light
b. particles
c. waves

4 Work in pairs. Talk about how we can prevent pollution. Use the ideas from the box, but remember to include your own ideas and opinions too.

Answers may include:

- We should use public transport.
- We shouldn't leave lights on when we leave a room.
- We should turn off the TV and computer if we aren't using them.
- We can reduce pollution by planting trees.

Activity Book answers / Audio CD2 track list

44

UNIT 8 **Energy**

1 What types of energy are being produced in the photos?

sound energy	thermal energy	light energy
kinetic energy	electrical energy	chemical energy

2 What other things produce these types of energy? Complete the table.

sound energy	thermal energy	light energy
violin	barbecue	light bulb
Open answers	Open answers	Open answers
kinetic energy	electrical energy	chemical energy
bikes	microwave	petrol
Open answers	Open answers	Open answers

44

45

3 Match and write true sentences about light energy.

Light is the fastest form	of seven different colours: red, orange, yellow, green, blue, indigo and violet.
Light from the Sun is made up	of energy. It travels at about 300 000 km per second.
Light travels in all directions	behave differently, depending on the surface it hits.
When something gets in its way, light can	from its source. One light bulb can light an entire room.

a. Light is the fastest form of energy. It travels at about 300 000 km per second.
b. Light from the Sun is made up of seven different colours: red, orange, yellow, green, blue, indigo and violet.
c. Light travels in all directions from its source. One light bulb can light an entire room.
d. When something gets its way, light can behave differently, depending on the surface it hits.

4 Write sentences about light energy which contain the following information:

a. transparent
Light passes through transparent materials. These materials do not scatter the light so we can see the image clearly

b. opaque
Light cannot pass through opaque materials. These materials reflect or absorb light.

c. translucent
Light passes through translucent materials. These materials scatter the light which means the image isn't clear.

d. eight minutes
It takes eight minutes for light from the Sun to reach us.

45

46

UNIT 8

5 Complete the tables.

heat conductors	heat insulators
iron	wood
copper	plastic
aluminium	wool

6 Complete the sentences about thermal energy using the words in the box

~~0°C~~ ~~100°C~~ ~~thermal~~ ~~water~~ ~~state~~

a. When we heat an object, we are increasing its temperature, as well as its amount of thermal energy.
b. A change in the thermal energy of a substance can change its state.
c. If we heat ice to a temperature of 0°C or higher, it will change into water.
d. If we heat water to a temperature of 100°C or higher, it will become steam.

7 Label the different characteristics of sound. Match the definitions to the correct picture.

a pitch | b intensity | c tone

Definitions
1. This is how we identify the source of a sound. c
2. This depends on the strength of the vibrations that produce the sound. b
3. This depends on how quickly the vibrations are produced. a

46

47

8 Complete the sentences about sound energy. Match the sentences to the correct picture.

~~sonic boom~~ ~~reflect~~ ~~air~~ ~~changes~~ ~~directions~~ ~~solid~~

1. Sound travels in all directions from its source.
2. It can travel through solid, opaque objects.
3. Sound can reflect off an object. If the object is far away, we hear an echo.
4. It cannot travel when there is no air.
5. Sound can produce changes in other objects.
6. When an object travels faster than the speed of sound, it produces a sonic boom.

a 6 | b 3 | c 2 | d 4 | e 1 | f 5

9 Do these sentences apply to light, sound or thermal energy?

a. We can change the state of an object by increasing or decreasing this type of energy. thermal energy
b. This is the fastest form of energy. Most of this energy comes from the Sun. light energy
c. This type of energy is produced when objects vibrate. Vibrations move through the air in waves. sound energy

47

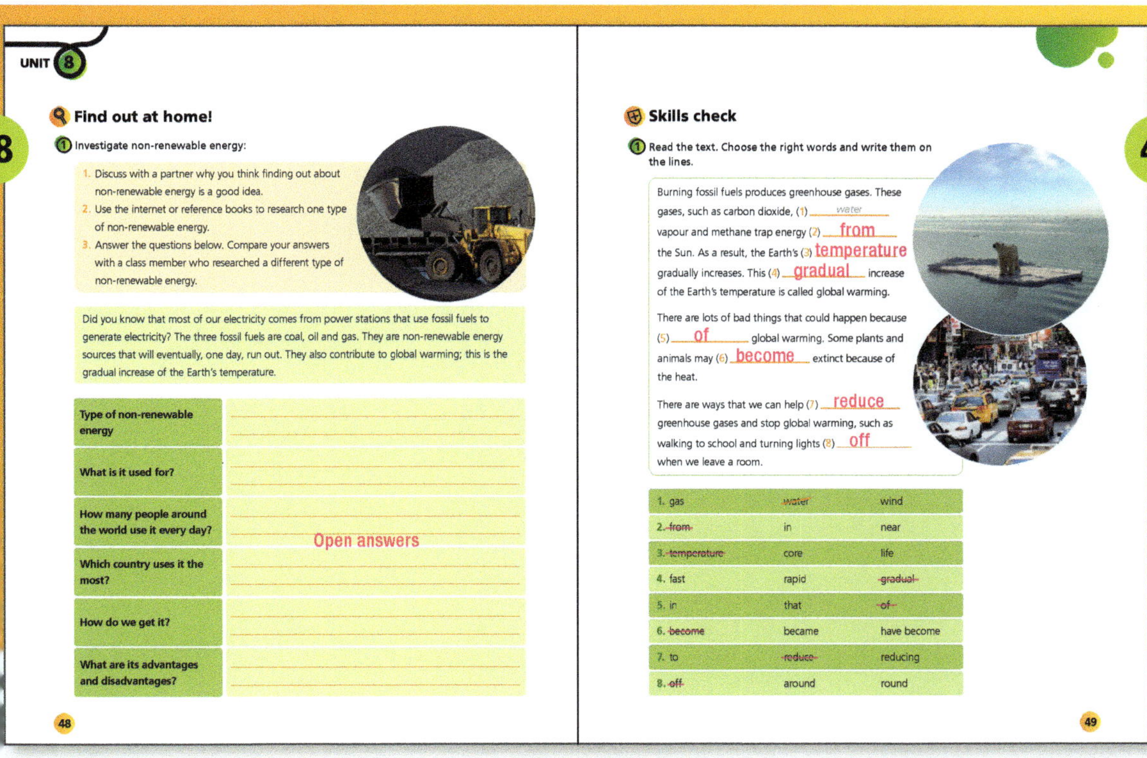

UNIT 8

Find out at home!

1. Investigate non-renewable energy:

1. Discuss with a partner why you think finding out about non-renewable energy is a good idea.
2. Use the internet or reference books to research one type of non-renewable energy.
3. Answer the questions below. Compare your answers with a class member who researched a different type of non-renewable energy.

Did you know that most of our electricity comes from power stations that use fossil fuels to generate electricity? The three fossil fuels are coal, oil and gas. They are non-renewable energy sources that will eventually, one day, run out. They also contribute to global warming; this is the gradual increase of the Earth's temperature.

Type of non-renewable energy	
What is it used for?	
How many people around the world use it every day?	Open answers
Which country uses it the most?	
How do we get it?	
What are its advantages and disadvantages?	

48

Skills check

1. Read the text. Choose the right words and write them on the lines.

Burning fossil fuels produces greenhouse gases. These gases, such as carbon dioxide, (1) *water* vapour and methane trap energy (2) **from** the Sun. As a result, the Earth's (3) **temperature** gradually increases. This (4) **gradual** increase of the Earth's temperature is called global warming.

There are lots of bad things that could happen because (5) **of** global warming. Some plants and animals may (6) **become** extinct because of the heat.

There are ways that we can help (7) **reduce** greenhouse gases and stop global warming, such as walking to school and turning lights (8) **off** when we leave a room.

1. gas	~~water~~	wind
2. ~~from~~	in	near
3. ~~temperature~~	core	life
4. fast	rapid	~~gradual~~
5. in	that	~~of~~
6. ~~become~~	became	have become
7. to	~~reduce~~	reducing
8. ~~off~~	around	round

49

Unit 8 Audio CD2 track list

TRACK	ACTIVITY
32	**Pupil's Book page 113,** Unit introduction
33	**Pupil's Book page 113,** Song *Energy*
34	**Pupil's Book page 114,** Story: *A trip to a wind farm*
35	**Pupil's Book page 116,** Types of energy
36	**Pupil's Book page 118,** Light energy
37	**Pupil's Book pages 119,** Thermal energy
38	**Pupil's Book page 119,** Change of state
39	**Pupil's Book pages 119,** Movement of thermal energy
40	**Pupil's Book page 120,** Sound energy
41	**Pupil's Book page 121,** Characteristics of sound

UNIT 9 Machines

CONTENT	EVALUATION CRITERIA
Simple and complex machines.	Identify the main characteristics of simple and complex machines and give examples of both.
Electricity.	Know the basic characteristics and some of the effects of energy as well as the elements of an electrical circuit.
Machines and energy.	Understand that machines use different forms of energy, have different uses and must be used carefully.
Scientists.	Know about some of the famous scientists of history.
First approaches to scientific activity and the scientific method. Use of different information sources (direct and indirect). Use ICTs.	Obtain relevant information about specific phenomena, make predictions, integrate information from direct and indirect observation and communicate the results.
First approaches to simple experiments and investigations.	Conjecture as to the results of natural occurrences and of simple experiments and investigations.
Individual and group work.	Work independently and proactively and develop strategies for working in a group.
Planning a project and presenting a report.	Carry out a project and present a report.

LEARNING STANDARDS	KEY COMPETENCES	PAGES
Identifies the parts of different complex and machines and how they work.	MST, LTL	128, 129
Defines the different simple machines: wedge, inclined plane, pulley, wheel and axle, screw and lever.	MST, SLIN	130, 131
Observes and identifies some of the applications of machines and how they contribute to making our lives easier.	MST, SOC	128-131, 135
Knows the basic characteristics and some of the effects of electricity.	MST	132
Knows the elements of an electrical circuit.	MST	133
Understands that machines use different forms of energy and can be used for many different things.	MST	134, 135
Uses machines with the care and attention they deserve.	MST, LTL	135
Knows the biography of one or more famous scientists from history and values what they contributed to human knowledge.	MST, CUL, SOC	128, 137
With help, selects and organises specific and relevant information; analyses it and draws conclusions; reflects on the experience and the process; presents the results.	MST, LTL	129, 136
Use books, libraries, etc. and collaborate in the care and maintenance of all the materials available in the school and the classroom.	MST, LTL	127-139
Shows autonomy in the planning of activities and tasks and shows initiative in decision taking.	LTL, AUT	129, 136, 137
With help, carries out simple experiments or investigations, and conjectures as to the results.	MST, LTL, AUT	136, 137
Uses strategies to help their own learning, as well as asking for help and information.	LTL, AUT	129, 138
First approaches to cooperative learning.	SOC, LTL	127, 137
Begins observation, using relevant instruments and consulting written documents and images.	LTL, AUT	129, 136
Shows autonomy and proactiveness in the planning of and carrying out of actions.	AUT	136, 137
Presents work clearly and in an organised fashion.	LIN, LTL, AUT	136, 137
With help, carries out a project and presents a report, using paper and/or digital means, collecting information from different sources, presenting the results orally and with the support of images and short texts.	LIN, LTL, AUT, DIG	136, 137

UNIT INFORMATION

UNIT SUMMARY

In this unit, pupils will review and extend their knowledge of machines and energy, looking at simple and complex machines. Pupils will understand some basic concepts of physics and explore how simple machines make up complex machines. They will learn to classify complex machines by energy sources and by functions.

At the beginning of the unit, pupils will revise simple machines and forces. This subject area is covered in the opening illustration with the help of the course characters, Carla and Alex, who are on a school trip to the Archaeological Museum. The school trip continues in the story and, on their return to school, Carla and Alex carry out a School trip project to review some of the simple machines they have seen. These opening pages are designed to test pupils' prior knowledge and provoke interest and participation.

This is followed by hands-on activities which challenge pupils to work collaboratively, to plan, design and make a simple machine (levers). This activity aims to consolidate what pupils have learned while also providing concrete experiences for them to develop critical and creative thinking skills.

This unit provides pupils with a variety of opportunities to develop scientific skills including observation, planning and problem-solving.

EXPERIMENT

Find out

IIn the *Find out* activity on page 136, your pupils will prepare an investigation to observe how inclined planes work.

The pupils will need:

- elastic band
- books
- marbles
- long wooden ruler
- bag

Further ideas

Pupils can continue their exploration of simple machines by setting up investigations of other simple machines such as pulleys etc. using everyday objects.

VALUES AND ATTITUDES

In this unit, your pupils will recognise simple machines and how they work and also identify them in complex machines, valuing their importance in making work easier and our lives better. Through hands-on activities, they will build confidence in manipulating different materials and in planning and designing machines. Throughout the unit, encourage pupils to think about the important role that simple and complex machines play in our lives. Encourage them also to explore how things work around them.

Think about it

The *Think about it* page in this unit focuses on a famous scientist, Isaac Newton. Pupils will learn about Newton's discoveries and will also investigate and present the work of a scientist of their choice.

EVALUATION MATERIAL

These documents can be downloaded from the *Teachers* section of the digital component and printed .

The materials include:

- **Unit diagnostic test**: provides an overview of the unit and allows you to assess the pupils' prior knowledge.
- **End-of-unit test**: in addition to the *Review* section at the end of each unit, this summative test can be used to evaluate pupils' progress after studying the unit content.
- **Class unit evaluation grid**: based on the evaluation criteria and learning standards of the unit.

DIGITAL RESOURCES

Presentations

- **Unit summary**: a simple slide presentation with text, images and audio to review the main ideas of the unit. It can be used at the beginning of the unit to test pupils' prior knowledge of the unit content or at the end of the unit as a revision tool.
- **Find out**: a slide presentation of the unit's *Find out* page with text, photos and audio. The slide presentation is perfect for a heads-up class, showing the steps one by one. Use this tool to get the pupils to predict the next steps (with their books closed) or to focus their attention on each step as they carry out the project themselves.

Activities

Activities vary per unit and include the following:

- **Memory game**: useful activity for reviewing key vocabulary and modelling pronunciation.
- **Labelling**: pupils label a diagram by dragging and dropping key terms.
- **Spelling**: pupils drag and drop letters to spell key terms.
- **Read and reveal**: pupils read sentences and guess the missing words, which are revealed by clicking the spaces.
- **Classification:** pupils drag and drop concepts and key terms in a simple classification table.
- **Wordsearch:** pupils find key terms hidden in the wordsearch.
- **Definitions:** pupils drag and drop words to complete definitions.

Song lyrics

Listen to the song *Simple machines* and follow the lyrics line by line.

Posters

Attractive and informative posters to display in class. You can use them to review key concepts and vocabulary.

Videos

Use the video links in this unit to present content in a dynamic, real-life context while reinforcing the pupils' listening skills.

Teachers

Digital flashcards and wordcards: topics include *Simple machines, Electricity* and *Machines and energy.*

Downloadable PDFs: evaluation tests, evaluation grids, templates, useful links and further information..

PAGES 126–127 Machines

PAGE SUMMARY

The aim of the unit opener is to develop your pupils' observation skills and find out what they already know about the topic of the unit. Use the picture to elicit vocabulary related to simple and complex machines, as well as action verbs that describe what is going on in the scene and elements to describe the various characters and objects. Get your pupils to work in groups to complete activities 1–4 and to have fun listening to the song and completing activity 5.

LANGUAGE

- Question words: *what, which, how many,* etc.
- Vocabulary: *simple machines, complex machines, cranes, bulldozers, effort, wheel and axle, pulley, wedge, inclined plane, screw, lever, slide, seesaw, bike, lift, knife, bottle top*

ADDITIONAL MATERIALS

- Digital flashcards
- Digital wordcards
- Extra classroom materials: a pencil sharpener, a pair of scissors, a mobile phone, a computer and a stapler

OPENING ACTIVITIES

- Remind pupils that they studied machines the previous year. Organise the class into small groups and ask them to work together to make a list of the things they remember about machines. Say: **Machines help us do work with less effort. What else do you remember about machines?** Write their information on the board.
- If you are using an interactive whiteboard, focus only on the illustration of the building site, not the questions. Pre-teach the words *cranes* and *bulldozer*. Either elicit ideas (*Alex is using a stapler; Carla is making notes*, etc.) or ask questions indicating each part of the picture: **How many cranes can you see in the picture? What type of protective clothing are the people wearing? What do we use a bulldozer for?**

MAIN ACTIVITIES

Page 127, Unit introduction (CD2 track 42)

- Read the unit introduction at the top of page 127. You can play the audio of the unit introduction first, with pupils reading along with it, and then ask one or two pupils to read aloud. This way, pupils will feel more self-assured when it comes to pronouncing new words.

- Divide pupils into small groups to answer the questions at the top of page 127. Then invite different groups to compare their answers with each other.

① Which complex machines can you see in the picture?

- If you have pre-taught the words *crane* and *bulldozer,* pupils will quickly identify these machines. Ask them to explain what these machines do. *Cranes, bulldozers, drills, wheel barrows, spades, cement mixers,* etc.

② Which simple machines do these complex machines use?

- Ask pupils to explain which parts of the machine are made up of the simple machines. *Wheel and axle, pulleys, levers, wedges, inclined planes, screws*

③ Make a list of machines that make your life easier at home.

- Elicit the fact machines make our lives easier and there are many examples at home. *Open answer*

④ How many of these machines need electricity to work?

- Extend this question by asking pupils to identify if the machines use mains electricity, batteries or both. *Open answer*

⑤ Listen to the song. Match the simple machines you hear in the song to the photos.

- Play the song *Simple machines* **(CD2 track 43)** and ask pupils to match the simple machines in the song to the correct photo. *Pulley – lift; inclined plane – slide; screw – bottle top; wheel and axle – bike; wedge – knife; lever - seesaw*

CD2 • track 43

Simple machines
How many are there?
There are six.
One: *Tell me about a pulley*
A pulley has a wheel and rope
We use it to lift and lower an object
[chorus]Simple machines …
Two: *Tell me about an inclined plane*
It's a slanting surface
We use it to move objects up and down
[chorus]Simple machines …
Three: *Tell me about a screw*
A screw is an inclined plane wrapped around a cylinder
We use it to hold things and to lift things
[chorus]Simple machines …
Four: *Tell me about a wheel and axle*
We use it to move objects
From one place to another
[chorus]Simple machines …
Five: *Tell me about a wedge*
It has at least one slanted edge
We use it to cut things
[chorus]Simple machines …
Six: *Tell me about a lever*
It's a rigid bar with a fulcrum
We use it to lift objects
Simple machines, simple machines
Reduce the force we need
And make our lives easier

ANSWERS AT A GLANCE

① Cranes, bulldozers, drills, wheelbarrows, spades, cement mixers, etc.

② Wheel and axle, pulleys, levers, wedges, inclined planes, screws.

③ Open answer.

④ Open answer.

⑤ Pulley – lift; inclined plane – slide; screw – bottle top; wheel and axle – bike; wedge – knife; lever – seesaw

PAGES 128–129 A trip to the Archaeological Museum

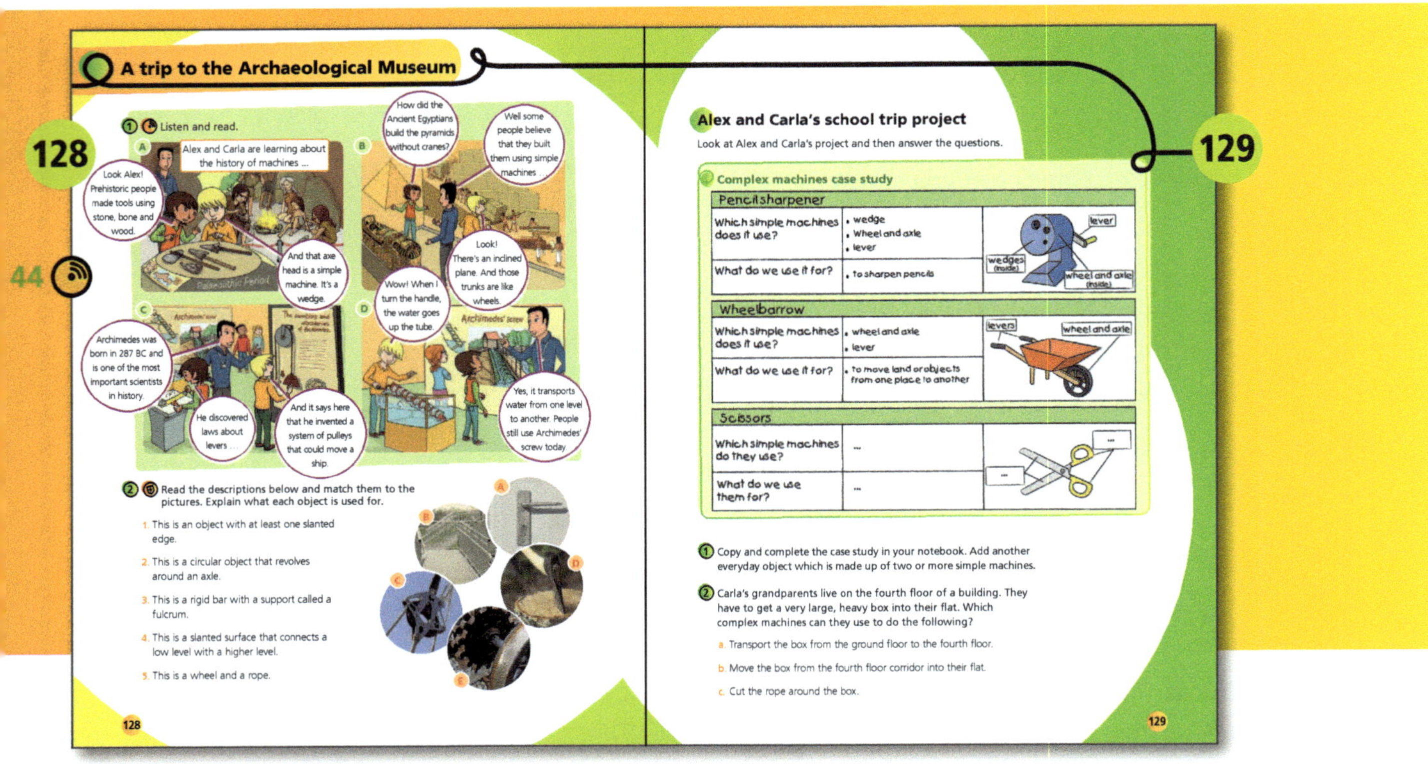

PAGE SUMMARY

This double-page spread opens with a story in which your pupils have the opportunity to see Carla and Alex at a particular moment of their school trip to the Archaeological Museum. Carla and Alex are talking to the museum guide and showing their knowledge of simple machines. The story is reinforced with an exam-style matching activity that is related to the story and opening double-page spread. On page 129, pupils can study Carla and Alex's school trip project about complex machines and the simple machines they are made up of.

LANGUAGE

- Present simple
- Past tense
- Infinitive of purpose
- Vocabulary: *tools, stone, bone, wood, axe head, pyramids, trunk, wheels, laws, levers, pulleys, slanted, edge, circular, rigid, bar, rope, revolve, BC, Archimedes, Archimedes' screw*

ADDITIONAL MATERIALS

- Digital flashcards
- Digital wordcards

OPENING ACTIVITIES

- Play the *Simple machines* song **(CD2 track 43)** and encourage pupils to sing along.
- Place the wordcards *pulley, wheel and axle, inclined plane, lever, screw* and *wedge* on the board. Read the definitions of simple machines from page 128 and ask pupils to identify the simple machine you are describing. Invite volunteers to give examples for each simple machine and write them on the board.

MAIN ACTIVITIES

1 Listen and read. (CD2 track 44)

- Draw the pupils' attention to the story at the top of page 128 and explain to them that they are going to listen to a story about Alex and Carla's trip to to the Archaeological Museum. Say **Let's listen and read**. Play the audio.
- Ask pupils to look at each of the illustrations and describe what is happening in each one using their own words. For example: *There are some Palaeolithic tools. Alex is looking at a model of Ancient Egyptains building the pyramids.*
- Divide pupils into groups of three and ask them to choose a character from the story – Alex, Carla or the museum guide. Pupils then read their part of the story aloud in their small group. You can invite a group to the front of the class to act the story out.

- Check for comprehension: Ask: **What were the Palaeolithic tools made of?** (*Stone, bones and wood*); **Which simple machines did the Ancient Egyptians use?** (*Inclined planes*); **When was Archimedes born?** (*In 287 BC*); **Which laws did he discover?** (*Ones about levers*); **What kind of system did he invent?** (*Pulleys*); **What do we use Archimedes' screw for?** (*To transport water from one level to another*)

(2) Read the descriptions below and match them to the pictures. Explain what each object is used for.

- This activity aims to introduce some new vocabulary, reinforce what pupils have learned in the story and refresh concepts studied in previous levels. Ask pupils to work with a partner to match the description to the pictures. *1-D, 2-E, 3-A, 4-B, 5-C*

SCHOOL TRIP PROJECT

- Explain to pupils that following their trip to the Archaeological Museum, Carla and Alex have done a project to summarise what they have learned about simple and complex machines.
- Tell pupils to look at the pictures on page 129 and ask a volunteer to read the questions about the pencil sharpener and invite other pupils to answer. Write on the board: T*his is a* _____. *It's made up of* ________ . *We use it to* __________. Ask a volunteer to complete the sentences about the sharpener. Repeat the procedure with the case studies of the wheelbarrow and the scissors.

(1) Copy and complete the case study in your notebook. Add another everyday object which is made up of two or more simple machines.

- Tell pupils to copy the case studies into their notebook and to add one other object. Tell them not to show their partner the extra object. Ask them to find out their partner's object by asking the same questions from the case studies. *Wedges and levers. To cut things.*

(2) Carla's grandparents live on the fourth floor of a building. They have to get a very large, heavy box into their flat. Which complex machines can they use to do the following?

- Ask pupils to work individually to answer the question. Check their answers and ask them to copy the question and answers into their notebook.

a. *A pulley system*

b. *A trolley*

c. *A knife or scissors*

(+) CLOSING ACTIVITIES

- Divide the class into two teams. Place two chairs at the front of the class, each facing their team. Ask one pupil from each team to come and sit on the chair, facing their team. Write the name of a machine on the board behind pupils' backs. Tell the teams to mime the word on the board to their team member who must guess what it is. The team member who guesses first wins a point for their team. Two new team members then come to the chairs.

(+) EXTRA IDEAS

- Ask pupils to find out information about Archimedes. This activity can be done at home with the help of parents, in small study groups on a computer or in the library. Ask them also to look for more information about Archimedes' screw.

ANSWERS AT A GLANCE

Page 128

(1) 1 - D; 2 – E; 3 – A; 4 – B; 5 – C

Page 129

(1) Wedges and levers. To cut things.

(2) a. A pulley system, b. A trolley, c. A knife or scissors.

PAGES 130–131 Simple machines

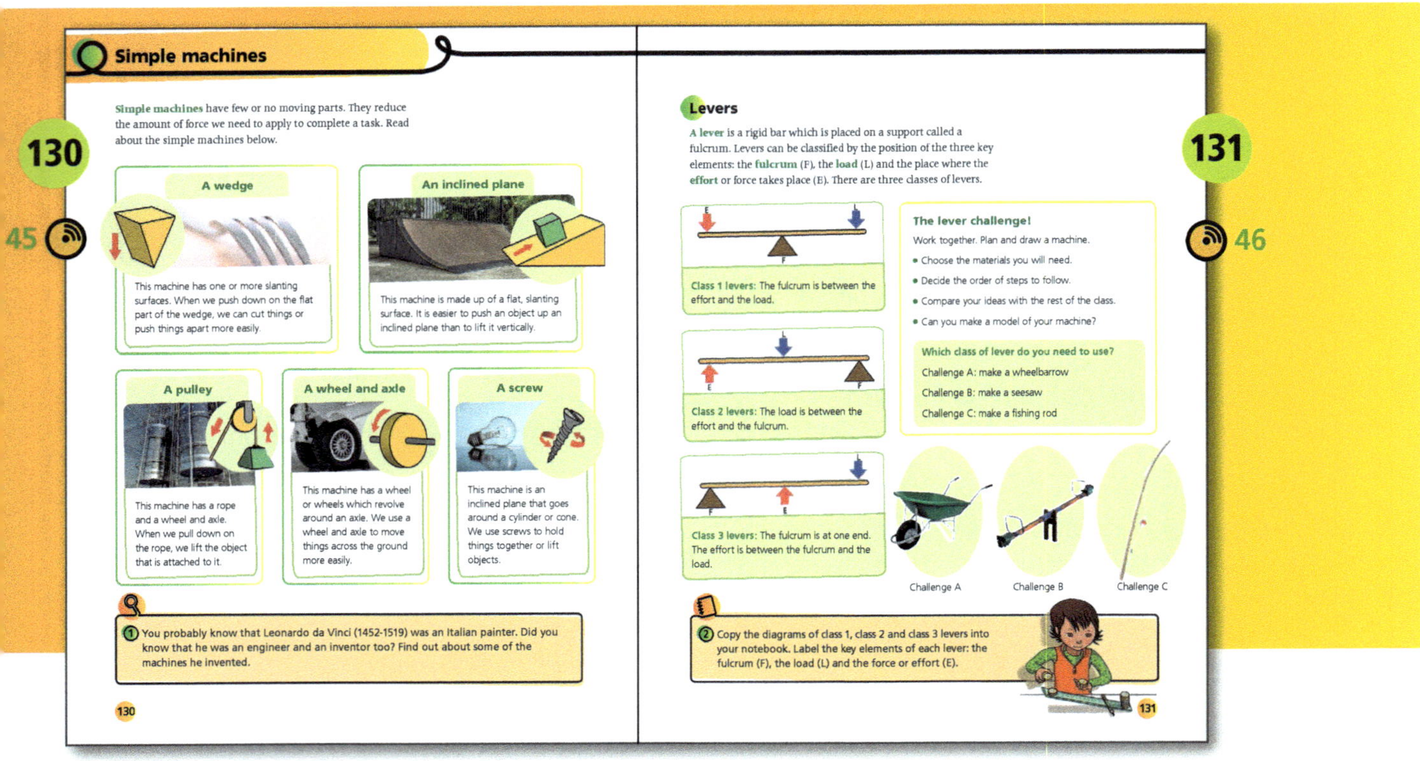

PAGE SUMMARY

This double-page spread reviews the six simple machines. Pupils are familiar with this topic and should have no difficulty with either the vocabulary or concepts. However, they will extend their knowledge by observing and investigating the three classes of lever. Pupils will observe the different parts and use the illustrations and photos to identify simple machines which make up complex machines. Encourage pupils to actively explore the objects in their environment and find out how things work around them.

LANGUAGE

- Imperatives: *choose, decide, make,* etc.
- Prepositions of movement: *up, down, from, to,* etc.
- Infinitive of purpose: *to cut paper*
- Vocabulary: *wedge, inclined plane, pulley, wheel and axle, screw, lever, rigid, bar, fulcrum, load, effort, slanting, rope, cylinder, cone*

ADDITIONAL MATERIALS

- Digital flashcards and wordcards
- Extra classroom materials: a stapler, a CD player, walnuts, nutcrackers

OPENING ACTIVITIES

- Draw pupils' attention to the stapler and CD player on the table. Point out that they are both complex machines. Ask a volunteer to explain what a complex machine is. *(It's made up of two or more parts.)* Say: **They are both complex machines but how are they different?** *(The CD player needs electricity to work.)* Point out that the stapler doesn't need electricity but it does need energy to work.
- Ask **What is the energy source that makes a stapler work?** Elicit that it's a person. Take the stapler and staple two pieces of paper together. Ask **How did I make it work?** Elicit that you pushed the top of the stapler down. Ask **What is a push or a pull?** *(It's a force.)* Explain that we use pushes and pulls when we use a simple machine. The simple machine makes them stronger, so our work is easier.
- **NB.** Check for nut allergies before doing this activity. Hand out a walnut to each pupil and ask them to try to open it with their hands. Now ask pupils to use the nutcrackers to open it. Explain that the nutcrackers multiply the force acting on the walnut

MAIN ACTIVITIES

Pages 130, Simple machines (CD2 track 45)

- Play the audio **(CD2 track 45)** and ask pupils to listen and read. Pause after each section and check for any problems with vocabulary. Ask pupils to read the texts again silently. Now ask them to work with a partner to ask and answer questions about the six simple machines. Tell them to use page 130 to help them. **Which simple machine has a rope and a wheel?** (*A pulley*); **What do we use screws for?** (*To hold things together*)

Pages 131, Levers (CD2 track 46)

- Ask pupils to open their books on page 131 and read the title. Alternately keep the books closed and present this entire page on the interactive whiteboard. Play the audio **(CD2 track 46)** and ask pupils to listen and read.
- Show the class a ruler, a pencil and a rubber and explain that you are going to make the three different types of levers. Elicit that the ruler is the rigid bar, the pencil is the fulcrum and the rubber is the load. Ask the class to take out a ruler, a rubber and a pencil from their pencil cases. Read the descriptions of the levers and encourage pupils to make the levers as you are making the examples.

Pages 131, The lever challenge!

- Invite volunteers to read the steps for the lever challenge. Explain that they are going to have a chance to use what they have learned about levers to make their own model. Divide pupils into groups and instruct them to choose a machine and plan the materials, tools and steps to build it. Ask: **Which class of lever is challenge A?** (*Class 2*); **Which class of lever is challenge B?** (*Class 1*); **Which class of lever is challenge C?** (*Class 3*) You may decide to continue this lesson during the following class to give pupils time to bring the materials they will need to make their lever.

1 You probably know that Leonardo da Vinci (1452-1519) was an Italian painter. Did you know that he was an engineer and an inventor too? Find out about some of the machines he invented.

- This activity can be done at home with the help of parents, in small study groups on a computer or in the library. *Open answer*

2 Copy the diagrams of class 1, class 2 and class 3 levers into your notebook. Label the key elements of each lever: the fulcrum (F), the load (L) and the force or effort (E).

- Before asking pupils to draw the diagrams in their notebooks, draw them on the board, out of order and ask them to identify them. Erase your diagrams and invite pupils to draw the three classes of levers on the board. Ask **How do we know this is a class 2 lever?** (*The load is between the effort and the fulcrum.*)

+ CLOSING ACTIVITIES

- Give pupils the following situations and ask pupils to decide which simple machine could best be used to help them. **You need to open a tin but the lid is very tight.** (*Lever*); **You have a heavy box and it has to be put in a lorry.** (*Inclined plane*); **You want to get a sofa into a fourth floor flat.** (*Pulley*); **Your school bag is heavy and hurts your back.** (*Wheel and axle*); **Your shoe laces are in a knot and you can't untie them.** (*Wedge*); **You need to join two pieces of wood.** (*Screw*) Ask pupils to invent more situations that can be solved by using a simple machine.

+ EXTRA IDEAS

- Ask pupils to work with a partner to find pictures of everyday objects for the six simple machines in order to make a chart. *A slide is an inclined plane; a bottle opener is a lever, etc.*

ANSWERS AT A GLANCE

1 Open answer.

2 Diagrams in notebook.

PAGES 132–133 Electricity

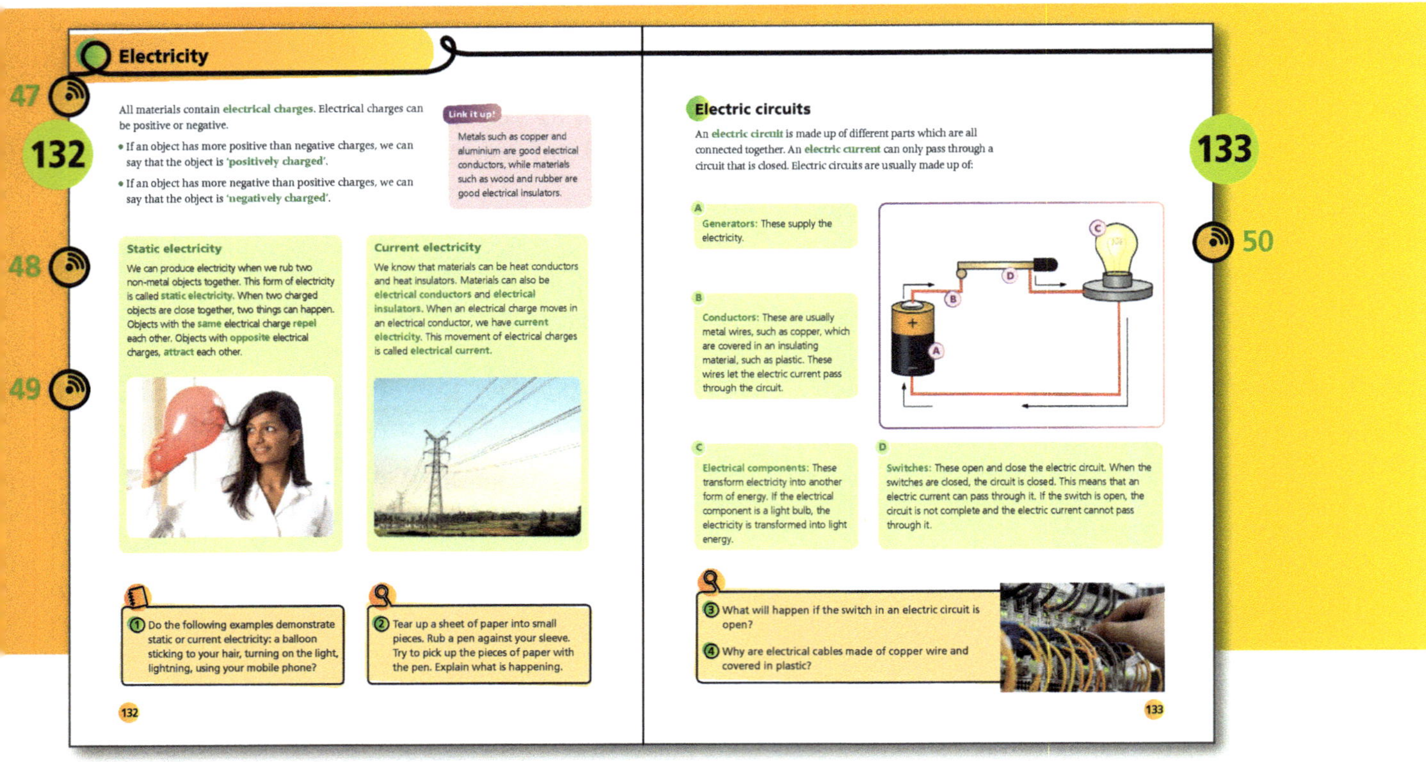

Electricity

47

132

All materials contain **electrical charges**. Electrical charges can be positive or negative.

- If an object has more positive than negative charges, we can say that the object is '**positively charged**'.
- If an object has more negative than positive charges, we can say that the object is '**negatively charged**'.

Link it up!

Metals such as copper and aluminium are good electrical conductors, while materials such as wood and rubber are good electrical insulators.

48

Static electricity

We can produce electricity when we rub two non-metal objects together. This form of electricity is called **static electricity**. When two charged objects are close together, two things can happen. Objects with the **same** electrical charge **repel** each other. Objects with **opposite** electrical charges, **attract** each other.

Current electricity

We know that materials can be heat conductors and heat insulators. Materials can also be **electrical conductors** and **electrical insulators**. When an electrical charge moves in an electrical conductor, we have **current electricity**. This movement of electrical charges is called **electrical current**.

49

1. Do the following examples demonstrate static or current electricity: a balloon sticking to your hair, turning on the light, lightning, using your mobile phone?
2. Tear up a sheet of paper into small pieces. Rub a pen against your sleeve. Try to pick up the pieces of paper with the pen. Explain what is happening.

132

Electric circuits

133

An **electric circuit** is made up of different parts which are all connected together. An **electric current** can only pass through a circuit that is closed. Electric circuits are usually made up of:

50

A **Generators:** These supply the electricity.

B **Conductors:** These are usually metal wires, such as copper, which are covered in an insulating material, such as plastic. These wires let the electric current pass through the circuit.

C **Electrical components:** These transform electricity into another form of energy. If the electrical component is a light bulb, the electricity is transformed into light energy.

D **Switches:** These open and close the electric circuit. When the switches are closed, the circuit is closed. This means that an electric current can pass through it. If the switch is open, the circuit is not complete and the electric current cannot pass through it.

3. What will happen if the switch in an electric circuit is open?
4. Why are electrical cables made of copper wire and covered in plastic?

133

PAGE SUMMARY

This double-page spread introduces pupils to the concept of electricity. The pupils will investigate static electricity and current electricity. On page 132, they will see for the first time the components of an electrical circuit and learn how electricity can pass through a closed circuit. There is a lot of new vocabulary and concepts on this double page. Do not expect pupils at this stage to absorb all of the information; the main learning aim is to understand the basic concepts of electricity in preparation for later courses.

LANGUAGE

- Questions words: *where, what, why*, etc.
- Vocabulary: *electricity, current electricity, static electricity, electrical charge, positive, negative, same, opposite, repel, attract, metal, copper, aluminium, wood, rubber, lightning, components, generators, conductors, switch, component, wire, insulating, circuit, insulators, supply, transform*

ADDITIONAL MATERIALS

- Digital flashcards
- Digital wordcards

OPENING ACTIVITIES

- Place the wordcards *kinetic, thermal, light, sound, chemical* and *electrical* on the board. Invite pupils to come to the board to draw a symbol to represent that type of energy. Invite other pupils to describe the energy. *Kinetic energy if found in all moving things*, etc.
- Remove all the wordcards except *electrical*. Remind the pupils that we use a lot of electrical energy at home, school and work. Draw the shape of a power station on the board and ask pupils what is used to produce electricity in power stations. Elicit *coal, gas and oil* and *fossil fuels*. Write these words to the left of the drawing and the word *electricity* to the right.
- Ask **What type of energy can electrical energy transform into?** As pupils name the different types of energy, encourage them to name a machine as an example. (*Light energy – light bulb; thermal energy – radiator and fridge; sound energy – CD player; kinetic energy – washing machine; chemical energy – batteries*, etc.)

MAIN ACTIVITIES

Page 132, Electricity (CD2 track 47)

- Read the introductory text with the class. Ask the class if they have ever touched an object or a person and received an electric shock. Explain that this happens because of electrically charged particles. Say **Let's find out more.**

Page 132, Static electricity (CD2 track 48)

- The pupils listen and read the text on page 132. Check understanding. **What happens when objects with the same charge are close together?** (*They repel each other.*) **What happens when objects with the opposite charge are together?** (*They attract each other.*) Tell the pupils to look at the photo. **Do the girl's hair and the balloon have the same electrical charge or the opposite electrical charge?** (*The opposite charge*)

Page 132, Current electricity (CD2 track 49)

- Before you read the text, ask the pupils what they can see in the photo. Explain that the power lines are how the electricity travels from power stations to our homes. Pupils listen and read the text. This is a good moment to draw the pupils' attention to the *Did you know?* box. Point out the similarities between heat and electrical conductors and insulators.

1 Do the following examples demonstrate static or current electricity: a balloon sticking to your hair, turning on the light, lightning, using your mobile phone?

- Point out that mobile phones have to be charged by current electricity and remind them that batteries contain chemical energy. Depending on the level of the class you may also like to go into more detail about how lightning is formed. *See Answers at a glance*

2 Tear up a sheet of paper into small pieces. Rub a pen against your sleeve. Try to pick up the pieces of paper with the pen. Explain what is happening.

- Ask the pupils to work with a partner to do this investigation. Suggest they also try to pick up the pieces of paper with a pen they haven't rubbed against their sleeve. *See Answers at a glance*

Page 133, Electric circuits (CD2 track 50)

- Ask the pupils to open their books on page 133 and look at the diagram of the electrical circuit. Tell them to follow the path of electricity through the circuit as you read or play the audio **(CD2 track 50)**. Ask **What is the generator in this diagram?** (*The battery*); **What is the component?** (*The light bulb*); **What is the conductor made of?** (*Copper wire*); **Which part of the circuit can stop the electric current?** (*The switch*) You may like to ask the pupils to copy and label the diagram in their notebooks.

3 What will happen if the switch in an electric circuit is open?

- Ask the pupils to work with a partner to answer questions 3 and 4. *The electric current will stop.*

4 Why are electrical cables made of copper wire and covered in plastic?

- Suggest they look at the *Did you know?* box to find the answer. *See Answers at a glance*

CLOSING ACTIVITIES

- Ask pupils to read pages 132 and 133 and to write five statements about electricity. The statements can be true or false. Tell them to play the true or false game with a partner. *Lightning comes from current electricity. (False, it is static electricity.) A light bulb is a generator. (False, it's an electrical component.)*

ANSWERS AT A GLANCE

1 Static electricity: a balloon sticking to your hair and lightning. Current electricity: turning on the light and using your mobile phone.

2 We can produce static electricity when we rub two non-metal objects together. By rubbing the pen against your sleeve, it becomes electrically charged. The pen's charge is the opposite to that of the pieces of paper. The papers are, as a result, attracted to the pen.

3 The electric current will stop.

4 Copper is an electrical conductor and plastic is an insulator. The copper wire allows electricity to pass through it. The plastic stops the electricity passing to us and giving us an electric shock.

PAGES 134–135 Machines and energy

134 135
51 52

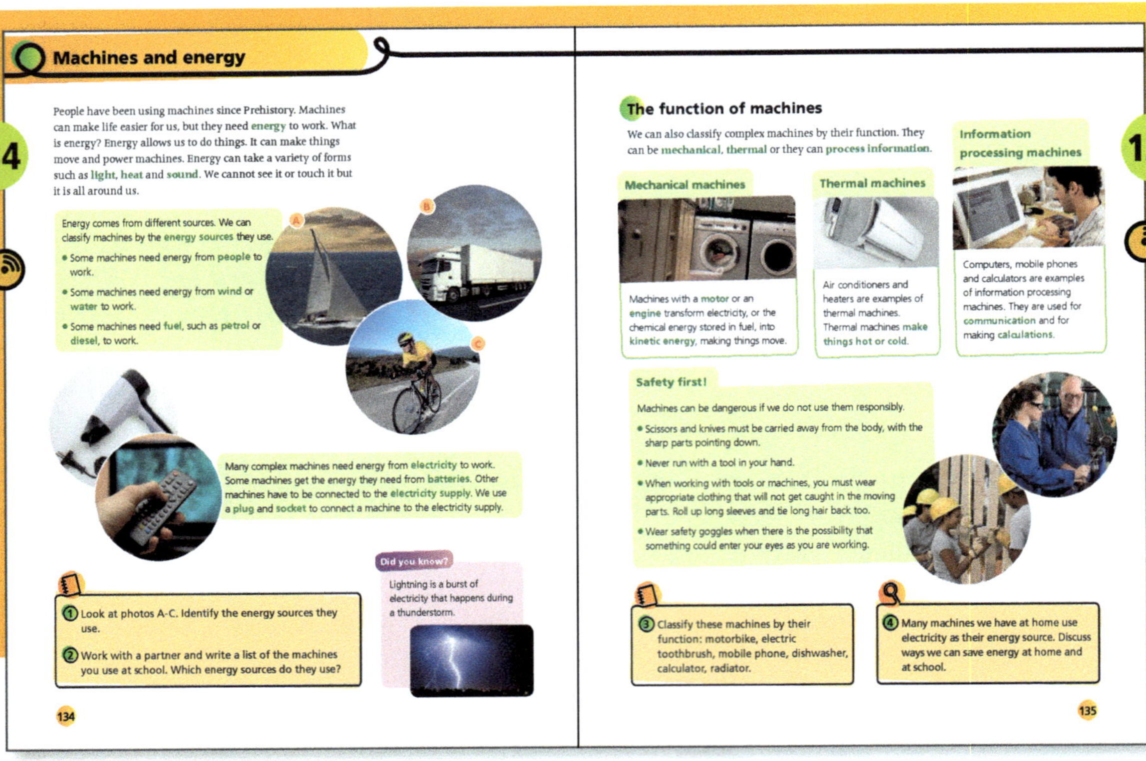

Machines and energy

People have been using machines since Prehistory. Machines can make life easier for us, but they need **energy** to work. What is energy? Energy allows us to do things. It can make things move and power machines. Energy can take a variety of forms such as **light**, **heat** and **sound**. We cannot see it or touch it but it is all around us.

Energy comes from different sources. We can classify machines by the **energy sources** they use.

- Some machines need energy from **people** to work.
- Some machines need energy from **wind** or **water** to work.
- Some machines need **fuel**, such as **petrol** or **diesel**, to work.

A B C

Many complex machines need energy from **electricity** to work. Some machines get the energy they need from **batteries**. Other machines have to be connected to the **electricity supply**. We use a **plug** and **socket** to connect a machine to the electricity supply.

Did you know?

Lightning is a burst of electricity that happens during a thunderstorm.

1. Look at photos A-C. Identify the energy sources they use.
2. Work with a partner and write a list of the machines you use at school. Which energy sources do they use?

134

The function of machines

We can also classify complex machines by their function. They can be **mechanical**, **thermal** or they can **process information**.

Mechanical machines

Machines with a **motor** or an **engine** transform electricity, or the chemical energy stored in fuel, into **kinetic energy**, making things move.

Thermal machines

Air conditioners and heaters are examples of thermal machines. Thermal machines **make things hot or cold**.

Information processing machines

Computers, mobile phones and calculators are examples of information processing machines. They are used for **communication** and for making **calculations**.

Safety first!

Machines can be dangerous if we do not use them responsibly.

- Scissors and knives must be carried away from the body, with the sharp parts pointing down.
- Never run with a tool in your hand.
- When working with tools or machines, you must wear appropriate clothing that will not get caught in the moving parts. Roll up long sleeves and tie long hair back too.
- Wear safety goggles when there is the possibility that something could enter your eyes as you are working.

3. Classify these machines by their function: motorbike, electric toothbrush, mobile phone, dishwasher, calculator, radiator.
4. Many machines we have at home use electricity as their energy source. Discuss ways we can save energy at home and at school.

135

PAGE SUMMARY

On this double-page spread pupils learn how to classify complex machines. They will see that they can be classified by energy source and by function. Pupils will look at the different sources of energy and, depending on the level of your class, this can be done in greater or lesser detail. Page 135 introduces pupils to the basic safety rules to follow when using tools or machines. The important learning aim is to show how machines need energy to work. Throughout the lesson encourage pupils to think about the importance of energy and why we should find ways to save it.

LANGUAGE

- Imperatives
- Vocabulary: *Energy, light, heat, sound, electrical, kinetic, thermal, chemical, fuel, petrol, diesel, wind, water, people, plug, socket, electrical*

ADDITIONAL MATERIALS

- Digital flashcards
- Digital wordcards
- Extra classroom materials: CD player, a pencil sharpener and a paper windmill

OPENING ACTIVITIES

- Place the unplugged CD player, a pencil sharpener and a paper windmill on the table. Press the play button and wait. Ask **Why isn't the machine working?** Elicit that it needs electricity or electrical energy to work. Put a pencil into the sharpener and wait. Ask **Why isn't the machine working?** Elicit that it needs energy from a person to work. Hold up the windmill and wait. Ask **Why isn't the machine working?** Elicit that it needs energy from the wind to work.
- Place the wordcards *electrical, light, thermal, sound, kinetic* and *chemical* on the board. Say that these are some of the different types of energy. Ask pupils to suggest where they come from. *Light can come from the Sun or light bulbs. Kinetic from anything that moves. Chemical energy can come from food,* etc.

MAIN ACTIVITIES

Pages 134, Machines and energy (CD2 track 51)

- Tell pupils to open their books on page 134 and read the texts as a group. You can use the *Read and repeat* activity (See *Helpful tips,* pages 20-23). Check for understanding. **Which energy sources have you read about?** (*People, wind, fuel and electricity*); **Do all machines need electricity to work?** (*No*); **Can you name two fuels?** (*Petrol and diesel*); **Where do machines get the electrical energy they need?** (*From the electricity supply and batteries*)

1 Look at photos A-C. Identify the energy sources they use.

- Ask pupils to match the photos to the energy source. Tell them to copy the answer into their notebooks. *A-wind; B-fuel; C-people*

2 Write a list of the machines you use at school. Which energy sources do they use?

- Ask pupils to work with a partner to make the list. Remind them to also identify the energy source they need. Ask them to name different areas in the school where there are machines (the office, laboratories, kitchens, etc.). Invite volunteers to give feedback to the rest of the class. *Open answer*

Pages 135, The function of machines (CD2 track 52)

- Draw pupils' attention to the photos and ask them to name the groups of machines. You can play the audio and encourage pupils to listen and read. Ask pupils to name more examples of mechanical, thermal and information machines.
- Draw pupils' attention to the information box *Safety first!* Invite volunteers to read the rules to the rest of the class. Check for understanding. **How should you carry scissors?** (*The sharp parts pointing down*); **What must you never do with tools in your hands?** (*Run*); **Why should you roll up your sleeves?** (*So that they don't get caught in the moving parts*); **Which part of the body do safety goggles protect?** (*Eyes*)

1 Classify these machines by their function: motorbike, electric toothbrush, mobile phone, dishwasher, calculator, radiator.

- Ask pupils to work with a partner to answer the question. Ask them to also identify the energy source they use. *See Answers at a glance*

2 Many machines we have at home use electricity as their energy source. Discuss ways we can save energy at home and at school.

- Explain that today most of our electricity comes from power stations. These stations make electricity by burning fossil fuels. Find out if they know the problems of using fossil fuels. *(They are non-renewable and will run out, as well as causing pollution.)* Ask the groups to discuss how we can use less electricity. *See Answers at a glance for example answer.*

+ CLOSING ACTIVITIES

- Describe the function of different machines and ask pupils to guess which machine you are describing and to classify it by its function. **We use this machine to do Maths.** (*Calculator – information processing*); **We use this machine to cook our food.** (*Cooker and oven - thermal*) ,etc.

+ EXTRA IDEAS

- Ask pupils **Have you got a bike?** Encourage them to tell you about their cycling, for example, where they ride their bike and what protection they use. Ask them to work in groups to make a safety list of DO's and DON'Ts about riding a bike. When they have finished, have each group share their list with the class.

ANSWERS AT A GLANCE

1. A-wind; B-fuel; C-people.
2. Open answer.
3. Mechanical machines – motorbike, electric toothbrush, dishwasher; Thermal machines – radiator; Information processing machines – mobile phone, calculator.
4. Example answer: Use renewable energy sources and ecological light bulbs. Turn off light, TVs and computers when you aren't using them.

PAGES 136–137 Find out / Think about it

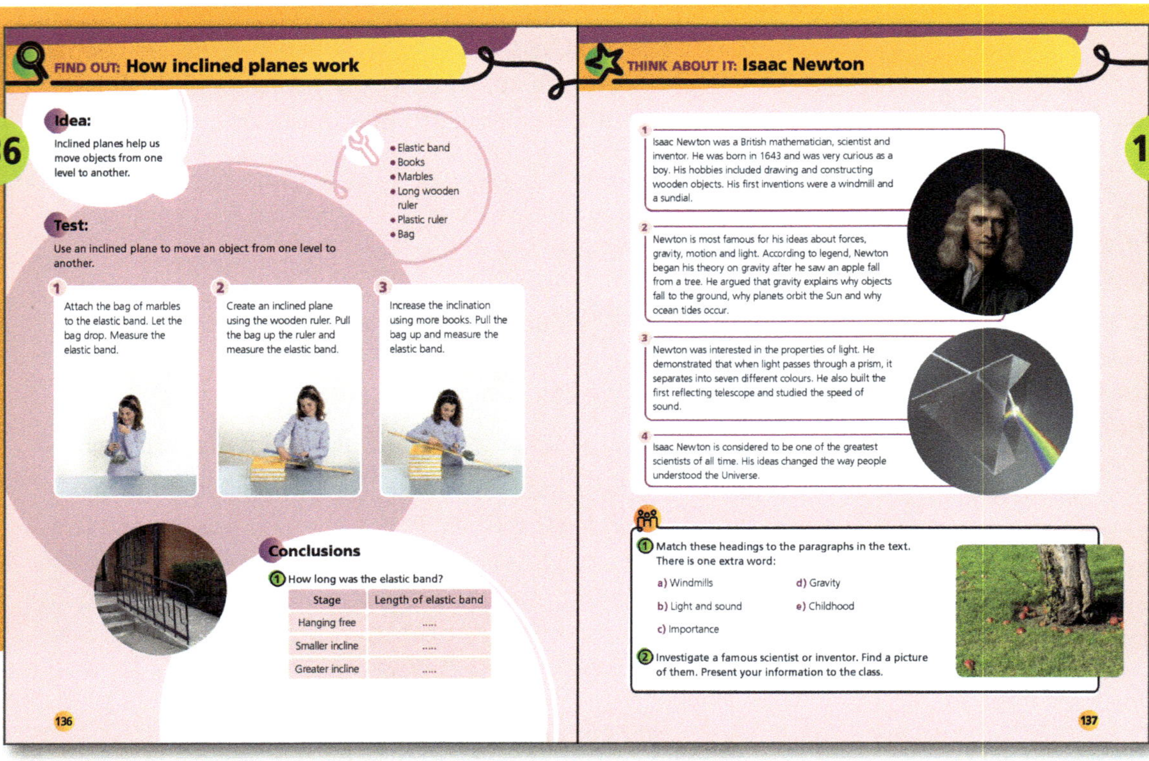

PAGE SUMMARY

In the first of these two pages (*Find out*), pupils carry out an investigation to see how inclined planes can help us move objects from one level to another. The second page (*Think about it*), provides pupils with the opportunity to learn about one of the greatest scientists of all time, Isaac Newton. They will also investigate another scientist of their choice and present their project to the class.

LANGUAGE

- Imperatives: *attach, let, measure, create, pull, increase*
- Past tense
- Vocabulary: *inclination, windmill, sundial, legend, theory, tides, prism, speed, argue, according to*

ADDITIONAL MATERIALS

- Digital flashcards
- Digital wordcards
- Extra materials: rulers, pencils, rubbers, CDs

FIND OUT

OPENING ACTIVITIES

- Place the wordcards of the simple machines on the board. Point to the first card and ask: **Who can tell me what this simple machine helps us do?** *Pulleys help us lift and lower heavy objects,* etc. Give the card to the pupil who gives the correct definition.
- Ask pupils to take out a ruler, a pencil and a rubber from their pencil cases. Ask them to work with a partner to make a class 1 lever. Invite volunteers to come to the board to draw the diagram of a class 1 lever. Ask: **Where is the fulcrum? Where is the load? Where is the effort?** Encourage them to write the letters on the diagrams. Repeat this procedure with class 2 and class 3 levers.

MAIN ACTIVITIES

- Ask pupils to open their books on page 136. Explain that they will be doing a simple investigation to observe how inclined planes can make our work easier. Ask pupils to read the steps on page 136. Then, tell them to write the materials and the three steps in their notebook. If you are using the book on the interactive whiteboard, you can play the audio of the steps.
- You may choose to do this investigation together as a class or allow small groups to go through the steps independently.

- Demonstrate the meaning of a small incline and a greater incline. Ask pupils to predict the results before beginning the investigation. The stretching of the elastic band shows the amount of effort needed to do the work. The stretching will be less using an inclined plane. (The smaller incline requires less effort.)

⊕ CLOSING ACTIVITIES

- Suggest pupils carry out the investigation twice before writing the conclusions in their notebooks in order to check the measurements. Encourage pupils to answer in full sentences. *The elastic band was X cms when it was hanging free*. Encourage them to compare results and ask them to decide if an inclined plane reduces the effort we need to make and if so which inclined plane is the best one to use.

1 How long was the elastic band?

- *Open answer but the smaller incline is more efficient.*

THINK ABOUT IT

⊕ OPENING ACTIVITIES

- In small groups, or pairs, ask pupils to talk about gravity. Give them questions to discuss. **What is gravity?** (*It's a force*); **What would happen if there were no gravity on Earth?** (*Everything would fly off into space*); Ask pupils if people have always known that gravity exists? Ask them to write, in their notebooks, which century they think gravity was discovered (*17th century*). They can check their predictions against the text in the next stage.

MAIN ACTIVITIES

- Ask pupils to open their books on page 137 and say **Let's read about an important scientist and inventor**. If you are using the interactive whiteboard, you can play the audio and encourage pupils to read along in their books. Check for understanding after each section. **What were his first inventions?** (*The windmill and sundial*); **How did he begin his theory on gravity?** (*He saw an apple fall*); **What happens to light when it passes through a prism?** (*It separates into seven colours*); **Why is he considered to be one of the greatest scientists?** (*He changed the way people understood the Universe*); **What is he most famous for?** (*His ideas about forces, gravity, motion and light*)
- Hand out the CDs and ask pupils to try to see the colours on the silver side of the disc. Tell them to move and tip the disc. Ask which colours they can see. Tell them that light separates into red, orange, yellow, green, blue, indigo and violet.
- Ask pupils to read the texts again with their partner. Then focus their attention on question 1.

⊕ CLOSING ACTIVITIES

1 Match these headings to the paragraphs in the text. There is one extra word: a) Windmills b) Light and sound c) Importance d) Gravity e) Childhood

- Ask pupils to work with their partner to match the headings to the correct paragraph. Correct as a class activity. *1e, 2d, 3b, 4c*

2 Investigate a famous scientist or inventor. Find a picture of them. Present your information to the class.

- Ask pupils to tell you the names of any scientists or inventors that they know. They may have heard of Fleming, Watt, Bell, Einstein, Gutenberg, Pasteur, Marie Currie, Morse, etc. This activity can be done at home with the help of parents, in small study groups on a computer or in the library. *Open answer*

PAGES 138–139 Look back: Machines

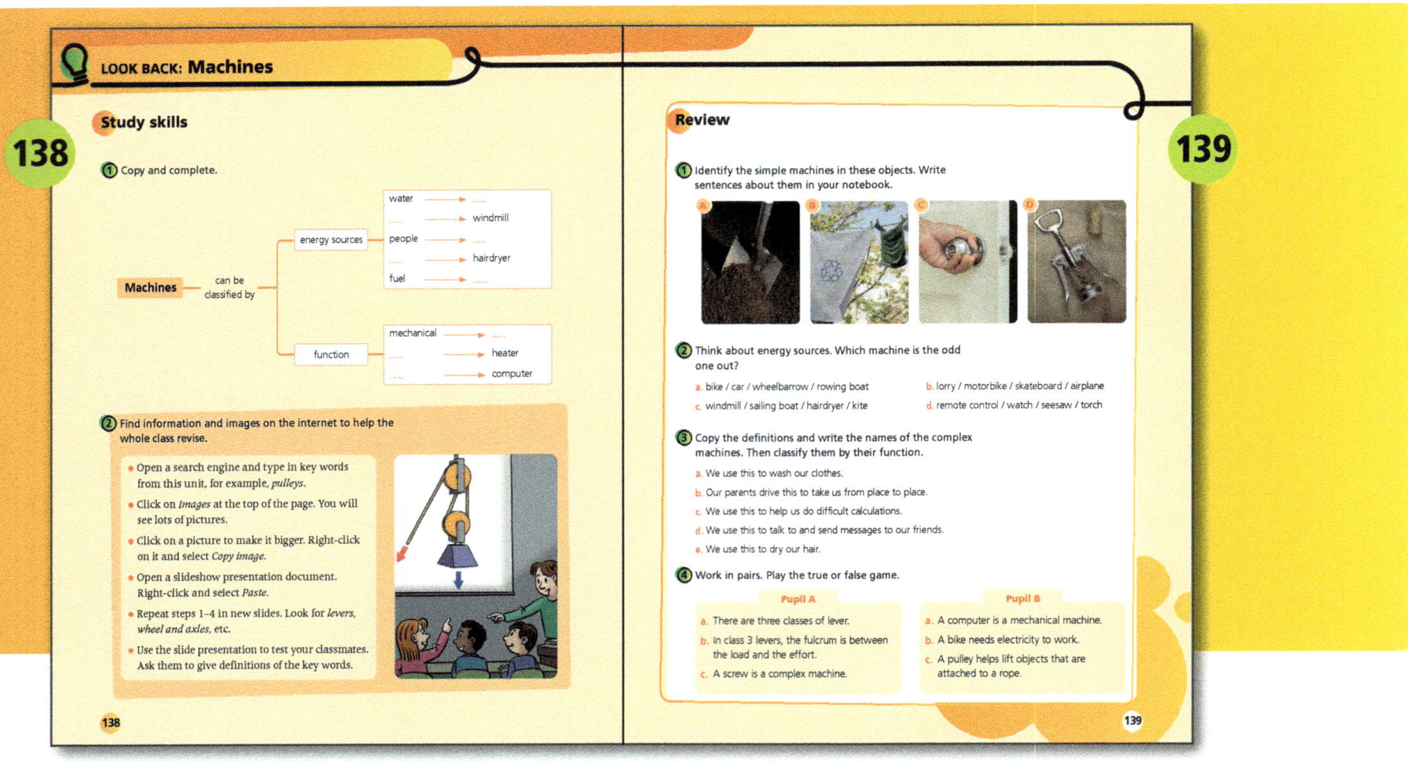

PAGE SUMMARY

This double-page spread allows pupils the opportunity to organise what they've learned in the unit by means of a concept map. They can also learn a new study skill in which pupils design a slide show to help the whole class revise. On the *Review* page, pupils complete activities individually to check their understanding of the material covered in this unit. Activity 4 is a pair work speaking activity. It is also a peer evaluation opportunity.

LANGUAGE

- Imperatives: *complete, write, copy, identify, classify, work, open, click on, use*
- Present tense
- Infinitive of purpose
- Encourage pupils to speak and write in complete sentences.

ADDITIONAL MATERIALS

- Digital flashcards
- Digital wordcards
- Extra classroom materials: computer with internet access and slide presentation software.

OPENING ACTIVITIES

- Explain that you are going to play a word chain game. The first person names a machine. The second classifies it by its function and the third classifies it by its energy source. The next person names a new machine. Tell them that they must differentiate between mains electricity and batteries. If a mistake is made or a machine is repeated, the pupil is eliminated from the game and must fold their arms to show that the turn must pass to the next player. The game is more fun if it's played fast.
- Organise the class into small groups. Ask them to look through the unit and make questions to test the rest of the class. Suggest that they make a variety of question styles: true or false, odd one out, definitions, etc. Monitor their preparation and check they are making grammatically correct questions.
- Draw a chart with three columns on the board. Write the headings *Complex machine, Energy source* and *Function* at the top of each column. Write the names of complex machines in the first column: computer, car, microwave, bicycle, waterwheel, etc. Invite pupils to come and complete the information on the chart.
- Invite different pupils to come to the front of the class to mime using one of the simple machines, e.g. pulling on a rope of a pulley. The rest of the class should watch and identify the machine.

MAIN ACTIVITIES

Page 139, Study skills

1 Copy and complete.

- Remind pupils that organising new information makes it easier to understand and remember. Focus pupils' attention on the concept map and ask them to tell you which words are missing. Encourage them to make full sentences, such as *Electricity is the energy source for a hairdryer. A toaster is a thermal machine.*
- Tell them to copy and complete the concept map in their notebooks.

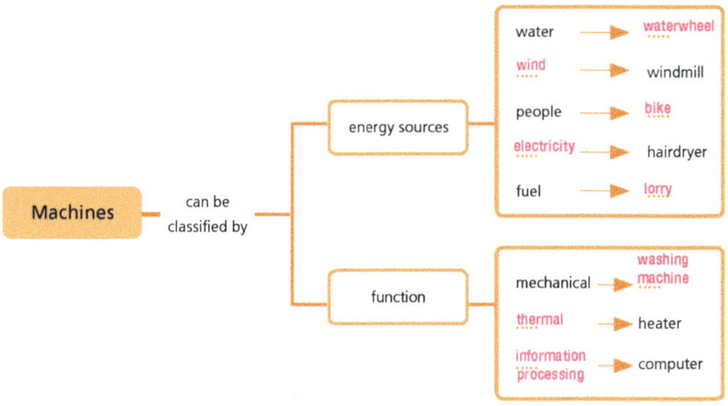

2 Find information and images on the internet to help the whole class revise.

- You will need the following materials: a computer with internet access and slide presentation software. Show pupils how to do a key-word search for images on internet and how to copy and paste photos into a slide presentation document. Pupils can resize and move photos around on each slide.

Page 139, Review

Note: This part of the review can be done with minimal teacher guidance. You may wish to work through the activities as a class or in small groups or partners. Alternatively, you can ask pupils to do them individually as self-evaluation. This review could also be done as homework.

1 Identify the simple machines in these objects. Write sentences about them in your notebook.

A. Lever

B. Pulley

C. Wheel and axle

D. Screw and lever

2 Think about energy sources. Which machine is the odd one out?

a. Car

b. Skateboard

c. Hairdryer

d. Seesaw

3 Copy the definitions and write the names of the complex machines. Then classify them by their function.

a. Washing machine – mechanical

b. Car – mechanical

c. Calculator – information processing

d. Phone – information processing

e. Hairdryer – thermal

4 Work in pairs. Play the true or false game.

Pupil A

a. True

b. False. The fulcrum is at one end. The effort is between the fulcrum and the load.

c. False. A screw is a simple machine.

Pupil B

a. False. A computer is an information processing machine.

b. False. A bike needs people to work.

c. True

Activity Book answers / Audio CD2 track list

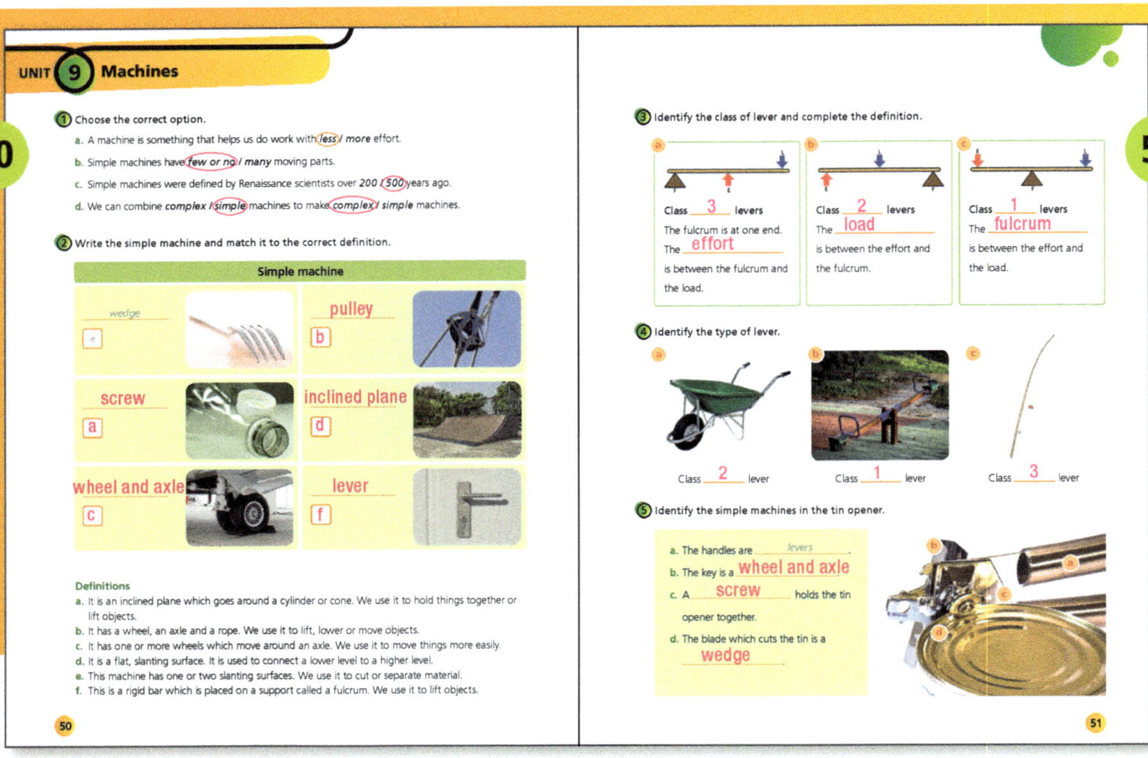

50

UNIT 9 Machines

1 Choose the correct option.

a. A machine is something that helps us do work with (less) / *more* effort.

b. Simple machines have (*few or no*) / *many* moving parts.

c. Simple machines were defined by Renaissance scientists over *200* / (*500*) years ago.

d. We can combine *complex* / (*simple*) machines to make (*complex*) / *simple* machines.

2 Write the simple machine and match it to the correct definition.

Simple machine	
wedge [e]	pulley [b]
screw [a]	inclined plane [d]
wheel and axle [c]	lever [f]

Definitions

a. It is an inclined plane which goes around a cylinder or cone. We use it to hold things together or lift objects.
b. It has a wheel, an axle and a rope. We use it to lift, lower or move objects.
c. It has one or more wheels which move around an axle. We use it to move things more easily.
d. It is a flat, slanting surface. It is used to connect a lower level to a higher level.
e. This machine has one or two slanting surfaces. We use it to cut or separate material.
f. This is a rigid bar which is placed on a support called a fulcrum. We use it to lift objects.

50

51

3 Identify the class of lever and complete the definition.

a. Class 3 levers. The fulcrum is at one end. The effort is between the fulcrum and the load.

b. Class 2 levers. The load is between the effort and the fulcrum.

c. Class 1 levers. The fulcrum is between the effort and the load.

4 Identify the type of lever.

a. Class 2 lever
b. Class 1 lever
c. Class 3 lever

5 Identify the simple machines in the tin opener.

a. The handles are levers.
b. The key is a wheel and axle.
c. A screw holds the tin opener together.
d. The blade which cuts the tin is a wedge.

51

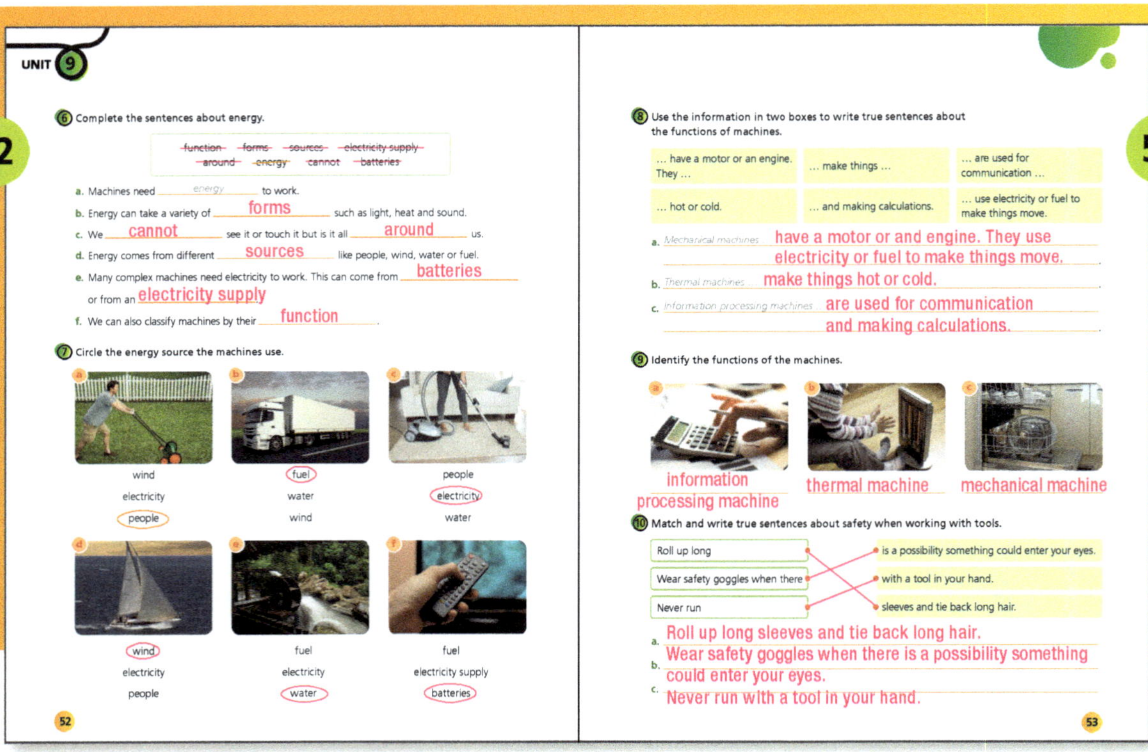

52

UNIT 9

6 Complete the sentences about energy.

~~function~~ ~~forms~~ ~~sources~~ ~~electricity supply~~ ~~around~~ ~~energy~~ ~~cannot~~ ~~batteries~~

a. Machines need energy to work.
b. Energy can take a variety of forms such as light, heat and sound.
c. We cannot see it or touch it but is it all around us.
d. Energy comes from different sources like people, wind, water or fuel.
e. Many complex machines need electricity to work. This can come from batteries or from an electricity supply.
f. We can also classify machines by their function.

7 Circle the energy source the machines use.

a. wind / electricity / (people)
b. (fuel) / water / wind
c. people / (electricity) / water
d. (wind) / electricity / people
e. fuel / electricity / (water)
f. fuel / electricity supply / (batteries)

52

53

8 Use the information in two boxes to write true sentences about the functions of machines.

… have a motor or an engine. They …	… make things …	… are used for communication …
… hot or cold.	… and making calculations.	… use electricity or fuel to make things move.

a. Mechanical machines … have a motor or and engine. They use electricity or fuel to make things move.
b. Thermal machines … make things hot or cold.
c. Information processing machines … are used for communication and making calculations.

9 Identify the functions of the machines.

a. information processing machine
b. thermal machine
c. mechanical machine

10 Match and write true sentences about safety when working with tools.

Roll up long	is a possibility something could enter your eyes.
Wear safety goggles when there	with a tool in your hand.
Never run	sleeves and tie back long hair.

a. Roll up long sleeves and tie back long hair.
b. Wear safety goggles when there is a possibility something could enter your eyes.
c. Never run with a tool in your hand.

53

4

UNIT 9

Find out at home!

1 Experiment with a lever:

1. Make a first class lever:
   - Tape a marker onto a table so that it does not move.
   - Place a ruler on top.
2. Place a rubber on one end of the lever. Place coins on the other end of the lever so that they lift the rubber. Add the information to the chart below.
3. Experiment moving the ruler so that the marker is at different distances from the rubber. Complete the chart below.

Distance of marker from rubber	Number of coins needed to lift rubber
Open answers	

2 Complete the sentences.

a. When the fulcrum is near the load, we need less effort to lift the load

b. When the fulcrum is near the effort, we need more effort to lift the load

c. In this experiment, the fulcrum is the maker

d. In this experiment, the load is the rubber

e. In this experiment, the effort is the coins

54

55

Skills check

1 Read the information about a class at a local museum. Complete the notes.

Do you like science?
Are you an inventor?

If you are between 8 and 14 years old, you are invited to attend a beginner's engineering class.

We will:
- learn about simple and complex machines
- learn about how we can use renewable energy sources
- carry out experiments
- have a great time

Price: €10
Saturday 20 April
10.00 – 12.00

MUNICIPAL SCIENCE MUSEUM

Hi! Shall we go to the engineering class together? My mum can take us home but we will have to take the bus there. See you tomorrow!
Carol

Notes	
1. Place:	*Municipal Science Museum*
2. Day:	Saturday 20th April
3. Price:	10 euros
4. Travel there by:	bus
5. Go with:	Carol
6. Age of participants:	8-14 years old

55

Unit 9 Audio CD2 track list

TRACK	ACTIVITY
42	**Pupil's Book page 127,** Unit introduction
43	**Pupil's Book page 127,** Song *Simple machines*
44	**Pupil's Book page 128,** Story: *A trip to the Archaeological Museum*
45	**Pupil's Book page 130,** Simple machines
46	**Pupil's Book page 131,** Levers
47	**Pupil's Book pages 132,** Electricity
48	**Pupil's Book page 132,** Static electricity
49	**Pupil's Book pages 132,** Current electricity
50	**Pupil's Book page 133,** Electric circuits
51	**Pupil's Book page 134,** Machines and energy
52	**Pupil's Book page 135,** The function machines

CONTENT	EVALUATION CRITERIA
The internet and other advances.	Value the importance of technological advances such as the internet and acknowledge the possible risks of new inventions.
First approaches to scientific activity and the scientific method. Use of different information sources (direct and indirect). Use ICTs.	Obtain relevant information about specific phenomena, make predictions, integrate information from direct and indirect observation and communicate the results.
First approaches to simple experiments and investigations.	Conjecture as to the results of natural occurrences and of simple experiments and investigations.
Individual and group work.	Work independently and proactively and develop strategies for working in a group.
Planning a project and presenting a report.	Carry out a project and present a report.

LEARNING STANDARDS	LINKEY COMPETENCES	PAGES
Values the importance of technological advances such as the internet but acknowledges some of the possible risks and disadvantages.	MST, SOC	140, 141
Carries out guided searches for information on the internet.	LTL, AUT	140, 141
Knows and applies the correct behaviour when using the internet.	LTL, AUT	140, 141
With help, selects and organises specific and relevant information; analyses it and draws conclusions; reflects on the experience and the process; presents the results.	MST, LTL	140, 141
Use books, libraries, etc. and collaborate in the care and maintenance of all the materials available in the school and the classroom.	MST, LTL	140, 141
Shows autonomy in the planning of activities and tasks and shows initiative in decision taking.	LTL, AUT	140, 141
With help, carries out simple experiments or investigations, and conjectures as to the results.	MST, LTL, AUT	140, 141
Uses strategies to help their own learning, as well as asking for help and information.	LTL, AUT	140, 141
First approaches to cooperative learning.	SOC, LTL	140, 141
Begins observation, using relevant instruments and consulting written documents and images.	LTL, AUT	140, 141
Shows autonomy and proactiveness in the planning of and carrying out of actions.	AUT	140, 141
Presents work clearly and in an organised fashion.	LIN, LTL, AUT	140, 141
With help, carries out a project and presents a report, using paper and/or digital means, collecting information from different sources, presenting the results orally and with the support of images and short texts.	LIN, LTL, AUT, DIG	140, 141

PAGES 140–141 Think together: The internet

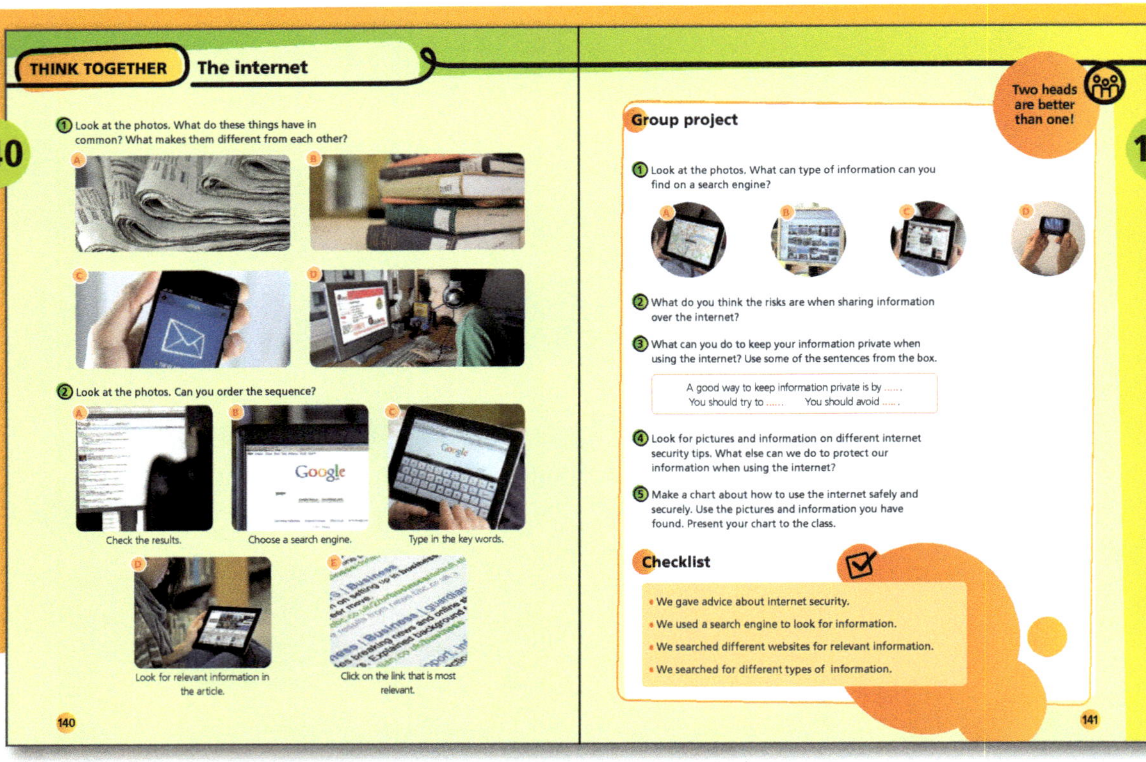
THINK TOGETHER The internet

140

1 Look at the photos. What do these things have in common? What makes them different from each other?

2 Look at the photos. Can you order the sequence?

Check the results.

Choose a search engine.

Type in the key words.

Look for relevant information in the article.

Click on the link that is most relevant.

140

Two heads are better than one!

141

Group project

1 Look at the photos. What can type of information can you find on a search engine?

2 What do you think the risks are when sharing information over the internet?

3 What can you do to keep your information private when using the internet? Use some of the sentences from the box.

A good way to keep information private is by ......
You should try to ...... You should avoid ......

4 Look for pictures and information on different internet security tips. What else can we do to protect our information when using the internet?

5 Make a chart about how to use the internet safely and securely. Use the pictures and information you have found. Present your chart to the class.

Checklist

- We gave advice about internet security.
- We used a search engine to look for information.
- We searched different websites for relevant information.
- We searched for different types of information.

141

PAGE SUMMARY

On these pages, pupils will revise the importance of the internet and ICT in our daily lives. The different activities will be done following different cooperative learning structures that will provide the optimal learning experience for the pupil and will guarantee the involvement of all the members of the group.

LANGUAGE

- Question words: *what, how,* etc.
- Making comparisons: *Picture B shows a printed sources, but Picture D shows are digital source*
- Vocabulary: *newspaper, book, smart phone, internet, computer, search engine, link, article, risk, security*

ADDITIONAL MATERIALS

- Digital flashcards
- Digital wordcards

OPENING ACTIVITIES

- Before doing these activities using different cooperative learning structures, you should form the groups. Teachers should form the groups rather than letting the pupils choose their own group members. Remember to form heterogeneous groups of three or four students.
- Tell the pupils what they will be doing in their groups, what procedures you will follow, and what your expectations are. If during these activities any group is having difficulty, spend some time in class on the relevant team skills.

MAIN ACTIVITIES

1 Look at the pictures. What do these people have in common? What makes them different from each other?

- This is a *Think–pair check* activity. Focus your pupils' attention on the four photos at the top of page 140.
- Ask your pupils to look at the photos and think independently about the questions: what do all of them have in common? How are they different?
- Tell them to discuss their answers in pairs. Ensure that each pupil shares something with their partner.
- Then, ask the pairs to share their answers with the rest of the class.

② Look at the photos. Can you order the sequence?

- This is a *Round robin* activity. Pupils work in groups of five. Focus your pupils' attention on the five photos at the bottom of page 140.
- Using the zoom on the interactive whiteboard, show the pupils each of the five photos. Give each group a sheet of paper and a pencil.
- The first pupil in the group writes the first stage of the sequence, the second pupil writes the second stage, etc.
- When each group has completed the sequence, they can review their answer as a whole and discuss any changes they think are necessary.

GROUP PROJECT

① Look at the photos. What type of information can you find using a search engine?

- Ask pairs to compare the photos from activity 1. Ask them to look closely at what each screen is showing and why people use these types of information.

② What do you think the risks are when sharing information over the internet?

- This is a *Think–write–pair check* activity.
- Ask your pupils to think about the question. If they are having difficulty, ask them to think of what type of information share over the internet and how people could abuse this information.
- Ask your pupils to write their ideas.
- Once they have finished, ask them to pair up and discuss their ideas with a partner.

③ What can you do to keep your information private when using the internet? Use some of the sentences from the box.

- This is a *Group members consult* activity.
- Ask your pupils to put their pencils down in the middle of the table.
- Ask your pupils to look at the words in the box. All members of the team should contribute in answering the question, but they don't all have to suggest the same things.
- When everyone in the group has decided on their answer, ask them to pick up their pencils and write it down.

④ Look for pictures and information on different internet security tips. What else can we do to protect our information when using the internet?

- Pupils can look for pictures and more information in reference books, higher-level school books or on the internet.

⑤ Make a chart about how to use the internet safely and securely. Use the pictures and information you have found. Present your chart to the class.

- This is a *Group project* activity.
- Clearly explain the project the groups are going to do and the amount of time they have to complete it. Assign roles:

  captain (in charge of managing the group and assigning the different roles)

  materials manager

  spokesperson

  timekeeper
- After distributing the materials, ask your pupils to work to complete the task.
- Monitor your pupils.
- Ask the groups to share their project with the class.

CHECKLIST

- Group assessment is essential in cooperative learning to ensure that there is analysis of interactions and promotion of teamwork. Pupils should understand that how they work together affects the quality and quantity of concepts that they learn and understand.
- Ask pupils to discuss and reflect on how the group worked together and identify ideas and actions that helped the group achieve its goals.
- Once they have shared their results, ask them to reflect on how the project could be done better next time.
- Invite your pupils to share their conclusions with the class.

PAGES 142–143 Review

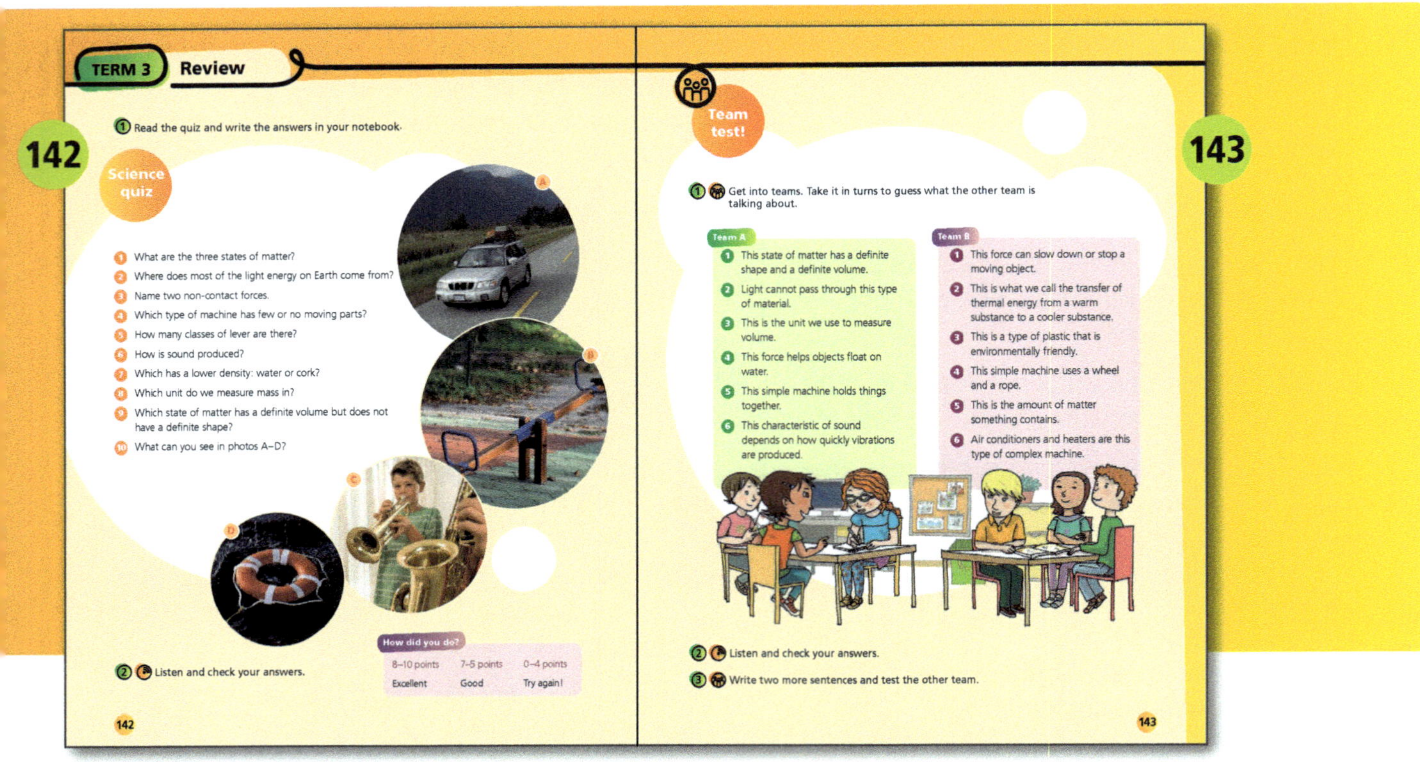
TERM 3 Review

142

① Read the quiz and write the answers in your notebook.

Science quiz

1. What are the three states of matter?
2. Where does most of the light energy on Earth come from?
3. Name two non-contact forces.
4. Which type of machine has few or no moving parts?
5. How many classes of lever are there?
6. How is sound produced?
7. Which has a lower density: water or cork?
8. Which unit do we measure mass in?
9. Which state of matter has a definite volume but does not have a definite shape?
10. What can you see in photos A–D?

② Listen and check your answers.

How did you do?

8–10 points	7–5 points	0–4 points
Excellent	Good	Try again!

142

Team test!

143

① Get into teams. Take it in turns to guess what the other team is talking about.

Team A

1. This state of matter has a definite shape and a definite volume.
2. Light cannot pass through this type of material.
3. This is the unit we use to measure volume.
4. This force helps objects float on water.
5. This simple machine holds things together.
6. This characteristic of sound depends on how quickly vibrations are produced.

Team B

1. This force can slow down or stop a moving object.
2. This is what we call the transfer of thermal energy from a warm substance to a cooler substance.
3. This is a type of plastic that is environmentally friendly.
4. This simple machine uses a wheel and a rope.
5. This is the amount of matter something contains.
6. Air conditioners and heaters are this type of complex machine.

② Listen and check your answers.

③ Write two more sentences and test the other team.

143

PAGE SUMMARY

The aim of the *Term Review* is to review and recycle what pupils have learned over the term and encourage a positive attitude towards revision as a group and as individuals. Before you begin the *Science quiz,* decide if you'd prefer this to be an individual or collaborative revision activity and if you want pupils to use what they know or to look back for the answers. The *Team test!* can be done in two teams or in small groups of two teams. Pupils should be encouraged to correct their own work, or peer correct. You can check the answers to both activities using the audio.

LANGUAGE

- Vocabulary: *matter, light energy, non-contact force, machine, lever, sound, density, mass, volume, shape, float, vibrations, thermal energy, plastic, environmentally friendly, wheel, rope, air conditioner, heater*

ADDITIONAL MATERIALS

- A clock for visual time keeping

SCIENCE QUIZ

① Read the quiz and write the answers in your notebooks.

1. What are the three states of matter?

The three states of matter are solid, liquid and gas.

2. Where does most of the light energy on Earth come from?

Most of the light energy on Earth comes from the Sun.

3. Name two non-contact forces.

Gravity and magnetism are two examples of non-contact forces.

4. Which type of machine has few or no moving parts?

Simple machines have few or no moving parts.

5. How many classes of lever are there?

There are three classes of lever.

6. How is sound produced?

Sound is produced when objects vibrate. This causes air particles to vibrate through the air until they reach our ear. We cause these vibrations sound waves.

7. Which has a lower density: water or cork?

Cork has a lower density than water. This is why cork floats on water.

8. Which unit do we use to measure mass?

We measure mass in grams.

9. Which state of matter has a definite volume but does not have a definite shape?

Liquid has a definite volume but does not have a definite shape.

10. What can you see in photos A-D?

Photo A shows a car. Cars are made of a variety of materials such as steel, aluminium, glass, rubber and plastic.

Photo B shows a seesaw. A seesaw is an example of a class 1 lever, in which the fulcrum is between the effort and the load.

Photo C shows a trumpet and a saxophone. These musical instruments have different tones, which is why they sound different.

Photo D shows a buoy floating on water. Buoyancy, a contact force, is acting on the buoy, helping it to float.

2 Listen and check your answers. (CD. track 113)

- Pupils can check their own answers or check a partner's or another group's answers.

TEAM TEST!

1 Get into teams. Take it in turns to guess what the other team is talking about.

1. Team A: This state of matter has a definite shape and a definite volume. Answer: *solid*

1. Team B: This force can slow down or stop a moving object. Answer: *friction*

2. Team A: Light cannot pass through this type of material. Answer: *an opaque material*

2. Team B: This is what we call the transfer of thermal energy from a warm substance to a cooler substance. Answer: *heat*

3. Team A: This is the unit we use to measure volume. Answer: *millilitres*

3. Team B: This is a type of plastic that is environmentally friendly. Answer: *bioplastics*

4. Team A: This force helps objects float on water. Answer: *buoyancy*

4. Team B: This simple machine uses a wheel and a rope Answer: *pulley*

5. Team A: This simple machine holds things together. Answer: *a screw*

5. Team B: This is the amount of matter something contains. Answer: *mass*

6. Team A: This characteristic of sound depends on how quickly vibrations are produced. Answer: *pitch*

6. Team B: Air conditioners and heaters are this type of complex machine. Answer: *thermal machines*

2 Listen and check your answers. (CD. track 114)

- Pupils can check the other group's answers.

3 Write two more sentences and test the other team.

- Give pupils a limited amount of time to go through the units and make up two more sentences to test their classmates. Circulate and check accuracy and suitability.
- At the end of the test, the winning team can choose either a video link or song from the unit, or request a particular game you play in class to close the lesson.

Notes

Notes